ESSENTIAL SKILLS IN MATHS

BOOK 5

Nelson

Graham Newman and Ron Bull

First published in 1997 by:
Thomas Nelson and Sons Ltd

Reprinted in 2001 by:
Nelson Thornes Ltd
Delta Place
27 Bath Road
CHELTENHAM
GL53 7TH
United Kingdom

ISBN 0-17-431444-2
02 / 10 9 8

Printed in China

Contents

NUMBER

ALGEBRA

SHAPE, SPACE AND MEASURES

HANDLING DATA

Number

1/ MENTAL ARITHMETIC: MULTIPLICATION AND DIVISION

To multiply or divide a decimal number by a power of ten it is only necessary to move the decimal point.

EXAMPLE

► Write down the answer to (a) 542×1000 (b) $768 \div 100$.

(a) Multiplying by 1000 means multiplying by 10 three times, so move the decimal point three places to the right:

$$542 \times 1000 = 542\,000$$

(b) Dividing by 100 means dividing by 10 twice, so move the decimal point two places to the left:

$$768 \div 100 = 7.68$$

When multiplying or dividing a number by a multiple of 10, the problem can be broken down so the calculation can be done mentally.

EXAMPLE

► Write down the answer to (a) 172×4000 (b) $245 \div 700$.

(a) $172 \times 4000 = 172 \times 4 \times 1000 = 688 \times 1000 = 688\,000$

(b) $245 \div 700 = 245 \div 7 \div 100 = 35 \div 100 = 0.35$

Exercise 1A

Write down the answer to each of the following problems. All working must be done in your head.

1 74×50	**2** 68×300	**3** $950 \div 50$	**4** 22×80
5 $502 \div 200$	**6** 38×600	**7** 32×5000	**8** $342 \div 300$
9 $3588 \div 40$	**10** 33×3000	**11** 85×20	**12** 55×100
13 $2000 \div 5000$	**14** 29×900	**15** $1758 \div 600$	**16** $2940 \div 70$
17 41×300	**18** $2427 \div 3000$	**19** 105×40	**20** $3008 \div 400$
21 76×6000	**22** $1312 \div 80$	**23** $1812 \div 200$	**24** $6300 \div 90$
25 297×800	**26** 186×2000	**27** $3060 \div 500$	**28** 766×400
29 $6704 \div 800$	**30** $3792 \div 6000$		

Exercise 1B

Write down the answer to each of the following problems. All working must be done in your head.

1 11×70	**2** 37×30	**3** 14×600	**4** $1390 \div 50$
5 $1674 \div 200$	**6** 23×300	**7** 56×700	**8** $2880 \div 50$

9 $2082 \div 300$	**10** 40×1000	**11** $1164 \div 4000$	**12** $3668 \div 70$
13 52×600	**14** $3224 \div 400$	**15** 245×50	**16** 125×400
17 $4270 \div 5000$	**18** 306×3000	**19** $4650 \div 600$	**20** $2456 \div 80$
21 147×900	**22** 720×6000	**23** $4023 \div 900$	**24** 352×20
25 $6825 \div 700$	**26** $4770 \div 6000$	**27** 124×500	**28** $7592 \div 8000$
29 $2052 \div 90$	**30** 140×8000		

2/ USING A CALCULATOR

A calculator is a useful tool for performing calculations but it must be used properly and accurately. The order in which a calculation is entered is important. Good use can be made of MEMORY and PARENTHESES (the brackets on a calculator).

The following should be worked out first, or separately:

anything in brackets
anything with a power or under a square-root sign
anything written as a denominator (the bottom part of a fraction)

EXAMPLE

► Work out (a) $\left(\dfrac{3127}{4.5 \times 14.2}\right)^2$ (b) $\dfrac{8193}{412} + \dfrac{219}{1.8}$ (c) $4.1 + \sqrt[3]{\dfrac{3.2 + 4.7}{(0.9)^2}}$

(a) Stage 1: work out the bottom separately: $\left(\dfrac{3127}{4.5 \times 14.2}\right)^2 = \left(\dfrac{3127}{63.9}\right)^2$

Stage 2: work out the fraction: $= 48.9358^2$

Stage 3: square the result: $= 2394.716$

Note: You could store the bottom number in the memory then do $3127 \div$ MEMORY, or use the brackets on your calculator and do $(3127 \div (4.5 \times 14.2))^2$.

(b) Stage 1: work out the fractions: $\dfrac{8193}{412} + \dfrac{219}{1.8} = 19.8859 + 121.6667$

Stage 2: add the decimals: $= 141.553$

(c) Stage 1: work out the fraction parts: $4.1 + \sqrt[3]{\dfrac{3.2 + 4.7}{(0.9)^2}} = 4.1 + \sqrt[3]{\dfrac{7.9}{0.81}}$

Stage 2: work out the fraction: $= 4.1 + \sqrt[3]{9.753}$

Stage 3: take the cube root: $= 4.1 + 2.13655$

$= 6.237$

Note: You could do $(3.2 + 4.7) \div 0.9^2 =$, and then do $\sqrt[3]{\ } + 4.1$.

Exercise 2A

Use a calculator to work out the following. Give your answers correct to 3 decimal places.

1 $\dfrac{3290}{707 \times 2.43}$

2 $\dfrac{457.3}{14.7} - \dfrac{327.5}{54.2}$

3 $\sqrt{\dfrac{64.9 + 22.4}{12.5 - 3.4}}$

4 $\dfrac{9.74 \times 8.91}{2.97 \times 8.15}$

5 $\dfrac{3}{4.972 \times 2.13}$

6 $\dfrac{127.3 \times 10.81}{41.55}$

7 $\dfrac{108.7}{63.9} + \dfrac{19.31}{4.27}$

8 $\dfrac{0.876^2 + 0.0039^2}{0.08^2}$

9 $\dfrac{812.7 \times 89.25}{89.1 \times 4.97}$

10 $\dfrac{81.95 \times 42.55}{29.75}$

11 $\dfrac{104.7}{15.4} - \dfrac{214.3}{55.9}$

12 $\dfrac{81.5}{21.34 \times 33.7}$

13 $\sqrt{\dfrac{48.9 \times 3.61}{298}}$

14 $\dfrac{9}{(0.23 + 3.72)^2}$

15 $\dfrac{87.01}{3.23} + \dfrac{95.56}{19.42}$

16 $\dfrac{33.4 \times 24.2}{7.45 \times 9.819}$

17 $\dfrac{429.3}{47.13 \times 49.77}$

18 $\dfrac{5.4^2}{2.7^2 + 9.6^2}$

19 $\sqrt{\dfrac{99.24 \times 77.08}{411 \times 31.2}}$

20 $\dfrac{445.56}{8.72} - \sqrt{\dfrac{89}{0.08}}$

21 $\dfrac{555.9}{2.27 \times 49.5}$

22 $\dfrac{38.72 \times 5.32}{\sqrt{491.3}}$

23 $\dfrac{243.5}{4.28 \times 49.7}$

24 $\dfrac{\sqrt{5987}}{14.4 \times 21.7}$

25 $\dfrac{15.3^2 - 4.1^2}{\sqrt{4217}}$

26 $\dfrac{21.76^2 \times 0.089}{3.42 + 3.7^2}$

27 $\dfrac{4955 \times 8.9}{184 \times 3.14 \times 32.9}$

28 $\dfrac{42.9}{3.14} + \dfrac{55.6}{18.7} + \dfrac{30.5}{18.4}$

29 $\dfrac{2.97}{0.08} + \sqrt{\dfrac{21.76}{0.085}}$

30 $\dfrac{89.4 \times 34.7 \times 3.34}{81.2 \times 47.2 \times 35.4}$

Exercise 2B

Use a calculator to work out the following. Give your answers correct to 3 decimal places.

1 $\dfrac{974.3}{23.7} - \dfrac{317.6}{9.5}$

2 $\sqrt{\dfrac{2105}{60.4 \times 79.1}}$

3 $\dfrac{2.91}{4.87} + \dfrac{82.2}{4.7}$

4 $\dfrac{47.89 \times 471.5}{94.12}$

5 $\dfrac{89.14}{5.42} + \dfrac{47.63}{1.43}$

6 $\dfrac{54.6 \times 81.7}{2.21 \times 49.1}$

7 $\left(\dfrac{8.14 \times 227.2}{353}\right)^2$

8 $\dfrac{98.5 \times 489}{49.7 \times 89.15}$

9 $\sqrt{\dfrac{2140}{92.1 \times 3.67}}$

10 $\dfrac{3.212}{0.21} + \dfrac{231.4}{14.75}$

11 $\dfrac{348.4 \times 7.8 \times 42.4}{340^2}$

12 $\dfrac{421.2 \times 98.71}{189.7}$

13 $\sqrt{\dfrac{82.5 \times 968}{1012 + 132}}$

14 $\dfrac{354.4}{14.3} - \dfrac{321.4}{19.9}$

15 $\dfrac{2.7^2}{3.5^2 + 8.4^2}$

16 $\dfrac{42.7}{8.275 \times 426.5}$

17 $3.45 + \sqrt{\dfrac{18.7}{2.21}}$

18 $\dfrac{7.62}{252} + \sqrt{\dfrac{703}{5.51}}$

19 $\dfrac{13.4^2 + 5.2^2}{3.5^2 - 1.4^2}$

20 $\dfrac{812.7 \times 2.97}{81.5 \times 89.2}$

21 $\dfrac{\sqrt{21510}}{14.3 \times 21.4}$

22 $\sqrt{\dfrac{3290}{807 \times 2.43}}$

23 $\left(\dfrac{42.8}{8.82}\right)^2 + \left(\dfrac{50.4}{3.15}\right)^2$

24 $\dfrac{812.2}{9.87 \times 97.82}$

25 $\dfrac{85.47^2 - 41.4^2}{\sqrt{132}}$

26 $\dfrac{123.7}{97.8 \times 29.9}$

27 $\dfrac{4.79}{5.2} + \dfrac{18.17}{2.4} + \dfrac{4.93}{1.52}$

28 $\dfrac{492 + 53.4}{153.4 + 27.4 - 3.2}$

29 $\dfrac{42.96^2 \times 3.82 \times 84}{1.965 \times 4250}$

30 $\dfrac{108.74 \times 42.9}{81.7 \times 39.4 \times 19.7}$

3/ ESTIMATES FOR CALCULATIONS

To make an estimate of the answer to a calculation round each number to 1 significant figure.

EXAMPLE

► Find an estimated answer to each of the following.

(a) 4.977×243.5 (b) $815.7 \div 5.579$ (c) $\dfrac{42.97 \times 55.56}{3.142 \times 18.9}$

(a) $4.977 \times 243.5 \approx 5 \times 200 = 1000$

(b) $815.7 \div 5.579 \approx 800 \div 6 = 133\frac{1}{3}$

(c) $\dfrac{42.97 \times 55.56}{3.142 \times 18.9} \approx \dfrac{40 \times 60}{3 \times 20} = \dfrac{2400}{60} = \dfrac{240}{6} = 40$

Exercise 3A

Find an estimated answer to each of the following.

1 421.3×89.7

2 10.87×8.76

3 217.5×4.7

4 14.98×1.79

5 $\dfrac{3.6 \times 9.1}{1.6}$

6 $\dfrac{72}{21 \times 18}$

7 $\dfrac{1.3 \times 4.9}{5.2}$

8 $\dfrac{21.7 \times 3.4}{1.8 \times 1.5}$

9 $\dfrac{41 \times 23.2}{1.6}$

10 $\dfrac{17.5 \times 15}{5 \times 42}$

11 $\dfrac{89.4}{1.46 \times 3.65}$

12 $\dfrac{4.27 \times 1.89}{6.43}$

13 $\dfrac{19.2 \times 88.2}{4.1 \times 4.6}$

14 $\dfrac{17 \times 61}{1.4 \times 3.4}$

15 $\dfrac{18.4 \times 48.5}{4.5 \times 2.1}$

16 $\dfrac{57.3 \times 11.4}{5.2}$

17 $\dfrac{24.4 \times 8.12}{9.6 \times 1.4}$

18 $\dfrac{472.8 \times 24.93}{213.9 \times 1.47}$

19 $\dfrac{14.9 \times 89.4}{225}$

20 $\dfrac{26 \times 14.5}{28 \times 17.5}$

21 $\dfrac{49 \times 53}{35 \times 14}$

22 $\dfrac{44 \times 48.4}{9.7 \times 2.1}$

23 $\dfrac{219.7 \times 897.6}{6.25 \times 4.19}$

24 $\dfrac{99 \times 8.1}{1.4 \times 1.5}$

25 $\dfrac{8.52 \times 124}{47.8}$

26 $\dfrac{2.4 \times 1.5 \times 4.2}{4.8 \times 1.8}$

27 $\dfrac{897.6 \times 913.3}{81.54 \times 95.89}$

28 $\dfrac{(2.49)^2 \times 49.72}{1.4 \times 21.74}$

29 $\dfrac{82.7 \times 8.97 \times 3.72}{3.29 \times 3.14}$

30 $\dfrac{3.2 \times 12.4 \times 35}{7.5 \times 2.1 \times 6.1}$

Exercise 3B

Find an estimated answer to each of the following.

1 18.97×41

2 43.23×24.85

3 $17.86 \times 31.9 \times 43.2$

4 11.5×2.3

5 $\dfrac{14.9}{1.19 \times 2.2}$

6 21.4×83.2

7 $\dfrac{8.3 \times 27}{6.1 \times 12}$

8 $\dfrac{36}{1.85 \times 2.1}$

9 $\dfrac{11.3 \times 49.4}{1.7 \times 5.2}$

10 $\dfrac{2.3 \times 7}{1.6 \times 1.5}$

11 $\dfrac{41.2 \times 22.9}{1.6}$

12 $\dfrac{36 \times 128}{9.4 \times 1.6}$

13 $\dfrac{13.4 \times 1.42}{1.2}$

14 $\dfrac{24.4 \times 39.5}{1.3 \times 2.1}$

15 $\dfrac{670 \times 130}{9.6 \times 2.4}$

16 $\dfrac{45.6 \times 39.2}{1.3 \times 2.23}$

17 $\dfrac{267}{124 \times 1.15}$

18 $\dfrac{32.4 \times 2.1}{3.89 \times 5.4}$

19 $\dfrac{62.4 \times 35.3}{3.2 \times 1.2}$

20 $\dfrac{42 \times 23}{18 \times 14}$

21 $\dfrac{25.4 \times 4.87}{4.5 \times 3.1}$

22 $\dfrac{(4.1 \times 2.3)^2}{1.6}$

23 $\dfrac{(131 \times 14.3)^2}{12.4^2}$

24 $\dfrac{81 \times 155}{42.4 \times 2.4}$

25 $\dfrac{74.3 \times 48.2}{4.1 \times 6.6}$

26 $\dfrac{264 \times 145}{18 \times 17.4}$

27 $\dfrac{8194 \times 119.7}{413}$

28 $\dfrac{42.5 \times 50.4}{8.82 \times 1.15 \times 4.5}$

29 $\dfrac{7.62 \times 703 \times 60.4}{25 \times 6.51 \times 252}$

30 $\dfrac{8.42 \times 10.9 \times 246}{507 \times 4.45}$

4/ MEASUREMENT AS AN APPROXIMATION

When a measurement is taken it is always an approximation, or rounding, of the value. This could be as a result of the accuracy of the measuring instrument. The rounding is within half a unit.

EXAMPLE

► For each measurement write down (i) the minimum (ii) the maximum value it could be.
(a) 14 kg (b) 7.9 ml (c) 4.233 km

(a) 14 kg	(i) minimum is 13.5 kg	(ii) maximum is 14.5 kg
(b) 7.9 ml	(i) minimum is 7.85 ml	(ii) maximum is 7.95 ml
(c) 4.233 km	(i) minimum is 4.2325 km	(ii) maximum is 4.2335 km

Exercise 4A

For each measurement write down (a) the minimum (b) the maximum value it could be.

1 17 cm	**2** 23 cl	**3** 85 km	**4** 0.214 s	**5** 1.27 cm^2
6 4.274 kg	**7** 3.14 m^2	**8** 8.91 ml	**9** 26.2 *l*	**10** 97 m.p.h.
11 15.3 t	**12** 3.27 km^2	**13** 0.321 cm^3	**14** 51 g	**15** 55.555 m^3
16 4.404 t	**17** 96.5 m^2	**18** 12.421 m	**19** 12 km/h	**20** 78.5 s
21 2.75 g	**22** 10.5 cm^3	**23** 33.333 km	**24** 2.26 cm	**25** 27.545 m^3
26 82 km	**27** 0.665 kg	**28** 43.1 ml	**29** 7.424 s	**30** 1.2005 *l*

Exercise 4B

For each measurement write down (a) the minimum (b) the maximum value it could be.

1	32 *l*	**2**	103 t	**3**	94 km^2	**4**	1.03 cl	**5**	4.446 t
6	7.253 cm^3	**7**	4.19 cm^2	**8**	23.853 m^3	**9**	4.277 t	**10**	1.88 cl
11	5.707 cm^3	**12**	21 km/h	**13**	17.413 m	**14**	85.7 s	**15**	3.257 m^3
16	35.7 ml	**17**	4.331 m	**18**	75 m.p.h.	**19**	3.125 kg	**20**	18.8 g
21	7.864 cm	**22**	66.8 s	**23**	52.4 m^2	**24**	4.224 km	**25**	8.59 *l*
26	40 km^2	**27**	0.52 s	**28**	6.70 cm^2	**29**	2.5995 *l*	**30**	3.44 ml

5/ EXPRESSING A POSITIVE INTEGER AS A PRODUCT OF PRIMES

A **prime number** is a number that has no factors other than 1 and itself, for example:
2, 3, 5, 7, 11, 13, ...
Note: 1 is not a prime number.
Any number can be broken down into prime factors which, when multiplied together, will give that number.

EXAMPLE

► Write each number as a product of prime factors.
(a) 36 (b) 720 (c) 65

Begin with the smallest prime number and divide this into the number repeatedly, where possible. Continue with the next prime factor.

(a)
```
2) 36
2) 18
3)  9
3)  3
    1
```

(b)
```
2) 720
2) 360
2) 180
2)  90
3)  45
3)  15
5)   5
     1
```

(c)
```
 5) 65
13) 13
     1
```

$36 = 2 \times 2 \times 3 \times 3$
$= 2^2 \times 3^2$

$720 = 2 \times 2 \times 2 \times 2 \times 3 \times 3 \times 5$
$= 2^4 \times 3^2 \times 5$

$65 = 5 \times 13$

Exercise 5A

Express each number as a product of primes.

1	20	**2**	75	**3**	42	**4**	110	**5**	44	**6**	182
7	418	**8**	76	**9**	42	**10**	18	**11**	605	**12**	48
13	325	**14**	759	**15**	1000	**16**	54	**17**	56	**18**	99
19	28	**20**	390	**21**	116	**22**	345	**23**	108	**24**	170
25	351	**26**	25935	**27**	92	**28**	532	**29**	289	**30**	360

Exercise 5B

Express each number as a product of primes.

1 28	**2** 70	**3** 84	**4** 114	**5** 195	**6** 52
7 322	**8** 45	**9** 144	**10** 374	**11** 102	**12** 92
13 726	**14** 715	**15** 189	**16** 425	**17** 230	**18** 637
19 44	**20** 625	**21** 238	**22** 2090	**23** 15	**24** 72
25 174	**26** 279	**27** 148	**28** 162	**29** 30030	**30** 2700

6/ STANDARD FORM: CONVERTING TO ORDINARY NUMBERS

$A \times 10^n$

This number, which is in **standard form**, has two parts to it:

(1) a decimal number A, with the decimal point after the first digit,

(2) a power of 10, to the power n, by which you should multiply the decimal to change it back into an ordinary number.

Standard form is a way of representing large numbers on a calculator display.

$\boxed{4.231^{\ 05}}$ means 4.231×10^5

Remember: Include the '× 10' when you write the number.

EXAMPLE

► Write as ordinary numbers (a) 4.213×10^6 (b) 1.45×10^2.

(a) $4.213 \times 10^6 = 4.213 \times 1\,000\,000 = 4\,213\,000$

(b) $1.45 \times 10^2 = 1.45 \times 100 = 145$

The positive power of ten is also the number of places the decimal point is moved to the right in the number.

Exercise 6A

Write each of the following numbers as an ordinary number.

1 1.95×10^3	**2** 5.34×10^2	**3** 1.17×10^3	**4** 2.27×10^2
5 3.215×10^4	**6** 2.72×10^3	**7** 2.1×10^3	**8** 4.01×10^2
9 8.94×10^4	**10** 9.4×10^3	**11** 8.203×10^3	**12** 9.1×10^2
13 4.912×10^5	**14** 3.5×10^2	**15** 1.913×10^6	**16** 9.875×10^5
17 1.981×10^6	**18** 1.49×10^2	**19** 5.8124×10^7	**20** 9.02×10^5
21 4.121×10^3	**22** 3.117×10^2	**23** 4.92×10^5	**24** 1.459×10^2
25 1.397×10^4	**26** 3.1×10^3	**27** 3.821×10^6	**28** 2.047×10^3
29 6.49×10^4	**30** 6.2821×10^6		

Exercise 6B

Write each of the following numbers as an ordinary number.

1 8.37×10^{4}	**2** 1.36×10^{3}	**3** 9.77×10^{3}	**4** 8.098×10^{5}
5 1.35×10^{2}	**6** 4.042×10^{4}	**7** 3.45×10^{2}	**8** 4.203×10^{2}
9 3.142×10^{3}	**10** 1.306×10^{4}	**11** 4.2×10^{2}	**12** 1.017×10^{3}
13 4.189×10^{5}	**14** 1.222×10^{3}	**15** 1.801×10^{6}	**16** 8.796×10^{7}
17 1.759×10^{5}	**18** 1.39×10^{2}	**19** 8.525×10^{3}	**20** 3.14×10^{4}
21 1.603×10^{3}	**22** 1.301×10^{5}	**23** 4.127×10^{2}	**24** 1.432×10^{6}
25 1.611×10^{3}	**26** 2.7×10^{2}	**27** 1.872×10^{4}	**28** 2.814×10^{3}
29 3.824×10^{2}	**30** 4.815×10^{4}		

Standard form can also be used to represent very small numbers.

[4.231 $^{-05}$] means $4.231 \times 10^{-5} = 4.231 \times \frac{1}{100\,000} = 0.000\,042\,31$

EXAMPLE

► Write as ordinary numbers (a) 8.703×10^{-4} (b) 2.329×10^{-2}.

(a) $8.703 \times 10^{-4} = 8.703 \div 10\,000 = 0.000\,870\,3$

(b) $2.329 \times 10^{-2} = 2.329 \div 100 = 0.023\,29$

Exercise 6C

Write each of the following numbers as an ordinary number.

1 4.85×10^{-3}	**2** 8.7×10^{-2}	**3** 2.41×10^{-1}	**4** 4.72×10^{-2}
5 4.91×10^{-3}	**6** 9.12×10^{-2}	**7** 2.255×10^{-4}	**8** 1.923×10^{-2}
9 4.216×10^{-1}	**10** 2.4721×10^{-5}	**11** 9.47×10^{-2}	**12** 5.715×10^{-3}
13 3.104×10^{-1}	**14** 5.84×10^{-4}	**15** 4.213×10^{-6}	**16** 2.525×10^{-1}
17 6.125×10^{-5}	**18** 3.128×10^{-3}	**19** 1.427×10^{-1}	**20** 8.014×10^{-4}
21 3.768×10^{-2}	**22** 5.71×10^{-1}	**23** 6.127×10^{-3}	**24** 4.191×10^{-2}
25 3.47×10^{-3}	**26** 3.012×10^{-4}	**27** 7.118×10^{-2}	**28** 1.792×10^{-6}
29 8.129×10^{-3}	**30** 2.17×10^{-5}		

Exercise 6D

Write each of the following numbers as an ordinary number.

1 9.23×10^{-2}	**2** 2.3×10^{-3}	**3** 7.63×10^{-2}	**4** 3.12×10^{-3}
5 9.128×10^{-1}	**6** 4.197×10^{-4}	**7** 8.199×10^{-5}	**8** 5.573×10^{-1}
9 9.08×10^{-4}	**10** 9.147×10^{-3}	**11** 3.289×10^{-2}	**12** 7.525×10^{-1}
13 1.472×10^{-4}	**14** 7.29×10^{-2}	**15** 9.147×10^{-3}	**16** 2.12×10^{-2}
17 8.232×10^{-4}	**18** 4.79×10^{-1}	**19** 4.721×10^{-3}	**20** 8.125×10^{-1}
21 9.14×10^{-2}	**22** 6.732×10^{-4}	**23** 2.55×10^{-3}	**24** 4.129×10^{-5}
25 2.8×10^{-1}	**26** 7.129×10^{-6}	**27** 2.176×10^{-3}	**28** 8.7×10^{-2}
29 4.991×10^{-4}	**30** 8.92×10^{-2}		

7/ STANDARD FORM: CONVERTING FROM ORDINARY NUMBERS

EXAMPLE

▶ Write in standard form (a) 41 000 (b) 5714 (c) 70.

(a) $41\,000 = 4.1 \times 10\,000 = 4.1 \times 10^4$

(b) $5714 = 5.714 \times 1000 = 5.714 \times 10^3$

(c) $70 = 7.0 \times 10 = 7.0 \times 10^1$

The positive power of ten is the number of places the decimal point must be moved to the left to put it after the first significant figure.

Exercise 7A

Write each of these numbers in standard form.

1	29 000	**2**	4850	**3**	600	**4**	4300
5	113 000 000	**6**	742	**7**	9172	**8**	760 000
9	56 000 000	**10**	628 000	**11**	190 000	**12**	10 000
13	21 000 000	**14**	4020	**15**	58 300	**16**	57 800
17	3700	**18**	2 743 000	**19**	45 000	**20**	676 000
21	72 900 000	**22**	70 700	**23**	328 400	**24**	511 200
25	727 000 000	**26**	24 000	**27**	573 400	**28**	510 000
29	2 500 000	**30**	254 127				

Exercise 7B

Write each of these numbers in standard form.

1	32 000	**2**	573 000	**3**	7000	**4**	270 000
5	9 300 000	**6**	18 340	**7**	70 000	**8**	226 000 000
9	92 700	**10**	46 600	**11**	7050	**12**	59 000 000
13	72 100	**14**	452	**15**	100 000	**16**	330 000
17	283 000	**18**	21 403	**19**	104 000 000	**20**	209 450
21	42 100 000	**22**	290 010	**23**	240 000	**24**	9 870 000
25	4 853 450	**26**	27 000 000	**27**	3 900 000	**28**	150 000
29	2 750 000	**30**	78 196				

EXAMPLE

▶ Write in standard form (a) 0.0312 (b) 0.000 49 (c) 0.8.

(a) $0.0312 = 3.12 \div 100 = 3.12 \times 10^{-2}$

(b) $0.000\,49 = 4.9 \div 10\,000 = 4.9 \times 10^{-4}$

(c) $0.8 = 8.0 \div 10 = 8.0 \times 10^{-1}$

The negative power of ten is the number of places the decimal point must be moved to the right, to put it after the first significant figure.

Exercise 7C

Write each of these numbers in standard form.

1	0.09	**2**	0.006	**3**	0.000 04	**4**	0.017
5	0.0101	**6**	0.000 56	**7**	0.009 02	**8**	0.1
9	0.004 39	**10**	0.000 068 5	**11**	0.000 27	**12**	0.004
13	0.000 025	**14**	0.0062	**15**	0.000 861	**16**	0.0032
17	0.000 82	**18**	0.000 011 7	**19**	0.098	**20**	0.001 662
21	0.000 004	**22**	0.008 219	**23**	0.001 001	**24**	0.2
25	0.000 763	**26**	0.000 027	**27**	0.008 129	**28**	0.0761
29	0.000 010 1	**30**	0.004 72				

Exercise 7D

Write each of these numbers in standard form.

1	0.007	**2**	0.02	**3**	0.0003	**4**	0.000 557
5	0.001 000 1	**6**	0.000 85	**7**	0.0871	**8**	0.000 72
9	0.008 47	**10**	0.01	**11**	0.000 84	**12**	0.0027
13	0.000 25	**14**	0.033	**15**	0.072 36	**16**	0.0034
17	0.000 242	**18**	0.000 09	**19**	0.087 64	**20**	0.000 024 2
21	0.000 101	**22**	0.0072	**23**	0.0002	**24**	0.0044
25	0.007	**26**	0.000 034 7	**27**	0.001 01	**28**	0.021 37
29	0.000 497	**30**	0.003 637				

8/ CALCULATING WITH STANDARD FORM

EXAMPLE

▶ Calculate (a) $(420\,000)^3$ (b) $2.19 \times 10^4 + 5.41 \times 10^5$.

(a) $(420\,000)^3 = 420\,000$ [x^y] $3 =$ [$7.4088\ ^{16}$] $= 7.4088 \times 10^{16}$

(b) 2.19 [EE] 4 + 5.41 [EE] 5 = 562 900 = 5.629×10^5

Note: [EE] is a common button on a scientific calculator which allows you to enter a standard-form number. Some calculators have similar buttons such as [EXP] or [E]. Consult the handbook for your calculator if you have any doubt as to how a standard form should be entered.

Exercise 8A

Write your answers in standard form, giving the decimal part correct to 3 decimal places where appropriate.

1 $(2.3 \times 10^3) \times (6 \times 10^{-7})$

2 $(5.4 \times 10^3) + (7.2 \times 10^2)$

3 $(6.4 \times 10^3) \div (8 \times 10^{-4})$

4 $(5 \times 10^6) \times (2 \times 10^2)$

5 $(450\,000)^2$

6 $(3.7 \times 10^8) \times (2 \times 10^{-3})$

7 $(4 \times 10^8) \times (6 \times 10^{-3})$

8 $(0.0008)^3$

9 $\dfrac{8.2 \times 10^8}{2 \times 10^6}$

10 $\dfrac{9 \times 10^8}{3 \times 10^3}$

11 $(8.4 \times 10^9) - (9.2 \times 10^8)$

12 $(8 \times 10^{-3}) \times (4 \times 10^{-4})$

13 $\dfrac{6.5 \times 10^9}{5 \times 10^7}$

14 $\dfrac{2.1 \times 10^{12}}{3 \times 10^5}$

15 $(4.8 \times 10^8) \times (8 \times 10^{-4})$

16 $(4.75 \times 10^{-5}) - (9.2 \times 10^{-6})$

17 $\dfrac{3 \times 10^6}{4 \times 10^2}$

18 $(130\,000)^4$

19 $\dfrac{(1.9 \times 10^3) \times (2.3 \times 10^4)}{(4.8 \times 10^{16})}$

20 $\dfrac{(7.6 \times 10^{-4}) \times (5.2 \times 10^{-5})}{(8.9 \times 10^{-8})}$

21 $\dfrac{3.8 \times 10^{-5}}{(9.7 \times 10^3) \times (8.4 \times 10^4)}$

22 $\dfrac{4.72 \times 10^{-7}}{(2.4 \times 10^{-6}) \times (3.2 \times 10^{-4})}$

23 $\dfrac{(3.91 \times 10^2) \times (2.56 \times 10^3)}{(3.1 \times 10^5) \times (4.2 \times 10^4)}$

24 Light travels at 9.461×10^{12} km per year. How far does light travel in 5000 years?

25 A book has 545 pages and a thickness of 19.5 mm. Find the thickness of one page.

26 A proton has a mass of 1.673×10^{-24} grams. Calculate the total mass of six million protons.

27 A femtosecond is 1×10^{-15} second. What length of time, in seconds, is 700 femtoseconds?

28 An elementary particle has a mass of 1.783×10^{-27} grams. Calculate the total mass of $2\frac{1}{2}$ million particles.

29 The Earth is 9.296×10^7 miles from the Sun. The speed of light is 1.86×10^5 miles per second. Calculate the time for light to travel from the Sun to the Earth. Give your answer to the nearest second.

30 The mass of the Earth is 5.974×10^{24} kg. The mass of Neptune is 17.1 times that of the Earth. Find the mass of Neptune.

Exercise 8B

Write your answers in standard form, giving the decimal part correct to 3 decimal places where appropriate.

1 $(0.000\,072)^2$

2 $(6 \times 10^5) \times (2 \times 10^2)$

3 $\dfrac{7 \times 10^2}{2 \times 10^6}$

4 $\dfrac{8 \times 10^8}{2 \times 10^2}$

5 $(6.4 \times 10^{-3}) \div (8 \times 10^{-6})$

6 $(54\,000)^4$

7 $(9.9 \times 10^{-6}) \times (5.8 \times 10^4)$

8 $(8.1 \times 10^{-5}) \times (9.4 \times 10^{-3})$

9 $(6 \times 10^5) \times (2 \times 10^{-3})$

10 $(5.6 \times 10^7) + (3.1 \times 10^6)$

11 $\dfrac{4.2 \times 10^9}{7 \times 10^5}$

12 $\dfrac{6 \times 10^9}{1.5 \times 10^5}$

13 $(7.61 \times 10^{-3}) - (8.4 \times 10^{-4})$

14 $(7.2 \times 10^{-7}) \times (9 \times 10^3)$

15 $\dfrac{1.26 \times 10^{-4}}{2.52 \times 10^{-9}}$

16 $\dfrac{9 \times 10^{10}}{1.8 \times 10^{-4}}$

17 $(7\,900\,000)^2$

18 $\dfrac{3 \times 10^{-6}}{4 \times 10^{-4}}$

19 $\dfrac{(5 \times 10^{-5}) \times (4.2 \times 10^{-7})}{(3.1 \times 10^{-8})}$

20 $\dfrac{(2.3 \times 10^7) \times (3.4 \times 10^6)}{(7.4 \times 10^2)}$

21 $\dfrac{(4.86 \times 10^{-5})}{(5.1 \times 10^2) \times (7.3 \times 10^3)}$

22 $\dfrac{(1.26 \times 10^{-4})}{(2.52 \times 10^{-6}) \times (3.4 \times 10^{-5})}$

23 $\dfrac{(6.43 \times 10^2) \times (3.27 \times 10^3)}{(5.4 \times 10^4) \times (7.4 \times 10^5)}$

24 The mass of the Earth is 5.974×10^{24} kg. The mass of Saturn is 95.2 times that of the Earth. What is the mass of Saturn?

25 In astronomy 1 AU is 1.496×10^8 km. The distance from the Sun to Jupiter is 5.2 AU. Write this distance in kilometres.

26 An electron has a mass of 9.109×10^{-31} grams. Calculate the total mass of five million electrons.

27 A ream of paper has 500 sheets and is 3.5 cm thick. Calculate, in millimetres, the thickness of one sheet of paper.

28 The nearest star, Proxima Centauri, is 4.22 light years away. A light year is equivalent to 9.461×10^{12} km. Find, in kilometres, the distance to the nearest star.

29 A femtosecond is 1×10^{-15} second. What length of time, in seconds, is 125 femtoseconds?

30 A neutron has a mass of 1.675×10^{-27} grams. Calculate the total mass of 2.4 million neutrons.

REVISION

Exercise A

1 Without using a calculator write down the answer to each of the following.
(a) $4168 \div 200$ (b) 314×5000 (c) $906 \div 3000$ (d) 207×90

2 Use a calculator and give your answers correct to 3 decimal places.
(a) $\dfrac{12.42 \times 14.974}{3.27 \times 5.41}$ (b) $\sqrt{\dfrac{27.41}{5.214 - 3.975}}$ (c) $\dfrac{21.4^2 - 5.63^2}{\sqrt{9.42}}$
(d) $\dfrac{42.47}{5.81} + \dfrac{83.73}{9.05}$

3 Use rounding to 1 significant figure to estimate the answer to each of the following.
(a) 23.4×39.75 (b) $\dfrac{82.4 \times 31.3}{6.43 \times 42.7}$ (c) $\dfrac{3.41^2 \times 47.4}{1.87 \times 8.64}$
(d) $\dfrac{24.3}{1.32 \times 4.273}$

4 Express each number as a product of primes.
(a) 720 (b) 2016 (c) 1215 (d) 2940

5 Write each of the following as an ordinary number.
(a) 5.217×10^5 (b) 4.596×10^{-2} (c) 8.104×10^7 (d) 2.375×10^{-6}

6 Write each of the following in standard form.
(a) 3 000 000 (b) 0.000 79 (c) 750 000 000 (d) 0.000 009

Exercise AA

1 Jill has bought 28 ink-pens at £1.95 each. Write down an estimate of the total cost.

2 Approximately how many 19p stamps can be bought with £8?

3 A group of 11 people are to share prize money of £503.25. Work out an estimate for the amount each person will receive.

4 A box of knives weighs 4.95 kg. What is the approximate weight of 78 boxes?

5 Write each piece of information as a standard-form number.
(a) The diameter of the Sun is 865 000 miles.
(b) The average distance of Pluto from the Sun is 3 670 000 000 miles.
(c) The speed of light is approximately 300 000 000 m/s.

6 The length of a car is measured as 4.55 metres, to the nearest centimetre. Write down
(a) the minimum (b) the maximum length it could be.

7 The diameter of a water tank is 83 centimetres, to the nearest centimetre. Write down
(a) the minimum (b) the maximum diameter it could be.

8 The weight of a tool is 84.3 grams, to the nearest tenth of a gram. Write down
(a) the minimum (b) the maximum weight it could be.

9 The flash of a camera has been timed as 0.075 second, to the nearest thousandth of a second. Write down (a) the minimum (b) the maximum time it could be.

10 Light travels at 298 000 kilometres per second. Calculate how far light travels in a year of 365 days. Give your answer in kilometres, correct to 3 significant figures.

11 The mass of an electron is 9.2×10^{-28} grams. Find the mass of three million electrons. Give your answer in standard form.

12 The distance from Earth to Mars is 2.3×10^8 km. A space-craft takes 715 days to travel from Earth to Mars. Find its average speed, in km/h, correct to 1 significant figure.

13 The mass of the Earth is 5.974×10^{24} kg. The mass of Jupiter is 317.8 times that of the Earth. Find the mass of Jupiter.

14 A book has 380 pages and a thickness of 1.3 cm. Find, in millimetres, the thickness of one page.

15 A femtosecond is 1×10^{-15} second. How many seconds are there in 600 femtoseconds?

9/ DIRECT PROPORTION

Direct proportion is when two quantities are directly related; an increase in one will result in a proportionate increase in the other.

EXAMPLE

► Five similar books cost £49.75. How much will eight books cost?

5 books cost £49.75

1 book costs £49.75 ÷ 5 = £9.95

8 books cost £9.95 × 8 = £79.60

Exercise 9A

1 A clock gains 20 minutes in five days. How much does it gain in eight days?

2 A car travels 450 km on 30 litres of petrol. How far should it travel on 20 litres?

3 A carpet of area 12 m^2 costs £108. What is the cost of a carpet of area 18m^2?

4 A hotel charges £180 for a stay of four days. How much would it charge for ten days at the same rate?

5 On five pages of a book there are 1900 words. How many words would you expect to find on nine pages?

6 It costs £323.82 to turf a lawn of area 63 m^2. How much would it cost to turf a lawn of area 56 m^2?

7 A machine in a milk-bottling factory fills 1240 bottles in eight hours. How many bottles will be filled in three hours?

8 Twenty children use 680 litres of water per day. How much water will be required by 37 children?

9 If 68 cm^3 of a metal has a mass of 561 grams. What is the mass of 40.8 cm^3?

10 The average rainfall in a town is 19.6 cm in four weeks. How much rain falls, on average, in 23 days?

11 Five wooden statues weigh 8 kg. What will be the weight of 11 statues?

12 A coach uses 33 litres of diesel to travel 132 miles. How far would it travel on 56 litres?

13 A train went 320 km in four hours. How long would it take to go 96 km?

14 A woman is paid £18.20 for seven hours' work. How much will she receive for five hours' work?

15 It costs £4.50 to feed a dog for 12 days. How much will it cost to feed the dog for 35 days?

16 Eight eggs from a farm cost 48p. Find the cost of half a dozen.

17 In a garden 32 tree seedlings need 24 cm^2 of space. How many seedlings can be planted in 27 cm^2 of space?

18 If 28 kg of oats cost £4.20, how much will a 72-kg bag cost?

19 It costs £40 to buy 25 metres of cloth. How many metres of the same material can be bought for £42.50?

20 A 6-kg bag of sprouts costs £2.97. What would an 8-kg bag cost?

Exercise 9B

1 Four tickets for a concert cost £39.20. How much would seven tickets cost?

2 Twelve books cost £72. Find the cost of 22 books.

3 A helicopter travels 288 km in $2\frac{1}{4}$ hours. How far will it travel in $1\frac{1}{4}$ hours?

4 The cost of printing a book with 160 pages is £5.76. What would be the cost of printing a book with 240 pages?

5 If 37 toy figures can be bought for £44.40, find the cost of buying 13 figures.

6 It costs £10.80 for 3 m^2 of floor covering. Find the cost of 7 m^2.

7 A pile of 500 sheets of card is 8 cm thick. How thick is a pile of 300 sheets of card?

8 Betty takes 50 minutes to walk 4 km. How long will it take her to walk 3 km?

9 Five similar books cost £29.95. How much will seven books cost?

10 In a cottage factory a dozen bars of soap weigh $1\frac{1}{2}$ kg. What would be the weight of 45 bars?

11 Six razor blades cost 42p. How much will ten blades cost?

12 In a school 15 pots of glue are ordered for every eight children. How many pots of glue are needed for 56 children?

13 Three metres of shelving are needed for 135 books. How many books would fit onto five metres of shelving?

14 A plane travels 5100 km in 6 hours. How far will it travel in 2 hours 6 minutes?

15 In four weeks 500 kg of coal is used to stoke a boiler. How many tonnes will be used in 18 weeks?

16 Cable costs £2.40 per 1.8-metre length. How much would 15 metres cost?

17 Four boxes weigh 30 kg. What weight will nine boxes be?

18 A hiker covers 12 km in four hours. How long will it take the hiker to cover 16 km?

19 Fencing costs £10.80 for nine metres. How much will it cost for seven metres?

20 Eight metres of chain cost £4.80. What is the cost of five metres?

10/ INVERSE PROPORTION

If two quantities, *A* and *B*, are **inversely proportional** then, as *A* increases, *B* decreases and, as *A* decreases, so *B* increases. For example, eight people will take less time to paint a wall than six people.

EXAMPLE

► Six workers can paint a fence in four days. How long will it take eight workers?

$6 \times 4 = 24$ man-days

So $24 \div 8 = 3$ days

Exercise 10A

In this exercise assume all rates remain constant.

1 Three women can do a job of work in four days. How long would it take eight women?

2 Forty pens are bought at 35p each. If the price rises to 40p, how many pens could then be bought?

3 Four men lay a cable in five days. How long would ten men take?
4 A secretary typed 3690 words in $4\frac{1}{2}$ hours. How long would it take to type 6642 words?
5 A loan is paid off at the rate of £15 for 25 weeks. How long would it take if £12.50 were paid off each week?
6 A large tin of chocolates is shared between a group of nine children. They get eight chocolates each. If there were only six children, how many would each get?
7 A rectangle measures 12 cm by 18 cm. A second rectangle has the same area as the first, and a width of 8 cm. What is its length?
8 A house can be built in ten weeks using 12 men. How long would it take if 18 men were employed?
9 A document fits onto 15 pages of text, with 30 lines per page. How many lines per page will there be if the document is written to fit onto nine pages?
10 A car took 45 minutes to make a journey at 70 m.p.h. The return journey took 50 minutes. What was the average speed on the return journey?
11 Six men can paint a house in ten days. How long would it take five men?
12 Four pipes fill a garden pond in 12 minutes. If one pipe were removed, how long would three pipes take to fill the pond?
13 Two painters can paint a classroom in 120 minutes. How long would three painters take?
14 If 18 workers are employed to do a job in six days. how long would it take 12 workers?
15 Vases are packed in 25 cases, each of which contains 12 vases. If the same batch was packed in boxes containing 15 vases each, how many boxes would there be?
16 Three painters can paint a town hall in 60 days. How long will it take five painters?
17 Seven machines are used to complete an order in 42 hours. How long would it take four machines to complete a similar order?
18 To complete a harvest a farmer needs two combine-harvesters for six days. How long would it take if he had three combine-harvesters?
19 Whilst travelling at 30 m.p.h. it takes a car five hours to complete a journey. How long would the journey take at a speed of 50 m.p.h.?
20 Three students can complete an exercise in 60 minutes. How long would it take five students working together?

Exercise 10B

1 Water from six taps fills an empty tank in $4\frac{1}{4}$ hours. How long would it have taken with only five taps?
2 It takes seven ladies six hours to complete a job of work. How long would it take eight ladies?
3 Six machines produce 840 toys in a day. How many would seven machines produce in a day?
4 A scarf is knitted with a length of 20 cm and a width of 48 stitches. It is unpicked and reknitted with a width of 60 stitches. What is its new length?
5 It takes nine workers 40 days to complete a contract. How long would it take 12 workers?
6 Whilst travelling at 40 m.p.h. it takes a car 5 hours to complete a journey. How long would it take at a speed of 60 m.p.h.?
7 Five machines take 40 hours to complete a production run. How long would it take three machines to produce a similar order?
8 A car uses seven litres of petrol for a 100-km journey. How far could the car go on eight litres?
9 The length of an article in a newspaper is 174 lines with an average of 16 words per line. If it is set out with 12 words per line, how many lines would there be?
10 A consultant charges £50 for work which took six hours. How much would she charge for nine hours' work?
11 Eight soldiers together can complete an engineering project in five hours. How long would six soldiers take?
12 A factory has 42 machines which together will complete the work on a contract in 63 days. How many machines will be required if the contract might need completion in 54 days?

13 A builder can build a house in 18 weeks using four men. How long will the job take with six men?
14 A field of grass feeds 48 cows for six days. How long would the same field feed 36 cows?
15 The length of a report is 348 lines with an average of 12 words per line. It is rewritten with an average of 14 words per line. How many lines will be needed?
16 Flagstones are arranged to make a terrace 30 metres by 20 metres. The same flagstones are rearranged to make a terrace 25 metres wide. What is the length of the terrace?
17 Four bricklayers can build a wall in ten days. How long would it take five bricklayers to do it?
18 Jill has an allowance of £12 each day to spend whilst on holiday for 15 days. If she books a 10-day holiday instead but takes the same amount of money, how much will she have to spend each day?
19 Eight machines are used to complete a job in 12 hours. How long would it take if 16 machines were used?
20 It takes 40 minutes to plant six trees. How long will it take to plant four more trees?

11/ SIMPLE INTEREST

Although in most cases interest is calculated using *compound* interest, **simple interest** can be used to find an approximate value for the interest. The **interest rate** is assumed to remain constant, and there is no attempt to add the interest each year.
The formula used is:

$$I = \frac{P \times R \times T}{100} = \frac{PRT}{100}$$

where I = interest, P = principal (sum of money), R = rate of interest (% p.a.), T = time (years), and p.a. means per annum or per year.

EXAMPLE

► Find the simple interest when £400 is invested for $2\frac{1}{2}$ years at an interest rate of $8\frac{1}{2}$% p.a.

$$I = \frac{PRT}{100} = \frac{£400 \times 8.5 \times 2.5}{100} = £85.00$$

EXAMPLE

► Find the approximate interest payable on an investment of £850 over 18 months at an interest rate of $11\frac{1}{4}$% p.a.

18 months = $1\frac{1}{2}$ years

$$I = \frac{PRT}{100} = \frac{£850 \times 1.5 \times 11.25}{100} = £143.4375 = £143.44 \text{ (to the nearest penny)}$$

Exercise 11A

Find the simple interest in each case. Give your answer to the nearest penny where appropriate.

1 £200 invested for 2 years at 4%
2 £400 invested for 2 years at 8%
3 £500 invested for 3 years at 7%
4 £700 invested for 3 years at $8\frac{1}{2}$%
5 £250 invested for 4 years at $7\frac{1}{2}$%
6 £350 invested for $3\frac{1}{2}$ years at 9%

7 £800 invested for 3 years at $11\frac{1}{2}$%

8 £450 invested for 4 years at $9\frac{1}{4}$%

9 £650 invested for $2\frac{1}{2}$ years at $10\frac{1}{2}$%

10 £910 invested for $3\frac{3}{4}$ years at $8\frac{1}{4}$%

11 £630 invested for $4\frac{1}{2}$ years at 7%

12 £890 invested for $2\frac{3}{4}$ years at $10\frac{3}{4}$%

13 £2560 invested for 1 year 9 months at 8%

14 £410 invested for 3 years 6 months at 10%

15 £1240 invested for 2 years 3 months at $9\frac{1}{2}$%

16 £683 invested for 3 months at 11%

17 £1040 invested for 1 year 9 months at $7\frac{1}{2}$%

18 £1270 invested for 6 months at $10\frac{1}{2}$%

19 £1125 invested for 2 years 3 months at $8\frac{1}{4}$%

20 £1450 invested for 1 year 9 months at $7\frac{3}{4}$%

Exercise 11B

Find the simple interest in each case. Give your answer to the nearest penny where appropriate.

1 £600 invested for 2 years at 7%

2 £500 invested for 2 years at 9%

3 £800 invested for 2 years at 12%

4 £1000 invested for 3 years at $9\frac{1}{2}$%

5 £650 invested for 3 years at 8%

6 £450 invested for $2\frac{1}{2}$ years at $7\frac{1}{2}$%

7 £250 invested for 2 years at $8\frac{1}{4}$%

8 £750 invested for 4 years at $12\frac{1}{2}$%

9 £850 invested for $3\frac{1}{4}$ years at $9\frac{3}{4}$%

10 £720 invested for $2\frac{3}{4}$ years at 11%

11 £440 invested for $4\frac{1}{4}$ years at 10%

12 £770 invested for $3\frac{3}{4}$ years at $8\frac{1}{2}$%

13 £840 invested for 2 years 6 months at 7%

14 £1840 invested for 1 year 3 months at 10%

15 £470 invested for 6 months at 8%

16 £872 invested for 1 year 9 months at $7\frac{1}{2}$%

17 £1140 invested for 3 years 6 months at $8\frac{1}{4}$%

18 £2750 invested for 3 months at 9%

19 £1450 invested for 2 years 9 months at $10\frac{1}{4}$%

20 £1850 invested for 1 year 3 months at $9\frac{3}{4}$%

EXAMPLE

► Approximately how long would it take for £400 to produce £50 simple interest at a rate of 8% p.a.? Give your answer to the nearest month.

$P = £400, I = £50, R = 8$

$$I = \frac{PRT}{100}$$

$$50 = \frac{400 \times 8 \times T}{100}$$

$$50 = 32T$$

$$T = \frac{50}{32} = 1.5625$$

Now 0.5625 years × 12 = 6.75 months

The time is 1 year 7 months (to the nearest month).

EXAMPLE

► Approximately how much money would need to be deposited in an account earning $7\frac{1}{2}$% p.a. interest, in order that interest of £80 is gained over a 2-year period? Give your answer to the nearest penny.

$R = 7\frac{1}{2}, I = £80, T = 2$

$$I = \frac{PRT}{100}$$

$$£80 = \frac{P \times 7.5 \times 2}{100}$$

$$£80 = 0.15P$$

$$\text{So } P = \frac{£80}{0.15} = £533.33$$

(to the nearest penny)

EXAMPLE

▶ Approximately what rate of interest is needed for £300 to earn £40 interest over a $1\frac{1}{2}$-year period. Give your answer correct to 2 decimal places.

$P = £300,\ I = £40,\ T = 1\frac{1}{2}$

$$I = \frac{PRT}{100}$$

$$£40 = \frac{£300 \times R \times 1.5}{100}$$

$$40 = 4.5R$$

$$\text{So } R = \frac{40}{4.5} = 8.89\% \text{ (correct to 2 d.p.)}$$

Exercise 11C

In this exercise give time to the nearest month, amounts of money to the nearest penny, and rates of interest to 2 decimal places.

Complete the table.

Question	*P*	*R*	*T*	*I*
1	£350		5 years	£105
2		$2\frac{1}{2}$%	5 years	£800
3	£350	8%		£42
4		9%	6 years	£351
5		14%	$4\frac{1}{2}$ years	£105
6	£250		4 years	£90
7	£500	7%		£35
8		$5\frac{1}{2}$%	8 years	£528
9	£350	8%		£126
10	£198	$7\frac{1}{2}$%		£84
11	£200		3 years	£30
12		4%	4 years	£360
13	£480		3 years	£36
14		9%	5 years	£333
15	£220		$2\frac{1}{2}$ years	£27.50
16		9%	4 years	£187.20
17	£1500	8%		£1440
18	£500	10%		£110
19		7%	$4\frac{1}{2}$ years	£300
20	£900		$3\frac{1}{2}$ years	£141.75

Exercise 11D

In this exercise give time to the nearest month, amounts of money to the nearest penny, and rates of interest to 2 decimal places.

Complete the table.

Question	P	R	T	I
1		6%	5 years	£120
2	£250		2 years	£12.50
3	£450	9%		£243
4	£420		4 years	£126
5		5%	5 years	£120
6		7%	5 years	£126
7	£500	8%		£170
8	£480	5%		£84
9	£900		6 years	£243
10	£500		3 years	£60
11	£200	7%		£14
12	£640		5 years	£200
13	£800	$7\frac{1}{2}$%		£450
14		$4\frac{1}{2}$%	5 years	£85.50
15		7%	4 years	£126
16	£850	11%		£200
17	£750		$2\frac{1}{2}$ years	£150
18	£150		3 years	£20.25
19		5%	2 years	£1000
20	£300	$8\frac{1}{4}$%		£40

12/ COMPOUND INTEREST

The usual way of calculating interest is by **compound** methods. Using this method the interest is added to the principal amount at various times. At each time the interest is added to the amount invested and the total then continues to earn interest.

The compound interest formula is:

$$A = P\left(1 + \frac{r}{100}\right)^n$$

where A = total final amount, P = principal, r = rate of interest for each payment period (not p.a.) and n = number of periods of interest payments.

EXAMPLE

► An amount of £650 is invested for $1\frac{1}{2}$ years at 7% p.a. compound interest, which is paid every 6 months. What is the total interest earned in this time?

Method 1

There are three 6-monthly intervals in $1\frac{1}{2}$ years. Six months is 0.5 of a year.

1st 6 months: $\frac{£650 \times 7 \times 0.5}{100} = £22.75$

Total amount: $£650 + £22.75 = £672.75$

2nd 6 months: $\frac{£672.75 \times 7 \times 0.5}{100} = £23.55$ (to the nearest penny)

Total amount: $£672.75 + £23.55 = £696.30$

3rd 6 months: $\frac{£696.30 \times 7 \times 0.5}{100} = £720.67$

Total amount: $£696.30 + £24.37 = £720.67$

Total interest earned = £720.67 – £650 = £70.67

Method 2

Using the compound interest formula:

$P = £650$, $r = 7 \times 0.5 = 3.5$, $n = 3$

So $A = £650\left(1 + \frac{3.5}{100}\right)^3$

$= 650 \times (1.035)^3$

$= £720.67$ (to the nearest penny)

Total interest earned = £720.67 – £650 = £70.67

Exercise 12A

In each question find the compound interest earned.

1 £250 invested for 2 years at 5% p.a., paid annually

2 £400 invested for 2 years at 7% p.a., paid annually

3 £500 invested for 3 years at 6% p.a., paid annually

4 £380 invested for 2 years at 6% p.a., paid annually
5 £780 invested for 3 years at 4% p.a., paid annually
6 £550 invested for 3 years at 6% p.a., paid annually
7 £825 invested for 3 years at 6% p.a., paid annually
8 £500 invested for 3 years at 9% p.a., paid annually
9 £180 invested for 4 years at $10\frac{1}{2}$% p.a., paid annually
10 £200 invested for 3 years at 4% p.a., paid annually
11 £186 invested for $1\frac{1}{2}$ years at 6% p.a., paid every 6 months
12 £370 invested for $1\frac{1}{2}$ years at $4\frac{1}{2}$% p.a., paid every 6 months
13 £700 invested for 2 years at $8\frac{1}{2}$% p.a., paid every 6 months
14 £300 invested for $1\frac{1}{2}$ years at $5\frac{1}{2}$% p.a., paid every 6 months
15 £800 invested for 1 year at 6% p.a., paid every 3 months
16 £200 invested for $1\frac{1}{2}$ years at $9\frac{1}{2}$% p.a., paid every 6 months
17 £280 invested for 2 years at $6\frac{1}{2}$% p.a., paid every 6 months
18 £181 invested for 2 years at 6% p.a., paid every 6 months
19 £1200 invested for $1\frac{1}{2}$ years at 7% p.a., paid every 3 months
20 £910 invested for 1 year at $8\frac{1}{4}$% p.a., paid every 3 months

Exercise 12B

In each question find the compound interest earned.

1 £520 invested for 2 years at 7% p.a., paid annually
2 £450 invested for 2 years at 6% p.a., paid annually
3 £400 invested for 3 years at 5% p.a., paid annually
4 £950 invested for 3 years at 4% p.a., paid annually
5 £700 invested for 2 years at $4\frac{1}{2}$% p.a., paid annually
6 £650 invested for 2 years at 7% p.a., paid annually
7 £200 invested for 3 years at $9\frac{1}{2}$% p.a., paid annually
8 £720 invested for 3 years at 8% p.a., paid annually
9 £475 invested for 2 years at 5% p.a., paid annually
10 £360 invested for 2 years at 3% p.a., paid annually
11 £200 invested for 4 years at 5% p.a., paid annually
12 £4000 invested for 4 years at 10% p.a., paid every 6 months
13 £500 invested for $1\frac{1}{2}$ years at 5% p.a., paid every 6 months
14 £408 invested for 2 years at 6% p.a., paid every 6 months
15 £80 invested for $1\frac{1}{2}$ years at $8\frac{1}{4}$% p.a., paid every 6 months
16 £200 invested for $1\frac{1}{2}$ years at 5% p.a., paid every 6 months
17 £312 invested for 2 years at $7\frac{1}{2}$% p.a., paid every 6 months
18 £900 invested for 1 year at 6% p.a., paid every 3 months
19 £2700 invested for 2 years at $6\frac{1}{2}$% p.a., paid every 6 months
20 £840 invested for 1 year at 7% p.a., paid every 3 months

13/ INVERSE PERCENTAGE

Inverse percentage is used when an amount is given after a percentage change, and the original amount is needed (that is, before the percentage change).

EXAMPLE

▶ The monthly rental of a satellite system is increased by 14% to £20.52. What was the charge before the increase?

The original amount is 100%.

£20.52 is 100% + 14% = 114% of the original price.

So 114% is £20.52

$$1\% \text{ is } \frac{£20.52}{114}$$

$$100\% \text{ is } \frac{£20.52}{114} \times 100 = £18.00$$

EXAMPLE

▶ The value of a motorbike has decreased by 32% to £5168. What was the original value?

The original amount is 100%.

£5168 is 100% – 32% = 68% of the original price.

So 68% is £5168

$$1\% \text{ is } \frac{£5168}{68}$$

$$100\% \text{ is } \frac{£5168}{68} \times 100 = £7600$$

Exercise 13A

1 A carpet is sold for £72 and this makes a profit of 20%. What did the carpet originally cost?

2 A car stereo has been increased in price by $7\frac{1}{2}$% to £172. What was its original price?

3 A table costs £282, including $17\frac{1}{2}$% VAT. What does the table cost without the VAT?

4 The price of a car has increased by 8% to £12 960. What is the amount of the increase?

5 An aeroplane ticket to Madrid has risen by 25% to £109. What was the price before the increase?

6 The weight of a van load increased by $22\frac{1}{2}$% to 122.5 kg. What was the original weight of the load?

7 A portfolio of shares is sold for £2112, which is a loss of 12%. What did it originally cost to buy the shares?

8 A holiday costs £715 after a 10% surcharge has been added. What does the holiday cost without the surcharge?

9 Car insurance is £320 after a 60% no-claims discount has been deducted. What is the full cost of the insurance?

10 A bathroom suite costs £305.50 inclusive of VAT at $17\frac{1}{2}$%. What is the cost of the bathroom suite without the VAT?

11 The price of a telephone has increased by 8% to £27. What was its original cost?

12 A radio is sold for £22. This is a profit of 10%. What did it originally cost?

13 A car costs £15 000 after the addition of 20% import duties. What would it cost without the duties?

14 A photocopier increases the size of a page by 24% to give an area of 465 cm^2. Find the original area of the page.

15 A worker's salary is £8679.75 after a wage increase of $6\frac{1}{2}\%$. What was the worker's salary before the wage increase?

16 The value of a house has increased by 15% and is now £69 000. What was its value originally?

17 During one year the price of a tin of ham increased by 4% to £1.56. What did it cost at the start of the year?

18 The price of a train ticket has gone up by 15% to £3.45. What was its original price?

19 During one month a plant increases its length by 25% to 15 cm. What length was it at the beginning of the month?

20 A newsagent delivers 168 papers each evening. This is 4% fewer than last year. How many newspapers were delivered last year?

Exercise 13B

1 A radio is reduced in price by 5% to £190. What was its original price?

2 A holiday costs £900 after a $12\frac{1}{2}\%$ surcharge was added. How much would the holiday cost without the surcharge?

3 A coat is reduced by $12\frac{1}{2}\%$ to £56 in a sale. What was the original price of the coat?

4 A building job costs £15 040 inclusive of $17\frac{1}{2}\%$ VAT. How much does it cost without the VAT?

5 A car insurance quotation is £400 after a 60% no-claims discount. How much is the car insurance without the discount?

6 A second-hand car has its price reduced by 15% to £6800. How much money has been taken off its price?

7 A suit costs £39 after a price increase of 30%. What was its original price before the increase?

8 The price of a vase is reduced by 10% to £36. What was its price before the reduction?

9 A cooker is priced at £728.50 inclusive of $17\frac{1}{2}\%$ VAT. What would the cooker cost without the VAT?

10 A calculator costs £3.80 after a 5% reduction in its price. What was the price of the calculator before the reduction?

11 A man weighs 220 kg, having lost 12% of his original weight. What was the original weight of the man?

12 In July there were 1008 pupils at a school. This is 12% more than in September. How many pupils were at the school in September?

13 A train ticket costs £18 after a 4% discount. How much did it cost before the discount?

14 A plant increases its height by 45%. It is now 58 cm. What was its original length?

15 By the end of a night-school course 25% of the students had dropped out. There were 18 students left. How many students started the course?

16 The value of a house increased by 8% and is now £70 200. What was its original value?

17 A tie is reduced by 15% in a sale to £13.60. What was the price of the tie before the sale?

18 The price of a typewriter is increased by 6% to £190.80. What was its original price?

19 A car has its price increased by 5% to £15 288. What was the price of the car before the increase?

20 Eileen has paid £26 103 off her mortgage. This is 42% of the value of the mortgage. What is the full value of the mortgage?

14/ GENERAL PROBLEMS

Exercise 14A

1 Find the $17\frac{1}{2}$% VAT on a £85.50 bill for a meal for four.

2 The cost of renting a photocopier for a year is made up of an annual charge of £120 plus a charge of 1.5p per copy. Over the first year 12 500 copies are made. (a) What is the cost of renting the copier for the year? (b) What is the average cost per copy over that year?

3 A mechanic works a basic $37\frac{1}{2}$-hour week, and overtime is paid at 'time and a half'. The basic hourly rate is £4.70 per hour. She works five hours' overtime (a total of $42\frac{1}{2}$ hours work). Calculate her weekly wage.

4 The insurance premium on a car was £350. (a) How much is payable with a 30% discount? (b) How much is payable if the premium is increased by 5% but there is also a 40% discount?

5 A television set which cost £350 last year is now £380. Find the percentage increase in cost.

6 Darren earns £50.80 for five hours' work at the weekend on 'double time'. What basic hourly rate is he paid during the week?

7 For each article up to a maximum of 200 a worker is paid 12p. Above this limit she is paid 15p. How much is she paid for making 300 articles?

8 A drum kit costs £1500 plus VAT at $17\frac{1}{2}$%. There is a 10% discount if payment is by cash. Calculate the cost if payment is by cash.

9 A 3-litre bottle of orange cordial was 55% full. A 2.5-litre bottle was three-quarters full. How much is in the bottle which contains the most orange cordial?

10 A car salesman receives 5% commission on the sale of a £12 000 car. How much is this?

11 The cost of a single ticket for a bus journey is 72p. A book of twelve single tickets is £8.40.
(a) How much is saved on each journey by buying a book of tickets?
(b) Express, correct to 1 decimal place, this saving as a percentage of the cost of buying a single ticket.

12 A kitchen table is offered for sale with a £200 cash price or a 20% deposit with ten payments of £21 each. Find (a) the cost of the credit terms (b) the difference between the credit cost and the cash price.

13 The number of students at a college rises from 1832 to 2009. What is this as a percentage increase?

14 An electricity bill is made up of a standing charge of £16.40 and a charge of 8.5p for each unit. Calculate the total bill when the number of units used is 750.

15 A man in a shop earns £1.83 per hour and commission of 8% on sales. How much is he paid for 38 hours' work and sales of £450 during the week?

16 A table is advertised at £98 plus VAT at $17\frac{1}{2}$%. What is the total purchase price?

17 A gardener needs weedkiller for a lawn of area 625 m^2. A can of weedkiller costing £5.69 will treat 125 m^2 of lawn. Calculate the total cost to treat the lawn.

18 The bill for a mobile telephone is made up of a line rental of £20 per month plus a charge of 62p per minute. Calculate a monthly bill if the telephone has been used for a total of 55 minutes.

19 Tina is paid 20p for each piece of work up to 100. After that she is paid a rate of 26p per piece. How much does she earn if she completes 130 pieces of work?

20 The credit agreement on a £4950 motorbike requires an initial deposit of 20% and 36 payments of £136.55. Find (a) the total cost of the credit terms (b) the difference in cost between the credit terms and the cash price.

Exercise 14B

1 A bill for a mobile telephone is made up of a line rental of £15 per month plus a charge of 90p per minute. Calculate a monthly bill if the telephone has been used for a total of 18 minutes.

2 Adam sells newspapers in the precinct. He is paid a basic rate of £1.30 per hour and $4\frac{1}{2}$% commission on sales. How much is he paid for 25 hours' work and sales of £190 during the week?

3 A man earns £154.44. He has worked 39 hours at a basic rate. What is his basic hourly rate of pay?

4 A distributor employs part-time staff to deliver leaflets at the rate of £5.20 for every complete 100 leaflets. How much is paid for the delivery of 1550 leaflets?

5 A lawnmower costs £155.80 plus VAT at $17\frac{1}{2}$%. What is the total cost of the lawnmower?

6 A garage offers $12\frac{1}{2}$% off a service normally costing £180. How much will the service now cost?

7 Photographic equipment costs £350. It can also be bought with a credit agreement which requires a 20% deposit and 30 payments of £14.90. Find (a) the total cost of the credit terms (b) the difference between the cost of the credit agreement and the cash price.

8 Helen works part time as a secretary and is paid £6.40 per hour. These are the hours she worked last week:
Mon. 9 a.m.–5 p.m., Tue. 9 a.m.–12 noon, Thu. 9 a.m.–5 p.m., Fri. 9 a.m.–3 p.m.
She has an hour off for lunch between 12 noon and 1 p.m. How much is she paid for this week's work?

9 Find the monthly repayments on a 9% p.a. loan of £16 540.

10 Last year a bicycle cost £120. Now its price is £126. By what percentage has the price increased?

11 An antique bookcase is sold for £846. An initial deposit of £165.60 is paid, followed by monthly repayments of £32.40 How long does it take to pay off the debt?

12 Ali is paid £4.25 each for the express delivery of container boxes. If he delivers more than 20 in a day, he is paid an extra 60p per box for those boxes over the first 20. How much will he be paid for delivering 28 boxes?

13 The cost of a satellite system has fallen from £240 to £210. What is the percentage decrease in price?

14 As a result of winning a competition Sandra can have either a two-thirds share of £139.53 or 49% of £186. What is the maximum amount of money she can win?

15 A telephone bill is £80.60 plus VAT at $17\frac{1}{2}$%. What is the total cost?

16 Off-peak electricity is charged at a cheaper tariff of 2.9p per unit but needs a special meter costing £2.50 a month. If 380 units are used in a month, calculate the total cost.

17 Shreena's basic week is 38 hours at £4.10 per hour. She also works five hours' overtime a week at 'time and a half'. Calculate her weekly wage.

18 A £225 electric typewriter can also be bought with a credit agreement requiring an initial deposit of 20%, plus 12 monthly payments of £18.99. Find (a) the total cost of the credit agreement (b) the difference between the cost of the credit agreement and the cash price.

19 Serafim is a keen squash player. The local club charges an annual subscription of £175 and 50p for each 20 minutes on the squash court. He likes to play for one hour, four times a week. How much will it cost him to play squash in one full year?

20 Sandra sells cosmetics at the door. She is paid £2.65 per hour and 15% commission on sales. How much is she paid for five hours' work and sales of £120?

15/ ADDITION OF FRACTIONS

EXAMPLES

▶ (a) $\frac{1}{4} + \frac{2}{5}$ (b) $\frac{3}{4} + \frac{5}{12}$ (c) $5\frac{1}{2} + 6\frac{5}{7}$

(a) $\frac{1}{4} + \frac{2}{5}$ — The denominators, 4 and 5, have a lowest common denominator of 20. Multiply top and bottom of $\frac{1}{4}$ by 5, and top and bottom of $\frac{2}{5}$ by 4.

$= \frac{5}{20} + \frac{8}{20}$ — These two fractions now have common denominators and can be added.

$= \frac{13}{20}$

(b) $\frac{3}{4} + \frac{5}{12}$ — The lowest common denominator is 12; only $\frac{3}{4}$ needs changing (multiply by 3).

$= \frac{9}{12} + \frac{5}{12}$

$= \frac{14}{12}$ — Cancel by 2.

$= \frac{7}{6}$ — Change the top-heavy fraction into a mixed number.

$= 1\frac{1}{6}$

(c) $5\frac{1}{2} + 6\frac{5}{7}$ — Add the whole numbers first.

$= 11\frac{1}{2} + \frac{5}{7}$ — The common denominator is 14.

$= 11\frac{7}{14} + \frac{10}{14}$

$= 11\frac{17}{14}$ — Change the top-heavy fraction into a mixed number.

$= 11 + 1\frac{3}{14}$

$= 12\frac{3}{14}$

Exercise 15A

1 $\frac{1}{4} + \frac{1}{12}$	**2** $\frac{1}{4} + \frac{1}{5}$	**3** $\frac{1}{3} + \frac{2}{5}$	**4** $\frac{3}{4} + \frac{1}{5}$	**5** $\frac{1}{4} + \frac{3}{7}$
6 $\frac{2}{5} + \frac{2}{9}$	**7** $\frac{4}{5} + \frac{7}{10}$	**8** $\frac{3}{4} + \frac{1}{6}$	**9** $\frac{7}{9} + \frac{3}{4}$	**10** $\frac{2}{3} + \frac{3}{4}$
11 $\frac{1}{2} + \frac{4}{5}$	**12** $\frac{5}{9} + \frac{3}{4}$	**13** $\frac{8}{9} + 4\frac{2}{3}$	**14** $4\frac{1}{7} + 6\frac{1}{2}$	**15** $4\frac{7}{8} + 2\frac{3}{4}$
16 $3\frac{4}{5} + 7\frac{7}{10}$	**17** $2\frac{3}{4} + 3\frac{2}{3}$	**18** $4\frac{3}{4} + 3\frac{4}{5}$	**19** $1\frac{5}{6} + 4\frac{1}{2}$	**20** $4\frac{8}{9} + 3\frac{3}{4}$
21 $7\frac{3}{8} + 1\frac{3}{4}$	**22** $3\frac{7}{10} + 4\frac{4}{5}$	**23** $3\frac{5}{12} + 4\frac{3}{8}$	**24** $2\frac{8}{9} + 1\frac{1}{4}$	**25** $2\frac{5}{6} + 3\frac{11}{15}$

26 A tin contains $5\frac{5}{8}$ litres of water. A further $3\frac{1}{4}$ litres of water are added to the tank. How much water is there now in the tank?

27 A farmer ploughed $2\frac{2}{3}$ hectares of land in the morning. In the afternoon he ploughs a further $3\frac{4}{9}$ hectares. What total area of land has been ploughed?

28 Two parcels are to be delivered to an address. Their weights are $2\frac{3}{4}$ kg and $3\frac{1}{2}$ kg. What is the total weight of the two parcels?

29 A triangle has sides of length $4\frac{1}{2}$ cm, $3\frac{2}{3}$ cm and $4\frac{1}{3}$ cm. Find the perimeter of the triangle.

30 Two pieces of wood, $3\frac{3}{4}$ metres and $2\frac{1}{2}$ metres in length, are fastened together, end to end. What is their total length?

Exercise 15B

1 $\frac{1}{4}+\frac{1}{6}$	**2** $\frac{1}{4}+\frac{1}{20}$	**3** $\frac{1}{3}+\frac{3}{5}$	**4** $\frac{2}{3}+\frac{1}{4}$	**5** $\frac{2}{7}+\frac{3}{8}$
6 $\frac{2}{5}+\frac{2}{7}$	**7** $\frac{2}{3}+\frac{5}{6}$	**8** $\frac{3}{4}+\frac{2}{5}$	**9** $\frac{2}{3}+\frac{1}{2}$	**10** $\frac{5}{6}+\frac{1}{5}$
11 $\frac{3}{5}+\frac{1}{2}$	**12** $\frac{7}{10}+\frac{2}{3}$	**13** $\frac{7}{12}+3\frac{3}{4}$	**14** $3\frac{1}{3}+2\frac{1}{2}$	**15** $4\frac{1}{2}+3\frac{3}{4}$
16 $2\frac{9}{10}+3\frac{19}{20}$	**17** $2\frac{3}{5}+3\frac{1}{4}$	**18** $3\frac{1}{3}+4\frac{11}{12}$	**19** $5\frac{5}{6}+2\frac{2}{3}$	**20** $8\frac{3}{10}+1\frac{2}{5}$
21 $4\frac{2}{3}+3\frac{3}{5}$	**22** $2\frac{1}{2}+4\frac{9}{11}$	**23** $2\frac{1}{2}+2\frac{3}{4}$	**24** $5\frac{1}{2}+3\frac{2}{7}$	**25** $2\frac{5}{8}+4\frac{1}{2}$

26 Two pieces of string, $5\frac{2}{3}$ metres and $6\frac{3}{4}$ metres long, are fastened together. What is the total length?

27 A triangle has sides of length $6\frac{1}{4}$ cm, $7\frac{5}{12}$ cm and $9\frac{2}{3}$ cm. Find the perimeter.

28 A tin can contains $2\frac{5}{8}$ litres of orange cordial. A further $1\frac{1}{2}$ litres are added. How much orange cordial is now in the tin?

29 Harold spent $\frac{3}{4}$ of his pocket money on Monday and $\frac{1}{7}$ of his money on Tuesday. What fraction of his pocket money did he have left?

30 Jeremy bought two fish of weights $1\frac{3}{4}$ kg and $1\frac{5}{6}$ kg. What is the total weight of the two fish?

16/ SUBTRACTION OF FRACTIONS

EXAMPLES

► (a) $\frac{3}{4} - \frac{2}{3}$ (b) $2\frac{1}{2} - 1\frac{1}{3}$ (c) $5\frac{1}{6} - 2\frac{2}{3}$

(a) $\frac{3}{4} - \frac{2}{3}$

The denominators, 4 and 3, have a lowest common denominator of 12. Multiply the top and bottom of $\frac{3}{4}$ by 3, and the top and bottom of $\frac{2}{3}$ by 4.

$= \frac{9}{12} - \frac{8}{12}$

$= \frac{1}{12}$

(b) $2\frac{1}{2} - 1\frac{1}{3}$

Subtract the whole numbers first and then the fractions.

$= 1\frac{1}{2} - \frac{1}{3}$

The lowest common denominator is 6.

$= 1\frac{3}{6} - \frac{2}{6}$

$= 1\frac{1}{6}$

(c) $5\frac{1}{6} - 2\frac{2}{3}$

Subtract the whole numbers first and then the fractions.

$= 3\frac{1}{6} - \frac{2}{3}$

The lowest common denominator is 6.

$= 3 + \frac{1}{6} - \frac{4}{6}$

Note: 1 – 4 = –3, giving the minus fraction $-\frac{3}{6}$.

$= 3 - \frac{3}{6}$

$= 2\frac{3}{6}$

$= 2\frac{1}{2}$

Exercise 16A

1 $\frac{1}{2} - \frac{1}{7}$	**2** $\frac{3}{5} - \frac{1}{10}$	**3** $\frac{7}{9} - \frac{1}{2}$	**4** $\frac{5}{8} - \frac{2}{5}$	**5** $\frac{7}{8} - \frac{1}{3}$
6 $\frac{2}{3} - \frac{3}{5}$	**7** $\frac{3}{4} - \frac{2}{5}$	**8** $6\frac{4}{5} - 3\frac{2}{9}$	**9** $7\frac{3}{4} - 4\frac{3}{5}$	**10** $9\frac{3}{4} - 2\frac{1}{10}$
11 $3\frac{7}{12} - 1\frac{2}{9}$	**12** $2\frac{1}{2} - 1\frac{1}{3}$	**13** $7\frac{9}{16} - 1\frac{1}{8}$	**14** $3\frac{3}{4} - 1\frac{1}{3}$	**15** $4\frac{4}{5} - 2\frac{7}{20}$
16 $9\frac{4}{5} - 1\frac{3}{8}$	**17** $7\frac{5}{6} - 3\frac{3}{10}$	**18** $3\frac{7}{9} - 1\frac{1}{2}$	**19** $4\frac{5}{6} - 1\frac{1}{3}$	**20** $7\frac{2}{9} - 4\frac{4}{9}$
21 $10\frac{1}{6} - 2\frac{2}{3}$	**22** $3\frac{7}{10} - 1\frac{2}{3}$	**23** $3\frac{7}{12} - 2\frac{2}{3}$	**24** $2\frac{4}{7} - 1\frac{4}{5}$	**25** $8\frac{1}{3} - 2\frac{4}{5}$

26 A hi-fi unit is delivered in a box. Together the unit and the box weigh $9\frac{3}{4}$ kg. The hi-fi unit weighs $8\frac{1}{5}$ kg. How heavy is the box and packaging?

27 A field has an area of $1\frac{3}{5}$ hectares. Vegetables are planted on $\frac{3}{8}$ hectare. What area of land is available for other crops?

28 A tank contains $2\frac{3}{8}$ litres of fruit juice. If $\frac{4}{5}$ litre is taken out, what amount of fruit juice is left?

29 A garden pond is $3\frac{1}{2}$ feet deep. After several weeks' drought its depth is $2\frac{2}{5}$ feet. By how much has the water level fallen?

30 A string has a length of $4\frac{1}{3}$ metres. A piece of length $1\frac{7}{10}$ metres is cut off. What length of string remains?

Exercise 16B

1 $\frac{3}{4} - \frac{1}{2}$	**2** $\frac{4}{5} - \frac{3}{10}$	**3** $\frac{3}{4} - \frac{3}{8}$	**4** $\frac{3}{5} - \frac{1}{2}$	**5** $\frac{3}{4} - \frac{2}{3}$
6 $\frac{4}{5} - \frac{1}{4}$	**7** $\frac{7}{9} - \frac{2}{3}$	**8** $8\frac{2}{3} - 4\frac{2}{5}$	**9** $4\frac{7}{8} - 2\frac{2}{3}$	**10** $6\frac{13}{16} - 4\frac{2}{3}$
11 $8\frac{11}{12} - 2\frac{4}{9}$	**12** $4\frac{7}{8} - 2\frac{1}{2}$	**13** $6\frac{4}{5} - 2\frac{3}{10}$	**14** $5\frac{9}{10} - 3\frac{1}{6}$	**15** $3\frac{5}{8} - 1\frac{1}{4}$
16 $3\frac{2}{3} - 1\frac{1}{4}$	**17** $3\frac{17}{20} - 2\frac{2}{3}$	**18** $8\frac{3}{8} - 4\frac{5}{6}$	**19** $4\frac{7}{12} - 1\frac{1}{3}$	**20** $4\frac{7}{10} - 2\frac{4}{5}$
21 $4\frac{3}{8} - 3\frac{3}{4}$	**22** $4\frac{1}{8} - 2\frac{3}{8}$	**23** $3\frac{1}{4} - 2\frac{4}{5}$	**24** $3\frac{1}{5} - 1\frac{1}{2}$	**25** $3\frac{2}{9} - 2\frac{4}{5}$

26 A can contains $7\frac{1}{2}$ litres of oil. If $2\frac{3}{8}$ litres of oil are poured out, how much oil remains?

27 A third of James' salary is spent on bills. A half is spent on food and household goods. What fraction of his salary is left?

28 A box is to be posted. The box weighs $1\frac{1}{4}$ kg. The box and its contents weigh $6\frac{7}{8}$ kg. What is the weight of the contents?

29 A plank of wood has a length of $5\frac{3}{8}$ metres. Then $2\frac{1}{2}$ metres is cut off the end. What length of wood remains?

30 The length of a patio is $8\frac{3}{5}$ metres. A section of $1\frac{3}{8}$ metres is to be converted into an area for barbecues. What length of patio will remain?

17/ MULTIPLICATION OF FRACTIONS

When multiplying fractions all mixed numbers must be changed into improper (top-heavy) fractions. Whole numbers cannot be dealt with separately.

EXAMPLES

► (a) $\frac{4}{9} \times \frac{7}{8}$ (b) $\frac{2}{3} \times 36$ (c) $5\frac{1}{4} \times 2\frac{2}{7}$ (d) $9\frac{1}{2} \times 3\frac{1}{2}$

(a) $\frac{4}{9} \times \frac{7}{8} = \frac{28}{72} = \frac{7}{18}$

(b) $\frac{2}{3} \times 36$ Write single whole numbers over 1.

$= \frac{2}{\cancel{3}_1} \times \frac{\cancel{36}^{12}}{1}$ The problem is made easier by cancelling numbers diagonally.

$= \frac{2}{1} \times \frac{12}{1}$

$= 24$

(c) $5\frac{1}{4} \times 2\frac{2}{7}$ Change mixed numbers to improper fractions.

$= \frac{\cancel{21}^{3}}{\cancel{4}_1} \times \frac{\cancel{16}^{4}}{\cancel{7}_1}$ Cancel, then multiply across.

$= \frac{12}{1}$

$= 12$

(d) $9\frac{1}{2} \times 3\frac{1}{2}$

$= \frac{19}{2} \times \frac{7}{2}$ It is not always possible to cancel.

$= \frac{133}{4}$ Simplify the answer: cancel if possible and then write as a mixed number.

$= 33\frac{1}{4}$

Exercise 17A

1 $\frac{3}{4} \times 8$	**2** $\frac{5}{8} \times 16$	**3** $\frac{3}{4} \times 2$	**4** $\frac{2}{3} \times 27$	**5** $\frac{4}{7} \times \frac{7}{8}$
6 $\frac{3}{5} \times \frac{4}{8}$	**7** $\frac{3}{4} \times \frac{4}{9}$	**8** $\frac{3}{7} \times \frac{1}{3}$	**9** $\frac{6}{7} \times \frac{5}{12}$	**10** $\frac{1}{8} \times \frac{2}{3}$
11 $\frac{4}{5} \times \frac{3}{8}$	**12** $\frac{3}{8} \times \frac{2}{3}$	**13** $\frac{2}{3} \times \frac{9}{10}$	**14** $2\frac{1}{2} \times \frac{3}{4}$	**15** $2\frac{3}{4} \times 4\frac{1}{2}$
16 $2\frac{1}{7} \times 1\frac{2}{5}$	**17** $5\frac{4}{9} \times 3\frac{5}{7}$	**18** $7\frac{1}{5} \times 2\frac{1}{4}$	**19** $8\frac{3}{4} \times 3\frac{5}{7}$	**20** $3\frac{3}{4} \times 2\frac{2}{5}$
21 $3\frac{1}{5} \times 2\frac{1}{3}$	**22** $3\frac{3}{7} \times 1\frac{1}{2}$	**23** $9\frac{1}{3} \times 4\frac{3}{4}$	**24** $1\frac{3}{5} \times 2\frac{1}{2}$	**25** $4\frac{4}{5} \times 2\frac{1}{6}$

26 A tin contains $1\frac{2}{3}$ litres of oil. If $\frac{3}{5}$ of the oil is taken out, how many litres of oil are removed?

27 A road is $2\frac{1}{2}$ km long and $\frac{2}{5}$ of the road needs new white lines. What length of road needs repainting?

28 A farmer grows apples on $\frac{3}{4}$ of his field, which is $2\frac{3}{5}$ hectares in area. What area of the field is used for growing apples?

29 A piece of cloth is $4\frac{1}{2}$ metres long. If $\frac{5}{8}$ of the length is cut away, what length of cloth remains?

30 Shelley has $1\frac{3}{4}$ litres of lemon drink. Tina has $2\frac{1}{2}$ times as much. How many litres has Tina?

Exercise 17B

1 $\frac{3}{7} \times 14$	**2** $\frac{4}{5} \times 5$	**3** $\frac{8}{9} \times 27$	**4** $\frac{3}{4} \times 40$	**5** $\frac{4}{5} \times \frac{3}{8}$
6 $\frac{5}{12} \times \frac{7}{15}$	**7** $\frac{7}{8} \times \frac{16}{21}$	**8** $\frac{4}{5} \times \frac{5}{8}$	**9** $\frac{3}{7} \times \frac{14}{15}$	**10** $\frac{2}{3} \times \frac{1}{4}$
11 $\frac{2}{3} \times \frac{6}{7}$	**12** $\frac{8}{9} \times \frac{3}{4}$	**13** $\frac{4}{5} \times \frac{15}{16}$	**14** $3\frac{3}{4} \times 1\frac{1}{2}$	**15** $7\frac{1}{2} \times \frac{1}{8}$
16 $1\frac{4}{5} \times 1\frac{2}{9}$	**17** $1\frac{1}{2} \times 1\frac{1}{2}$	**18** $6\frac{9}{10} \times 1\frac{1}{23}$	**19** $2\frac{1}{2} \times 4\frac{2}{5}$	**20** $3\frac{3}{8} \times 2\frac{2}{3}$
21 $7\frac{1}{7} \times 2\frac{4}{5}$	**22** $5\frac{1}{7} \times 2\frac{4}{9}$	**23** $3\frac{3}{4} \times 2\frac{3}{4}$	**24** $2\frac{3}{4} \times 1\frac{1}{4}$	**25** $2\frac{2}{3} \times 2\frac{1}{4}$

26 A field has an area of $1\frac{2}{3}$ hectares and $\frac{1}{3}$ of the field is used for grazing. What area of the field is used for grazing?

27 A box contains $2\frac{1}{3}$ kg of sand. If $\frac{2}{3}$ of the sand is removed, what weight of sand remains?

28 Amanda has $2\frac{3}{4}$ litres of orange cordial. Bill has $2\frac{1}{4}$ times as much. How many litres has Bill?

29 A tank contains $2\frac{1}{3}$ litres of water. Then $\frac{2}{5}$ of it is drained off. How many litres remain in the tank?

30 A waste tip covers an area of $5\frac{3}{5}$ hectares and $\frac{3}{4}$ of the tip is covered with waste. What area is free of waste?

18/ DIVISION OF FRACTIONS

The rule for dividing fractions is:
'Turn the fraction you are dividing by upside-down and multiply.'

EXAMPLES

▶ (a) $\frac{2}{5} \div \frac{3}{4}$ (b) $\frac{2}{3} \div 4$ (c) $2\frac{3}{4} \div 1\frac{1}{4}$

(a) $\frac{2}{5} \div \frac{3}{4} = \frac{2}{5} \times \frac{4}{3} = \frac{8}{15}$

(b) $\frac{2}{3} \div 4 = \frac{2}{3} \div \frac{4}{1}$

$= \frac{2}{3} \times \frac{1}{4}$

$= \frac{1}{6}$

(c) $2\frac{3}{4} \div 1\frac{1}{4} = \frac{11}{4} \div \frac{5}{4}$

$= \frac{11}{\cancel{4}_1} \times \frac{\cancel{4}^1}{5}$

$= \frac{11}{5}$

$= 2\frac{1}{5}$

Exercise 18A

1 $\frac{1}{4} \div 3$	**2** $\frac{3}{5} \div 2$	**3** $\frac{4}{9} \div 5$	**4** $2\frac{2}{3} \div 5$	**5** $1\frac{3}{8} \div 4$
6 $4\frac{7}{8} \div 2$	**7** $\frac{1}{2} \div \frac{2}{3}$	**8** $\frac{8}{15} \div \frac{4}{9}$	**9** $\frac{9}{16} \div \frac{3}{14}$	**10** $\frac{13}{14} \div \frac{2}{7}$
11 $\frac{7}{20} \div \frac{2}{5}$	**12** $\frac{13}{14} \div \frac{13}{15}$	**13** $3\frac{3}{4} \div 1\frac{1}{2}$	**14** $3\frac{1}{8} \div 2\frac{1}{2}$	**15** $9\frac{3}{8} \div 3\frac{3}{4}$
16 $8\frac{5}{8} \div 2\frac{1}{4}$	**17** $3\frac{3}{8} \div 2\frac{1}{4}$	**18** $2\frac{1}{7} \div 3\frac{3}{4}$	**19** $3\frac{3}{4} \div 7\frac{1}{2}$	**20** $4\frac{1}{2} \div 3\frac{1}{2}$
21 $1\frac{1}{2} \div 3\frac{3}{4}$	**22** $5\frac{1}{3} \div 2\frac{3}{4}$	**23** $3\frac{3}{4} \div 3\frac{3}{4}$	**24** $2\frac{1}{2} \div 1\frac{1}{4}$	**25** $3\frac{1}{3} \div 1\frac{1}{9}$

26 A metal sheet is $9\frac{3}{5}$ metres long. How many short strips, each $\frac{7}{10}$ metre long, can be cut from the sheet?

27 If $9\frac{1}{2}$ kg of coffee is put into $\frac{3}{4}$ kg packets, how many packets are needed?

28 A road is $5\frac{4}{5}$ km long. It is being resurfaced at the rate of $\frac{2}{3}$ km a day. How long will it take to resurface the road?

29 A tin contains $8\frac{2}{3}$ litres of water. How many $1\frac{1}{4}$ litre containers can be filled from the tin?

30 A woman can walk $1\frac{3}{4}$ km in an hour. How long will it take her to walk $15\frac{5}{6}$ km?

Exercise 18B

1 $\frac{2}{3} \div 3$ **2** $\frac{1}{2} \div 8$ **3** $\frac{3}{4} \div 4$ **4** $3\frac{1}{4} \div 4$ **5** $2\frac{1}{5} \div 3$

6 $5\frac{1}{5} \div 7$ **7** $\frac{4}{7} \div \frac{6}{7}$ **8** $\frac{9}{16} \div \frac{1}{2}$ **9** $\frac{11}{12} \div \frac{3}{4}$ **10** $\frac{13}{14} \div \frac{4}{7}$

11 $\frac{9}{16} \div \frac{2}{3}$ **12** $\frac{2}{5} \div \frac{3}{4}$ **13** $2\frac{1}{2} \div 3\frac{1}{3}$ **14** $6\frac{2}{3} \div 3\frac{3}{4}$ **15** $2\frac{4}{5} \div 1\frac{2}{5}$

16 $4\frac{4}{5} \div 1\frac{3}{5}$ **17** $3\frac{1}{5} \div 2\frac{2}{3}$ **18** $7\frac{1}{5} \div 2\frac{1}{4}$ **19** $3\frac{3}{4} \div 3\frac{1}{8}$ **20** $3\frac{1}{3} \div 1\frac{1}{4}$

21 $4\frac{5}{7} \div 1\frac{2}{7}$ **22** $3\frac{1}{2} \div 1\frac{3}{4}$ **23** $2\frac{2}{3} \div 1\frac{1}{6}$ **24** $5\frac{1}{4} \div 2\frac{1}{3}$ **25** $1\frac{1}{4} \div 2\frac{1}{5}$

26 If $12\frac{1}{2}$ kg of flour are packed into $1\frac{1}{4}$ kg packets, how many packets are needed?

27 A tank contains $12\frac{1}{4}$ litres of oil. How many $1\frac{3}{4}$ litre tins can be filled from the tank?

28 A plank of wood is $6\frac{3}{4}$ metres long. How many pieces of wood of length $1\frac{1}{3}$ metres can be cut from the plank?

29 A farmer has $25\frac{3}{4}$ hectares of land. He can plough $1\frac{2}{3}$ hectares every day. How many days will he take to plough the land?

30 A rope is of length $7\frac{2}{3}$ metres. How many $\frac{3}{4}$ metre pieces can be cut from the rope?

REVISION

Exercise B

1 Find the simple interest on £200 for 5 years at $7\frac{1}{2}$% p.a.
2 Find the time in which £150 will earn £30 simple interest at 6% p.a.
3 Find the principal amount which will earn £120 simple interest in 6 years at 4% p.a.
4 Find the rate (% p.a.) at which £200 will earn £70 simple interest in 5 years.
5 Find the compound interest when £507 is invested for 4 years at 5% p.a., paid annually.
6 Find the compound interest when £1200 is invested for 2 years at $6\frac{1}{2}$% p.a., paid annually.

7 (a) $\frac{1}{3} + \frac{3}{8}$ (b) $2\frac{7}{8} + 3\frac{9}{16}$ (c) $4\frac{7}{10} + 1\frac{1}{5}$

8 (a) $\frac{5}{8} - \frac{11}{24}$ (b) $8\frac{7}{8} - 7\frac{5}{6}$ (c) $6\frac{2}{7} - 2\frac{4}{5}$

9 (a) $\frac{4}{5} \times \frac{2}{3}$ (b) $\frac{2}{7} \times 2\frac{1}{3}$ (c) $3\frac{3}{4} \times 1\frac{2}{5}$

10 (a) $\frac{4}{7} \div 5$ (b) $\frac{13}{14} \div \frac{4}{7}$ (c) $7\frac{1}{8} \div 1\frac{3}{8}$

Exercise BB

1 A machine makes 245 parts in 35 minutes. How many will it make in one hour at the same rate?
2 If 1440 brass plates can be packed into 16 boxes, how many boxes are needed to pack 1080 brass plates?
3 An electric fire uses $12\frac{1}{2}$ units of electricity in five hours. How many units will it use in eight hours?

4 A field of grass feeds 24 cows for six days. For how long would the same field feed 18 cows?

5 A farmer employs 18 students in his orchard. It takes them three days to pick the apples. How long would it take 12 students?

6 Seven machines are used to do a job in 21 hours. How long would it take three machines to complete the job?

7 A load on a lorry is increased by 16% to 1102 kg. Find the original weight of the load.

8 An antique is bought and is then resold for £945, making a profit of $12\frac{1}{2}$%. What amount of profit was made?

9 A shop sells 72% of its stock in a closing-down sale. If 266 items are left, how many items were originally in the store?

10 A path has been increased in length by 16% to 377 metres. What was the actual increase, in metres?

11 Mary invests £84.50 from 1 January to 30 June at $12\frac{1}{2}$% p.a. interest. Approximately how much interest will she receive?

12 A bank account has £225 in it. Approximately how long will it take, at 5% p.a. interest, to become £300?

13 Derek wants to have £1500 available to make a cash payment in three years' time. Find how much Derek must invest now, at 5% p.a. throughout the term, to make this possible.

14 Sarah invests £125 for two years in an account which will give her 5% p.a. interest, paid every six months. Calculate the amount of interest received over this time.

15 Scott borrows £3500 at 8% p.a. interest, to be added every six months, and arranges to pay back £250 at the end of each six months. How much will he still owe after $1\frac{1}{2}$ years?

16 A rectangle has sides $4\frac{4}{5}$ cm and $3\frac{2}{3}$ cm. Find the perimeter of the rectangle.

17 A farmer had $3\frac{5}{8}$ tons of hay. If $1\frac{3}{5}$ tons has already been used, how much is left?

18 The area of a small island is $24\frac{1}{2}$ hectares. Of this $\frac{3}{5}$ is grassland. What area of the island is grassland?

19 A man can cycle $5\frac{1}{4}$ km in an hour. How long will it take him to travel $32\frac{2}{3}$ km?

20 A man spends $\frac{3}{5}$ of his money on food, and $\frac{1}{4}$ on clothes. He has £26.40 left. With how much did he start?

Algebra

19/ MAKING PREDICTIONS AND GENERALISING IN NUMBER SERIES

A rule is a short-cut, using calculation methods, to find later terms more easily.

EXAMPLE

► A sequence of numbers is given by the table:

Term (n)	1	2	3	4	5
Number	–1	1	3	5	7

(a) Find a rule, in words, to describe this series.
(b) Write the rule to represent the nth term in terms of n.
(c) Use the rule to find the 15th and 20th terms in the series.

(a) $1 \rightarrow -1$
$2 \rightarrow 1$
$3 \rightarrow 3$
$4 \rightarrow 5$
$5 \rightarrow 7$

In each case the first number is multiplied by 2, and 3 is taken away. The rule is 'Multiply by 2 and subtract 3'.

(b) In symbols: $n \times 2 - 3 = 2n - 3$

(c) The rule is $2n - 3$, so 15th term $= (15 \times 2) - 3 = 27$
20th term $= (20 \times 2) - 3 = 37$

EXAMPLE

► A sequence of numbers is given by the table:

Term (n)	1	2	3	4	5
Number	5	14	27	44	65

(a) Write the rule to represent the nth term in terms of n.
(b) Use the rule to find the 20th and 50th terms in the series.

(a) Since the differences between the numbers in the table (bottom row) do not remain the same there is probably an n^2 in the rule. It is sometimes useful to add this row to the table:

Term^2 (n^2)	1	4	9	16	25

$1 \rightarrow 1 + 1 + 3 = 5$
$2 \rightarrow 4 + 4 + 6 = 14$
$3 \rightarrow 9 + 9 + 9 = 27$
$4 \rightarrow 16 + 16 + 12 = 44$ etc.
The rule is 'term^2 + term^2 + (3 × term)' or $2n^2 + 3n$.

(b) 20th term $= 20^2 + 20^2 + 3 \times 20 = 860$
50th term $= 50^2 + 50^2 + 3 \times 50 = 5150$

Exercise 19A

In each question the first four numbers in a sequence are listed.
(a) Write the rule to represent the nth term in terms of n.
(b) Find the terms indicated in each question.

1 0, 2, 4, 6; 10th, 20th
2 5, 9, 13, 17; 15th, 20th
3 6, 9, 12, 15; 14th, 18th
4 –3, –1, 1, 3; 16th, 22nd
5 –1, 2, 5, 8; 12th, 20th
6 5, 7, 9, 11; 16th, 20th
7 4, 9, 14, 19; 13th, 18th
8 7, 10, 13, 16; 18th, 22nd
9 5, 11, 17, 23; 13th, 18th
10 9, 13, 17, 21; 14th, 20th
11 5, 12, 19, 26; 12th, 18th
12 0, 4, 8, 12; 15th, 20th
13 2, 5, 10, 17; 10th, 22nd
14 3, 12, 27, 48; 8th, 15th
15 –1, 2, 7, 14; 10th, 15th
16 0, 2, 6, 12; 10th, 12th
17 3, 8, 15, 24; 7th, 10th
18 1, 5, 11, 19; 10th, 15th
19 4, 10, 20, 34; 6th, 10th
20 4, 10, 18, 28; 8th, 12th
21 4, 8, 14, 22; 8th, 12th
22 5, 12, 21, 32; 7th, 10th
23 1, 7, 17, 31; 6th, 10th
24 4, 9, 16, 25; 8th, 12th
25 1, 6, 15, 28; 10th, 15th
26 4, 13, 28, 49; 7th, 10th
27 5, 14, 27, 44; 6th, 10th
28 5, 16, 33, 56; 7th, 10th
29 4, 11, 22, 37; 8th, 12th
30 6, 18, 38, 66; 6th, 10th

Exercise 19B

In each question the first four numbers in a sequence are listed.
(a) Write the rule to represent the nth term in terms of n.
(b) Find the terms indicated in each question.

1 4, 7, 10, 13; 15th, 20th
2 –2, 0, 2, 4; 20th, 25th
3 3, 7, 11, 15; 12th, 18th
4 6, 8, 10, 12; 15th, 20th
5 1, 4, 7, 10; 20th, 25th
6 8, 13, 18, 23; 10th, 15th
7 8, 10, 12, 14; 12th, 18th
8 0, 3, 6, 9; 15th, 20th
9 4, 10, 16, 22; 7th, 10th
10 1, 5, 9, 13; 12th, 20th
11 7, 12, 17, 22; 10th, 18th
12 11, 19, 27, 35; 10th, 15th
13 2, 8, 18, 32; 8th, 12th
14 4, 7, 12, 19; 15th, 20th
15 2, 6, 12, 20; 8th, 12th
16 –3, 0, 5, 12; 12th, 15th
17 –1, 0, 3, 8; 10th, 15th
18 6, 12, 22, 36; 8th, 12th
19 –1, 3, 9, 17; 10th, 15th
20 3, 10, 21, 36; 8th, 12th
21 4, 14, 30, 52; 7th, 10th
22 6, 10, 17, 24; 10th, 12th
23 4, 12, 24, 40; 8th, 10th
24 1, 10, 25, 46; 7th, 10th
25 2, 9, 20, 35; 8th, 12th
26 –2, –2, 0, 4; 10th, 15th
27 1, 8, 21, 40; 8th, 12th
28 0, 4, 12, 24; 8th, 12th
29 2, 10, 24, 44; 10th, 14th
30 4, 19, 44, 79; 8th, 12th

20/ MULTIPLICATION OF TERMS

When terms are multiplied together the coefficients are multiplied and the letters are arranged in alphabetical order.
When like terms are multiplied together the indices are added.

EXAMPLES

► $4 \times a \times c \times 3 \times b = 12abc$

$t^5 \times t^6 = t^{11}$

$(2p^2)^3 = 2p^2 \times 2p^2 \times 2p^2 = 8p^6$

$3y^3 \times 2y^6 = 6y^9$

Exercise 20A

Simplify.

1 $2x \times 2x$
2 $3c \times 4c$
3 $5ab \times 2ab$
4 $4y \times 2y \times y$

5 $x^3 \times x^2$	**6** $2y \times 6y \times y$	**7** $b \times 3b \times b$	**8** $y^3 \times y^3$
9 $4 \times 4x \times x$	**10** $(3a)^2$	**11** $5t \times 6t$	**12** $2ab \times 2ab$
13 $(2x^2)^2$	**14** $4y^2 \times 3y^3$	**15** $2c^3 \times 3c^3 \times c$	**16** $2y^4 \times y^3 \times 2y^2$
17 $7q \times 3r$	**18** $(3y)^3$	**19** $5f^3 \times 4f^4$	**20** $4p \times 4q \times 2$
21 $3y^4 \times 2y^5$	**22** $5d \times 4d$	**23** $3a \times 3c \times d$	**24** $ab \times ba$
25 $2eg \times ef$	**26** $(x^3)^2$	**27** $st \times 3t$	**28** $3gh \times 2gh$

Exercise 20B

Simplify.

1 $3x \times 4x$	**2** $3c \times 3c$	**3** $cd \times 3cd$	**4** $a \times 2a \times 3a$
5 $3 \times 2x \times x$	**6** $a \times a^4$	**7** $x \times 3x \times 2x$	**8** $x^2 \times x^6$
9 $(4b)^2$	**10** $4w \times 3w$	**11** $3x^2 \times 2x^6$	**12** $7g^5 \times 3g^3$
13 $(2ab)^2$	**14** $3cd \times 2cd$	**15** $5y^2 \times 3y^5$	**16** $4x^3 \times 2x \times 3x^2$
17 $4x \times 3y$	**18** $(2x^2)^3$	**19** $3c \times 2b \times 3a$	**20** $3x \times 3x$
21 $4a \times 2b \times 3c$	**22** $2xy \times 3y$	**23** $2 \times 5a \times 3b$	**24** $ab \times bc$
25 $(y^4)^3$	**26** $3cd \times 2d$	**27** $2e^2 \times 2d^2$	**28** $(3d^2)^3$

21/ DIVISION OF TERMS

When terms are divided common factors of the top and bottom are cancelled and the coefficients are divided.

When like terms are divided the indices are subtracted.

EXAMPLES

► $y^3 \div y^6 = \dfrac{y^3}{y^6} = \dfrac{1}{y^3}$ $\quad 5xy \div 5xy = \dfrac{5xy}{5xy} = 1$ $\quad 12a^2b \div 3ab = \dfrac{12a^2b}{3ab} = 4a$

Exercise 21A

1 $t^6 \div t^3$	**2** $8d \div 4$	**3** $f \div f$	**4** $21x \div 7$
5 $9cd \div 3cd$	**6** $x^6 \div x^5$	**7** $cd \div ce$	**8** $5ab \div ac$
9 $16f \div 4f$	**10** $18d^5 \div 6d^2$	**11** $2xy \div 8x$	**12** $f \div fg$
13 $t^3 \div t^5$	**14** $18xy \div 9y$	**15** $5pq \div 10qr$	**16** $12xy \div 4x$
17 $x^2 \div xy$	**18** $m^2n \div 2mn$	**19** $p^2q^3 \div p^2q$	**20** $10x^3y^2 \div 2x^2$
21 $30b^6 \div 15b^3$	**22** $y^2 \div y^5$	**23** $6wy \div 9wx$	**24** $2m^3n \div m^2n$
25 $a^3b^2 \div a^2b^3$	**26** $5xy \div 10y$	**27** $3pq \div 9p^2$	**28** $x^2y \div xy^2$
29 $9pqw \div 6pw^2$	**30** $6stu^2 \div 4s^2u$		

Exercise 21B

1 $f^5 \div f$	**2** $xy \div wy$	**3** $8g \div 2$	**4** $18c \div 9c$
5 $15y \div 3$	**6** $12g^8 \div g^3$	**7** $w^8 \div w^6$	**8** $h \div h$
9 $8de \div 2df$	**10** $20b^4 \div 10b^3$	**11** $k^2m^2 \div km$	**12** $j^4 \div j^5$
13 $12a^2b \div 4ab$	**14** $12fgh \div 6gh$	**15** $a^2 \div abc$	**16** $8ab \div 10b$
17 $x^6 \div 3x^5$	**18** $16abc \div 4bcd$	**19** $12xy \div 3y^2$	**20** $8mn \div 4m$
21 $3mn \div 9m$	**22** $27m^4 \div 9m^4$	**23** $5a^3 \div a^5$	**24** $6pq \div 12p$

25 $10x^3y \div y^4$ **26** $2mn^3 \div 2mn^2$ **27** $x^3y^2 \div x^4y^2$ **28** $3pq \div 3q^2$
29 $s^2t^3 \div t^3w$ **30** $8ab^2 \div 4ab$

22/ BRACKETS

When brackets are multiplied out this frequently leaves terms which can be collected together, or simplified further.

EXAMPLE

▶ Multiply out and simplify if possible (a) $xy(x + y)$ (b) $2(3x - 1) + 3(2x + 1)$

(a) $xy(x + y) = x^2y + xy^2$

(b) $2(3x - 1) + 3(2x + 1)$
$= 6x - 2 + 6x + 3$
$= 12x + 1$

When multiplying a bracket by a negative term, the negative sign outside the bracket has the effect of changing all the signs inside the bracket.

EXAMPLE

▶ Multiply out and simplify if possible: $9 - 2(a - 4)$.

$9 - 2(a - 4)$
$= 9 - 2a + 8$
$= 17 - 2a$

Exercise 22A

Multiply out and simplify if possible.

1 $3(x + 6) + 2(x + 1)$ **2** $3(x + 4) - 8$ **3** $(2m - 3m) - (m + m)$
4 $8x(2x - 5)$ **5** $5(x + 3) - 4(x - 7)$ **6** $8d - 3 - (3d - 1)$
7 $2x(3x^2 + 4)$ **8** $2c(2d + e + 3f)$ **9** $9(2x + 3) - 7(x - 6)$
10 $2x(3y + w) - 4xy$ **11** $3x^2(3x^2 + 2x - 7)$ **12** $4(5g - 4) - 3(g - 2)$
13 $1 - 5(x - 1)$ **14** $9 - 2(4 - 9t)$ **15** $7(3p + 2q) - 4(5p - q)$
16 $10a - 4(2a - 5)$ **17** $3(2x - y) - 2(x + 2y)$ **18** $5ab(2a + 4b)$
19 $3(7x - 2) - 5(3x - 5)$ **20** $2a(b - 4) - a(b + 3)$ **21** $5(1 - 3x) - (1 + x)$
22 $4x(y + 3) + x(4 - y)$ **23** $5(2b - 3) - (b + 16)$ **24** $2xy(3x^2 + 2y)$
25 $4a(b + c) - 2a(b - c)$ **26** $2(3x - 2) - 3(x - 8)$ **27** $5x(2xy^2 + 3x^2)$
28 $8(x + 2y) - 4(4y - x)$ **29** $11x - 2(x - y)$ **30** $8x - 2(3x - 4)$

Exercise 22B

Multiply out and simplify if possible.

1 $5(x + 3) + 2(x + 4)$ **2** $4(x + 2y) - 3y$ **3** $(9k + 5m) + 2(2k - 3m)$
4 $10(x + 1) - 3(x - 4)$ **5** $5x(x + 6)$ **6** $(9e + 1) - (7e - 2)$
7 $4x(2x^2 + 1)$ **8** $4(3x - 5) - 3(2x + 2)$ **9** $7(2 - x) - (1 + x)$
10 $8x(3x^2 - 6x + 1)$ **11** $5(2k - m) + 6(k - 2m)$ **12** $8 - 2(x + 3)$
13 $12u^2 - (8u^2 + 5)$ **14** $6pq + 3p(4 - 2q)$ **15** $8d - 2(3d - 3e)$
16 $7c(2d + e) + 3c(d - 3e)$ **17** $26 - 4(3g + 4)$ **18** $2pq(3p^2 + 4q)$

19 $5(3x + 2) - 4(2x + 3)$
20 $2c(d + 3e) - c(d - 2e)$
21 $19 - 3(4 + 3c)$
22 $x^2(1 + 2x)$
23 $8(3p + 2) - 3(5p + 1)$
24 $6x(a - 3b) - 2x(b - 4a)$
25 $4(1 + x) - 3(2x - 5)$
26 $3x^2(1 + x^2)$
27 $5(5c + 6d) - 4(3c + 7d)$
28 $4x - 8(6y - x)$
29 $5 - 3(6x - 5y)$
30 $8(5x + 2y) - 6(y - x)$

23/ EXPANSIONS

EXAMPLE

► Multiply out and simplify.
(a) $(2x + 3)(x - 2)$ (b) $(x - 3)^2$ (c) $(2x + y)(2x - y)$

(a) $(2x + 3)(x - 2) = (2x + 3)(x - 2)$
$= 2x^2 - 4x + 3x - 6$
$= 2x^2 - x - 6$

(b) $(x - 3)^2 = (x - 3)(x - 3)$
$= x^2 - 3x - 3x + 9$
$= x^2 - 6x + 9$

(c) $(2x + y)(2x - y) = 4x^2 - 2xy + 2xy - y^2$
$= 4x^2 - y^2$

Exercise 23A

Multiply out and simplify.

1 $(x + 7)(x + 3)$
2 $(x + 8)(x - 3)$
3 $(x - 4)(x + 2)$
4 $(x - 6)(x - 3)$
5 $(x + 4)^2$
6 $(x - 6)^2$
7 $(3x + 5)(x - 6)$
8 $(8x + 2)(3x + 4)$
9 $(4x - 1)(2x - 3)$
10 $(2x + 5)^2$
11 $(8x - 3)(2x + 1)$
12 $(x + 6)(x - 2)$
13 $(x - 4)(3x + 2)$
14 $(6x - 5)(6x + 5)$
15 $(2x - 9)(2x + 1)$
16 $(x + 5)(x + 3)$
17 $(2x - 3)(5x + 2)$
18 $(4x + 1)(4x - 1)$
19 $(2x - 5)(2x + 5)$
20 $(3x - 1)^2$
21 $(9x + 5)(9x - 5)$
22 $(6 - x)(5 + 2x)$
23 $(2a + 3b)(a - 2b)$
24 $(2a + b)(2a - b)$
25 $(5y - 4z)(4y + z)$
26 $(5t - 2)(5t + 2)$
27 $(5x + 2y)(2x + y)$
28 $(5x + 2y)(3x - y)$
29 $(6x + 5y)(x + 3y)$
30 $(2x + 3y)(x + y)$

Exercise 23B

Multiply out and simplify.

1 $(x + 5)(x + 2)$
2 $(x - 3)(x + 7)$
3 $(x + 9)(x - 2)$
4 $(x - 8)(x - 7)$
5 $(x - 2)^2$
6 $(x + 5)^2$
7 $(4x + 5)(2x + 1)$
8 $(5x - 4)(2x + 3)$
9 $(2x + 5)(3x - 4)$
10 $(3x + 4)(2x - 7)$
11 $(2x - 7)(3x - 4)$
12 $(5x + 2)(2x + 3)$
13 $(2x - 5)^2$
14 $(3x + 2)(3x - 2)$
15 $(5x + 2)(3x - 4)$
16 $(3x + 5)(4x - 1)$
17 $(4x + 9)(4x - 9)$
18 $(3x + 7)(3x - 5)$
19 $(8x + 5)(3x + 1)$
20 $(3x + 4)^2$
21 $(4x + 3)(3x - 7)$
22 $(8x + 3)(8x - 3)$
23 $(2x + 3)^2$
24 $(3x + y)(3x - 5y)$
25 $(3p - 5q)(6p + q)$
26 $(2x - 1)^2$
27 $(4x + 3y)(x + y)$
28 $(2x + 5)(5x - 2)$
29 $(4x - 3y)(4x + y)$
30 $(7x + 2y)(3x + 4y)$

24/ FACTORISING

To factorise an expression, identify the highest common factor of the terms in that expression, then rewrite it using brackets.

EXAMPLE

► Factorise (a) $a^2x + ax^2$ (b) $5y^3 + 10y^2 - 20y$ (c) $8a^2b^2 + 2ab$.

(a) $a^2x + ax^2$
$= ax(a + x)$

The highest common factor of both terms is ax.
Write the highest common factor outside the bracket.
Write terms inside the bracket so that, if the bracket is multiplied out, it gives the original expression.

(b) $5y^3 + 10y^2 - 20y$
$= 5y(y^2 + 2y - 4)$

The highest common factor is $5y$.

(c) $8a^2b^2 + 2ab$
$= 2ab(4ab + 1)$

The highest common factor is $2ab$.
Note: The second term in the bracket is 1 so that the bracket multiplies out to give the original expression.

Exercise 24A

Factorise each expression.

1	$100x - 10y$	**2**	$12u + 15uv$	**3**	$3a + 4ab$
4	$6p - 2q$	**5**	$xy - 5x$	**6**	$mn - 4n$
7	$5xy + 7x$	**8**	$3ab - 4ac + 5ad$	**9**	$5yz + 10z$
10	$c^2d - cd^2$	**11**	$3y - 2y^3$	**12**	$5s^3 + 20$
13	$14d + 35d^2$	**14**	$2ap + ap^3$	**15**	$6ab + 8bc - 4bd$
16	$5p^2q + 10pq^2$	**17**	$a^4bc - a^3b^2c$	**18**	$12u^2v + 16uv$
19	$8x^2 + 10x$	**20**	$9y^2 - 3y$	**21**	$2xy + y^2 + 5y$
22	$x^3 + 7x^2 + 4x$	**23**	$6xy - 9x^2$	**24**	$5x + 10x^2$
25	$4x^2y - 10xy^2$	**26**	$8ab + 4a^2b^2$	**27**	$3mn - 6m^2n^2$
28	$5y^3 + 10y^2 - 20y$	**29**	$2x^3 - 8x^2 + 2x$	**30**	$6d^4 - 6d^3$

Exercise 24B

Factorise each expression.

1	$2a + 4b$	**2**	$8gt + 12ht$	**3**	$5ab + 10bc$
4	$3xy + 6x$	**5**	$pqr + rst$	**6**	$4xy - 8x$
7	$2xy - 3xz$	**8**	$ut + 5t^2$	**9**	$4yz + 6z$
10	$36d^3 - 12d^2$	**11**	$5c^2 - 10cd$	**12**	$2ab^2 - 6ab + a$
13	$d - 6d^2$	**14**	$ax^2 + a^2x$	**15**	$5abc - bcd + 2cde$
16	$x^2yz + xy^2z + xyz^2$	**17**	$7ab^2 - 21a^2$	**18**	$2\pi r^2h + 2\pi rh$
19	$a^2 - 6ab^2$	**20**	$3x^3 + 15x^2 + 3x$	**21**	$9x^2 - 12x$
22	$8p^3 + 6p^2$	**23**	$2x - 8xy + 12x^2$	**24**	$x^3 + x^2y + xy^2$
25	$13gh^2 - g$	**26**	$18x^2 - 12xy$	**27**	$6pq - 5p^2q^2$
28	$2x^3 - 6x^2 + 8x$	**29**	$x^3y^3 - x^2y^2 + xy$	**30**	$8xy^2 - 4xy$

25/ SUBSTITUTION

EXAMPLE

▶ If $x = ab - c$ find x when $a = 4$, $b = \frac{1}{2}$ and $c = -5$.

$x = 4 \times \frac{1}{2} - (-5)$

$= 2 + 5 = 7$

Remember: When two negative numbers are multiplied together the result is a positive number.

EXAMPLE

▶ If $s = ut + \frac{1}{2}at^2$ find s when $u = 4$, $a = -5$ and $t = 2$.

$s = 4 \times 2 + \frac{1}{2} \times (-5) \times 2 \times 2$

$= 8 - 10$

$= -2$

Note: Answers can be negative.

EXAMPLE

▶ If $A = \frac{1}{2}(a + b)h$ find a when $b = 3$, $h = 10$ and $A = 40$.

$40 = \frac{1}{2}(a + 3)10$ — First multiply out the bracket.

$40 = 5a + 15$ — Move terms to simplify.

$40 - 15 = 5a$

$5a = 25$

$a = 5$

Exercise 25A

In questions 1–10, $a = \frac{2}{3}$, $b = 9$, $c = -3$. Find the value of x.

1 $x = ab + c$
2 $x = a + b + c$
3 $x = 2a^2$
4 $x = (a - c)^2$
5 $x = ab + ac$
6 $x = a^2 + b^2 + c^2$
7 $x = a^2 - bc$
8 $x = 3a - 2c$
9 $x = abc$
10 $x = c^2 - ab$

11 $a = b - \frac{1}{2}c$
(a) Find a when $b = 3.6$ and $c = 0.05$.
(b) Find c when $a = 6$ and $b = 10$.

12 $A = \pi rl$
(a) Find A when $\pi = \frac{22}{7}$, $r = 4$ and $l = 5$.
(b) Find r when $\pi = \frac{22}{7}$, $A = 308$ and $l = 28$.

13 $v = u + at$
(a) Find v when $u = 30$, $a = -10$ and $t = 2.5$.
(b) Find a when $v = 21.5$, $u = 4$ and $t = 7$.

14 $F = \frac{9C}{5} + 32$
(a) Find F when $C = -6$.
(b) Find C when $F = 42.8$.

15 $A = 4\pi r^2$
(a) Find A when $\pi = \frac{22}{7}$ and $r = \frac{2}{3}$.
(b) Find r when $\pi = \frac{22}{7}$ and $A = 616$.

16 $F = \dfrac{Gmn}{d^2}$

(a) Find F when $G = 6.6$, $m = 80$, $n = 300$ and $d = 6$.
(b) Find G when $d = 3$, $F = 10$, $m = 4$ and $n = 5$.

17 $v^2 = u^2 + 2as$

(a) Find v when $u = 3.27$, $a = 9.81$ and $s = 3.96$.
(b) Find u when $v = 5$, $a = 2$ and $s = 4$.

18 $t = \dfrac{(5 + n)}{l}$

(a) Find t when $n = 8.4$ and $l = 2.2$.
(b) Find n when $t = 4$ and $l = 3$.

19 $V = RI$

(a) Find V when $R = \frac{1}{3}$ and $I = 7.5$.
(b) Find I when $V = 5.8$ and $R = 0.2$.

20 $S = \dfrac{(u + v)t}{2}$

(a) Find S when $u = 4.2$, $v = 5.8$ and $t = 4.2$.
(b) Find v when $S = 22$, $u = 4$ and $t = 4$.

21 $V = w \times \sqrt{a^2 - x^2}$

(a) Find V when $w = \frac{1}{2}$, $a = 10$ and $x = 6$.
(b) Find a when $V = 40$, $w = 10$ and $x = 3$.

22 $T = 2\pi\sqrt{\dfrac{l}{g}}$

(a) Find T when $g = 9.81$, $\pi = 3.14$ and $l = 88.29$.
(b) Find g when $T = 9.42$, $\pi = 3.14$ and $l = 3$.

23 $P = ri^2$

(a) Find P when $r = 18$ and $i = \frac{1}{3}$.
(b) Find i when $P = 36$ and $r = 4$.

24 $s = ut + \frac{1}{2}at^2$

(a) Find s when $u = -6$, $a = 2\frac{1}{2}$ and $t = 8$.
(b) Find a when $s = 85$, $u = 2$ and $t = 5$.

25 $V = \pi r^2(h + \frac{2}{3}r)$

(a) Find V when $\pi = 3.14$, $h = 5.6$ and $r = 2.7$.
(b) Find h when $V = 84\,780$, $r = 30$ and $\pi = 3.14$.

26 $T = \dfrac{px}{a}$

(a) Find T when $p = \frac{1}{2}$, $x = 10$ and $a = 4$.
(b) Find x when $T = 9$, $p = 3$ and $a = 1.5$.

27 $d = \frac{1}{2}(u + v)t$

(a) Find d when $u = 3.3$, $v = 4.1$ and $t = 2.2$.
(b) Find v when $u = 3$, $t = 5$ and $d = 30$.

28 $E = \dfrac{px^2}{2a}$

(a) Find E when $p = \frac{1}{3}$, $x = 15$ and $a = 2$.
(b) Find a when $E = 4.8$, $p = 3$ and $x = 16$.

29 $s = ut + \frac{1}{2}at^2$

(a) Find s when $u = 5$, $a = \frac{1}{5}$ and $t = 10$.
(b) Find u when $t = 2$, $a = 5$ and $s = 16$.

30 $T = \frac{1}{2}a(b + c)$

(a) Find T when $a = 7$, $b = -4$ and $c = 8$.
(b) Find a when $b = 3$, $c = 5$ and $T = 20$.

Exercise 25B

In questions 1–10, $p = 18$, $q = \frac{5}{6}$ and $r = -9$. Find the value of x.

1 $x = p + qr$
2 $x = 2q^2$
3 $x = pq + qr$
4 $x = r^2 - pq$
5 $x = p + q + r$
6 $x = 12q + r$
7 $x = (pqr)^2$
8 $x = p^2 + q^2 + r^2$
9 $x = (q - r)^2$
10 $x = \dfrac{p}{q}$

11 $V = RI$

(a) Find V when $R = \frac{2}{3}$ and $I = 2.5$.
(b) Find I when $V = 56$ and $R = 8$.

12 $E = \frac{1}{2}mv^2$

(a) Find E when $m = 5$ and $v = 8$.
(b) Find v when $E = 100$ and $m = 8$.

13 $A = 4\pi r^2$

(a) Find A when $\pi = \frac{22}{7}$ and $r = 14$.
(b) Find r when $A = 616$ and $\pi = \frac{22}{7}$.

14 $P = Ri^2$

(a) Find P when $i = \frac{3}{4}$ and $R = 12$.
(b) Find i when $P = 48$ and $R = 3$.

15 $f = \dfrac{uv}{u + v}$

(a) Find f when $u = -12$ and $v = -4$.
(b) Find v when $f = 4$ and $u = 6$.

16 $v = u + at$

(a) Find v when $a = \frac{5}{6}$, $t = 48$ and $u = -12$.
(b) Find a when $v = 33$, $u = 5$ and $t = 4$.

17 $F = \dfrac{9C}{5} + 32$

(a) Find F when $C = -3$.
(b) Find C when $F = 23$.

18 $v^2 = u^2 + 2as$

(a) Find v when $u = -6$, $a = 7$ and $s = -2$.
(b) Find s when $v = 8$, $u = 4$ and $a = 3$.

19 $T = 2\pi\sqrt{\dfrac{l}{g}}$

(a) Find T when $g = 9.81$, $\pi = 3.142$ and $l = 1.7$.
(b) Find l when $T = 31.42$, $\pi = 3.142$ and $g = 4$.

20 $F = \dfrac{Gmn}{d^2}$

(a) Find F when $G = 5.6$, $d = 8$, $m = 50$ and $n = 200$.
(b) Find d when $F = 16$, $G = 20$, $m = 4$ and $n = 5$.

21 $A = \pi rl$

(a) Find A when $\pi = \frac{22}{7}$, $r = 21$ and $l = 9$.
(b) Find l when $A = 220$, $\pi = \frac{22}{7}$ and $r = 2$.

22 $C = \dfrac{5(F - 32)}{9}$

(a) Find C when $F = -58$.
(b) Find F when $C = 5$.

23 $s = ut + \frac{1}{2}at^2$

(a) Find s when $u = -4$, $t = 5$ and $a = 8$.
(b) Find t when $s = 14$, $a = 4$ and $u = 3$.

24 $V = \dfrac{mv}{m + M}$

(a) Find V when $m = \frac{1}{2}$, $M = 2$ and $v = 36$.
(b) Find m when $V = 3$, $v = 4$ and $M = 1$.

25 $d = \frac{1}{2}(u + v)t$

(a) Find d when $u = -8$, $v = 12$ and $t = 16$.
(b) Find u when $d = 18$, $t = 4$ and $v = 7$.

26 $E = \dfrac{px^2}{2a}$

(a) Find E when $p = \frac{1}{4}$, $x = 10$ and $a = 5$.
(b) Find x when $E = 4$, $p = 2.5$ and $a = 5$.

27 $V = w \times \sqrt{a^2 - x^2}$

(a) Find V when $w = \frac{1}{3}$, $a = 13$ and $x = 5$.
(b) Find x when $V = 16$, $w = 4$ and $a = 5$.

28 $T = \dfrac{px}{a}$

(a) Find T when $p = \frac{4}{5}$, $x = 10$ and $a = 2$.
(b) Find x when $T = 3$, $p = 9$ and $a = 15$.

29 $s = ut + \frac{1}{2}at^2$

(a) Find s when $u = -3$, $a = \frac{1}{3}$ and $t = 15$.
(b) Find u when $s = 5.5$, $t = 1$ and $a = 7$.

30 $A = 2\pi r(r + h)$

(a) Find A when $\pi = 3.142$, $r = \frac{1}{2}$ and $h = 1$.
(b) Find h when $\pi = 3.142$, $r = 10$ and $A = 942.6$.

26/ CHANGING THE SUBJECT OF A FORMULA (1)

To change the subject of a formula, the formula has to be rearranged so that the **subject** (the letter required) is left on one side of the formula on its own.

EXAMPLE

▶ Make x the subject of the formula in each of the following.
(a) $a = x - ab$ (b) $xy = w$ (c) $f = d(x + e)$

(a) $a = x - ab$
$a + ab = x$

(b) $xy = w$
$\frac{xy}{y} = \frac{w}{y}$
$x = \frac{w}{y}$

(c) $f = d(x + e)$ Multiply out the brackets.
$f = dx + de$ Move terms to leave x terms alone.
$f - de = dx$ Divide to leave x alone.
$\frac{f - de}{d} = x$

Exercise 26A

In questions 1–15 make x the subject of the formula.

1 $3x = b$
2 $\frac{x}{5} = d$
3 $f = 4 - x$
4 $g = x - h$
5 $3(2x - 3) = y$
6 $2(3x - 1) = 5y$
7 $5x + 9 = y$
8 $3x - 4 = y$
9 $2x + q = 3p$
10 $a(x + 3) = y$
11 $a(x - b) = 2$
12 $\frac{x}{2} - 3 = a$
13 $\frac{3x}{4} + 1 = d$
14 $\frac{x + b}{c} = a$
15 $\frac{x - p}{q} = t$

In questions 16–30 make the letter in brackets [ ] the subject of the formula.

16 $p = q + r$ [r]
17 $ab - d = c$ [a]
18 $k - pq = 3$ [k]
19 $r = s + t$ [t]
20 $p(q + r) = 1$ [q]
21 $l + m = n$ [m]
22 $p = \frac{Q + R}{3}$ [Q]
23 $S = 5t + v$ [t]
24 $\frac{s}{v} = \frac{1}{t}$ [s]
25 $2s = a + b + c$ [a]
26 $v^2 = u^2 - 2as$ [s]
27 $A = lb$ [b]
28 $S = 3t + u$ [t]
29 $A = h(a + b)$ [b]
30 $2(b + c) = 1$ [b]

Exercise 26B

In questions 1–15 make x the subject of the formula.

1 $4x = y$
2 $\frac{x}{2} = a$
3 $c = x - e$
4 $m = 5 - x$
5 $2(x - 4) = y$
6 $2(4x + 1) = 7y$
7 $2x + 3 = y$
8 $4x - 1 = y$
9 $3x - p = 2q$
10 $a(x - 4) = y$
11 $a(x + d) = c$
12 $\frac{x}{4} + 2 = a$

13 $\frac{3x}{4} - 2 = c$ 14 $\frac{x-5}{4} = y$ 15 $\frac{x-y}{2} = 3$

In questions 16–30 make the letter in brackets [ ] the subject of the formula.

16 $ab - d = c$ [d] 17 $r = s - t$ [s] 18 $y = xz$ [z] 19 $h - pq = 4$ [p]

20 $x(y - z) = 3$ [y] 21 $P = QR$ [Q] 22 $I = \frac{PRT}{100}$ [R] 23 $p^2 + q = 6$ [q]

24 $C = 2\pi r$ [r] 25 $v = u - gt$ [t] 26 $v = u + at$ [u] 27 $3(p - q) = 5$ [p]

28 $v^2 = u^2 + 2as$ [s] 29 $A = \frac{1}{2}h(a + b)$ [h] 30 $a = \frac{b+c}{2}$ [c]

27/ CHANGING THE SUBJECT OF A FORMULA (2)

EXAMPLE

► In each of the following make x the subject of the formula.

(a) $g = x^2y$ (b) $r = px + qx$ (c) $t = 2\sqrt{\frac{p}{x}}$

(a) $g = x^2y$

$$\frac{g}{y} = \frac{x^2y}{y}$$

$$x^2 = \frac{g}{y}$$

$$x = \sqrt{\frac{g}{y}}$$

(b) $r = px + qx$ If there is more than one x term, factorise.

$r = x(p + q)$ Divide both sides by the bracketed expression.

$$\frac{r}{p+q} = \frac{x(p+q)}{p+q}$$

$$x = \frac{r}{p+q}$$

(c) $t = 2\sqrt{\frac{p}{x}}$ Square everything to remove the square-root sign.

$t^2 = \frac{4p}{x}$ Multiply both sides by x to move the x to the top line.

$xt^2 = \frac{4px}{x}$ Cancel the x terms on the right-hand side and divide both sides by t^2 to leave x alone.

$$x = \frac{4p}{t^2}$$

Exercise 27A

In questions 1–15 make x the subject of the formula.

1 $ax = bx + c$ 2 $mx = u - 2x$ 3 $px + q = qx + d$ 4 $py = qx + 5x$

5 $ax - c = dx + e$ 6 $px = r - qx$ 7 $a(x + y) = bx$ 8 $x^2 + 4 = b$

9 $x^2 - a = b$ **10** $x^2 + a^2 = b^2$ **11** $\frac{x^2}{4} = y$ **12** $\sqrt{x - 2} = y$

13 $\sqrt{\frac{x}{p}} = q$ **14** $\sqrt{\frac{x}{2}} = d$ **15** $\sqrt{\frac{x-4}{5}} = 2y$

In questions 16–30 make the letter in brackets [ ] the subject of the formula.

16 $pq = r - ps$ [p] **17** $ab = c(b + a)$ [b] **18** $4p^2 = q$ [p] **19** $ab - c = ad$ [a]

20 $d = \sqrt{\frac{3g}{4}}$ [g] **21** $ab = c(b + a)$ [a] **22** $a = b\sqrt{c}$ [c] **23** $p(q + r) = q$ [p]

24 $\sqrt{x + a} = b$ [a] **25** $p^2 + q = 6$ [p] **26** $pq + qr + rp = 0$ [p] **27** $T = 2\pi\sqrt{\frac{l}{g}}$ [l]

28 $pr - p = qr + q$ [r] **29** $f = n\sqrt{\frac{T}{m}}$ [T] **30** $v = \frac{1}{3}\pi r^2 h$ [r]

Exercise 27B

In questions 1–15 make x the subject of the formula.

1 $px = r - qx$ **2** $tx = u - 3x$ **3** $xy = xz + 2$ **4** $ax + b = bx + c$

5 $px - r = qx + s$ **6** $dx = x + f$ **7** $px + qx = pq$ **8** $x^2 - 2 = y$

9 $x^2 + a = b$ **10** $x^2 - c^2 = d^2$ **11** $\frac{x^2}{3} = y$ **12** $\sqrt{x + a} = b$

13 $\sqrt{x - m} = n$ **14** $\sqrt{\frac{x}{3}} = y$ **15** $\sqrt{\frac{x+1}{2}} = 3y$

In questions 16–30 make the letter in brackets [ ] the subject of the formula.

16 $a + b = ac$ [a] **17** $\sqrt{p^2 + q^2} = r$ [p] **18** $ab + ac = d$ [a]

19 $pr - p = qr + q$ [q] **20** $a = \sqrt{bc}$ [c] **21** $a = 2\sqrt{p}$ [p]

22 $m^2 + n = p$ [m] **23** $a^2 + b = c$ [a] **24** $p(q + n) = q(n - p)$ [p]

25 $b = \sqrt{\frac{7c}{8}}$ [c] **26** $a = 2\sqrt{\frac{p}{q}}$ [q] **27** $ax + b = ay + c$ [a]

28 $\sqrt{a + b} = c$ [a] **29** $I = \frac{2mr^2}{5}$ [r] **30** $A = 3(R^2 - r^2)$ [R]

REVISION

Exercise C

In questions 1–4 the first four numbers in a sequence are listed.
(a) Write the rule using n to represent the nth term.
(b) Find the terms indicated in each question.

1 9, 13, 17, 21; 15th, 20th **2** 1, 7, 17, 31; 10th, 15th

3 6, 10, 17, 24; 10th, 15th **4** 4, 14, 30, 52; 15th, 20th

5 Simplify.
(a) $4a^2 + 8a^2 - 6a^2$ (b) $3ab + 2ba - ab$ (c) $2a + a^2 - a + 3a^2$ (d) $xy + 3cd + 3xy - cd$
(e) $x^3 \times x^5$ (f) $c \times 4c \times 2c$ (g) $(3b^2)^3$ (h) $4y^2 \times 2y^4$
(i) $p^4 \div p$ (j) $15ab \div 5b$ (k) $ab \div abc$ (l) $12pqr \div 3pqr$

6 Multiply out and simplify if possible.

(a) $3(x + 2) - 2(x - 4)$ (b) $2x(x^2 + 3)$ (c) $2 - 5(x - 4)$ (d) $4x + 2(3y - x)$

(e) $(x - 2)(x - 3)$ (f) $(2x + 1)(x - 3)$ (g) $(2x - 3)^2$ (h) $(5x - y)(2x + 3y)$

7 Make x the subject of the formula.

(a) $ax = bc$ (b) $b = x + cd$ (c) $a(x + 2) = c$ (d) $A = \frac{1}{2}h(x + y)$

(e) $ax + bx = c$ (f) $b = \sqrt{\frac{a}{x}}$

Exercise CC

In each of questions 1–4 the diagram shows the stages of blocks arranged in a pattern.

(a) State the rule to find the number of blocks in the nth stage.

(b) Use your rule to state the number of blocks in stages (i) 10 (ii) 15 (iii) 20.

1

2

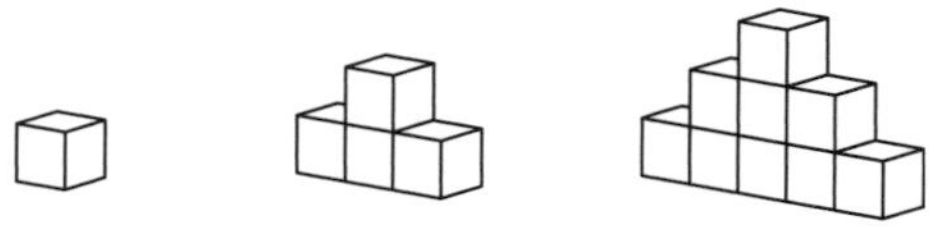

3

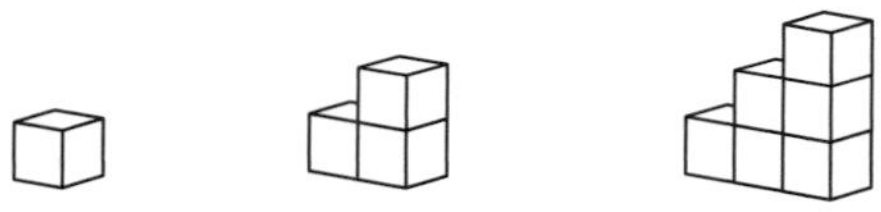

4

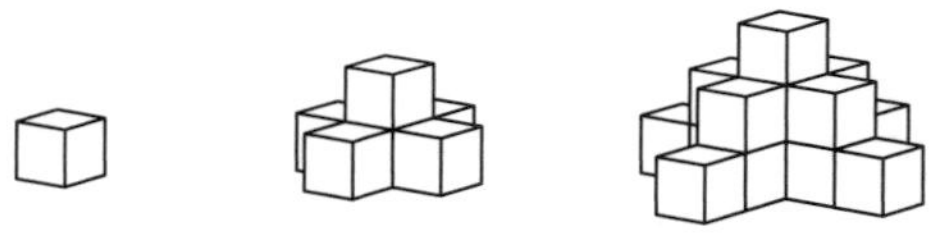

5 The perimeter, P metres, of a rectangle of length l metres and width w metres is given by the formula $P = 2(l + w)$.

(a) Find P when $l = 2.6$ metres and $w = 1.9$ metres

(b) Find l when $P = 24$ metres and $w = 3.2$ metres

(c) Find w when $P = 0.9$ metres and $l = 0.2$ metres

6 The formula for the volume V of a cone of radius r and height h is $V = \frac{1}{3}\pi r^2 h$.

(a) Calculate the value of V when $r = 14$, $h = 12$ and $\pi = \frac{22}{7}$.

(b) Calculate the value of h when $V = 29\frac{1}{3}$, $r = 4$ and $\pi = \frac{22}{7}$.

7 The formula for converting degrees Fahrenheit (°F) to degrees Celsius (°C) is $C = \frac{5}{9}(F - 32)$.

(a) Convert −4°F to degrees Celsius.

(b) Convert 5°C to degrees Fahrenheit.

8 This is a cube with edges of x cm. It has a hole with cross-sectional area of $8\,\text{cm}^2$ cut through it.

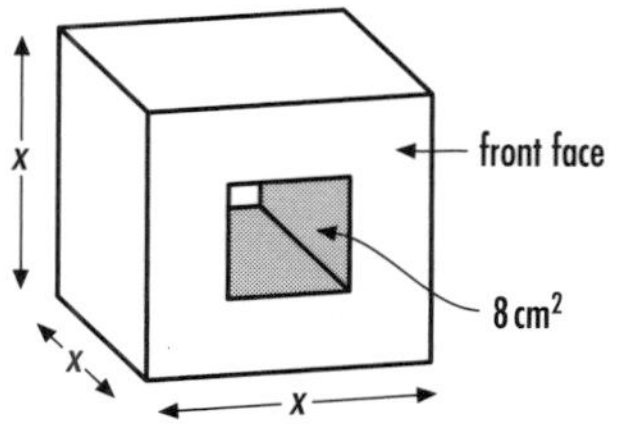

(a) Write down, in terms of x, the remaining area of the front face.

(b) Write down, in terms of x, the volume of the solid.

28/ SOLVING EQUATIONS

To solve an equation:

(a) expand any brackets and/or gather terms,

(b) collect numbers on one side of the equation and terms involving the unknown on the other side,

(c) gather number and/or algebra terms if necessary,

(d) multiply or divide both sides to ensure the unknown is on its own.

EXAMPLE

▶ Solve the equations (a) $5x + 4 = 11$ (b) $7(x - 2) = 7$.

(a)
$$5x + 4 = 11$$
$$5x = 11 - 4$$
$$5x = 7$$
$$x = \frac{7}{5} = 1\frac{2}{5}$$

(b)
$$7(x - 2) = 7$$
$$7x - 14 = 7$$
$$7x = 7 + 14$$
$$7x = 21$$
$$x = \frac{21}{7} = 3$$

EXAMPLE

▶ Solve the equations (a) $3x + x - 8 = 27 - 3x$ (b) $5(x - 1) = 2(x + 8)$.

(a)
$$3x + x - 8 = 27 - 3x$$
$$4x - 8 = 27 - 3x$$
$$4x + 3x = 27 + 8$$
$$7x = 35$$
$$x = \frac{35}{7} = 5$$

(b)
$$5(x - 1) = 2(x + 8)$$
$$5x - 5 = 2x + 16$$
$$5x - 2x = 16 + 5$$
$$3x = 21$$
$$x = \frac{21}{3} = 7$$

Exercise 28A

Solve the equations.

1 $5x + 7 = 32$

2 $7x + 4 = 25$

3 $2x + 8 = 13$

4 $2x + 9 = 20$

5 $4x + 3 = 8$

6 $6x - 3 = 15$

7 $10x + 2 = 16$

8 $3x - 1 = 10$

9 $4(2x - 1) = 28$

10 $2(x - 4) = 1$

11 $3(3x + 4) = 21$

12 $2(4x + 1) = 22$

13 $2(2x - 7) = 7$

14 $5(3x + 2) = 100$

15 $3(6x + 4) = 39$

16 $2(x - 7) = 3$

17 $5x + 7 + 2 = 12 + 3 - 3x$

18 $8x + 8 + 4x = 5x + 20 + 5x$

19 $7x + 6 - 5x + 2 = 11$

20 $14x - 8 + 24 - 6x = 36$

21 $12x + 7 + 4 = 6x + 17 + 14 + x$

22 $8x - 3x - 4 = 4 - 7x + 4$

23 $7x + 3x - 6x + 7 = 5x + 13 - 4x$

24 $4(4x + 1) = 3(5x + 4)$

25 $3(2x + 1) + 2(4x + 2) = 21$

26 $4(7x + 2) = 5(5x + 6)$

27 $3(2x + 1) = 2(2x + 7)$

28 $2(4x + 3) + 3(2x + 1) = 23$

29 $8(x + 1) + 5(2x + 3) = 4(4x + 9)$

30 $2(2x + 1) + 3(4x + 5) = 57$

Exercise 28B

Solve the equations.

1 $3x + 1 = 10$
2 $2x + 3 = 10$
3 $7x + 4 = 25$
4 $6x - 1 = 29$
5 $8x + 4 = 28$
6 $2x - 5 = 9$
7 $9x - 4 = 2$
8 $8x + 9 = 45$
9 $2(2x - 7) = 4$
10 $3(3x + 1) = 12$
11 $2(x - 3) = 5$
12 $4(5x - 6) = 16$
13 $5(2x - 3) = 10$
14 $7(5x - 3) = 84$
15 $2(5x - 9) = 27$
16 $3(x - 8) = 4$
17 $12x + 1 + 12 - 10x = 18$
18 $7x + 2 + 3x + 9 = 7x + 20$
19 $8x + 5 + 12 - 6x = 30$
20 $9x - 5x + 5 = 2x + 13 - 2$
21 $14x - 5 - 5x = 9 - x + 6$
22 $8x + 5 - 3x - 2x = 4x + 2x + 14 - 6x$
23 $7x + 6x - 2x = 16 + x + 5x + 9$
24 $4(5x + 2) = 9(2x + 2)$
25 $9(7x + 5) = 6(10x + 8)$
26 $2(x + 2) + 3(x + 4) = 31$
27 $3(6x - 3) = 4(5x - 4)$
28 $4(3x + 2) + 8(x + 1) = 56$
29 $6(x - 1) + 2(4x + 8) = 3(4x + 9)$
30 $4(2x + 2) + 2(x + 4) = 41$

Exercise 28C

Solve the equations.

1 $2x + 1 = 5$
2 $\frac{2x}{3} = 4$
3 $\frac{q}{5} - 6 = 2$
4 $3r - 16 = 4$
5 $6 + 4x = 2x + 16$
6 $2(t - 3) = 8$
7 $5 + 4p = 21$
8 $9y + 2(y + 7) = 36$
9 $60 - 3h = 2h + 10$
10 $12 - y = 5$
11 $6(2r - 7) = 0$
12 $\frac{7d}{2} = 21$
13 $5(h + 3) = 20$
14 $6x + 5 = 2(2x + 1)$
15 $2p - 7 = 5 - p$
16 $5(x + 4) - 2 = 3$
17 $5(3b - 4) = 8b + 1$
18 $4x - 6 = x$
19 $6 + r = 4 - 4r$
20 $5(3p - 1) - 9 = 16$
21 $8p + 2 = 50$
22 $16 + 3(y - 4) = 28$
23 $1 - 7x = 3x + 11$
24 $3(6h - 3) = 4(5h - 4)$
25 $3(2x - 3) - 2(1 - x) = 5$
26 $3 - 5y = 2(2y - 3)$
27 $6(x - 4) = 10(2x + 8) - 62$
28 $b + 5 = 8 - b$
29 $7(5x - 2) - 8(4x + 1) = 5$
30 $6(1 - x) + 5 = 3(2 - x) - 4$

Exercise 28D

Solve the equations.

1 $9 + 2x = 33$
2 $3k + 4 = 19$
3 $\frac{3y}{5} = 6$
4 $2y - 1 = 7$
5 $3(k + 5) - 14 = 25$
6 $\frac{4t}{7} = 8$
7 $1 - x = x - 1$
8 $3x - 6 = 14 + x$
9 $5(2s + 7) = 15$
10 $4x + 13 = 3$
11 $10y - 1 = 89$
12 $2(3k - 5) + 3(3k + 4) = 17$
13 $23 = 3 - 3m$
14 $7x - 1 = x - 7$
15 $2(2c - 1) - 7 = 11$
16 $\frac{3d}{4} = 45$
17 $9(w + 1) = 4(2w + 3)$
18 $5x - 20 = 80$
19 $6x + 4 = 5x + 1$
20 $4(p + 3) - 2 = 2$
21 $5 - 2c = 11 + c$
22 $1 - 2x = x - 8$
23 $10(2x + 3) = 10$
24 $t - 1 = 3(5 - t)$
25 $2(2x + 3) = 3(3x + 1)$
26 $4(6 - 2x) + 3(3 - 2x) = 5$
27 $4(4y + 1) = 3(5y + 4)$
28 $2x - 2(x - 3) = 6x + 3(2x + 2)$
29 $3(7x - 1) + 8(5 - 2x) = 17$
30 $5(7x - 1) = 11(3x + 2)$

29/ QUADRATIC EQUATIONS: SOLUTION BY TRIAL AND IMPROVEMENT

'Trial and improvement' is a recognised method of solving equations. The method is to try a possible answer; if this is not an exact answer, then try an answer which might be more accurate.

EXAMPLE

► Find a solution to the equation $2x^2 + x = 2$, to 2 decimal places.

Try $x = 0$:	$0 + 0 = 0$	too low
Try $x = 1$:	$(2 \times 1^2) + (1) = 3$	too high
Try $x = 2$:	$(2 \times 2^2) + (2) = 10$	too high

A solution seems to be between $x = 0$ and $x = 1$, but nearer to $x = 1$ than $x = 0$.

Try $x = 0.6$:	$(2 \times 0.6^2) + 0.6 = 1.32$	too low
Try $x = 0.7$:	$(2 \times 0.7^2) + 0.7 = 1.68$	too low
Try $x = 0.8$:	$(2 \times 0.8^2) + 0.8 = 2.08$	too high

The solution would appear to be between $x = 0.7$ and $x = 0.8$, but nearer to 0.8.

Try $x = 0.77$:	$(2 \times 0.77^2) + 0.77 = 1.9558$	too low
Try $x = 0.78$:	$(2 \times 0.78^2) + 0.78 = 1.9968$	too low
Try $x = 0.79$:	$(2 \times 0.79^2) + 0.79 = 2.0382$	too high

Of the last two results, 1.9968 is closer to 2 than 2.0382, so the solution, to 2 decimal places, is 0.78.

To find the second solution return to $x = 2$ and try increasing values of x to see whether solutions again approach a value of 2. If not, then try decreasing values of x (negative values). By this method the second solution can be found: $x = -1.28$.

Notes:

(1) If the equation is in a form such as $2x^2 + x - 2 = 0$, then rearrange the equation as $2x^2 + x = 2$ before looking for a solution by trial and improvement.

(2) A quadratic equation (with the term in x^2 as the highest power) normally has two solutions.

(3) A cubic equation (with the term in x^3 as the highest power) normally has only one solution which can be found by this method.

Exercise 29A

Use a 'trial and improvement' method to find any solutions to these equations. Find your answers to 2 decimal places.

1 $x^2 - 2x = 2$	**2** $x^2 - 3x = 3$	**3** $x^2 - 2x = 7$	**4** $x^2 + 3x = 6$
5 $x^3 = 4$	**6** $x^3 + x = 31$	**7** $x^2 - 4x = 6$	**8** $x^3 = 20$
9 $x^3 + 2x = 200$	**10** $x^3 - 4x + 2 = 0$	**11** $x^3 + x = 9$	**12** $2x^2 - 3x = 1$
13 $3x^2 + x = 2$	**14** $x^3 - 2x = 35$	**15** $4x^2 + x = 4$	**16** $2x^2 + 5x + 1 = 0$
17 $x^3 - 4x = 100$	**18** $3x^2 + 2x = 2$	**19** $x^3 + x^2 + x = 10$	**20** $2x^2 + x = 4$

Exercise 29B

Use a 'trial and improvement' method to find any solutions to these equations. Find your answers to 2 decimal places.

1 $x^2 - 2x = 6$ **2** $x^2 - 3x = 3$ **3** $x^2 + x = 7$ **4** $x^3 + x = 16$
5 $x^2 - 3x = 8$ **6** $x^3 = 10$ **7** $x^3 + 3x = 28$ **8** $2x^2 - 2x = 1$
9 $x^2 + 4x + 1 = 0$ **10** $x^3 = 45$ **11** $3x^2 - x = 1$ **12** $2x^2 - 2x = 8$
13 $x^3 + 2x = 15$ **14** $4x^2 - 3x = 4$ **15** $x^3 - x = 49$ **16** $x^2 + 3x + 1 = 0$
17 $2x^2 + 6x + 2 = 0$ **18** $x^3 + 3x = 47$ **19** $3x^2 + 4x = 3$ **20** $x^3 + x^2 + x = 12$

30/ SIMULTANEOUS EQUATIONS: SOLUTION BY ALGEBRAIC METHODS

EXAMPLE

► Solve these simultaneous equations.

(a) $x + 2y = 7$, $x + y = 4$ (b) $7x + 2y = 32$, $x + y = 1$ (c) $5x + 2y = 26$, $x - 3y = 7$

(a)
$$\begin{array}{r} x + 2y = 7 \\ x + y = 4 \\ \hline y = 3 \end{array}$$
Subtract equations.

Take $y = 3$ and substitute into one of the equations:
$x + y = 4$ so $x + 3 = 4$ and $x = 1$
Solution: $x = 1$, $y = 3$

(b)
$$\begin{array}{r} 7x + 2y = 32 \\ x + y = 1 \end{array}$$
Multiply the bottom equation by 2 to get the same coefficient of y.
$$\begin{array}{r} 7x + 2y = 32 \\ 2x + 2y = 2 \\ \hline 5x = 30 \\ x = 6 \end{array}$$
Subtract equations.

Take $x = 6$ and substitute into $x + y = 1$: $6 + y = 1$ so $y = -5$
Solution: $x = 6$, $y = -5$

(c) To get the same coefficient of x or y the equations need to be multiplied by two *different* numbers:
$$\begin{array}{rl} 5x + 2y = 26 & [\times 3] \\ 4x - 3y = 7 & [\times 2] \\ 15x + 6y = 78 & \\ 8x - 6y = 14 & \text{Add.} \\ \hline 23x = 92 & \\ x = \frac{92}{23} = 4 & \end{array}$$

Substitute into the equation $5x + 2y = 26$:
$$\begin{array}{r} (5 \times 4) + 2y = 26 \\ 20 + 2y = 26 \\ 2y = 26 - 20 \\ 2y = 6 \end{array}$$
Solution: $x = 4$, $y = 3$

Exercise 30A

Solve the simultaneous equations.

1 $x + y = 8$, $x - y = 4$
2 $x + y = 14$, $x - y = 4$
3 $x + y = 3$, $x + 4y = 12$
4 $x + 3y = 15$, $x - 2y = 5$

5 $x + 2y = 5$
$x + y = 3$

6 $3x + 9y = 21$
$3x + y = 5$

7 $4x - 2y = 6$
$4x - 5y = 3$

8 $3x + 5y = 21$
$3x + y = 9$

9 $5x + 2y = 12$
$3x + 2y = 8$

10 $x + 5y = 0$
$3x - 5y = 10$

11 $10x - 2y = 9$
$7x - 2y = 6$

12 $9x - 3y = 15$
$5x - 3y = 7$

13 $5x - 3y = 1$
$4x + 3y = 17$

14 $4x + y = 0$
$2x + y = 2$

15 $2x + 3y = 14$
$2x + y = 10$

16 $6x + 4y = 14$
$3x - y = 1$

17 $12x - 3y = 0$
$6x - y = 2$

18 $2x + y = 7$
$5x - 3y = 12$

19 $6x - 5y = 8$
$4x - 3y = 6$

20 $8x + 2y = 4$
$4x + 3y = 2$

21 $x + 5y = 9$
$2x + 3y = 11$

22 $3x + y = 14$
$2x + 3y = 28$

23 $4x + 3y = 31$
$2x - 6y = -22$

24 $4x - 3y = 1$
$5x - 2y = 10$

25 $6x + 7y = 12$
$4x + 3y = 18$

26 $2x - 3y = 5$
$3x + 2y = 40$

27 $5x + 3y = 4$
$3x - 2y = 10$

28 $2x + 3y = 7$
$3x + 4y = 11$

29 $11x - 3y = 8$
$9x + 4y = 13$

30 $2x - 5y = 22$
$3x + 7y = 4$

Exercise 30B

Solve the simultaneous equations.

1 $x + y = 11$
$x - y = 5$

2 $x + y = 3$
$x - y = 3$

3 $x + y = 1$
$x - y = 9$

4 $x - 5y = 2$
$x + 2y = 3$

5 $x - 3y = 6$
$x + 2y = 1$

6 $4x + 9y = 17$
$4x + 3y = 11$

7 $3x + 7y = 5$
$9x - 7y = 1$

8 $4x + 3y = 7$
$4x + y = 13$

9 $2x + 2y = 20$
$2x + 5y = 44$

10 $4x + 3y = 7$
$4x + y = 13$

11 $x - 2y = 7$
$x - 6y = 3$

12 $7x - 2y = 3$
$7x - 3y = 1$

13 $3x - y = 31$
$x - y = 7$

14 $4x - y = 18$
$2x + y = 6$

15 $2x + y = 5$
$3x - y = 5$

16 $4x - 2y = 10$
$2x + 4y = 10$

17 $2x + y = 14$
$x + 3y = 22$

18 $6x - 4y = 26$
$3x + 7y = 22$

19 $4x + 6y = 50$
$3x + 2y = 30$

20 $x + 5y = 20$
$2x + 3y = 19$

21 $3x - 4y = 0$
$9x + 8y = 60$

22 $5x + 3y = 14$
$4x + y = 7$

23 $3x + 2y = 7$
$x + 4y = 9$

24 $5x - 2y = 1$
$2x + 3y = 27$

25 $3x + 2y = 8$
$5x + 3y = 13$

26 $2x + 5y = 23$
$3x + 2y = 29$

27 $3x - 5y = 13$
$2x - 3y = 8$

28 $4x - 3y = 2$
$3x + 4y = 14$

29 $5x + 11y = -2$
$2x + 9y = 13$

30 $7x + 3y = 5$
$3x - 2y = 12$

EXAMPLE

► Four tins of peas and one tin of beans together weigh 1100 g. Five tins of peas weigh 100 g more than three tins of beans.
Find the weight of (a) a tin of peas (b) a tin of beans.

Write as two equations:

$4x + y = 1100$ (× 3)
$5x - 3y = 100$

$12x + 3y = 3300$
$5x - 3y = 100$ Add.
$17x = 3400$
$x = 3400 \div 17 = 200$

Substitute $x = 200$ into $4x + y = 1100$:
$4 \times 200 + y = 1100$
$800 + y = 1100$
$y = 300$

(a) The tin of peas weighs 200 g.
(b) The tin of beans weighs 300 g.

Exercise 30C

For each question write down a pair of simultaneous equations, and solve them to find the solution to the problem.

1. The sum of two numbers is 25. The difference between the two numbers is 13. What are the two numbers?
2. Two numbers have a sum of 39 and a difference of 11. Find the two numbers.
3. The sum of two numbers is 66 and the difference between them is 6. Find the two numbers.
4. Three rubbers and a protractor cost 54p. A rubber and two protractors cost 48p. Find the cost of (a) a rubber (b) a protractor.
5. Seven pens and five pencils have a total weight of 391 g. Four pens and nine pencils have a total weight of 377 g. Find the weight of (a) a pen (b) a pencil.
6. Three pounds of pears and two pounds of lemons cost £2.80. Five pounds of pears and three pounds of lemons cost £4.52. What is the price per pound of pears and lemons?
7. Four copies of one book and three copies of a second book cost £30; this is the same cost as three copies of the first book and six copies of the second book. Find the cost of both of the books.
8. A newspaper and a magazine together have a weight of 152 g. The magazine weighs 36 g more than the newspaper. Find the weight of (a) the magazine (b) the newspaper.
9. Three rollerball pens and two ink-pens cost £3.20. Four rollerball pens and three ink-pens cost £4.50. What is the price of (a) a rollerball pen (b) an ink-pen?
10. It takes 2 hours to wash and clean two family cars and three small cars; three family cars and five small cars take 3 hours 10 minutes. How long, on average, does it take to wash and clean (a) one family car (b) one small car?
11. On a market stall four cups and three saucers cost £5.40. Three cups and five saucers cost £5.70. Find the cost of (a) a cup (b) a saucer.
12. The perimeter of a rectangle is 38 metres. The difference between the length and the width is 3 metres. Find the length and the width.
13. A grandfather is twelve times older than his grandson. In 5 years' time the difference in their ages will be 55 years. How old will they each be in 5 years' time?
14. Five dot-matrix printers and two laser printers cost £1800. One dot-matrix printer and three laser printers cost £1400. Find the cost of (a) one laser printer (b) one dot-matrix printer.
15. A man is three times as old as his son. In 15 years' time the father will be twice as old as his son. What are their ages today?

Exercise 30D

For each question write down a pair of simultaneous equations and solve them to find the solution to the problem.

1. The sum of two numbers is 9. One of the numbers is 5 more than the other. What are the two numbers?
2. Two numbers have a sum of 27 and a difference of 9. Find the two numbers.
3. Two chocolate bars and one ice cream cost £1. Three chocolate bars and one ice cream cost £1.40. Find the cost of (a) a chocolate bar (b) an ice cream.
4. Sean has two sisters. Twice the age of the older, added to the age of the younger is 17 years. Four times the age of the older, minus the age of the younger is 25 years. What are the ages of his two sisters?
5. Six tapes and four CDs cost £136. Five tapes and four CDs cost £124. Find the cost of (a) a tape and (b) a CD.
6. Three pencils and five pens cost £1.70. Five pencils and three pens cost £1.66. Find the cost of (a) a pencil (b) a pen.

7 Four nails and a screw weigh 28 g; two nails and three screws weigh 34 g. Find the weight of (a) a nail (b) a screw.

8 Six adults and three children pay a total of £144 for a train journey. Four adults and three children pay £108 for the same train journey. Find the cost of a ticket for (a) one adult (b) one child.

9 A maths department can buy three logic calculators and four graphic calculators for £280 or six logic calculators and four graphic calculators for £460. Find the cost of (a) a logic calculator (b) a graphic calculator.

10 A mother is five times as old as her daughter. In 15 years' time the mother will be exactly twice as old as her daughter. What are their ages now?

11 A holiday for two adults and three children costs £1496. The same holiday for three adults and four children costs £2112. What would be the cost of the holiday for two adults and two children?

12 Six tins of dog food and three tins of cat food weigh 2550 grams. Four tins of dog food and one tin of cat food weigh 1450 grams. Find the weight of one tin of (a) dog food (b) cat food.

13 The age of a man and his son together total 27 years. In 4 years' time, the father will be exactly four times as old as his son. What age are they both now?

14 Metal rods of different lengths are classified by colour. Two red rods and one blue rod have a total length of 9 metres. Three red and five blue rods have a total length of 17 metres. Find the length of (a) a red metal rod (b) a blue metal rod.

15 Two T-shirts and a pair of jeans cost £28. Five T-shirts and a pair of the same jeans cost £43. How much is (a) a T-shirt (b) a pair of jeans?

31/ FINDING THE EQUATION OF A STRAIGHT-LINE GRAPH

All straight lines have an equation of the type $y = mx + c$, where m is the **gradient** of the line, and c is the point on the y-axis where the line crosses it.

The equation of a straight line can be found by examination of the graph.

EXAMPLE

► Write down the equation of this straight-line graph.

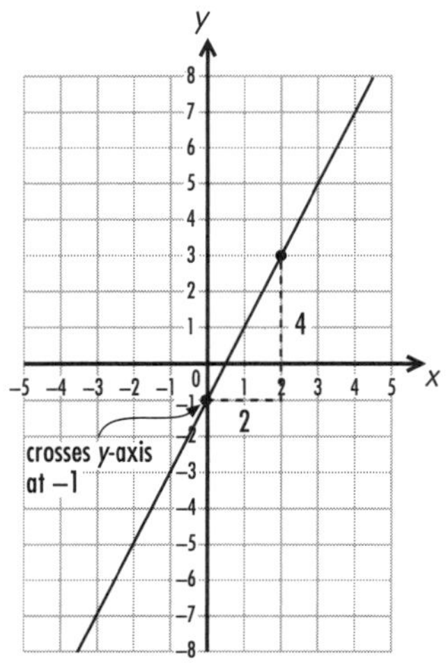

Draw a right-angled triangle using two points on the graph.

Gradient:

m = height of triangle ÷ base of triangle

$m = \frac{4}{2} = 2$

Also:

$c = -1$ (from the graph)

So the equation of the line is $y = 2x - 1$.

EXAMPLE

► Write down the equation of this straight-line graph.

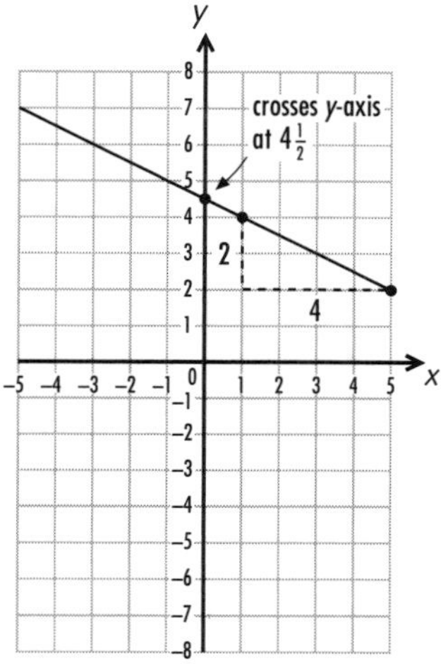

Draw a right-angled triangle using two points on the graph.

Gradient: height of triangle ÷ base of triangle

$$= \frac{2}{4} = \frac{1}{2}$$

However the gradient is negative (diagonally sloping downwards).

So: $m = -\frac{1}{2}$

$c = 4\frac{1}{2}$ (from the graph)

The equation of the line is $y = -\frac{1}{2}x + 4\frac{1}{2}$.

Note: This equation could be written a different way by multiplying the equation by 2:

$2y = -x + 9$ or $2y + x = 9$

Exercise 31A

Write down the equation of each of the lines.

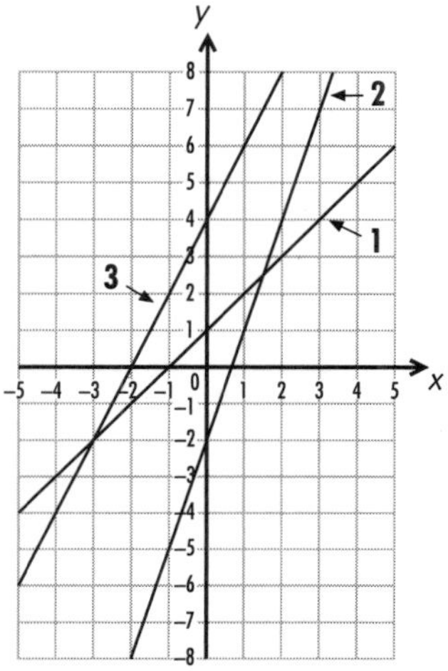

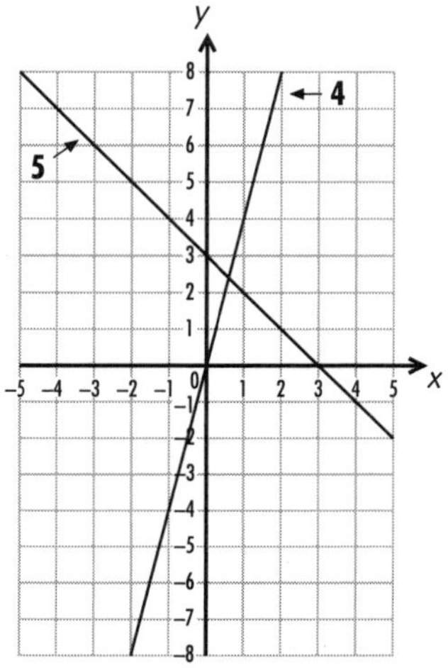

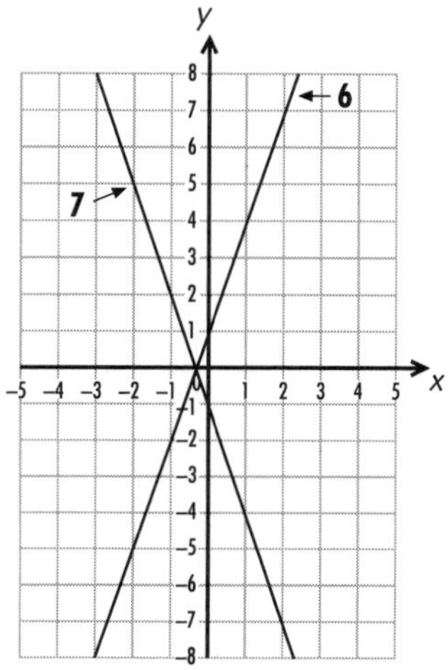

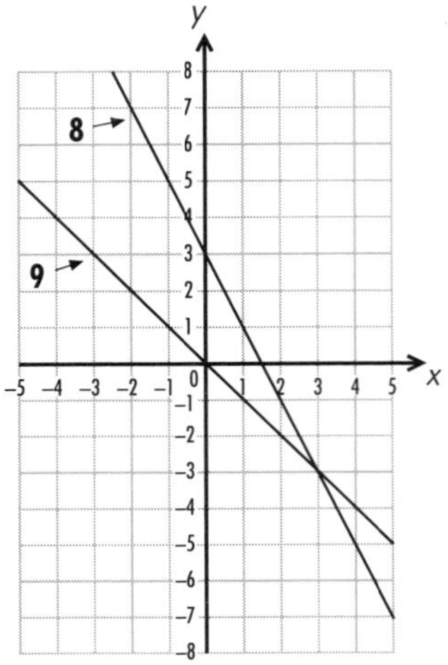

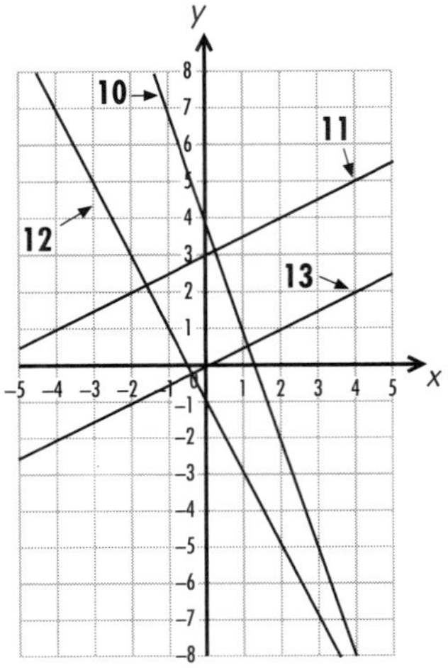

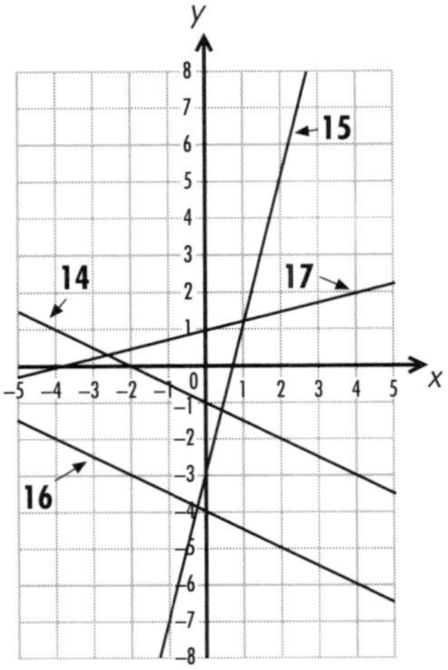

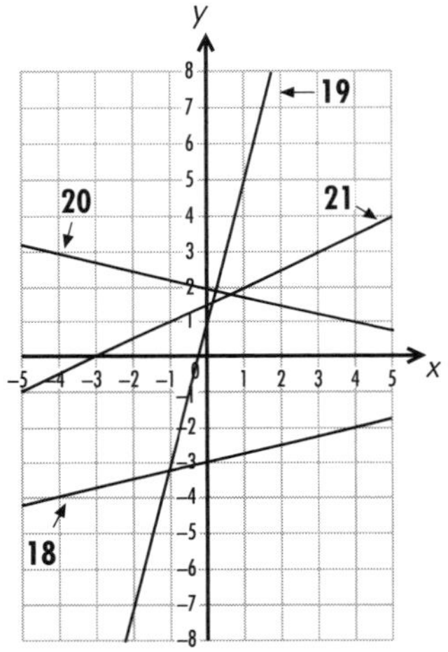

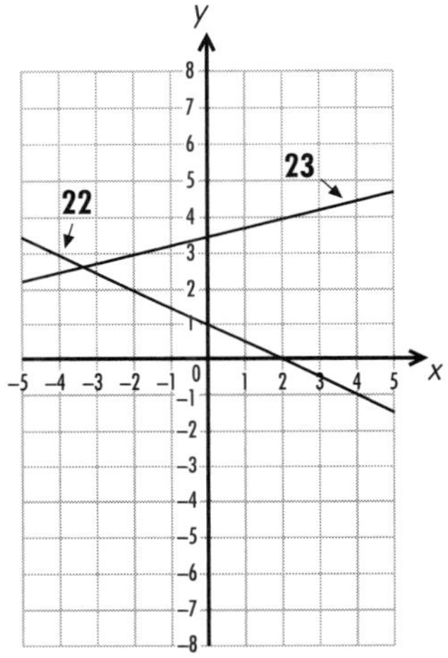

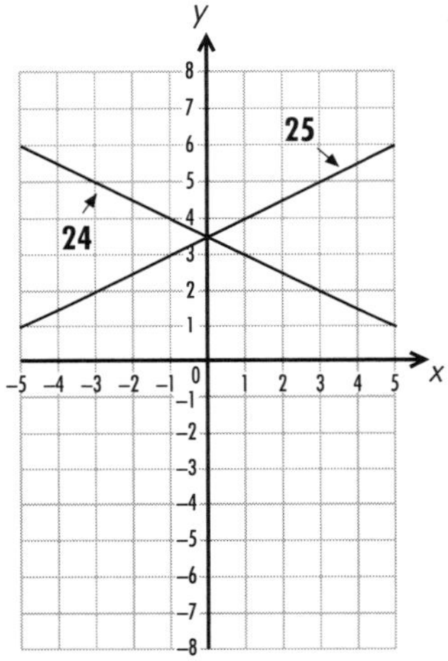

Exercise 31B

Write down the equation of each of the lines.

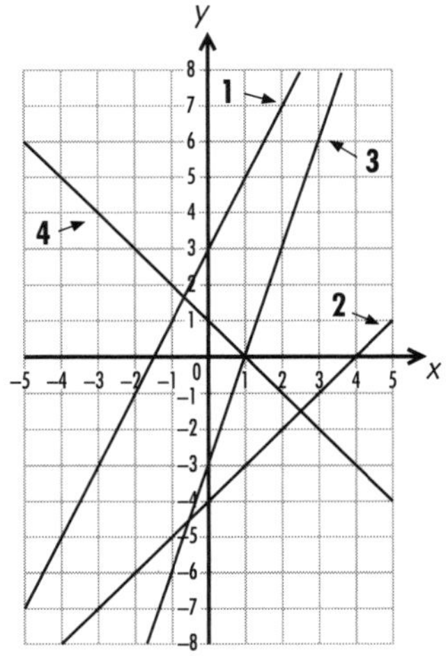

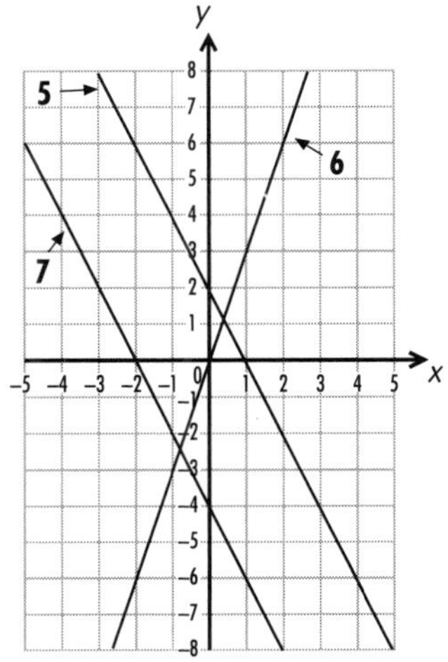

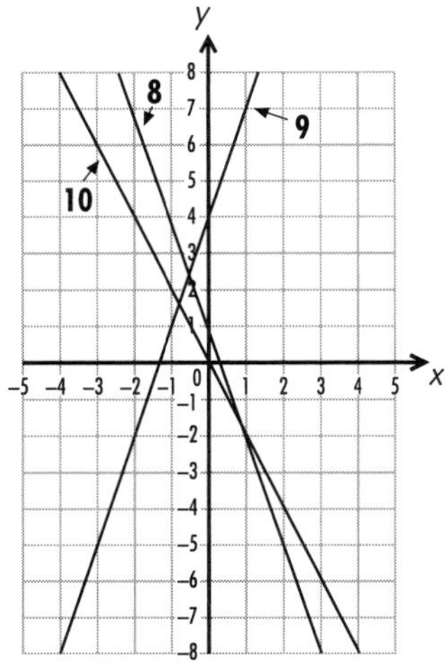

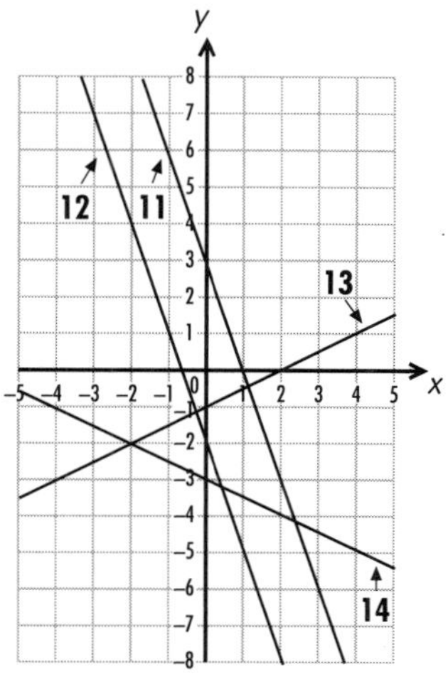
y
x
11
12
13
14

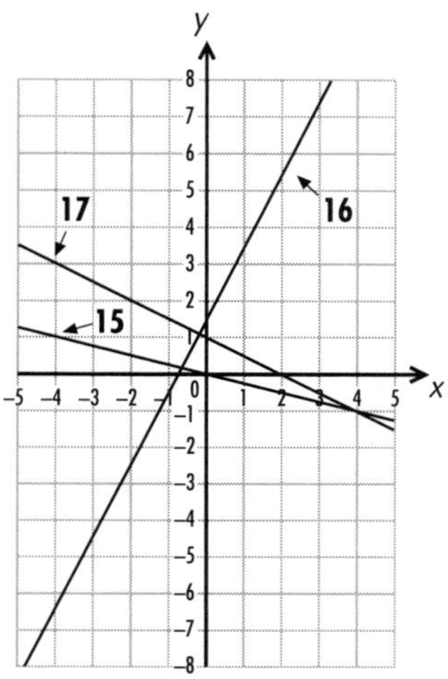
y
x
15
16
17

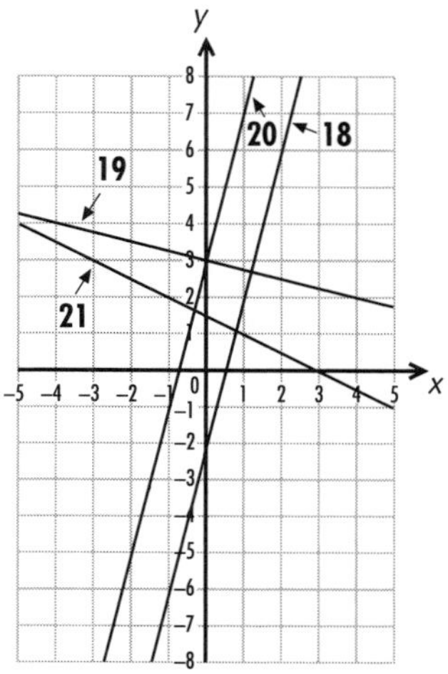
y
x
18
19
20
21

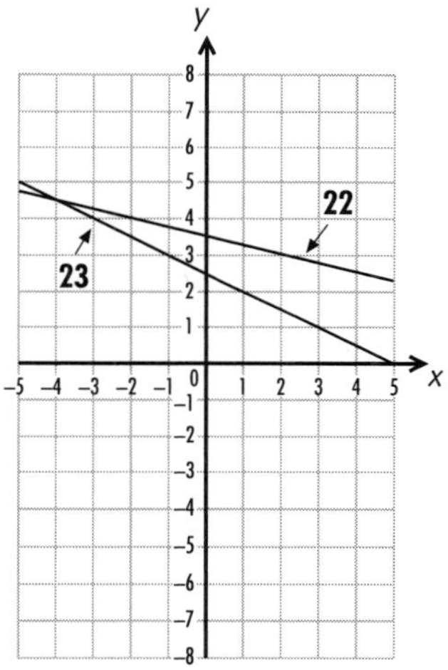
y
x
22
23

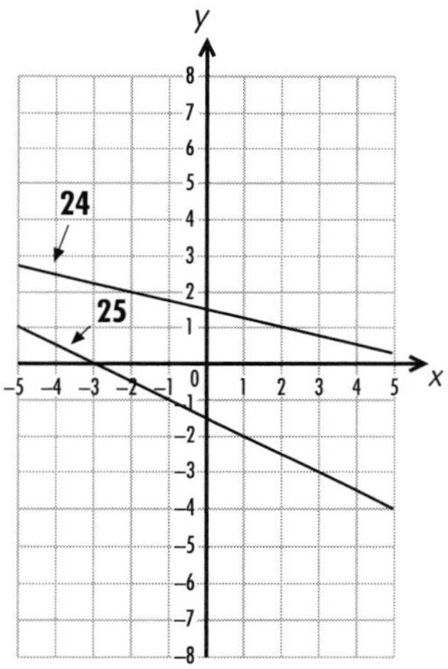
y
x
24
25

32/ DRAWING A STRAIGHT-LINE GRAPH FROM AN EQUATION

All straight lines have an equation of the type $y = mx + c$, where m is the **gradient** of the line, and c is the point on the y-axis where the line crosses it.
The straight-line graph of an equation can be drawn by examination of the equation.

EXAMPLE

► Draw the straight-line graph for the equation $y = 3x - 5$.

$$y = 3x - 5$$

Gradient (m) — Point where the line crosses the y-axis (c).

Plot the point (0, –5).
From this point, a gradient of 3 means that, for each square moved to the right, the line moves up by 3 squares. Use this pattern to plot a few points to help you draw the line.

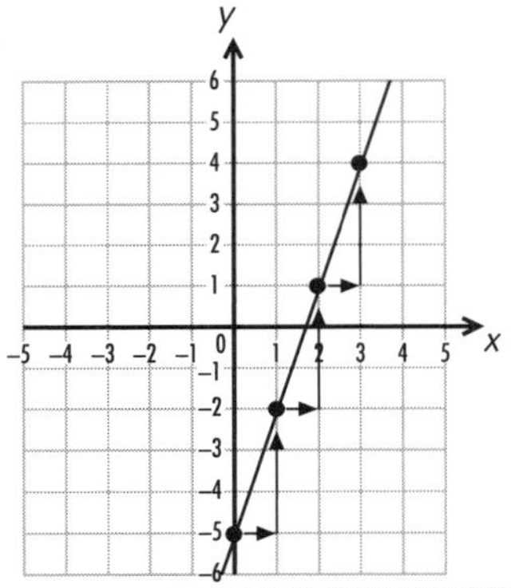

EXAMPLE

► Draw the straight-line graph for the equation $y = -\frac{1}{2}x + 3$.

$$y = -\frac{1}{2}x + 3$$

Gradient (m) — Point where the line crosses the y-axis (c).

Plot the point (0, 3).
From this point, a gradient of $-\frac{1}{2}$ means that, for each square moved to the right, the line moves *down* (because of the minus sign) by $\frac{1}{2}$ square. Use this pattern to plot a few points to help you draw the line.
Note: An equation written in the form $2y = x + 5$ should be rearranged as the type $y = mx + c$ first.
So $2y = x + 5$ becomes $y = \frac{1}{2}x + 2\frac{1}{2}$.

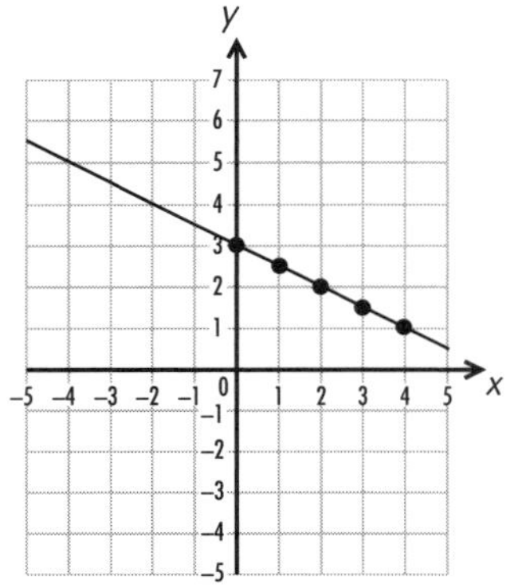

Exercise 32A

Draw axes of the size shown in the examples above; draw a straight-line graph for each of these equations.

1 $y = x + 3$	**2** $y = 3x - 1$	**3** $y = 2x - 4$	**4** $y = x$	**5** $y = 3x + 2$
6 $y = -2x + 4$	**7** $y = \frac{1}{2}x + 2$	**8** $y = -3x$	**9** $y = -2x - 2$	**10** $y = 4x - 4$
11 $y = -3x - 3$	**12** $y = -x - 4$	**13** $y = -\frac{1}{2}x$	**14** $y = \frac{1}{4}x + 2$	**15** $2y = x + 1$

16 $y = \frac{1}{2}x - 3$	**17** $y = -\frac{1}{4}x + 1$	**18** $y = 4x + 2$	**19** $4y = x + 6$	**20** $2y = -x - 8$
21 $4y = -x + 10$	**22** $2y = x - 3$	**23** $2y = -x - 5$	**24** $2y = -x + 7$	**25** $4y = -x + 2$

Exercise 32B

Draw axes of the size shown in the examples (page 58); draw a straight-line graph for each of these equations.

1 $y = 2x + 2$	**2** $y = 3x - 4$	**3** $y = -x - 3$	**4** $y = -2x + 1$	**5** $y = 3x + 3$
6 $y = \frac{1}{2}x - 2$	**7** $y = 2x$	**8** $y = -2x - 3$	**9** $y = -3x - 4$	**10** $y = -4x$
11 $y = -3x + 2$	**12** $y = -\frac{1}{2}x + 2$	**13** $y = \frac{1}{2}x + 4$	**14** $y = -\frac{1}{2}x - 2$	**15** $y = 4x - 2$
16 $y = \frac{1}{4}x$	**17** $4y = x + 10$	**18** $y = -\frac{1}{4}x - 3$	**19** $y = 4x + 4$	**20** $4y = x - 8$
21 $2y = x - 5$	**22** $2y = -x + 5$	**23** $4y = -x - 2$	**24** $2y = x - 7$	**25** $2y = -x + 3$

33/ SIMULTANEOUS EQUATIONS: SOLUTION BY GRAPHICAL METHODS

EXAMPLE

▶ Find the solutions of the simultaneous equations $4y = x + 2$ and $4y = -x + 6$.

The equations can be written as: $y = \frac{1}{4}x + \frac{1}{2}$ and $y = -\frac{1}{4}x + 1\frac{1}{2}$

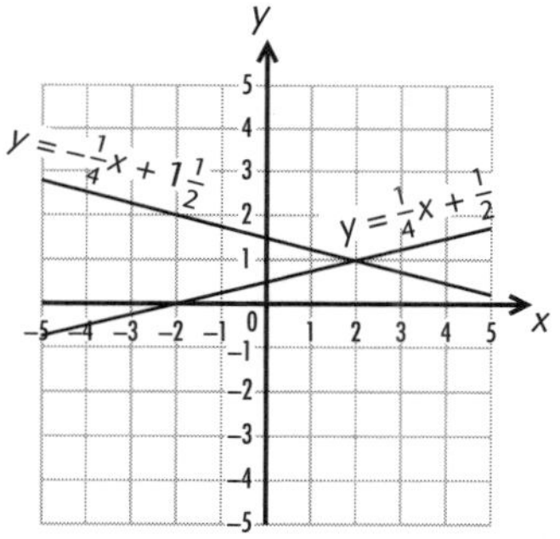

The diagram shows the graphs of the lines $y = \frac{1}{4}x + \frac{1}{2}$ and $y = -\frac{1}{4}x + 1\frac{1}{2}$.
The solution to the simultaneous equations is where the two graphs cross: at the point (2, 1).
The solution is $x = 2$, $y = 1$.

Exercise 33A

Write down the solution to each pair of simultaneous equations, which are shown as straight-line graphs.

1 $y = 2x - 2$
$y = -\frac{1}{2}x + 3$

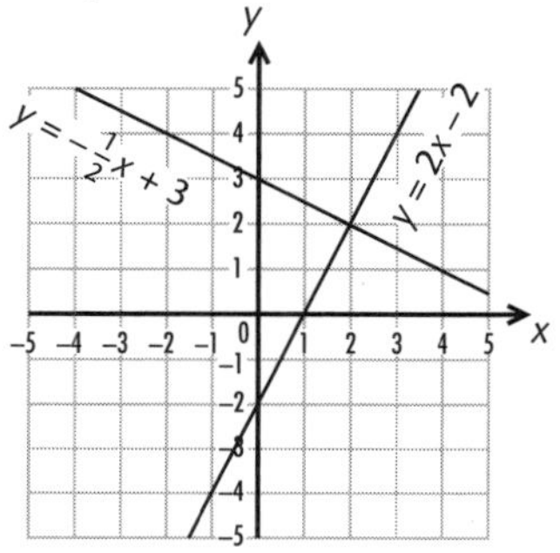

2 $y = 2x + 1$
$y = -x + 4$

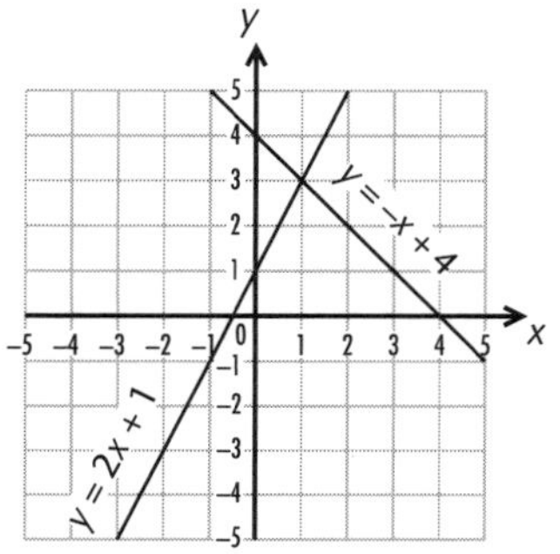

3 $y = -x + 1$
$y = \frac{1}{2}x + 1$

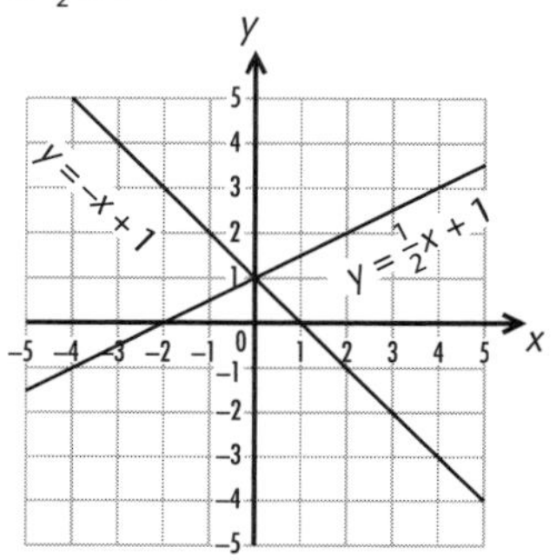

4 $y = -x + 4$
$y = 2x - 5$

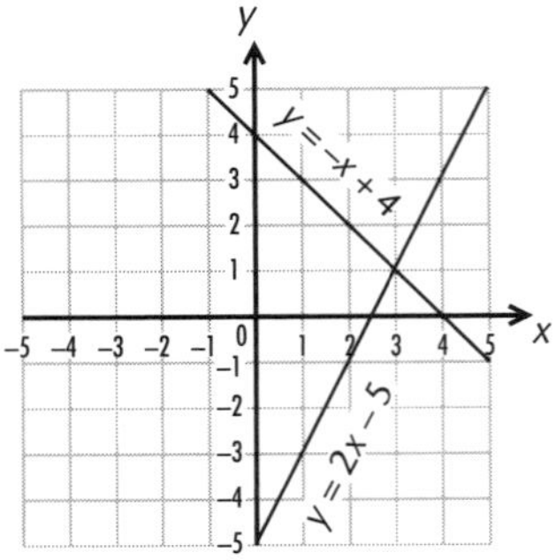

5 $y = -x - 2$
$y = \frac{1}{2}x + 1$

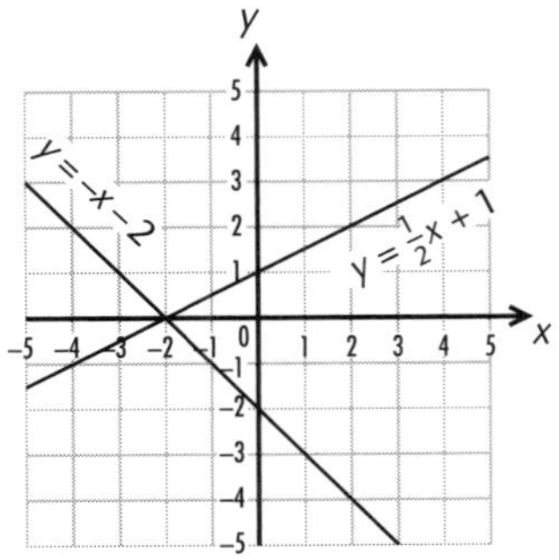

6 $y = -x + 1$
$y = -\frac{1}{2}x + 3$

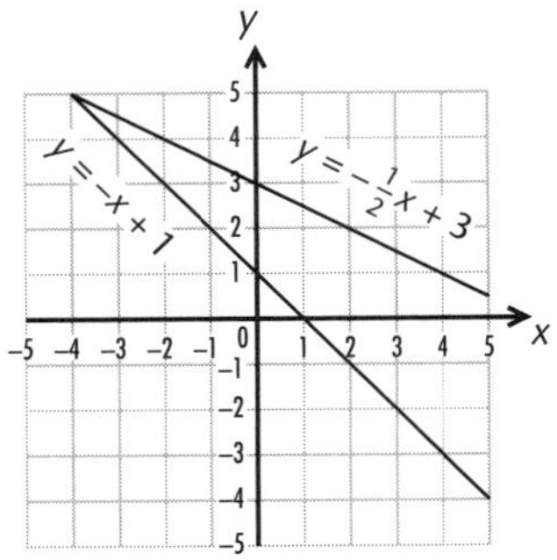

7 $y = -x + 4$
$y = -\frac{1}{2}x + 3$

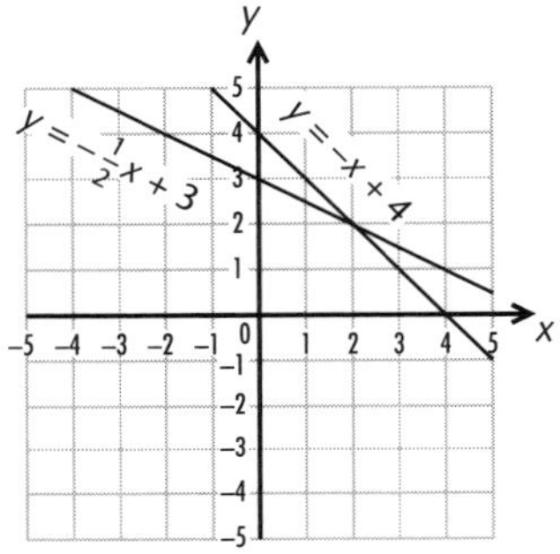

8 $y = -x - 2$
$y = 2x - 5$

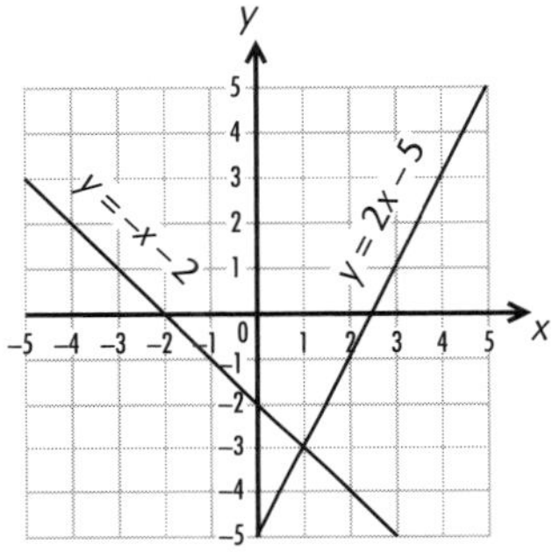

9 $y = \frac{1}{2}x + 1$
$y = 2x + 1$

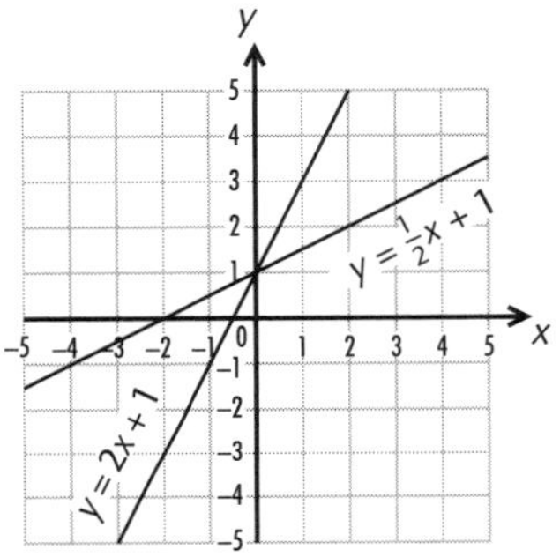

10 $y = -\frac{1}{2}x + 3$
$y = -x + 2$

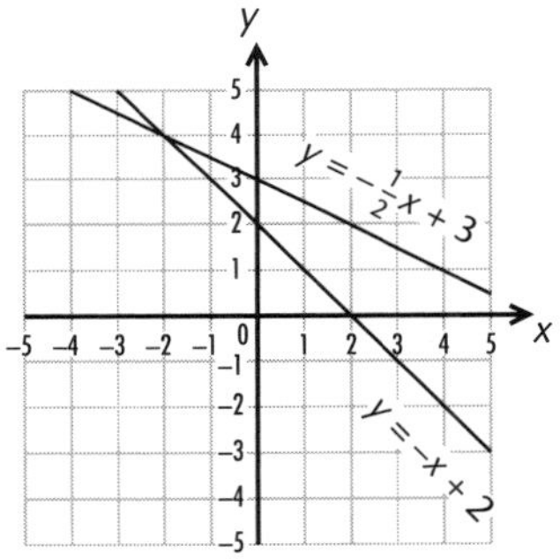

For each pair of equations:
(a) draw and label straight-line graphs representing both equations on the same axes,
(b) find the solution to the simultaneous equations.

11 $y = \frac{1}{2}x + 1$
$y = x - 1$

12 $y = -x + 1$
$y = x - 3$

13 $y = x + 2$
$y = -x - 2$

14 $y = x - 3$
$y = -x + 2$

15 $y = x - 1$
$4y = -x + 6$

16 $4y = -x + 6$
$y = 2x - 3$

17 $y = 2x - 3$
$y = x - 3$

18 $y = x + 4$
$y = -4x - 6$

19 $y = -x + 1$
$y = 2x - 2$

20 $y = -x + 1$
$y = x + 4$

Exercise 33B

Write down the solution to each pair of simultaneous equations, which are shown as straight-line graphs.

1 $y = -x + 4$
$y = \frac{1}{2}x + 1$

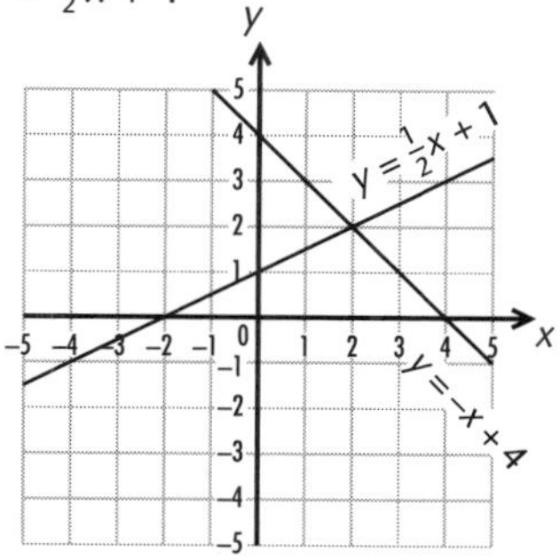

2 $y = 2x + 1$
$y = -x - 2$

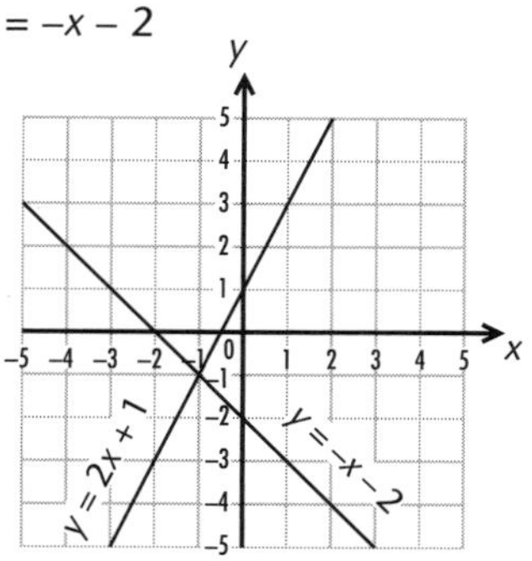

3 $y = 2x - 5$
$y = \frac{1}{2}x + 1$

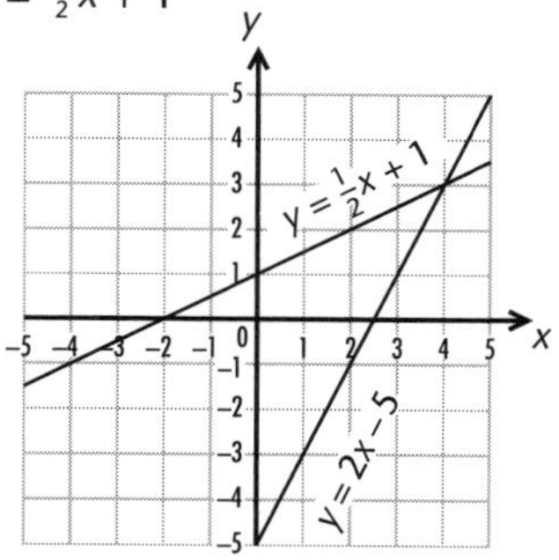

4 $y = -x + 2$
$y = -\frac{1}{2}x + 3$

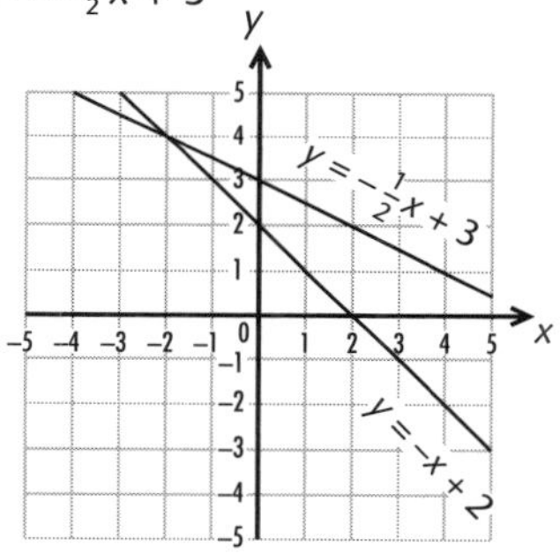

5 $y = 2x - 5$
$y = -x + 1$

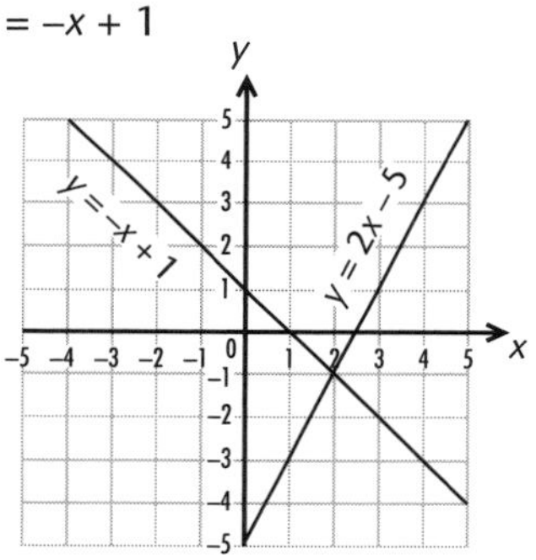

6 $y = -x + 4$
$y = x - 2$

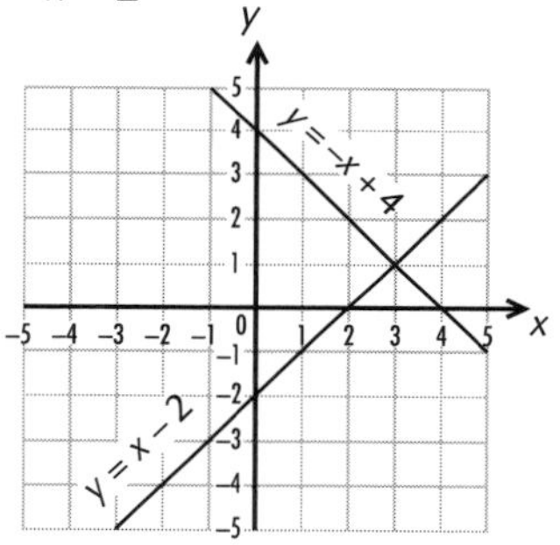

7 $y = x - 2$
$y = -x - 2$

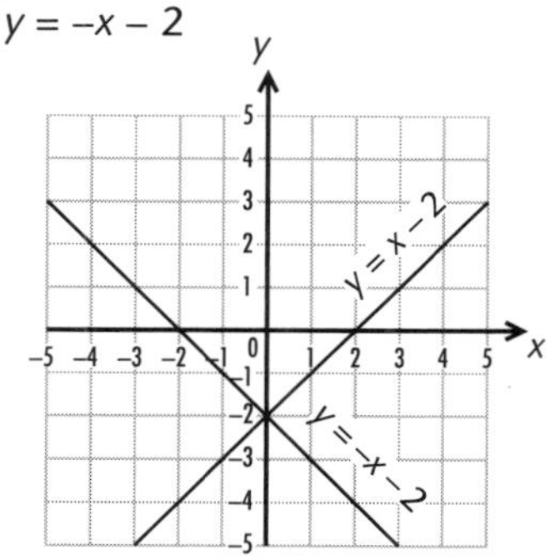

8 $y = -x + 2$
$y = x - 1$

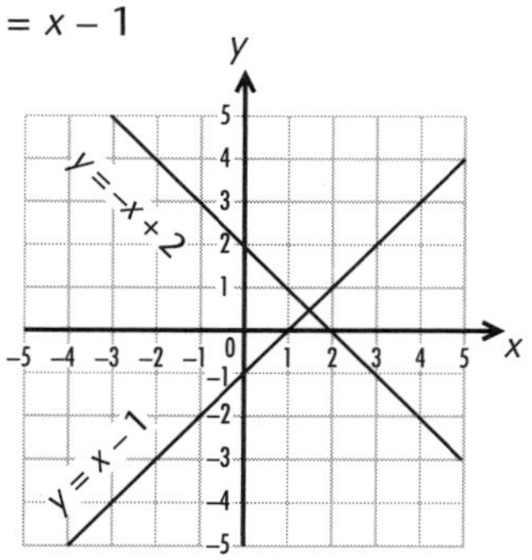

9 $y = -x + 4$
$y = x + 2$

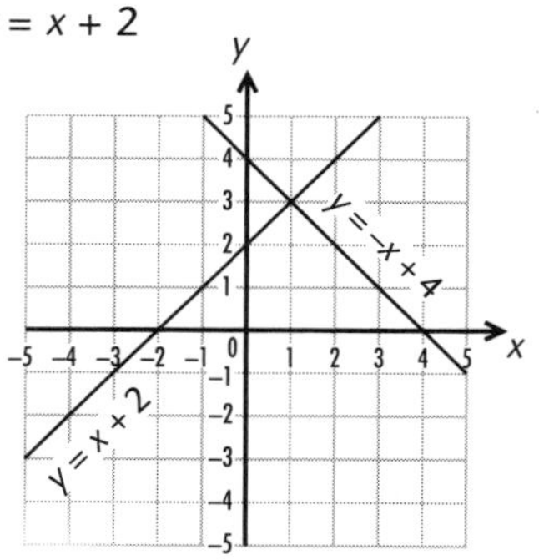

10 $y = x - 1$
$y = -x - 2$

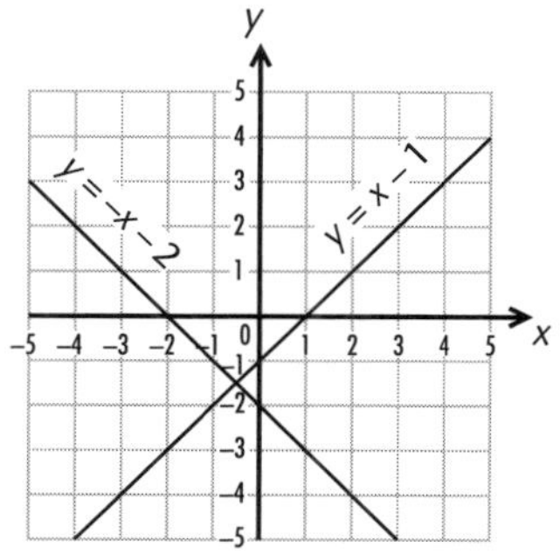

For each pair of equations:

(a) draw and label straight-line graphs representing both equations on the same axes,

(b) find the solution to the simultaneous equations.

11 $y = x + 2$, $y = -x + 1$

12 $y = x + 4$, $4y = -x + 6$

13 $y = -x + 4$, $y = x - 3$

14 $y = -4x - 6$, $4y = -x + 6$

15 $y = -x - 2$, $y = x - 3$

16 $y = -x + 2$, $y = x + 2$

17 $y = -x + 4$, $y = \frac{1}{4}x - 1$

18 $y = \frac{1}{4}x + 4$, $y = -x + 4$

19 $y = \frac{1}{4}x + 4$, $y = 2x - 3$

20 $y = x - 1$, $y = \frac{1}{4}x - 1$

34/ INTERPRETING TRAVEL GRAPHS

Travel graphs are used to show a comparison of distances travelled over a period of time. They are a useful way of representing a journey.

EXAMPLE

► The travel graph represents the journey of a cyclist.

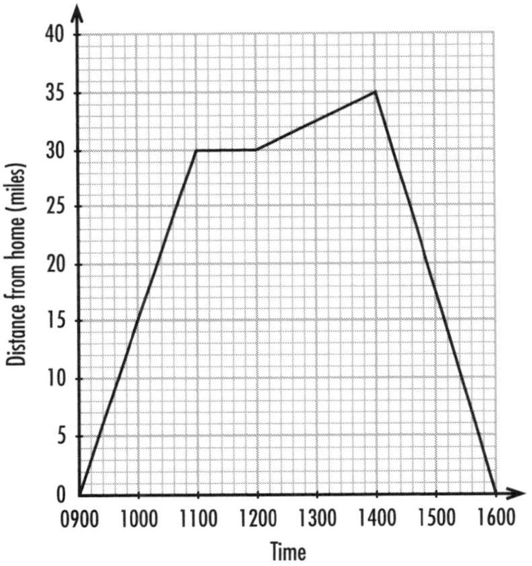

(a) What was the average speed of the cyclist between 0900 and 1100?
(b) Between which times was the cyclist stationary?
(c) Why does the graph slope downwards after 1400?
(d) At what time did the cyclist turn around and head for home?
(e) What is the average speed on the homeward journey?

(a) Average speed $= \dfrac{\text{distance}}{\text{time}} = \dfrac{30 \text{ miles}}{2 \text{ hours}} = 15$ m.p.h.

(b) Between 1100 and 1200, as here the graph is horizontal.

(c) The cyclist is returning home.

(d) At 1400 – the slope of the graph changes from upwards to downwards.

(e) Average speed $= \dfrac{\text{distance}}{\text{time}} = \dfrac{35 \text{ miles}}{2 \text{ hours}} = 17\frac{1}{2}$ m.p.h.

Exercise 34A

1 This graph represents a coach on a journey.

(a) What was the average speed of the coach during the first part of its journey?
(b) At what time did it begin to travel more slowly?
(c) How long was the total journey?
(d) How far had the coach gone at 1000?

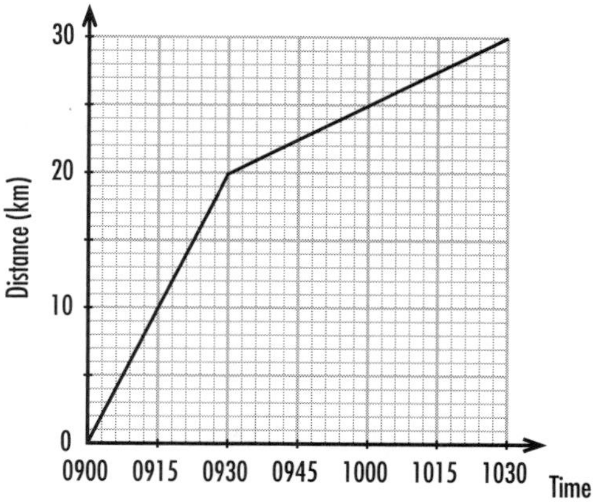

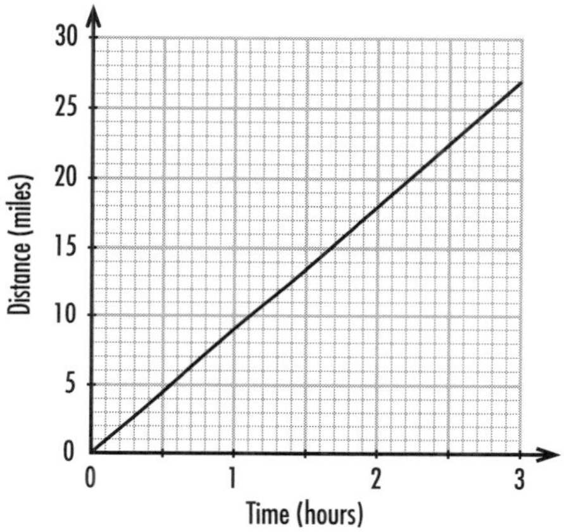

2 This graph represents a person running.

(a) How far had the runner gone in $2\frac{1}{2}$ hours?
(b) After what time had the runner gone 18 miles?
(c) What was the average speed of the runner?

3 This graph represents a car journey.

(a) At what time had the car gone 80 km?
(b) How far was travelled in the second part of the journey?
(c) What was the average speed of the second part of the journey?
(d) How far had the car travelled at 1330?

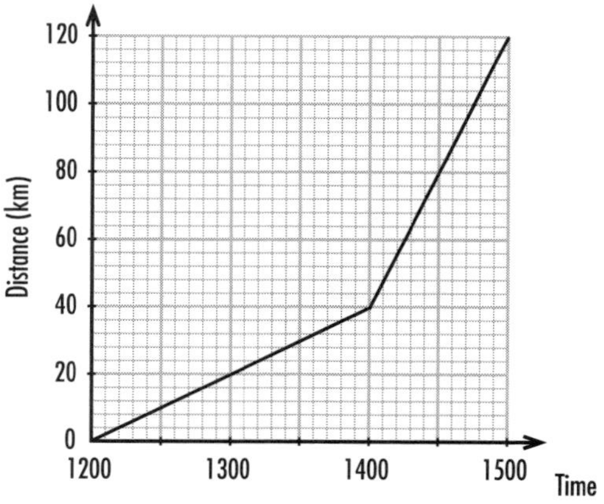

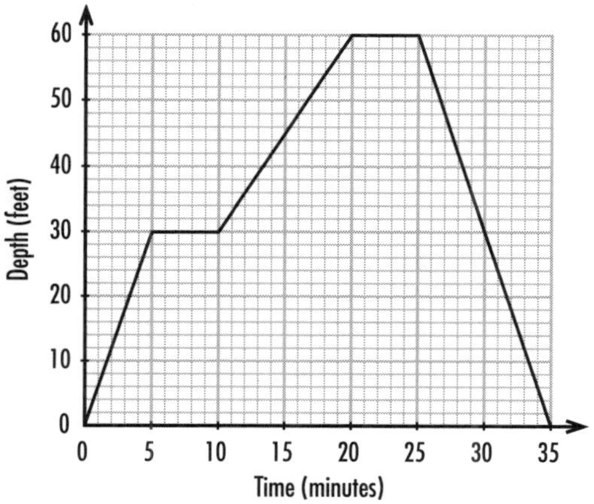

4 This graph represents the depth of a scuba diver.

(a) After how many minutes did the diver reach a depth of 54 feet?
(b) Describe why the graph is horizontal in two places.
(c) How deep was the diver after $\frac{1}{4}$ hour?
(d) What happened after 25 minutes?

5 This graph represents the rail journey of a Liverpool salesman.

(a) What happened 2 hours into the journey?
(b) After what time had the salesman travelled 200 miles?
(c) What was the average speed of his return journey?
(d) What was the total length of the journey?

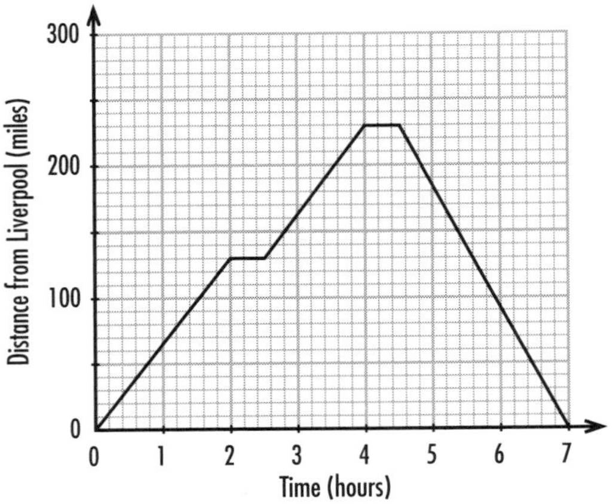

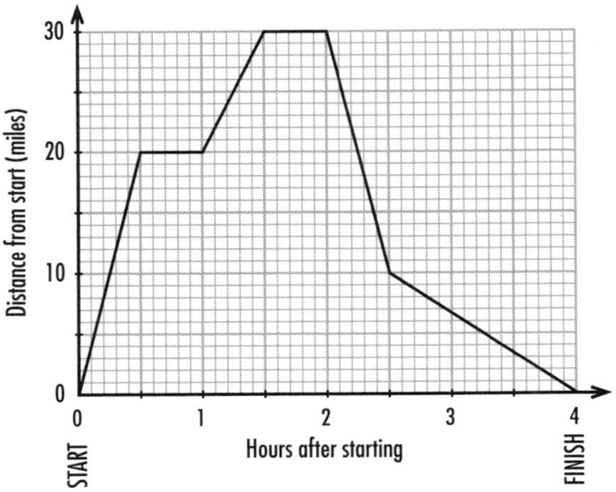

6 This graph represents the journey of a cyclist in a rally.

(a) At what time did the cyclist first stop?
(b) How far was the cyclist from the starting point after $1\frac{1}{4}$ hours?
(c) How long did it take to complete the last 3 miles?
(d) What was the average speed of the cyclist during the last $1\frac{1}{2}$ hours?

7 This graph represents the movement of an object across a field.

(a) During the entire journey, what was the total time spent stationary?
(b) Between which two times was the object travelling the fastest?
(c) At what distance did the object begin to return to the starting point?
(d) At what times was the object 80 metres from the starting point?

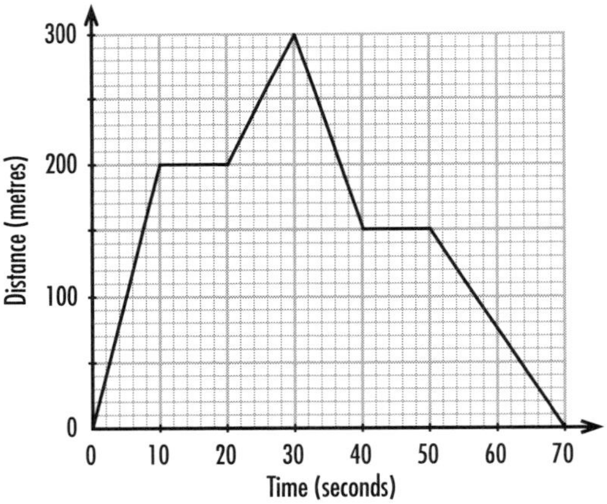

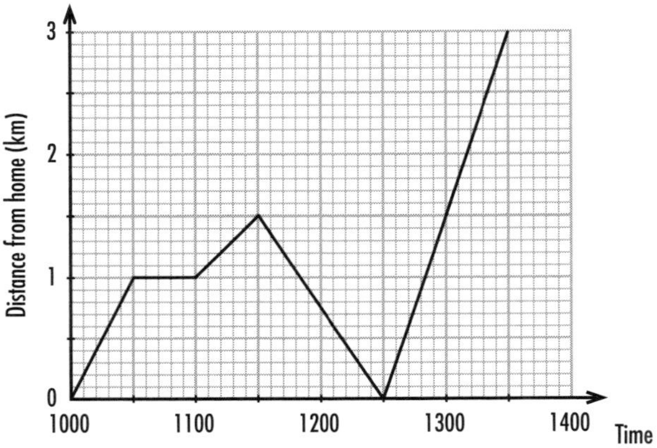

8 This graph represents the journey of a girl from her home.

(a) What happened at 1230?
(b) Between which times was the girl travelling the fastest?
(c) What was the total length of the journey?
(d) What was the average speed of the girl from 1130 to 1230?

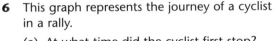

Exercise 34B

1 This graph represents the path of a walker.

(a) What was the average speed of the walker during the first part of the journey?
(b) At what time did the walker begin to walk more quickly?
(c) How long was the complete journey?
(d) At what time had the walker gone 20 miles?

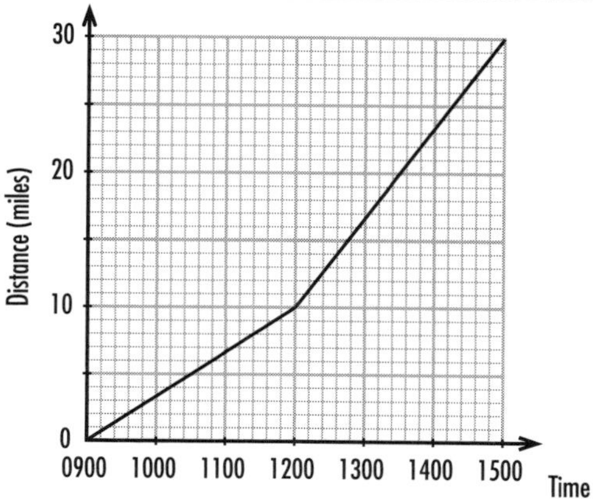

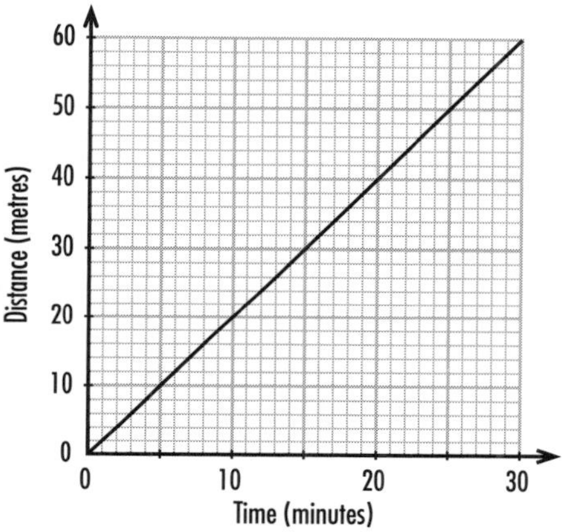

2 This graphs represents the journey of a lizard in the desert.

(a) What was the average speed of the lizard?
(b) At what time had the lizard travelled 50 metres?
(c) How far had the lizard gone after 18 minutes?

3 This graph represents the journey of a remote-control car.

(a) Between which two times was the car travelling the slowest?
(b) What was the average speed during the last part of the journey?
(c) At what time was the car the furthest from the starting point?
(d) How far was the car from the starting point after 15 seconds?

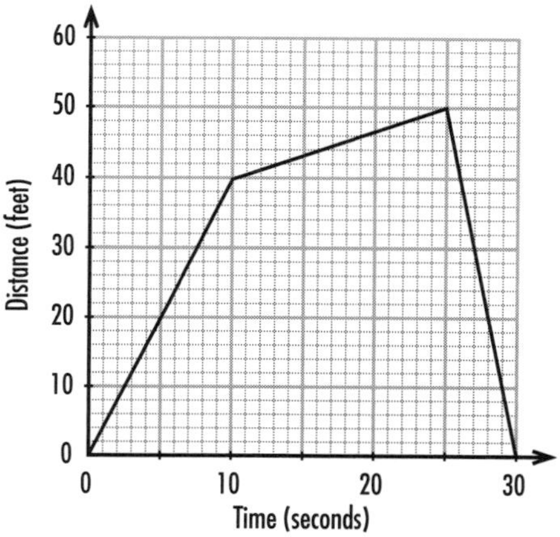

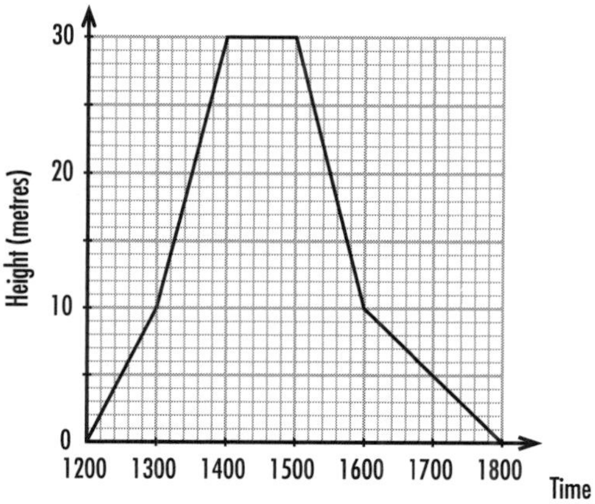

4 This graph represents the journey of a window-cleaner up the outside of a tall building.

(a) How high did the window-cleaner have to go?
(b) At what time did the window-cleaner begin to descend?
(c) The window-cleaner took a break. How long was the break?
(d) At what times was the window-cleaner 20 metres off the ground?

5 This graph represents the journey of a saleswoman to and from a meeting.

(a) How long did the meeting last?
(b) What was the average speed of the second stage of the journey, beginning after 30 km?
(c) How far had the saleswoman travelled after $1\frac{1}{4}$ hours?
(d) How long did it take the saleswoman to travel the last 20 km?

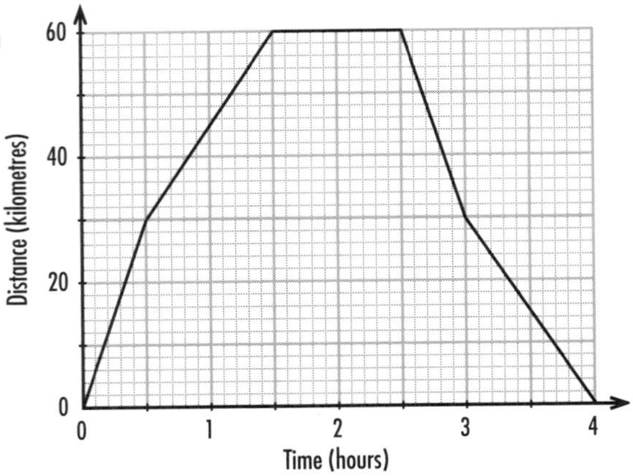

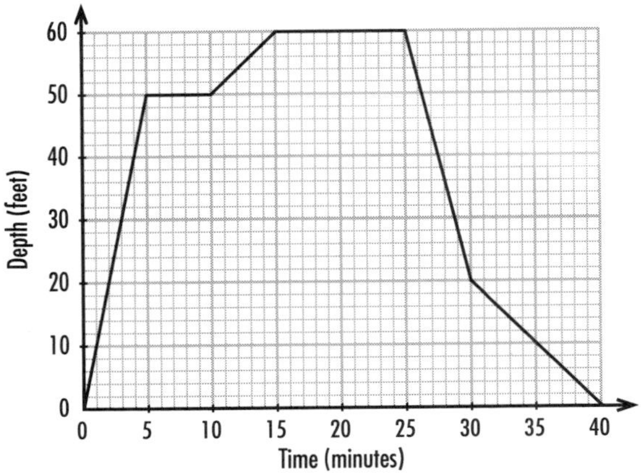

6 This graph represents the depth of a scuba diver.

(a) For how long did the diver remain at his deepest depth?
(b) How long did it take the diver to surface from 60 feet?
(c) What was the depth of the diver after 12 minutes?

7 This graph represents the journey of a moped rider.

(a) After how long did the moped rider stop?
(b) What was the total distance covered in the journey?
(c) What was the distance of the rider from the starting point after $4\frac{1}{2}$ hours?
(d) What was the average speed of the return journey from 4 to 6 hours?

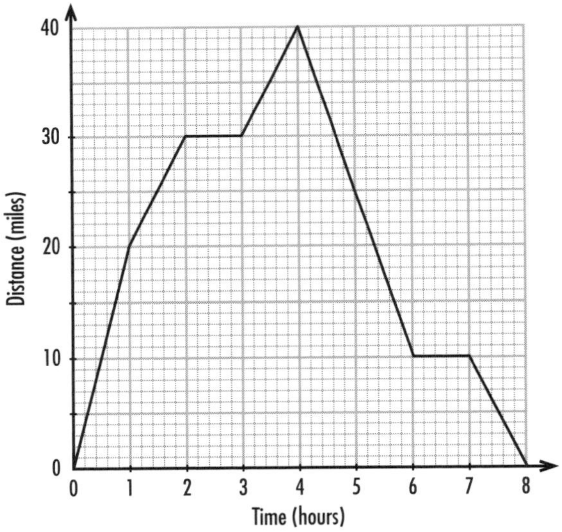

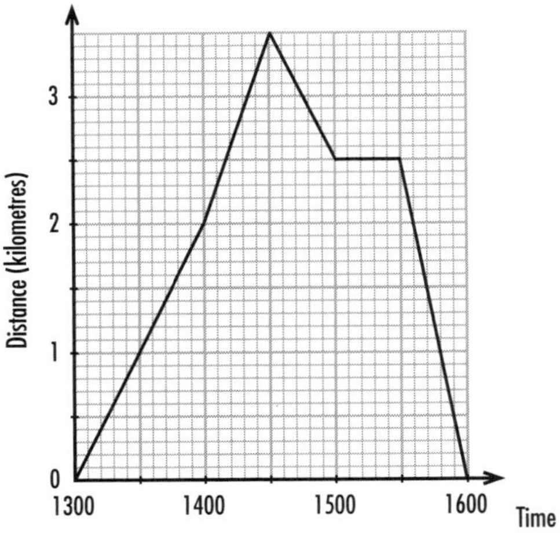

8 This graph represents the journey of a walker.

(a) After how long did the walker stop for a break?
(b) What was the average speed of the last part of the journey?
(c) What was the total length of the journey?
(d) At what times was the walker $1\frac{1}{2}$ km from the starting point?

35/ DRAWING QUADRATIC GRAPHS

An algebraic expression which has an x^2 term as the highest power is called a **quadratic** expression, for example: $x^2 + 5x + 2$.
The graph of a quadratic expression can be drawn; such a graph is called a **quadratic graph**.

EXAMPLE

► Draw the graph of $y = x^2 + 5x + 2$ for $-6 \le x \le 1$ and use the graph to answer the following questions.
(a) Write down the lowest value of $x^2 + 5x + 2$.
(b) Find the values of x for which $y = 5$.
(c) Find the value of y for which $x = -0.4$.

Use a table of values. The inequality $-6 \le x \le 1$ means take values of x between -6 and 1.
Write down each individual term in the table, working it out for each value of x required, then adding each column to give a corresponding value for y for each value of x.

x	−6	−5	−4	−3	−2	−1	0	1
x^2	36	25	16	9	4	1	0	1
$5x$	−30	−25	−20	−15	−10	−5	0	5
2	2	2	2	2	2	2	2	2
y	8	2	−2	−4	−4	−2	2	8

All the corresponding pairs of values for x and y are **coordinates**, which can be plotted on a grid and joined using a free-hand **curve**. The bottom of the curve should not be flat or pointed and should not bulge out between points. You will need to estimate the lowest point through which the curve should be drawn.

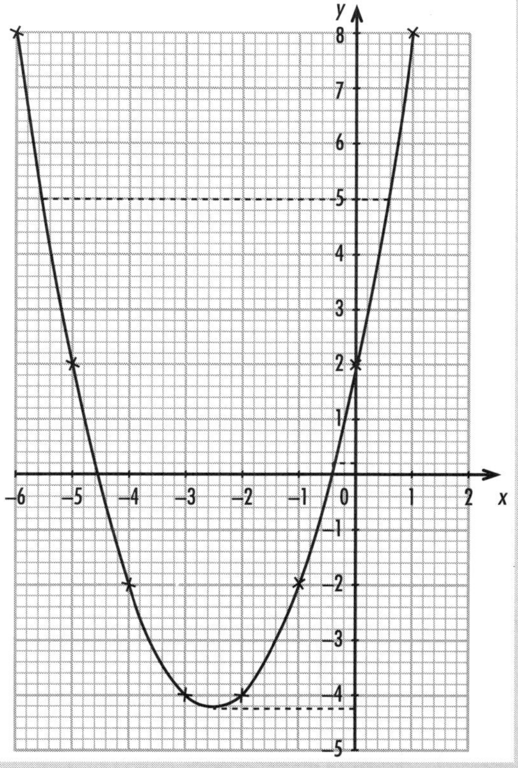

(a) The lowest value of $x^2 + 5x + 2$ is the lowest point of the graph: −4.25.
(b) At $y = 5$ draw a line across to the curve and then lines down to the x-axis to read off the values: $x = -5.5$ and $x = 0.5$.
(c) At $x = -0.4$ draw a line to the curve and then across to the y-axis to read off the value $y = 0.2$.

Exercise 35A

Draw a graph for each of the equations shown below and answer the questions using your graph.

1 $y = x^2 - 5x + 7$ for $0 \le x \le 5$
(a) Write down the lowest value.
(b) Find the value of y when $x = 3.5$.
(c) Find the values of x when $y = 4.8$.

2 $y = x^2 - 8x + 12$ for $1 \le x \le 7$
(a) Write down the lowest value.
(b) Find the value of y when $x = 5.4$.
(c) Find the values of x when $y = -2.04$.

3 $y = x^2 - 4x + 4$ for $0 \le x \le 5$
(a) Find the value of y when $x = 4.5$.
(b) Find the values of x when $y = 2.6$.

4 $y = x^2 - 3x$ for $-1 \le x \le 4$
(a) Write down the lowest value.
(b) Find the value of y when $x = -0.5$.
(c) Find the values of x when $y = 1.75$.

5 $y = x^2 - 3x - 1$ for $-1 \le x \le 5$
(a) Write down the lowest value.
(b) Find the value of y when $x = 4.4$.
(c) Find the values of x when $y = 2$.

6 $y = 2 + 4x - x^2$ for $0 \le x \le 5$
(a) Write down the highest value.
(b) Find the value of y when $x = 4.4$.
(c) Find the values of x when $y = 3$.

7 $y = x^2 - 6x + 8$ for $0 \le x \le 6$
(a) Find the value of y when $x = 0.5$.
(b) Find the values of x when $y = 1.8$

8 $y = x^2 - 4x + 3$ for $-1 \le x \le 5$
(a) Find the value of y when $x = 3.5$.
(b) Find the values of x when $y = 7$.

9 $y = 6x - x^2$ for $0 \le x \le 6$
(a) Find the value of y when $x = 4.5$.
(b) Find the values of x when $y = 3$.

10 $y = 2x^2 + 3$ for $-3 \le x \le 3$
(a) Find the value of y when $x = 1.4$.
(b) Find the values of x when $y = 10$.

11 $y = x^2 - 4x$ for $-1 \le x \le 5$
(a) Find the value of y when $x = 4.4$.
(b) Find the values of x when $y = 4$.

12 $y = 8 + 2x - x^2$ for $-2 \le x \le 4$
(a) Find the value of y when $x = -1.5$.
(b) Find the values of x when $y = 2$.

13 $y = x^2 - 7x + 10$ for $0 \le x \le 6$
(a) Write down the lowest value.
(b) Find the value of y when $x = 2.5$.
(c) Find the values of x when $y = 3$.

14 $y = 4x^2 - 12x + 9$ for $-1 \le x \le 4$
(a) Write down the lowest value.
(b) Find the value of y when $x = 2.5$.
(c) Find the values of x when $y = 12$.

15 $y = 4 + 3x - 2x^2$ for $-2 \le x \le 3$
(a) Write down the highest value.
(b) Find the value of y when $x = -1.5$.
(c) Find the values of x when $y = 1$.

16 $y = 2x^2 + 3x - 4$ for $-3 \le x \le 2$
(a) Write down the lowest value.
(b) Find the value of y when $x = 1.5$.
(c) Find the values of x when $y = -2.5$.

Exercise 35B

Draw a graph for each of the equations shown below and answer the questions using your graph.

1 $y = x^2 - 6x + 9$ for $0 \le x \le 6$
(a) Find the value of y when $x = 4.5$.
(b) Find the values of x when $y = 5$.

2 $y = x^2 - 8x + 15$ for $1 \le x \le 6$
(a) Find the value of y when $x = 1.8$.
(b) Find the values of x when $y = 1$.

3 $y = x^2 + 2x$ for $-3 \le x \le 2$
(a) Find the value of y when $x = 1.4$.
(b) Find the values of x when $y = -0.5$.

4 $y = x^2 - 10x + 25$ for $1 \le x \le 7$
(a) Find the value of y when $x = 2.2$.
(b) Find the values of x when $y = 2$.

5 $y = x^2 - 7x + 10$ for $0 \le x \le 6$
(a) Write down the lowest value.
(b) Find the value of y when $x = 0.5$.
(c) Find the values of x when $y = 2$.

6 $y = x^2 - 3x - 4$ for $-1 \le x \le 5$
(a) Write down the lowest value.
(b) Find the value of y when $x = 4.4$.
(c) Find the values of x when $y = -5$.

7 $y = x^2 - 2x - 8$ for $-2 \le x \le 4$
(a) Find the value of y when $x = -1.5$.
(b) Find the values of x when $y = -7$.

8 $y = x^2 - 2x + 3$ for $-2 \le x \le 4$
(a) Find the value of y when $x = 1.5$
(b) Find the values of x when $y = 8$.

9 $y = 3 + 6x - x^2$ for $0 \le x \le 6$
(a) Find the value of y when $x = 4.5$.
(b) Find the values of x when $y = 7$.

10 $y = 4x - x^2$ for $-1 \le x \le 5$
(a) Find the value of y when $x = 3.8$.
(b) Find the values of x when $y = -3$.

11 $y = x^2 - 7x + 7$ for $0 \le x \le 6$
(a) Write down the lowest value.
(b) Find the value of y when $x = 1.6$.
(c) Find the values of x when $y = -2$.

12 $y = 6 + x - x^2$ for $-2 \le x \le 4$
(a) Write down the highest value.
(b) Find the value of y when $x = 3.4$.
(c) Find the values of x when $y = 5$.

13 $y = 5 + 3x - x^2$ for $-2 \le x \le 4$
(a) Write down the highest value.
(b) Find the value of y when $x = -1.5$.
(c) Find the values of x when $y = 6$.

14 $y = 3x^2 - 3x - 2$ for $-2 \le x \le 3$
(a) Write down the lowest value.
(b) Find the value of y when $x = 1.8$.
(c) Find the values of x when $y = 6$.

15 $y = 2x^2 - 5$ for $-3 \le x \le 3$
(a) Find the value of y when $x = 2.5$.
(b) Find the values of x when $y = -4$.

16 $y = 2x^2 - 9x + 4$ for $0 \le x \le 5$
(a) Write down the lowest value.
(b) Find the value of y when $x = 4.5$.
(c) Find the values of x when $y = 1$.

36/ QUADRATIC EQUATIONS: SOLUTION BY GRAPHICAL METHODS

One way of solving an equation is to draw a graph of it and read off the solutions using the graph.

EXAMPLE

► Solve the equations.
(a) $x^2 + 5x + 2 = 0$
(b) $x^2 + 5x - 1 = 0$

(a) The expression $x^2 + 5x + 2$ is represented by the graph $y = x^2 + 5x + 2$ shown here. Read off the values of x where $y = 0$ to give $x = -0.4$, $x = -4.6$. The solutions to $x^2 + 5x + 2 = 0$ are $x = -0.4$ and $x = -4.6$.

(b) The expression $x^2 + 5x - 1$ is not the same as $x^2 + 5x + 2$. Rearrange it to give the expression drawn as a graph by adding 3 to both sides:

$$x^2 + 5x - 1 + 3 = 0 + 3$$
$$x^2 + 5x + 2 = 3$$

This is now represented by the graph $y = x^2 + 5x + 2$ where $y = 3$. Read off the values of x where $y = 3$, which gives $x = 0.2$, $x = -5.2$. The solutions to $x^2 + 5x - 1 = 0$ are $x = 0.2$ and $x = -5.2$.

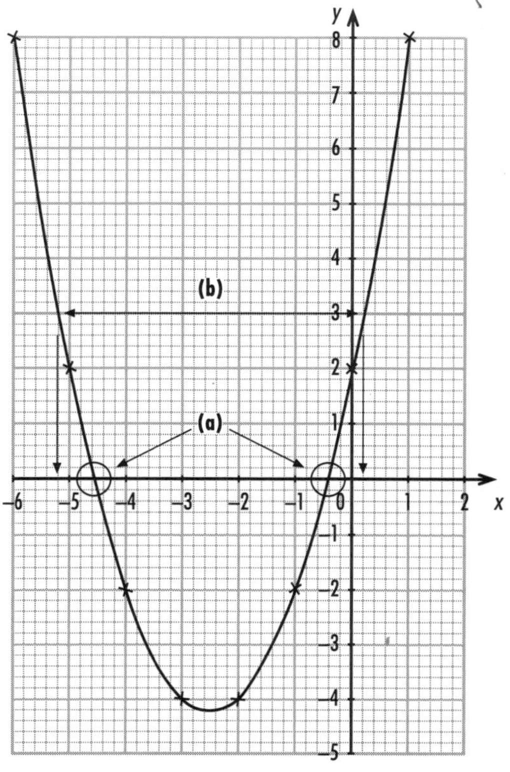

Exercise 36A

Use the corresponding graphs drawn in Exercise 35A to solve the equations in these questions.

1 (a) $x^2 - 5x + 7 = 2$ (b) $x^2 - 5x + 3 = 0$
2 (a) $x^2 - 8x + 12 = 0$ (b) $x^2 - 8x + 13 = 0$
3 (a) $x^2 - 4x + 4 = 0$ (b) $x^2 - 4x + 2 = 0$
4 (a) $x^2 - 3x = 0$ (b) $x^2 - 3x - 2 = 0$
5 (a) $x^2 - 3x - 1 = 0$ (b) $x^2 - 3x + 1 = 0$
6 (a) $2 + 4x - x^2 = 0$ (b) $4x - 2 - x^2 = 0$
7 (a) $x^2 - 6x + 8 = 0$ (b) $x^2 - 6x + 3 = 0$
8 (a) $x^2 - 4x + 3 = 0$ (b) $x^2 - 4x + 1 = 0$
9 (a) $6x - x^2 = 0$ (b) $6x - 6 - x^2 = 0$
10 (a) $2x^2 + 3 = 4$ (b) $2x^2 - 15 = 0$
11 (a) $x^2 - 4x = 0$ (b) $x^2 - 4x + 2 = 0$
12 (a) $8 + 2x - x^2 = 0$ (b) $2 + 2x - x^2 = 0$
13 (a) $x^2 - 7x + 10 = 0$ (b) $x^2 - 7x + 9 = 0$
14 (a) $4x^2 - 12x + 9 = 0$ (b) $4x^2 - 12x + 3 = 0$
15 (a) $4 + 3x - 2x^2 = 0$ (b) $6 + 3x - 2x^2 = 0$
16 (a) $2x^2 + 3x - 4 = 0$ (b) $2x^2 + 3x - 6 = 0$

Exercise 36B

Use the corresponding graphs drawn in Exercise 35B to solve the equations in these questions.

1 (a) $x^2 - 6x + 9 = 0$ (b) $x^2 - 6x + 6 = 0$
2 (a) $x^2 - 8x + 15 = 0$ (b) $x^2 - 8x + 13 = 0$
3 (a) $x^2 + 2x = 0$ (b) $x^2 + 2x - 2 = 0$
4 (a) $x^2 - 10x + 25 = 0$ (b) $x^2 - 10x + 22 = 0$
5 (a) $x^2 - 7x + 10 = 0$ (b) $x^2 - 7x + 11 = 0$
6 (a) $x^2 - 3x - 4 = 0$ (b) $x^2 - 3x - 2 = 0$
7 (a) $x^2 - 2x - 8 = 0$ (b) $x^2 - 2x - 5 = 0$
8 (a) $x^2 - 2x + 3 = 10$ (b) $x^2 - 2x - 2 = 0$
9 (a) $3 + 6x - x^2 = 5$ (b) $6x - 7 - x^2 = 0$
10 (a) $4x - x^2 = 0$ (b) $4x - x^2 - 2 = 0$
11 (a) $x^2 - 7x + 7 = 0$ (b) $x^2 - 7x + 5 = 0$
12 (a) $6 + x - x^2 = 0$ (b) $4 + x - x^2 = 0$
13 (a) $5 + 3x - x^2 = 0$ (b) $3 + 3x - x^2 = 0$
14 (a) $3x^2 - 3x - 2 = 0$ (b) $3x^2 - 3x - 11 = 0$
15 (a) $2x^2 - 5 = 0$ (b) $2x^2 - 3 = 0$
16 (a) $2x^2 - 9x + 4 = 0$ (b) $2x^2 - 9x + 8 = 0$

37/ DRAWING CUBIC AND RECIPROCAL GRAPHS

An algebraic expression which has an x^3 term as the highest power is called a **cubic expression**, for example: $x^3 - 6x^2 + 9x$.

EXAMPLE

▶ Draw a graph of the expression $x^3 - 6x^2 + 9x$ for $-1 \le x \le 4$.

x	-1	0	1	2	3	4
x^3	-1	0	1	8	27	64
$-6x^2$	-6	0	-6	-24	-54	-96
$9x$	-9	0	9	18	27	36
y	-16	0	4	2	0	4

Plot these points and join them using a free-hand curve. You may need to estimate parts of the path of the curve between these points or you could calculate additional intermediate points (for example $x = 0.5$) to help with drawing the curve.

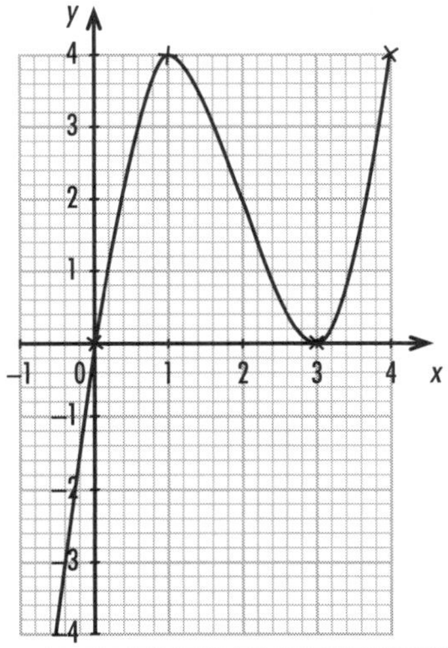

An algebraic expression which has an x in the denominator and a number in the numerator is called a **reciprocal expression**, for example: $y = \frac{3}{x}$.

EXAMPLE

► Draw a graph of the expression $\frac{3}{x}$ for $-4 \leq x \leq 4$.

x	–4	–3	–2	–1	0	1	2	3	4
y	–0.75	–1	–1.5	–3	E	3	1.5	1	0.75

Plot these points on a graph.

The calculation 3 ÷ 0 on the calculator causes an E (ERROR).
To help understand what happens near to $x = 0$, use additional values of x at 0.2, 0.4, 0.6. These values indicate the graph continues to increase (and decrease) near to the y-axis.
There is no point at (0, 0).

x	0.2	0.4	0.6
y	15	7.5	5

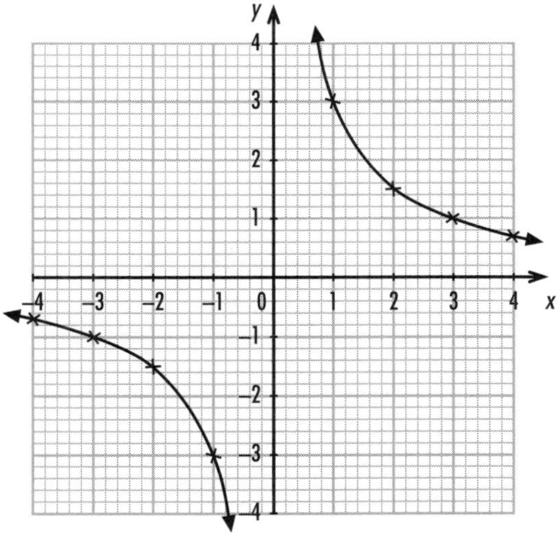

Exercise 37A

Draw a graph for each of the equations.

1 $y = \frac{1}{x}$ for $-4 \leq x \leq 4$

2 $y = x^3 - 9x$ for $-4 \leq x \leq 4$

3 $y = x^3 - 9x + 2$ for $-3 \leq x \leq 3$

4 $y = x^3 - 4x^2 + 6$ for $-1 \leq x \leq 4$

5 $y = \frac{4}{x}$ for $-4 \leq x \leq 4$

6 $y = x^3 - x^2 - 6x$ for $-3 \leq x \leq 3$

7 $y = x^3 - 2x^2 - 10$ for $-2 \le x \le 4$

8 $y = x^3 - 3x^2$ for $-1 \le x \le 4$

9 $y = x^3 - x^2 - 2x$ for $-2 \le x \le 3$ and at $x = -0.5$

10 $y = \frac{7}{x}$ for $-4 \le x \le 4$

11 $y = 9x - x^2 - x^3$ for $-3 \le x \le 3$

12 $y = x + 4x^2 - x^3$ for $-1 \le x \le 4$

Exercise 37B

Draw a graph for each of the equations.

1 $x^3 - 4x$ for $-3 \le x \le 3$

2 $y = \frac{2}{x}$ for $-4 \le x \le 4$

3 $y = x^3 - 6x + 1$ for $-3 \le x \le 3$

4 $y = x^3 - 4x - 2$ for $-2 \le x \le 3$

5 $y = x^3 + 2x^2$ for $-3 \le x \le 2$

6 $y = \frac{5}{x}$ for $-4 \le x \le 4$

7 $y = 3x^2 - x^3$ for $-2 \le x \le 4$

8 $y = x^3 - x - 2$ for $-2 \le x \le 2$ and at $x = -0.5$, $x = 0.5$

9 $y = x^3 - 2x^2 - 5x$ for $-3 \le x \le 4$

10 $y = \frac{8}{x}$ for $-4 \le x \le 4$

11 $y = x^3 - 4x^2 + 3x$ for $-2 \le x \le 3$

12 $y = 4x + 4x^2 - x^3$ for $-2 \le x \le 4$

38/ RECOGNISING TYPES OF GRAPH FROM EQUATIONS

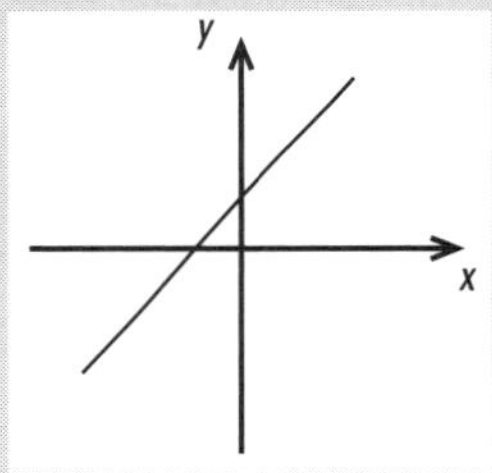

The **straight-line graph** has an equation of the form $y = mx + c$, where m is the gradient and c is the point where the line crosses the y-axis. If m is negative the graph slopes downwards.

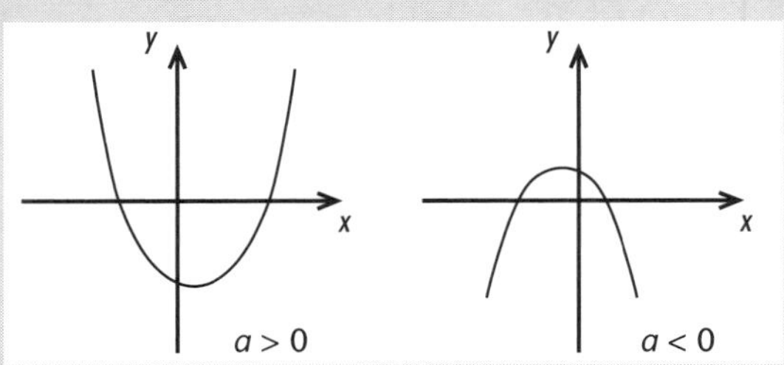

The **quadratic curve** has an equation of the form $y = ax^2 + bx + c$, where c is the point at which the line crosses the y-axis. A quadratic curve has one turning point, which is either a maximum or a minimum point. Graphs with a negative value for a are inverted.

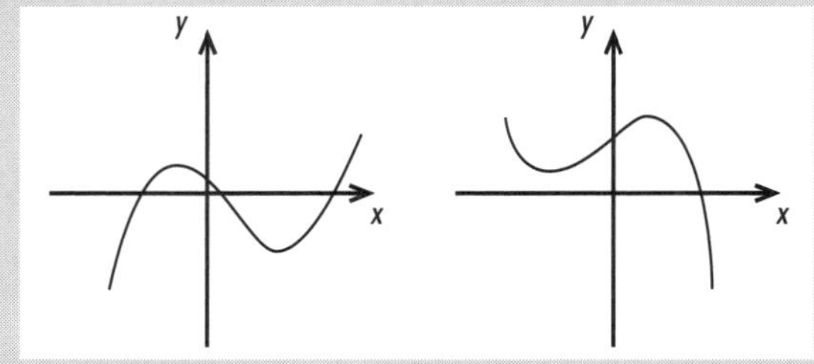

A **cubic curve** has an equation of the form $y = dx^3 + ax^2 + bx + c$, where c is the point at which the line crosses the y-axis.
A cubic curve usually has two turning points.

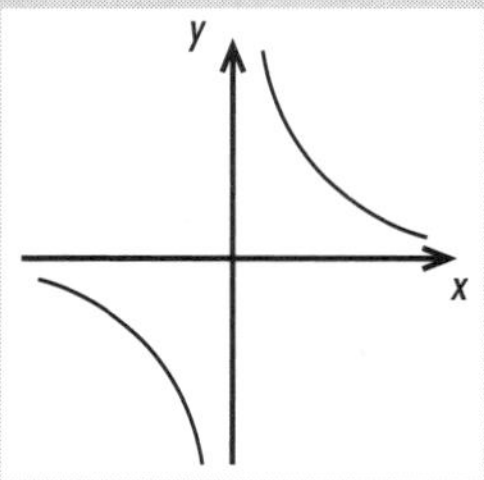

A **reciprocal graph** has an equation of the form $y = \frac{a}{x}$. Its shape is quite distinctive and the graph is in two parts.

Exercise 38A

Write down the letter of the graph which matches the equation in each question.

1	$y = x^3 - 4x$	**2**	$y = -x$	**3**	$y = -x^2 - x + 6$	**4**	$y = x^3 + x^2 + 2$
5	$y = x + 3$	**6**	$y = -x^2 - 4$	**7**	$y = \dfrac{2}{x}$	**8**	$y = x^2 + 3x$
9	$y = x^3$	**10**	$y = 3x + 3$	**11**	$y = -x^3 + 2x^2 + 2$	**12**	$y = x - 3$
13	$y = x^3 - 3x - 4$	**14**	$y = -\dfrac{1}{2}x$	**15**	$y = \dfrac{10}{x}$	**16**	$y = 3x^2 + x + 1$
17	$y = x^2 + 2x - 4$	**18**	$y = -x - 2$	**19**	$y = x - x^3$	**20**	$y = 2x - x^2$

A
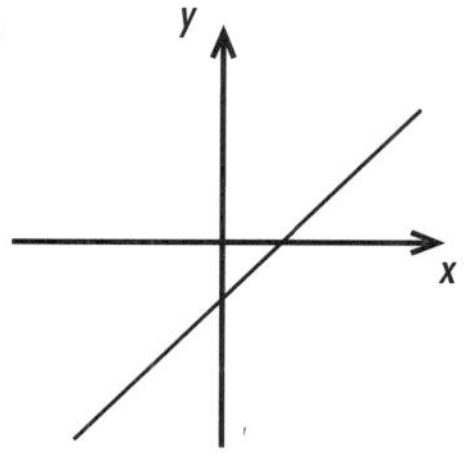

B
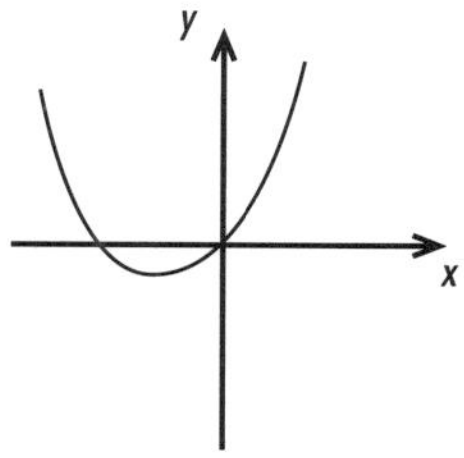

C
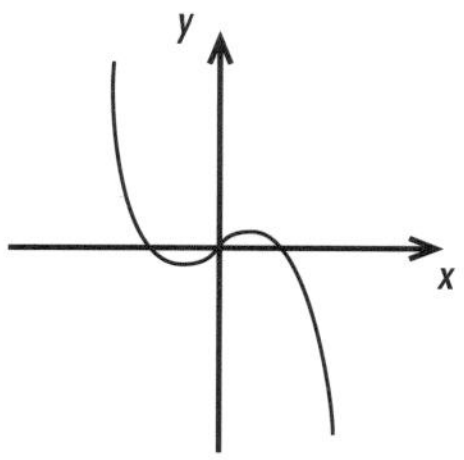

D
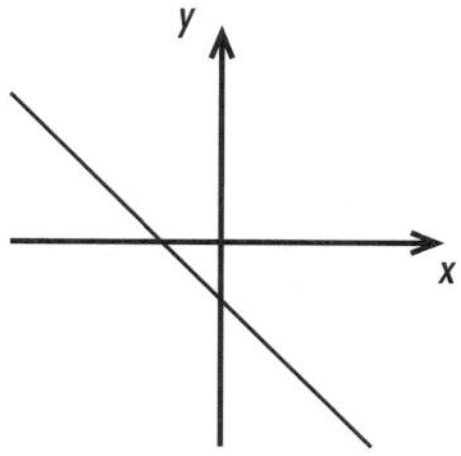

E
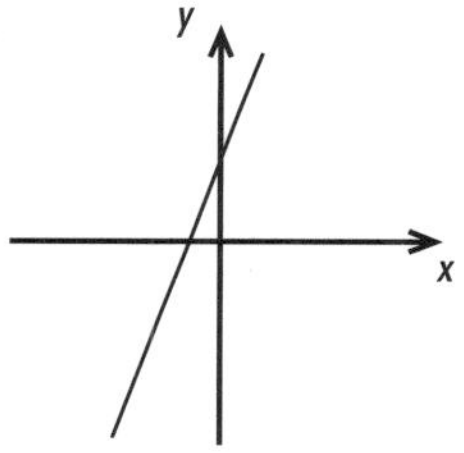

F
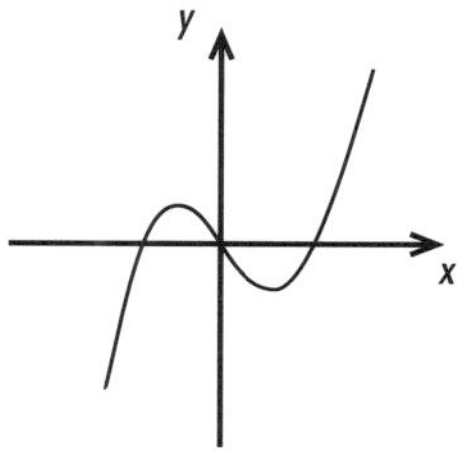

G
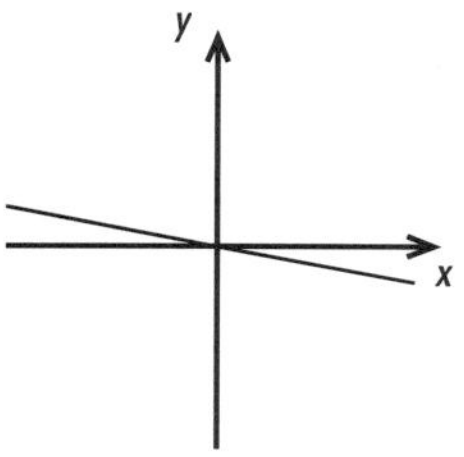

H
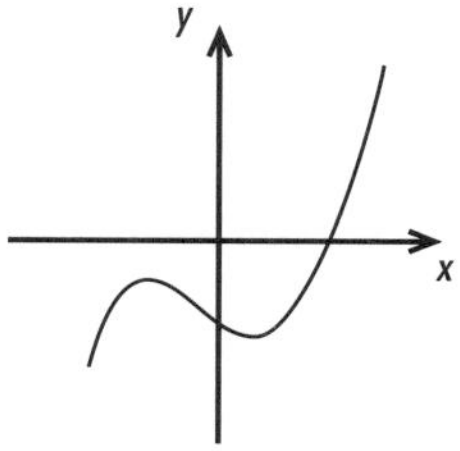

I
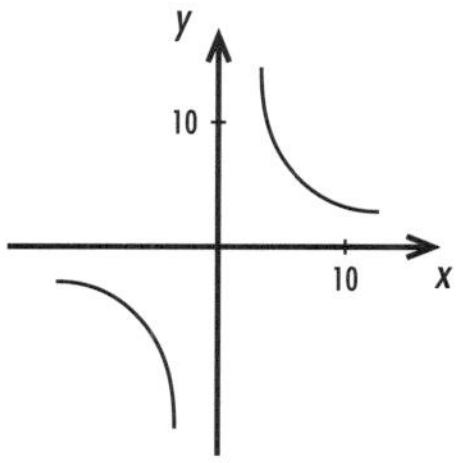

J
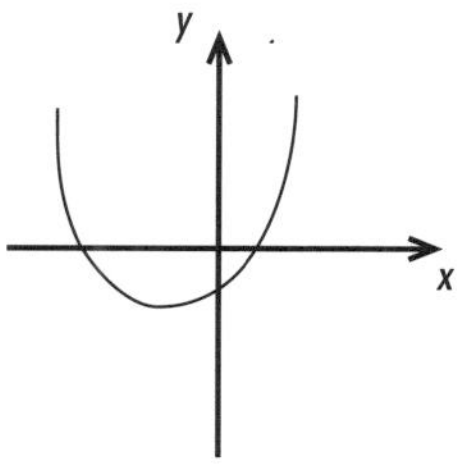

K
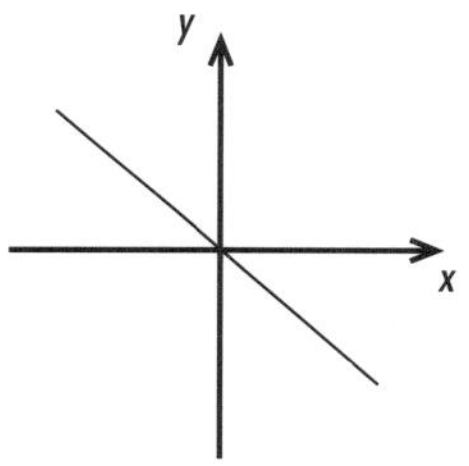

L
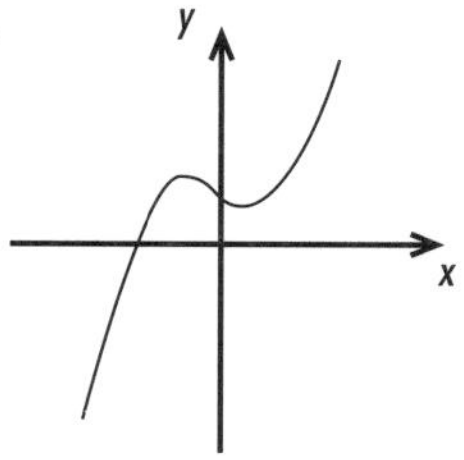

M
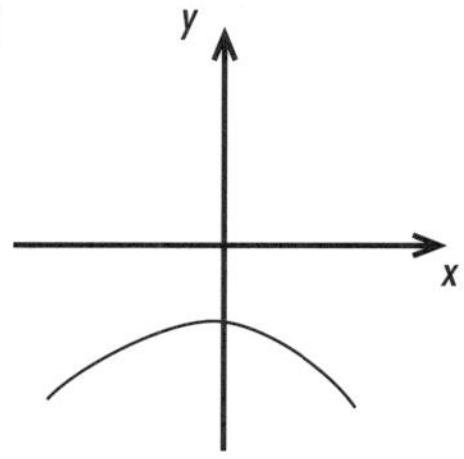

N
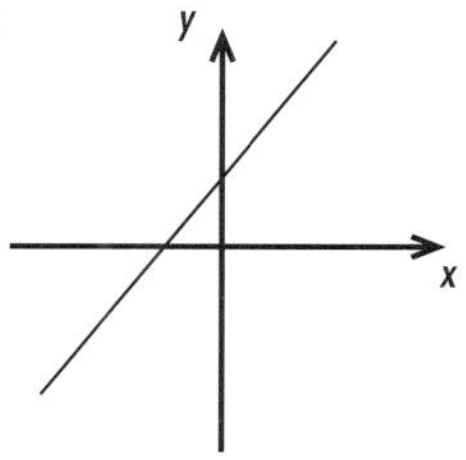

O
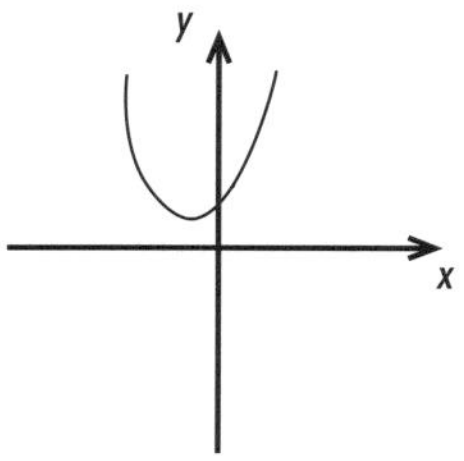

P
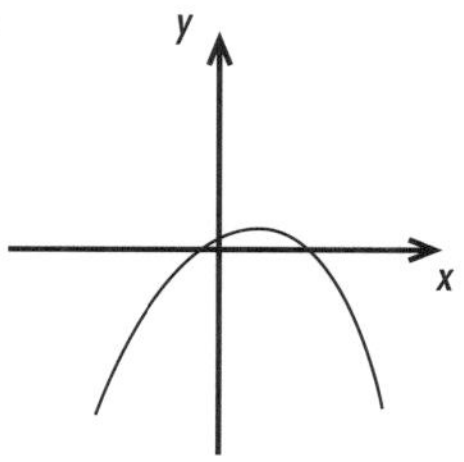

Q
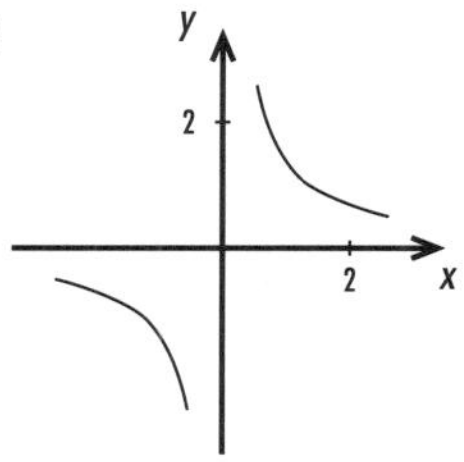

R
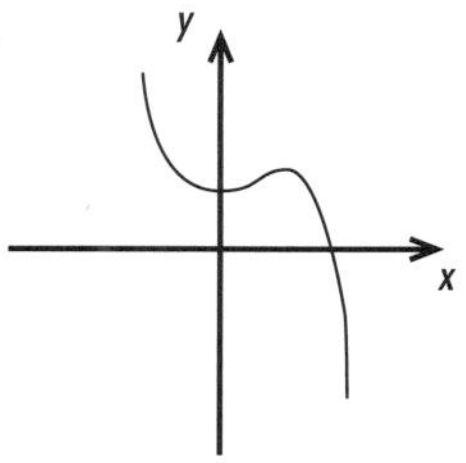

S
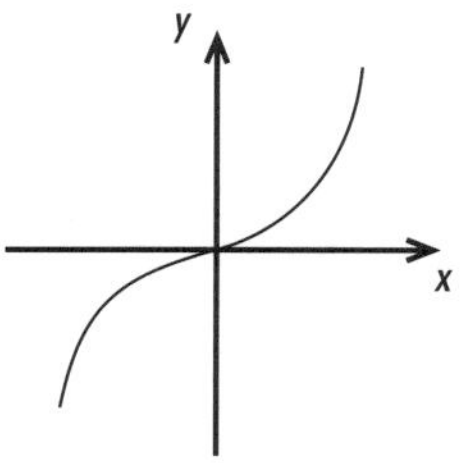

T
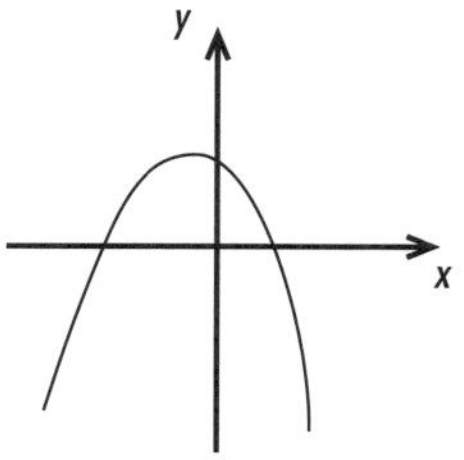

Exercise 38B

Write down the letter of the graph which matches the equation in each question.

1 $y = x + 4$

2 $y = x^2 + 3x - 5$

3 $y = 2x + 4$

4 $y = \frac{8}{x}$

5 $y = x^3 - 2x$

6 $y = 2x^2 + x + 3$

7 $y = x$

8 $y = 4x^2$

9 $y = -x^3 + x^2 + 3$

10 $y = x - 2$

11 $y = 3x - 2x^2$

12 $y = x^3 - 2x - 3$

13 $y = -x + 4$

14 $y = x^3 - 2x + 4$

15 $y = -x^3$

16 $y = -2x^2 - 3x + 8$

17 $y = \frac{1}{2}x$

18 $y = -3x^2 - x - 4$

19 $y = \frac{4}{x}$

20 $y = 4x - x^3$

A

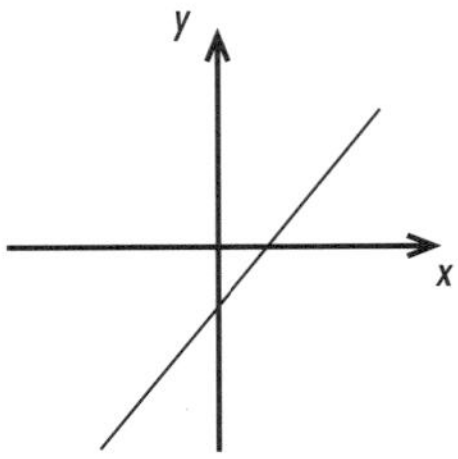

B

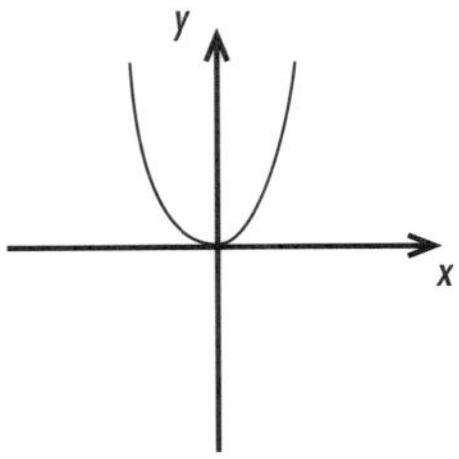

C

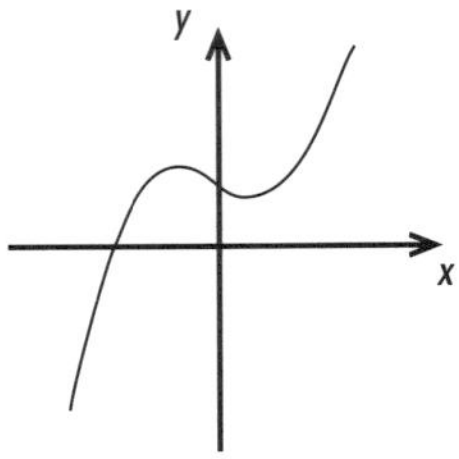

D

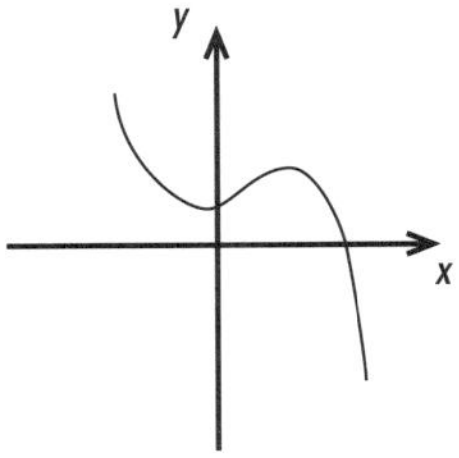

E

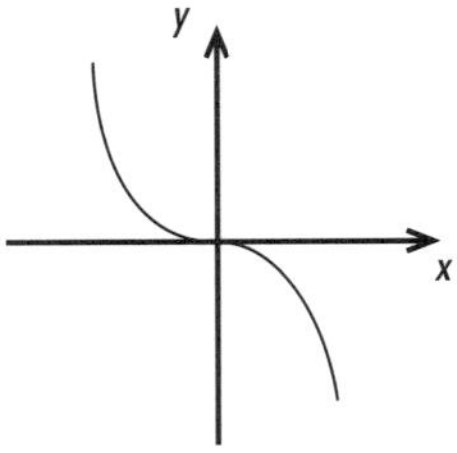

F

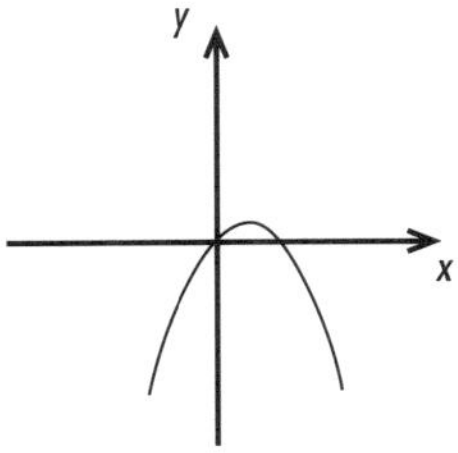

G

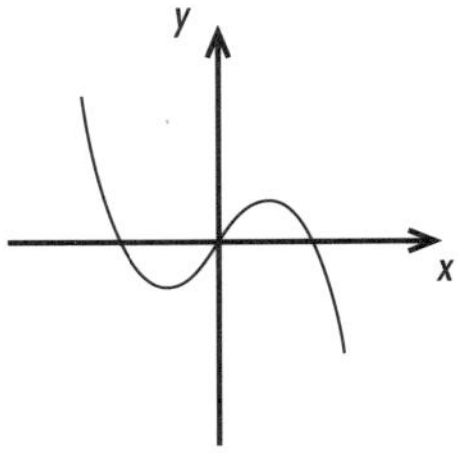

H

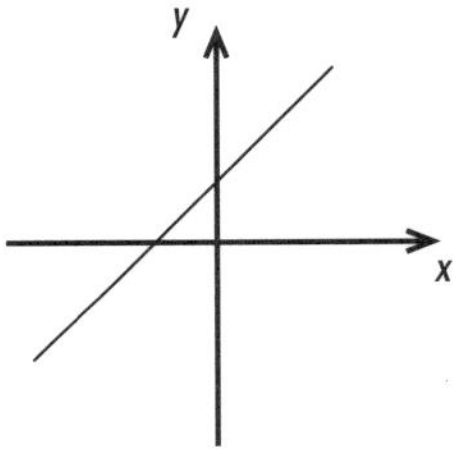

I

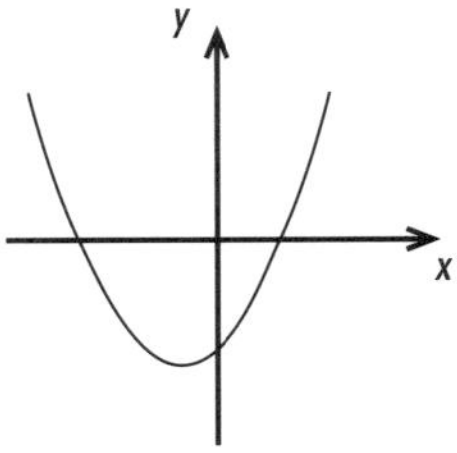

J

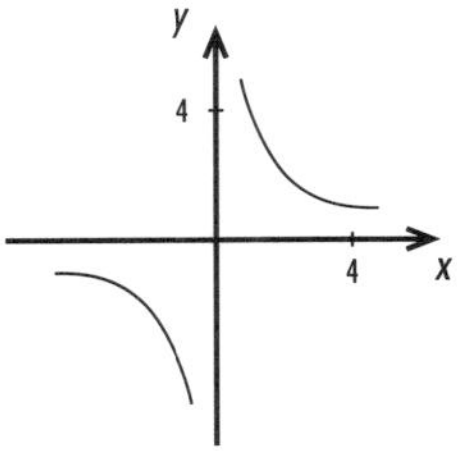

K

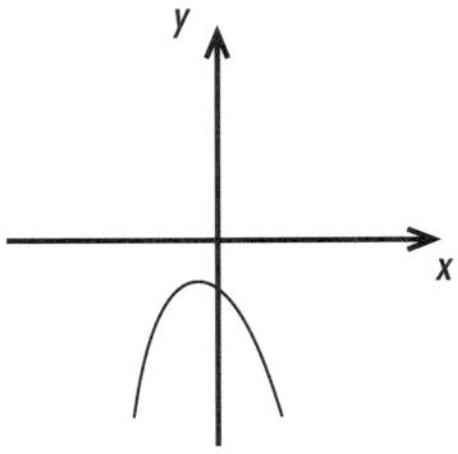

L

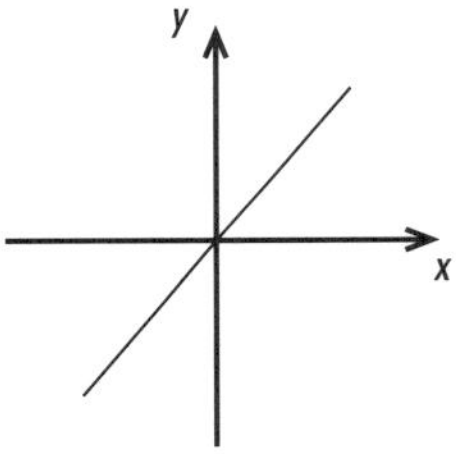

M

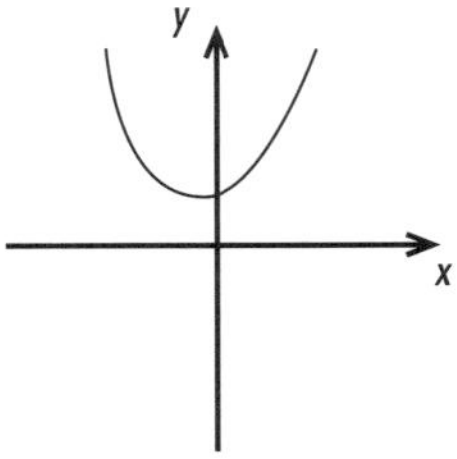

N

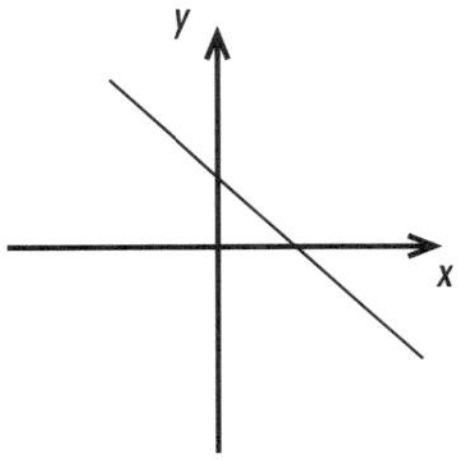

O

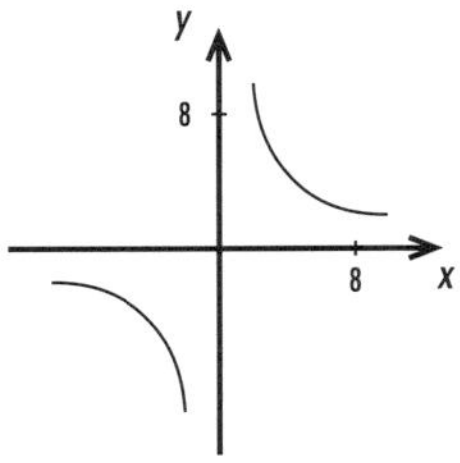

P

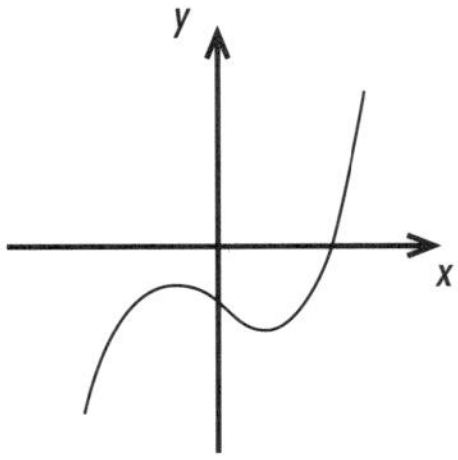

Q

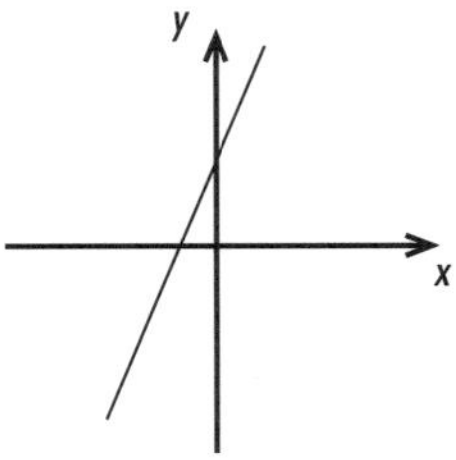

R

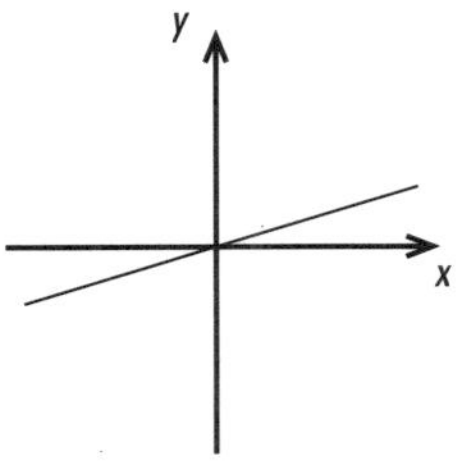

S

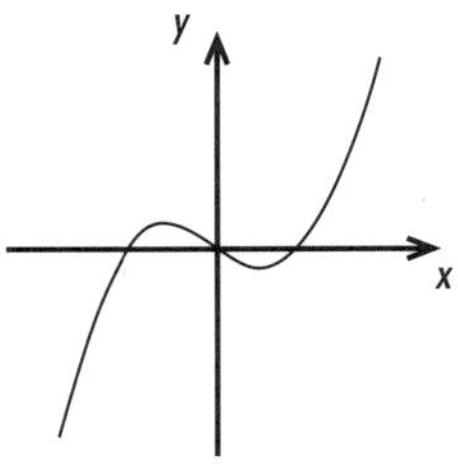

T

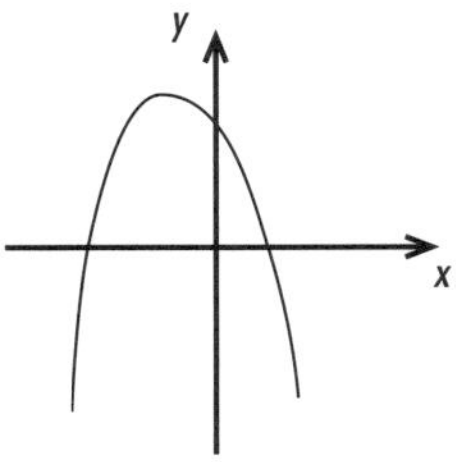

An **inequality** can be represented on a number line.
An empty circle means the value circled is *not* included in the inequality.
A filled circle means the value circled *is* included in the inequality.
Common notation includes:

$>$ for 'more than'	$\geq$ for 'more than or equal to'
$<$ for 'less than'	$\leq$ for 'less than or equal to'

The notation $-2 < x \leq 5$ means x is between -2 and 5; it does not include -2 but does include 5.

EXAMPLE

▶ Write down the inequality.

(a) 

(b) 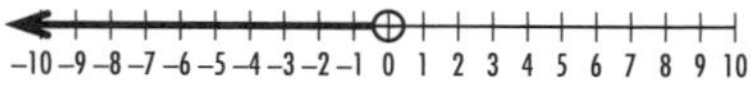

(c) 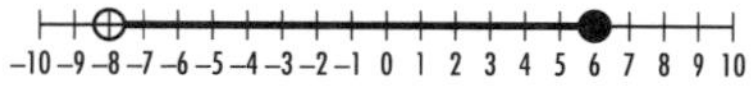

(a) $x \geq -5$ (b) $x < 0$ (c) $-8 < x \leq 6$

EXAMPLE

▶ Draw, on a number line, the part indicated by the inequality.
(a) $x > 4$ (b) $x \leq -3$ (c) $-4 < x \leq 5$

(a) 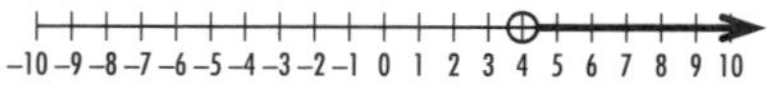

(b) 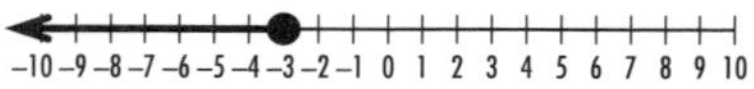

(c) 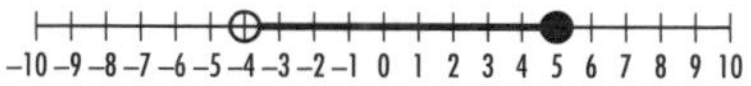

Exercise 39A

Write down the inequality shown on each of the number lines.

1

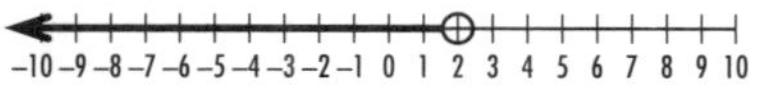

2

3

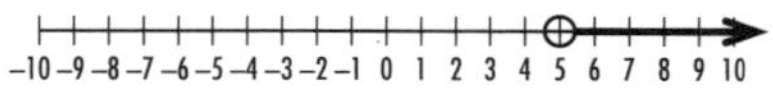

4

5

6

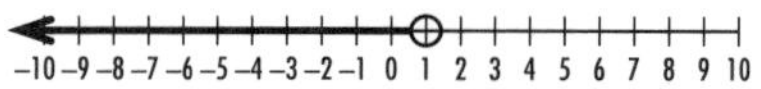

7

8

9

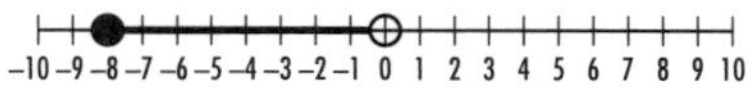

10

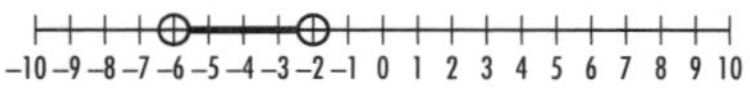

11

12

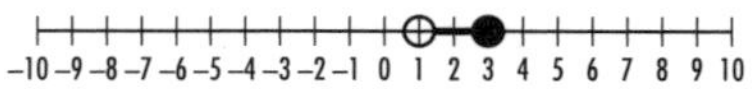

13

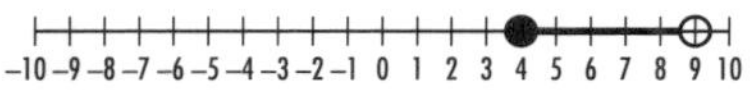

14

15

For each question draw a number line from –10 to 10 and draw the part included in the inequality.

16 $x \le 6$ **17** $x \le -7$ **18** $x < -5$ **19** $x \ge -3$ **20** $x < 8$
21 $x < -4$ **22** $x \le 7$ **23** $x \le -6$ **24** $-8 < x \le -4$ **25** $-5 \le x < 5$
26 $0 < x \le 8$ **27** $-6 < x \le 0$ **28** $2 < x < 5$ **29** $-7 \le x \le -2$ **30** $6 \le x < 7$

Exercise 39B

Write down the inequality shown on the following number lines.

1

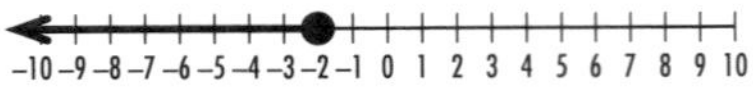

2

3

4

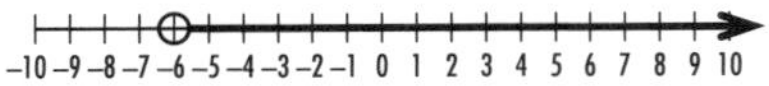

5

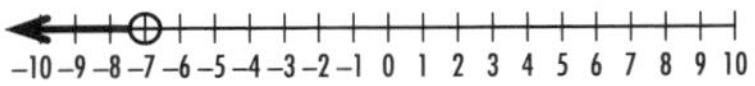

6

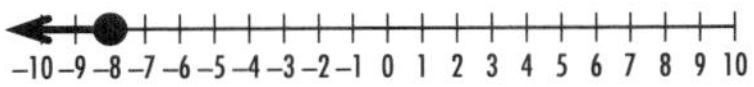

7

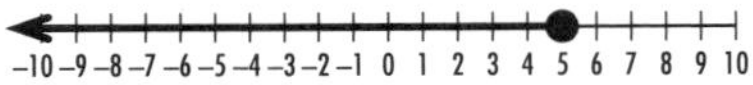

8

9

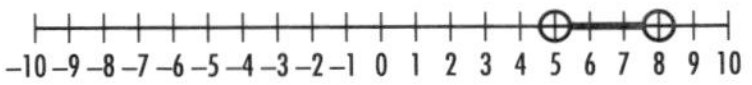

10

11

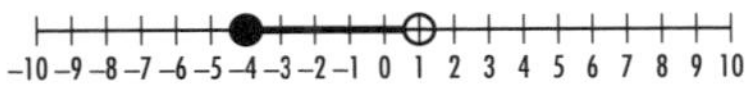

12

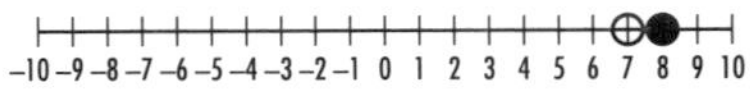

13

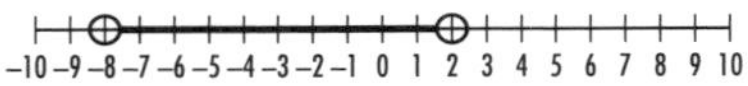

14

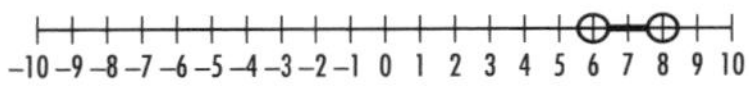

15

For each question draw a number line from –10 to 10 and draw the part included in the inequality.

16 $x \ge -7$ **17** $x < 9$ **18** $x \le -5$ **19** $x < -2$ **20** $x \le 8$
21 $x > -2$ **22** $x \le -4$ **23** $x < 6$ **24** $-5 < x \le -3$ **25** $2 < x < 7$
26 $4 \le x < 5$ **27** $0 < x \le 6$ **28** $5 \le x \le 7$ **29** $5 < x < 7$ **30** $-6 < x < 5$

EXAMPLE

▶ Write down all the possible integer values of x if:
(a) $-6 \le x < 1$ (b) $5 < x < 8$.

(a) 6, –5, –4, –3, –2, –1, 0 (The 1 is not included.)
(b) 6, 7 (Neither the 5 nor the 8 is included.)

Exercise 39C

Write down all possible integer values of x in each of the following inequalities.

1 $-3 < x < 0$ **2** $-4 < x \le -1$ **3** $6 \le x < 7$ **4** $-7 \le x \le -4$
5 $2 < x < 5$ **6** $-3 \le x \le 1$ **7** $-5 \le x \le 0$ **8** $-8 < x \le 0$

Write down all possible even values of x in each of the following.

9 $3 < x < 8$ **10** $7 \le x < 9$ **11** $8 \le x \le 10$ **12** $4 < x < 8$
13 $0 < x \le 1$ **14** $-6 < x \le 0$ **15** $-5 < x \le -3$ **16** $9 < x \le 10$

Write down all possible odd values of x in each of the following.

17 $3 < x < 7$ **18** $4 \le x \le 6$ **19** $-8 \le x \le -3$ **20** $4 < x \le 5$

21 $2 < x < 9$ **22** $5 \le x \le 8$ **23** $-4 \le x < 1$ **24** $1 < x < 5$

Exercise 39D

Write down all possible integer values of x in each of the following inequalities.

1 $3 < x < 7$ **2** $-4 \le x < 0$ **3** $-4 < x \le 2$ **4** $6 < x \le 9$

5 $0 \le x < 5$ **6** $-8 < x < -2$ **7** $3 \le x < 4$ **8** $5 < x \le 9$

Write down all possible even values of x in each of the following.

9 $2 < x < 7$ **10** $2 \le x \le 6$ **11** $-8 < x \le -4$ **12** $1 \le x \le 7$

13 $-7 \le x < 8$ **14** $0 < x < 9$ **15** $7 < x \le 8$ **16** $0 \le x \le 9$

Write down all possible odd values of x in each of the following.

17 $4 \le x \le 8$ **18** $-8 \le x \le 4$ **19** $-6 < x < -4$ **20** $1 < x < 9$

21 $0 \le x < 4$ **22** $0 < x \le 8$ **23** $6 \le x \le 8$ **24** $-7 < x < 1$

40/ INEQUALITIES AND REGIONS

An inequality can be represented by a **region** on a grid.
Note: The shading shows the *required* region.

EXAMPLE

► On a grid show the region where $x \ge 3$ and $y \le 4$.

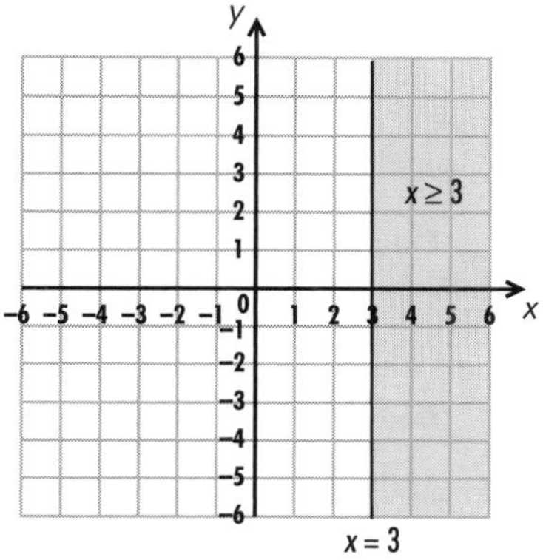

All points to the right of the line $x = 3$ have an x coordinate greater than 3.

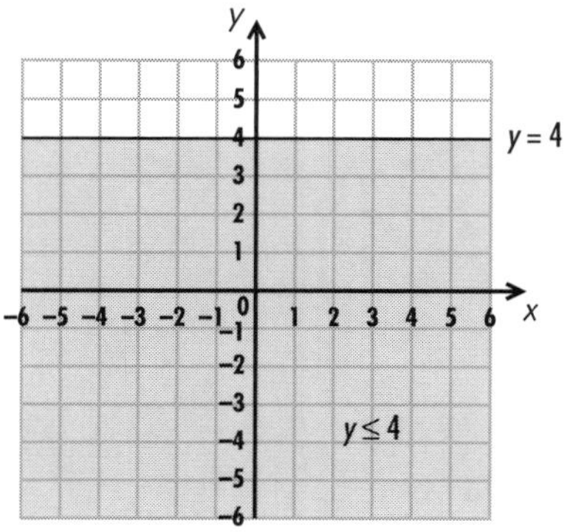

All points below the line $y = 4$ have a y coordinate less than 4.

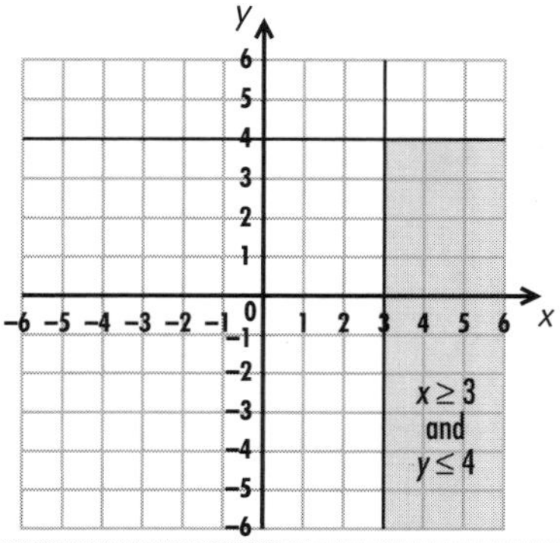

The shaded region shows the combined region $x \ge 3$, $y \le 4$.

EXAMPLE

▶ Write inequalities to describe the regions.

(a)

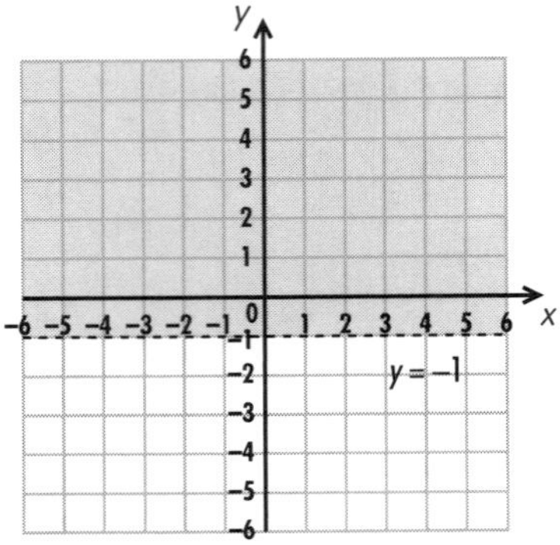

(b)

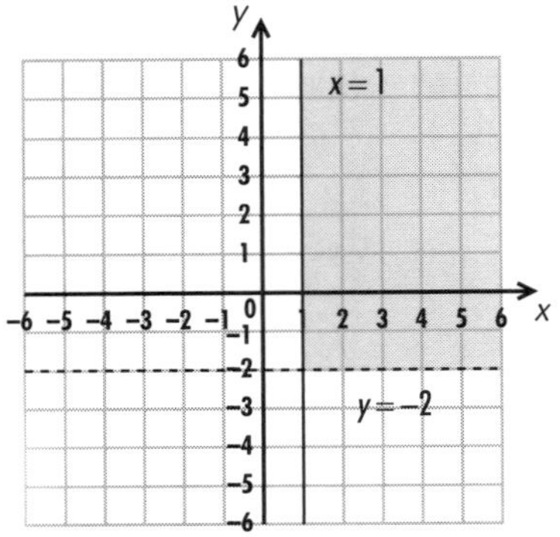

(a) The dotted line means the region does not include points on the line. The region is $y > -1$.

(b) $x \geq 1$ and $y > -2$

Exercise 40A

Write down inequalities to describe each of the shaded regions.

1

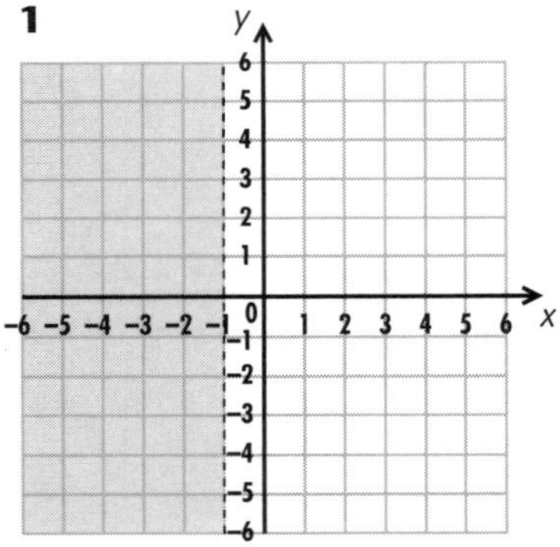

2

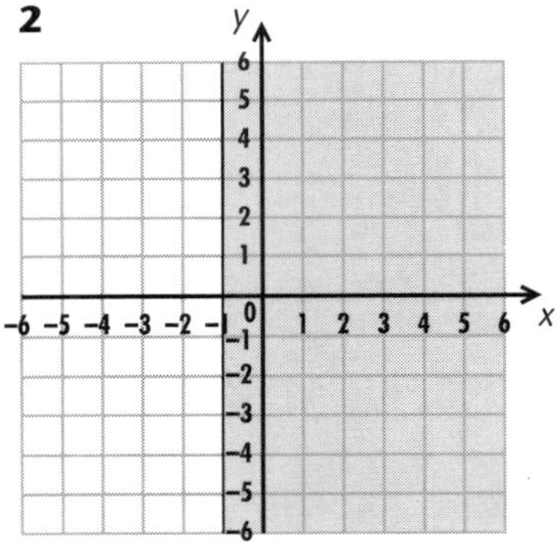

3

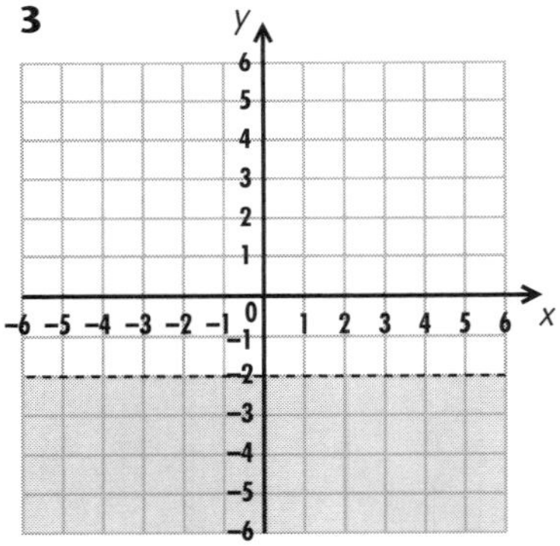

4

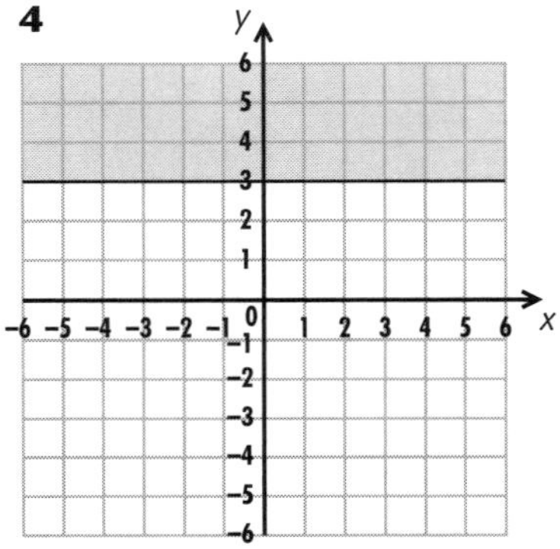

5

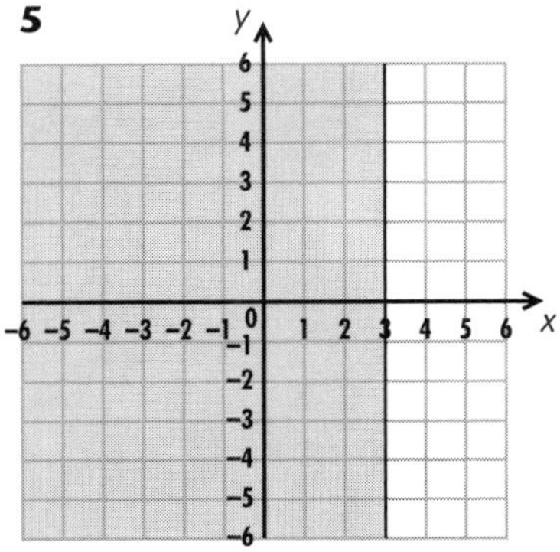

6

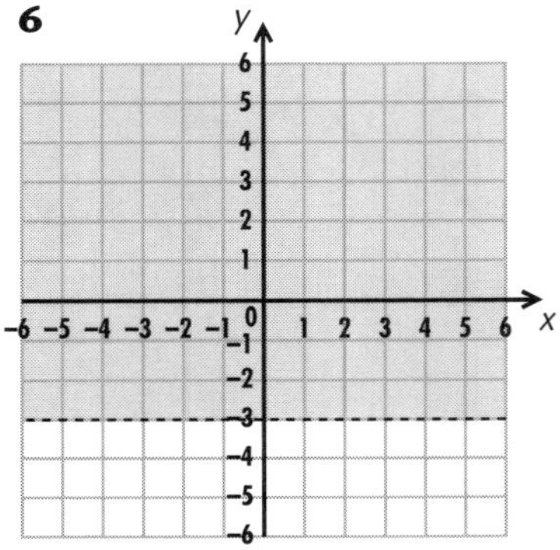

7

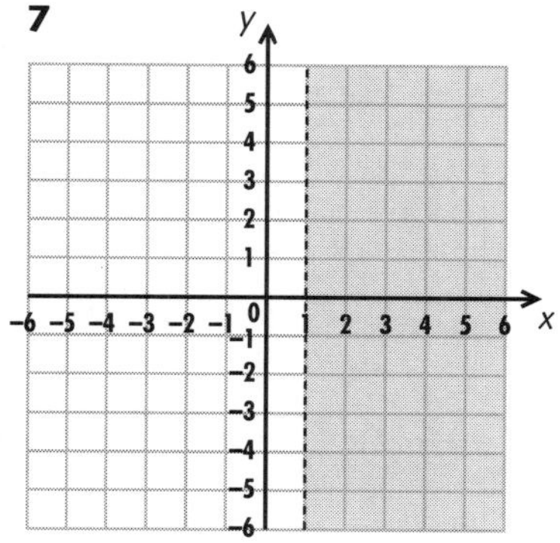

8

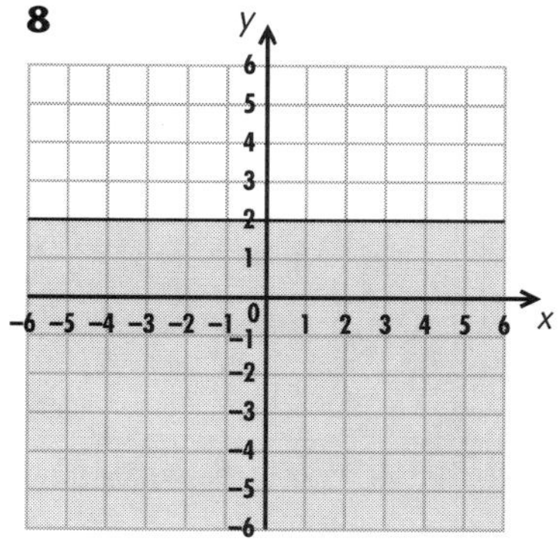

9

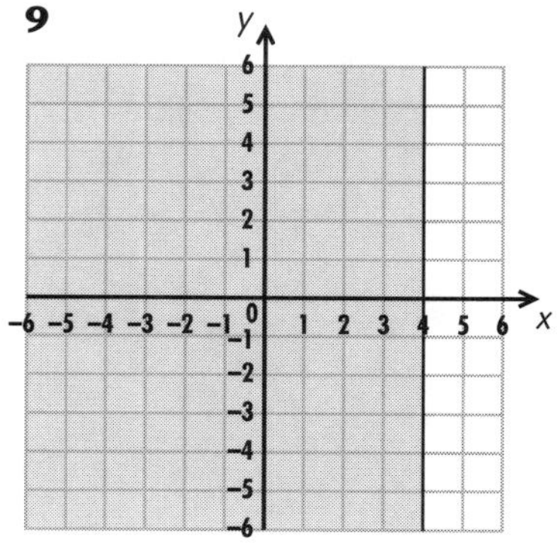

10

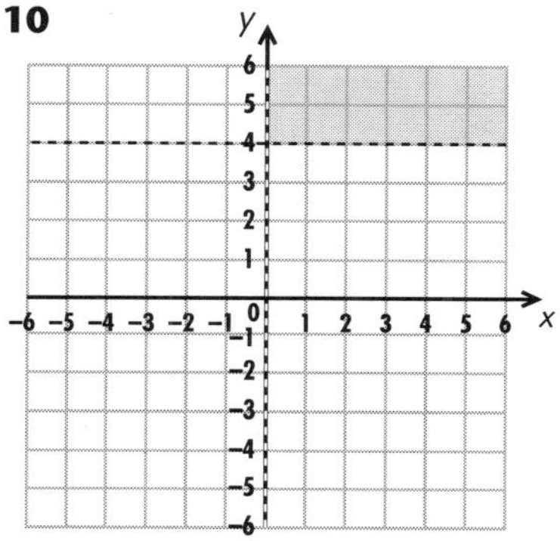

11

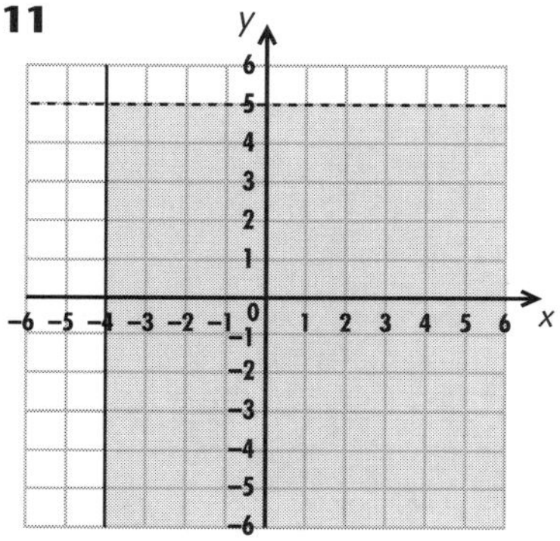

12

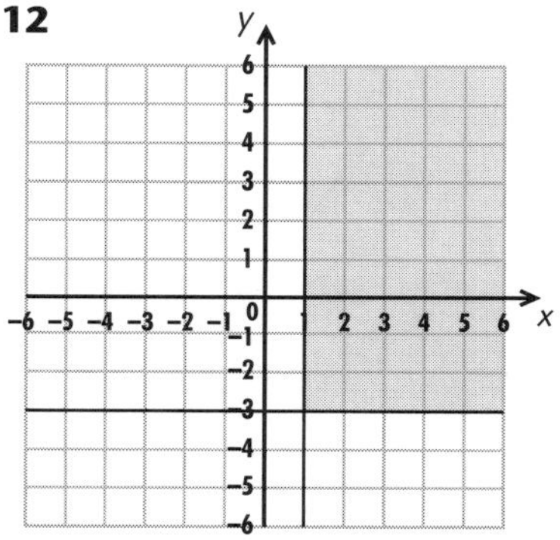

13

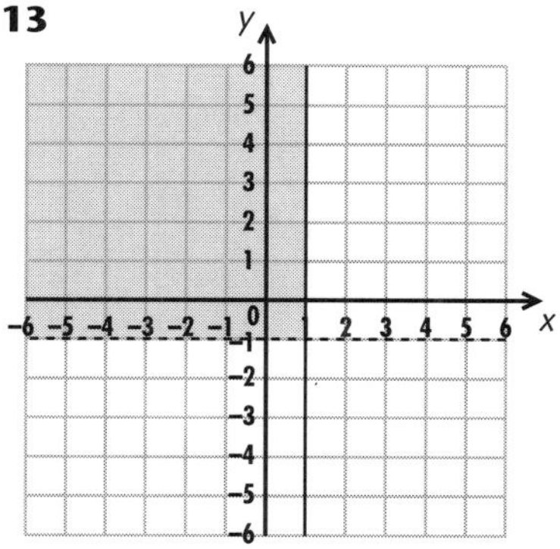

14

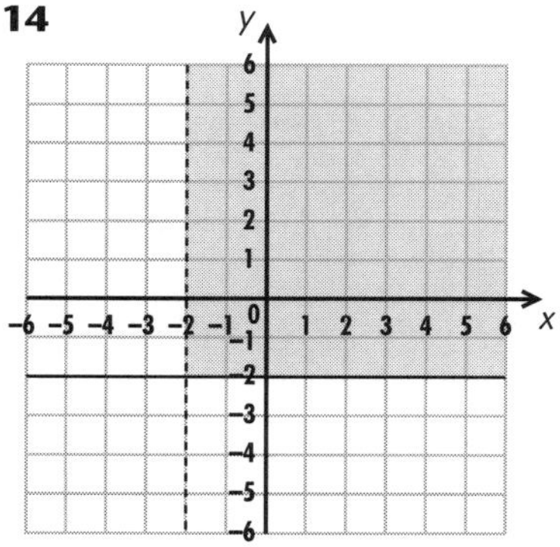

15

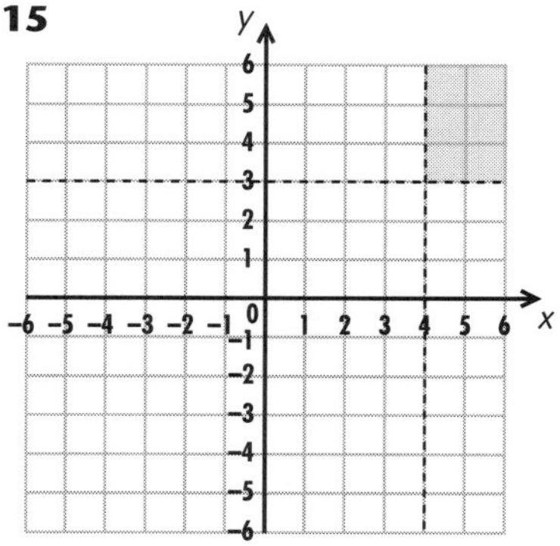

Use a grid, as in the previous diagrams, to show each of the inequalities as a shaded region.

16 $x < -4$

17 $y > 2$

18 $x \geq 3$

19 $x \leq 0$

20 $y \geq -1$

21 $x > 5$

22 $y < 0$

23 $x < 2$

24 $y \geq 1$

25 $x > -3,\ y \geq 2$

26 $x \geq 4,\ y \leq 1$

27 $x \leq -2,\ y \leq 5$

28 $x < 2,\ y < -1$

29 $x < 0,\ y \geq 4$

30 $x < 3,\ y > -2$

Exercise 40B

Write down inequalities to describe each of the shaded regions.

1

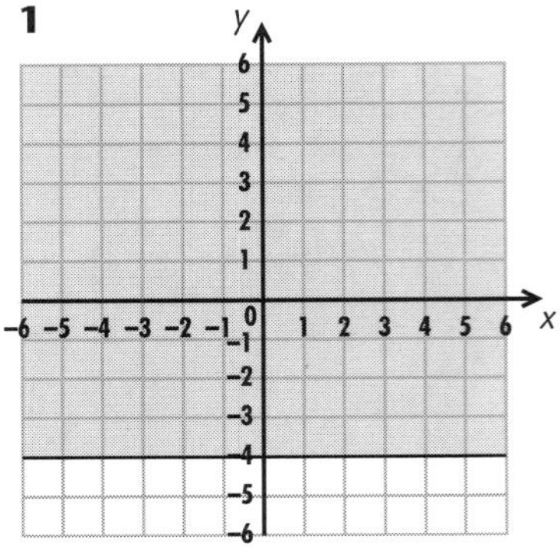

2

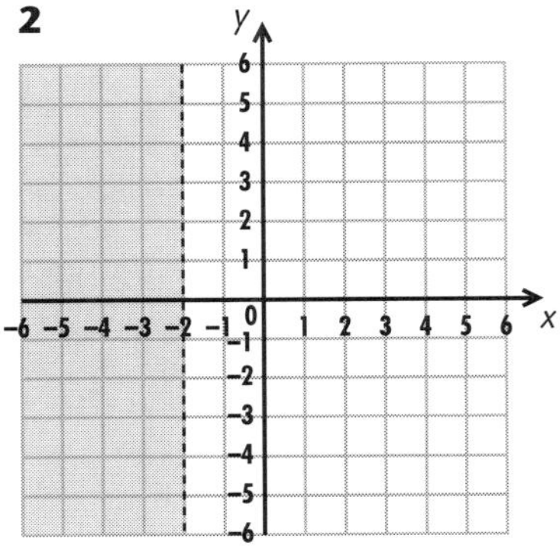

3

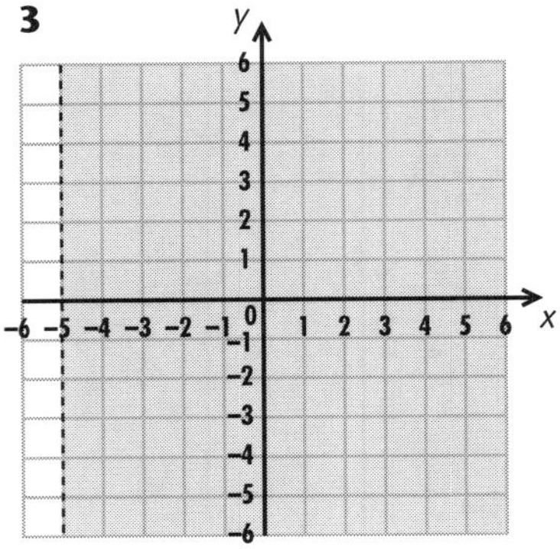

4

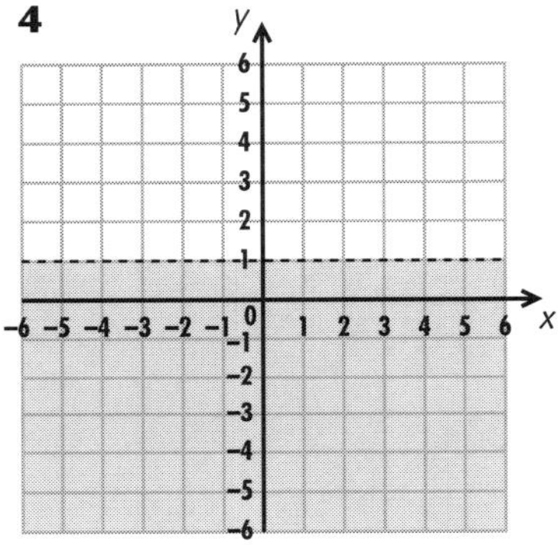

5

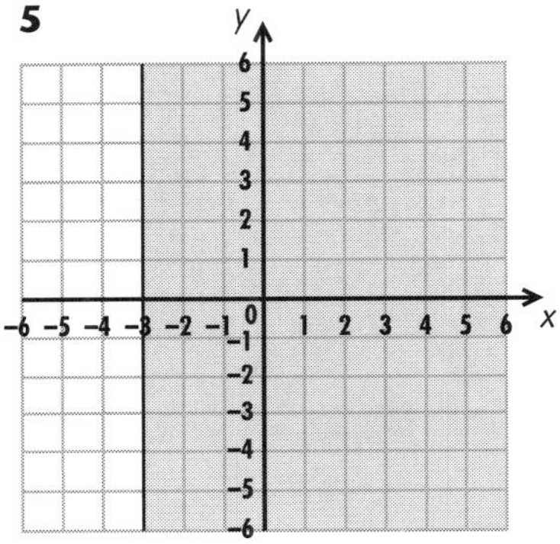

6

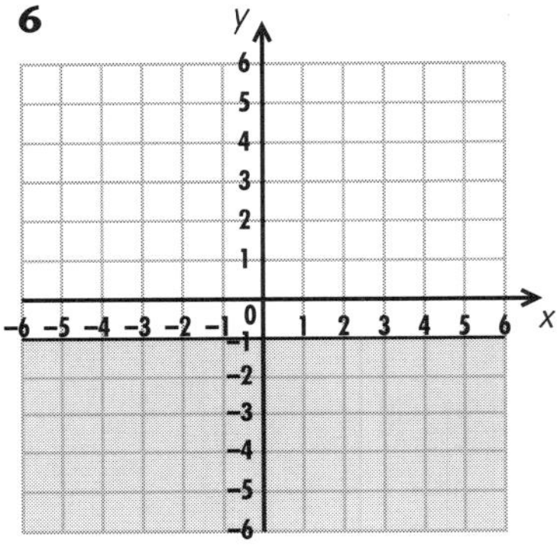

7

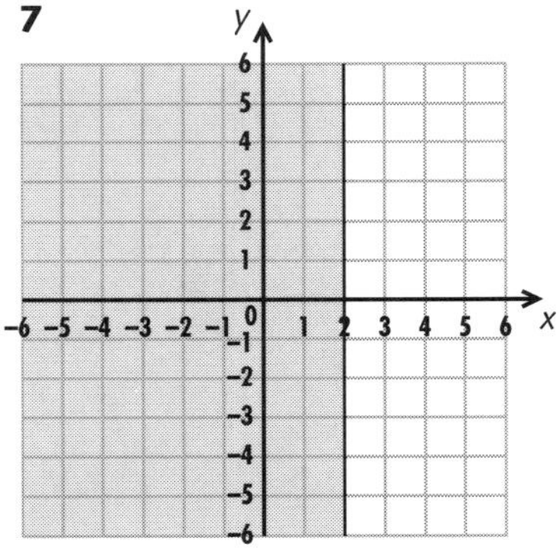

8

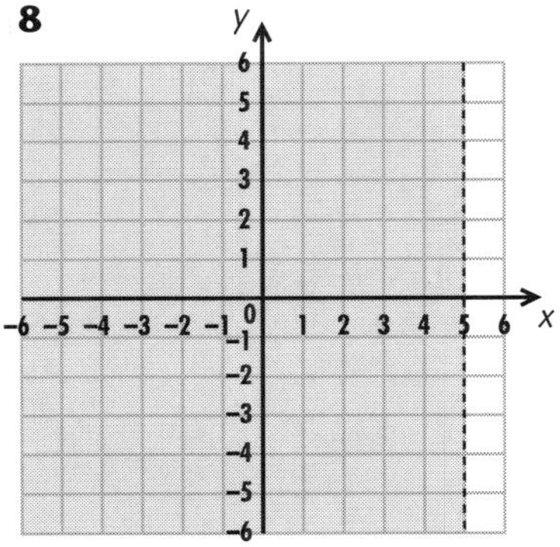

9

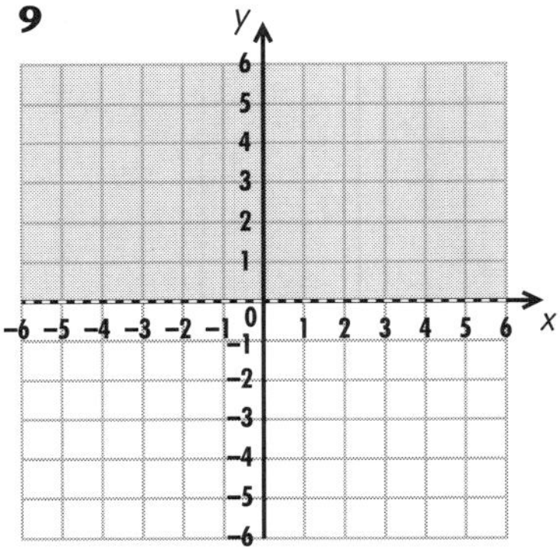

10

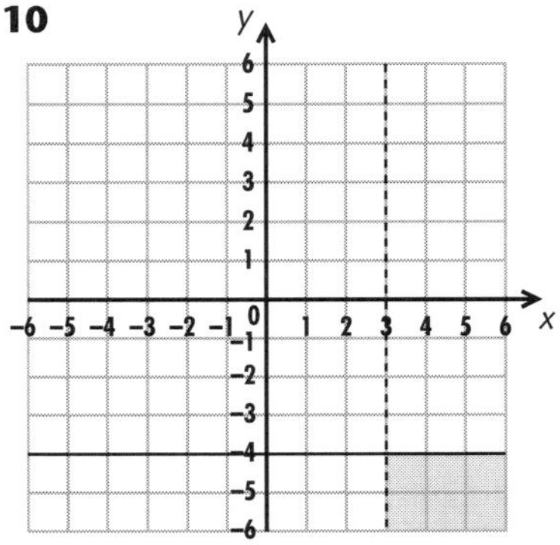

11

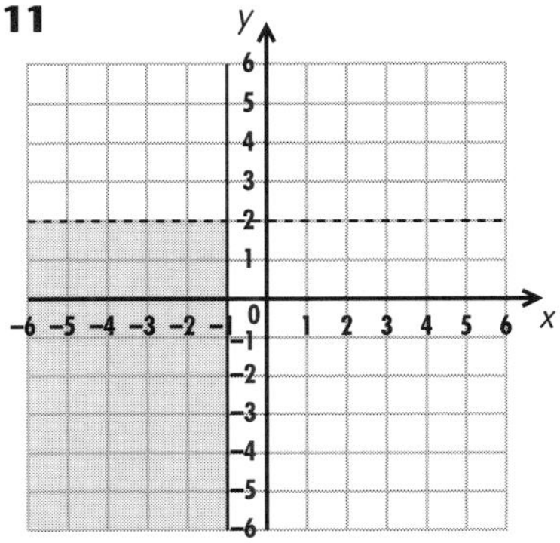

12

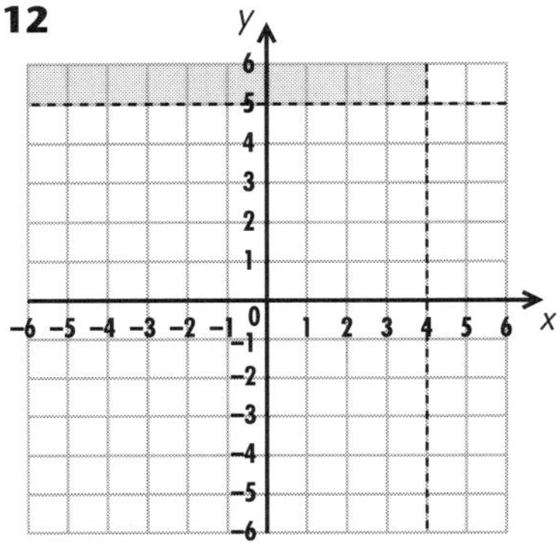

13

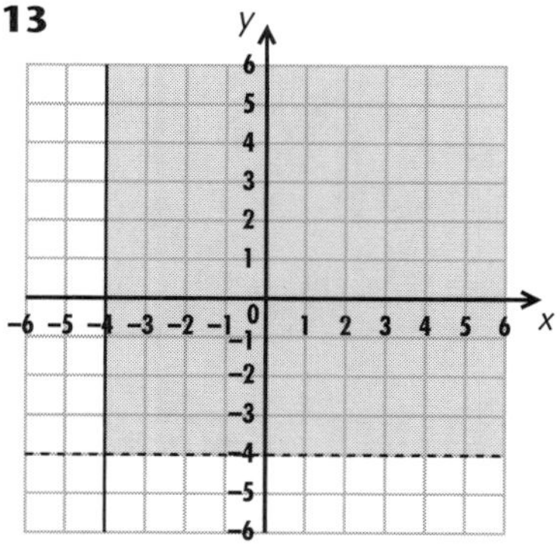

14

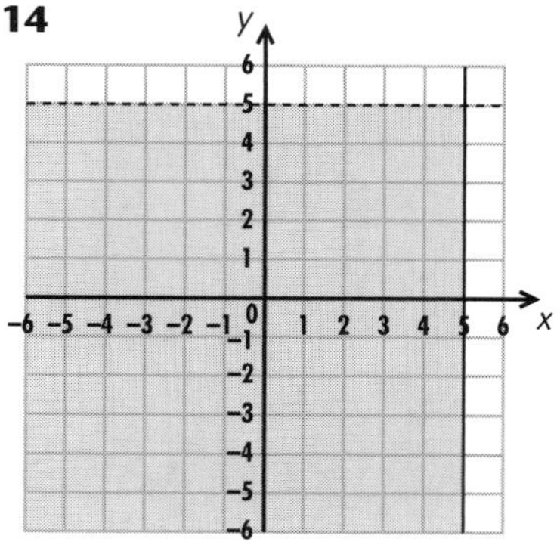

15

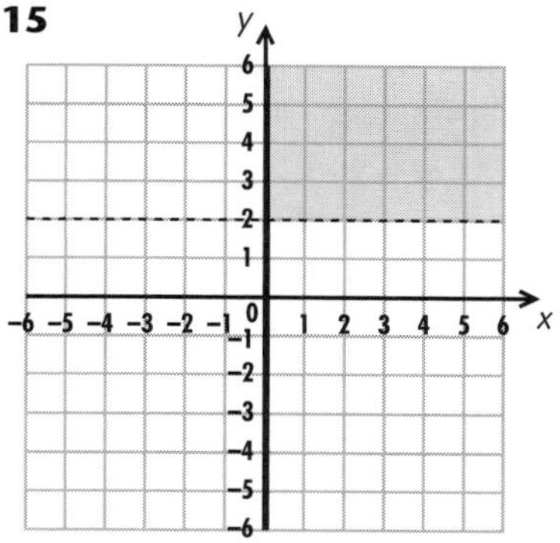

Use a grid, as in the previous diagrams, to show each of the inequalities as a shaded region.

16	$y < 3$	**17**	$x > 2$	**18**	$y \geq 0$
19	$x \leq 1$	**20**	$y < -3$	**21**	$y > 1$
22	$x \geq -2$	**23**	$x < -3$	**24**	$y \leq 4$
25	$x < 1, y \leq -2$	**26**	$x > -4, y \leq 3$	**27**	$x > 0, y \geq 5$
28	$x \leq -3, y < 4$	**29**	$x \geq 5, y \leq 0$	**30**	$x < 6, y \leq -3$

EXAMPLE

► Shade the region which satisfies the three inequalities.
$y < 4 - x$, $x \geq 0$ and $y > 1$

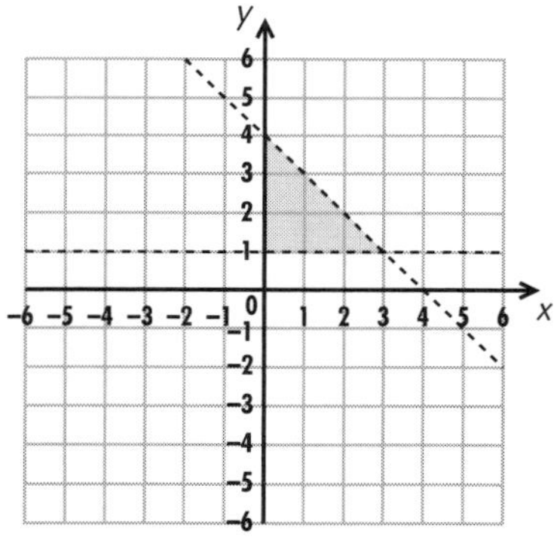

EXAMPLE

► Write down inequalities to describe the shaded region.

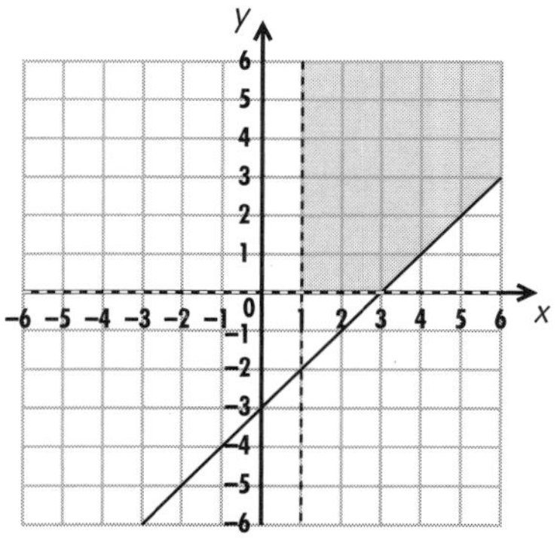

$y \geq x - 3$, $x > 1$, $y > 0$

Exercise 40C

Write down inequalities to describe the shaded region in each diagram.

1

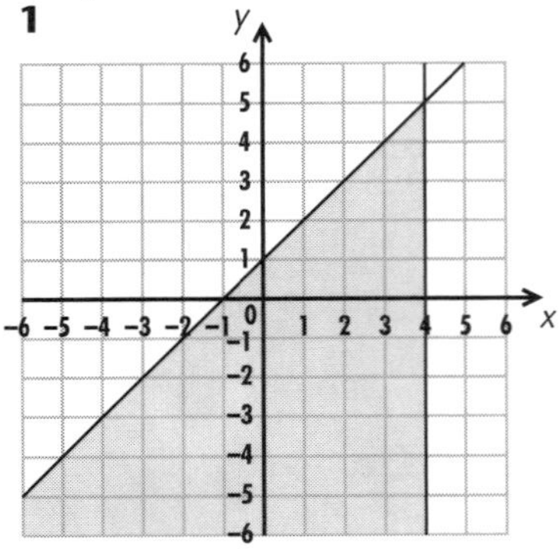

2

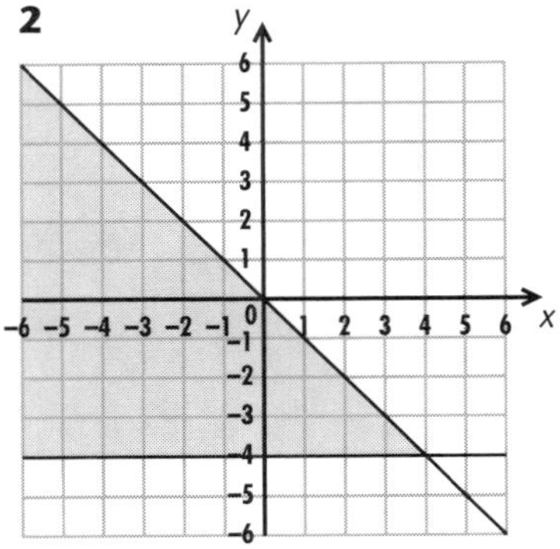

3

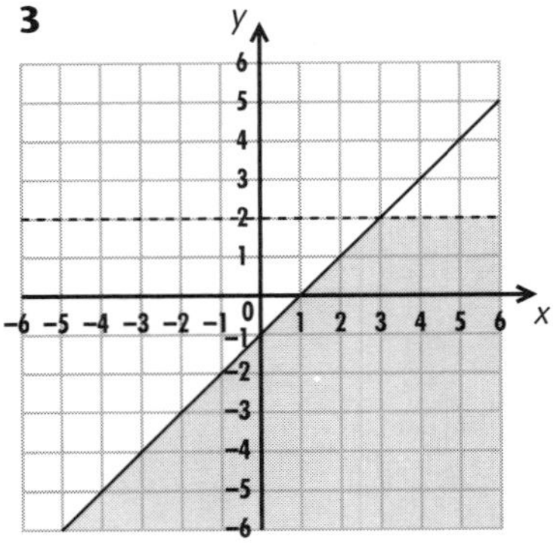

4

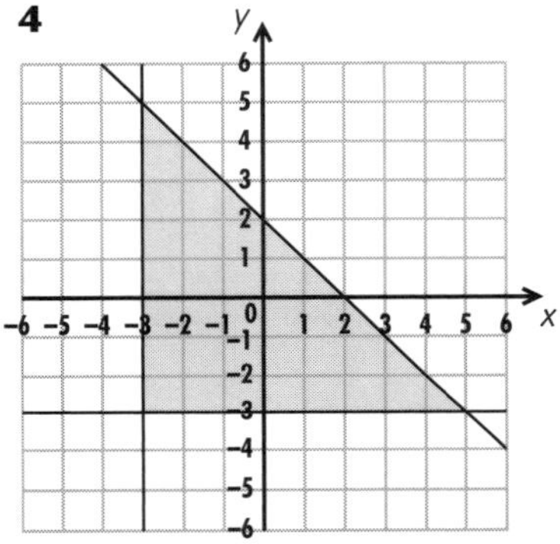

5

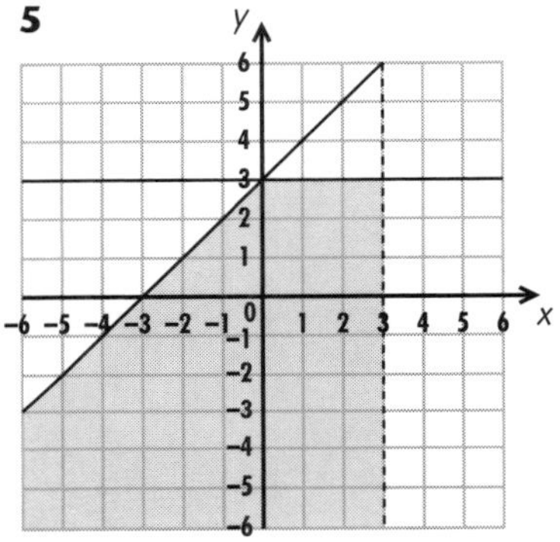

6

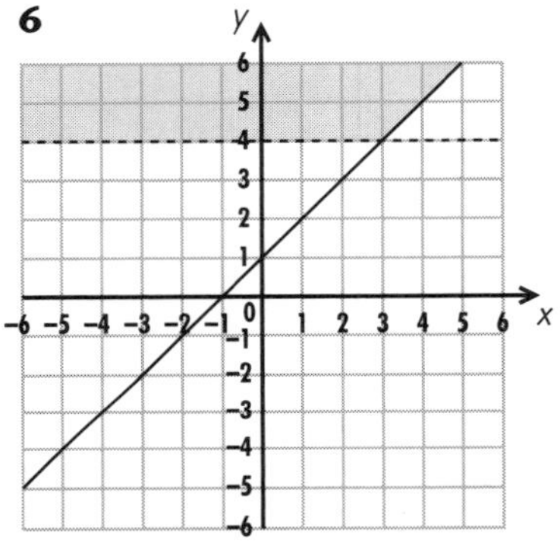

7

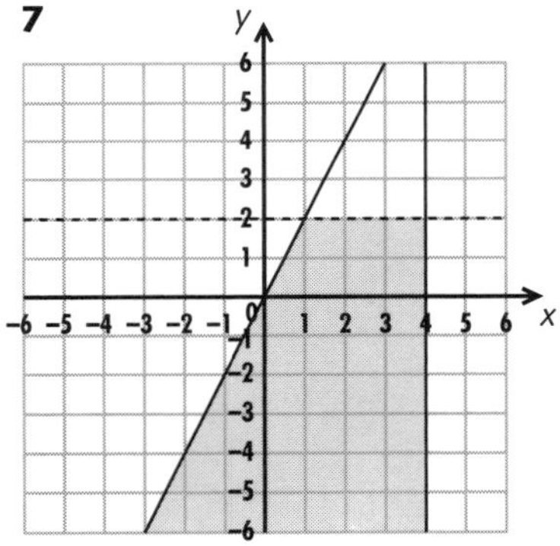

8

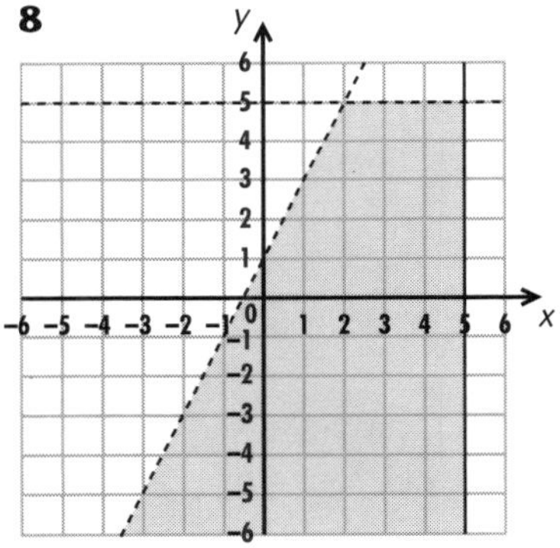

9

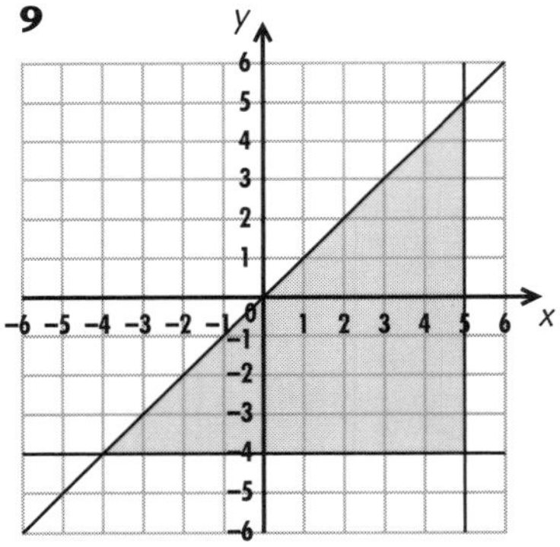

10

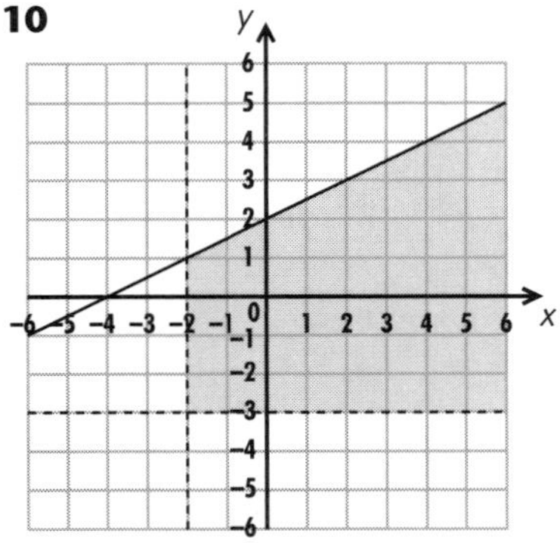

In each question use a grid, as in the previous diagrams, to shade the region which satisfies the inequalities.

11 $y \le x - 3$, $x < 4$

12 $y \ge x$, $y > 2$

13 $y \ge 2 - x$, $y \le 5$, $x \le 2$

14 $y \le 4$, $y \ge x + 1$

15 $y \le 2$, $x \ge -3$, $y \ge 2x$

16 $y \le 3x - 4$, $x \le 3$, $y \ge -3$

17 $y \ge 2x + 1$, $y \le 4$, $x > -3$

18 $y > -x$, $x \ge -2$

19 $y \ge \frac{1}{2}x + 1$, $x < 2$, $y < 4$

20 $y > x + 1$, $x \ge -4$, $y \le 3$

Exercise 40D

Write down inequalities to describe the shaded region in each diagram.

1

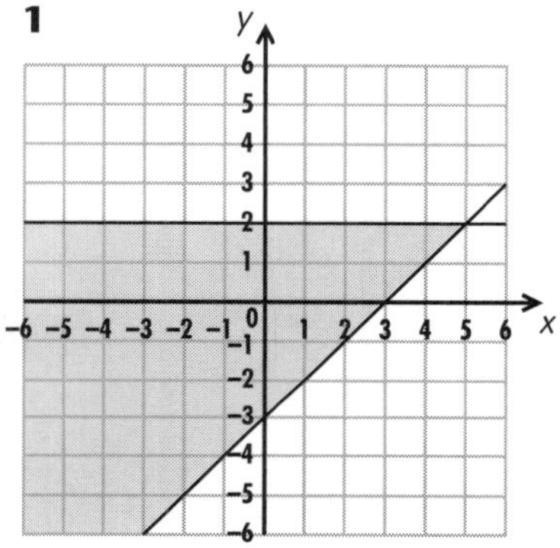

2

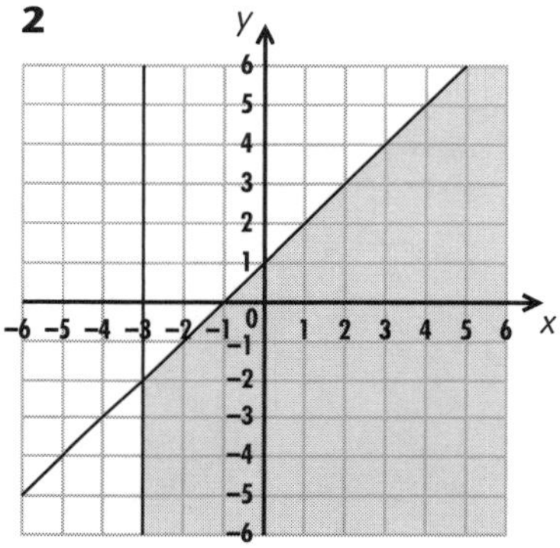

3

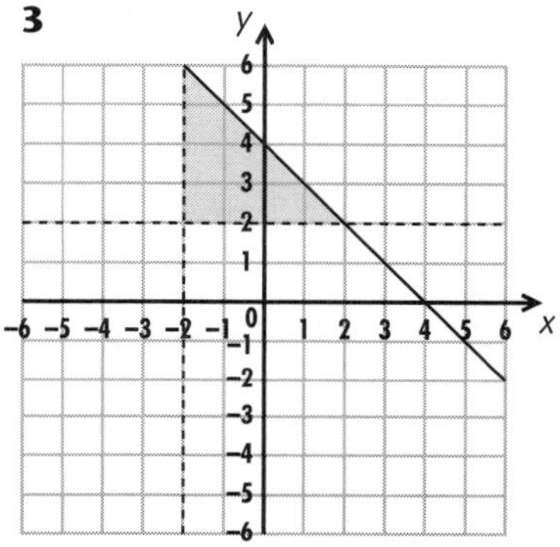

4

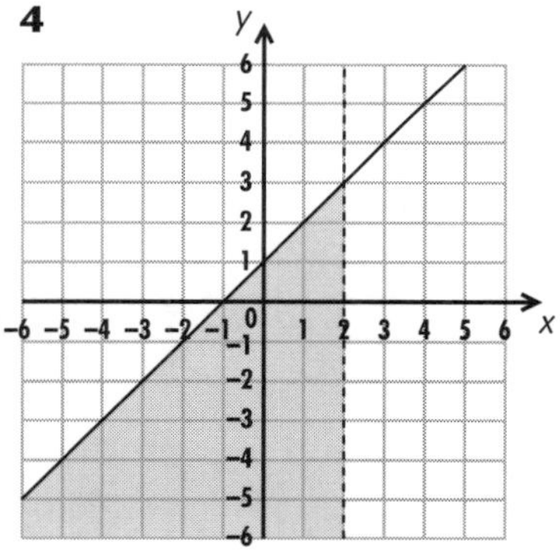

5

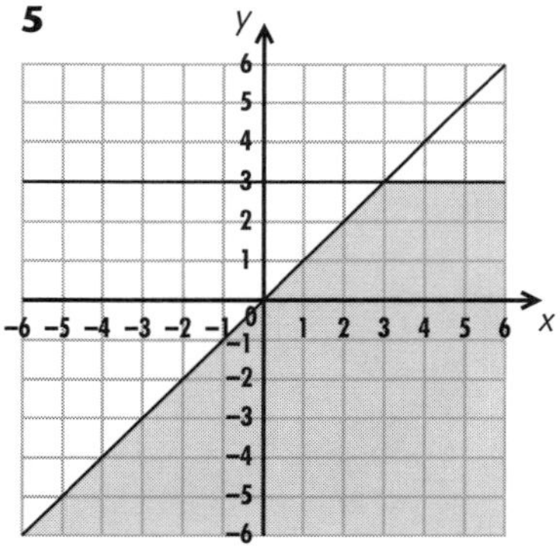

6

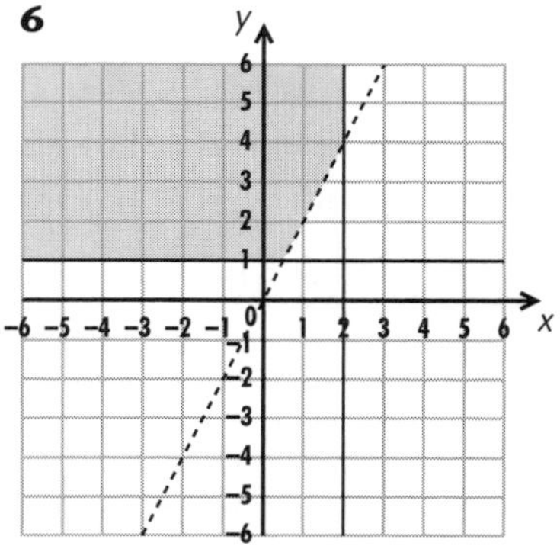

7

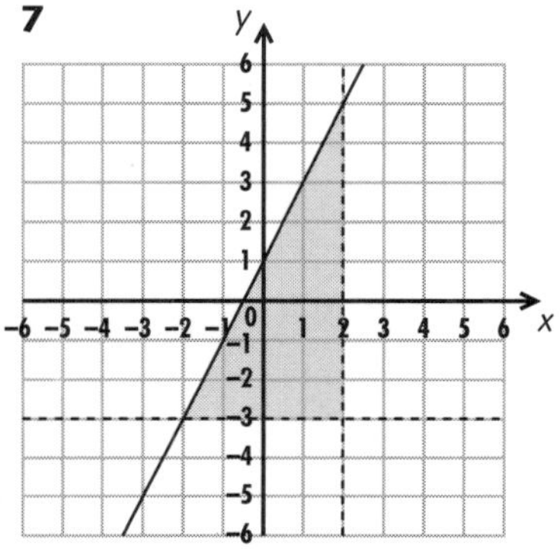

8

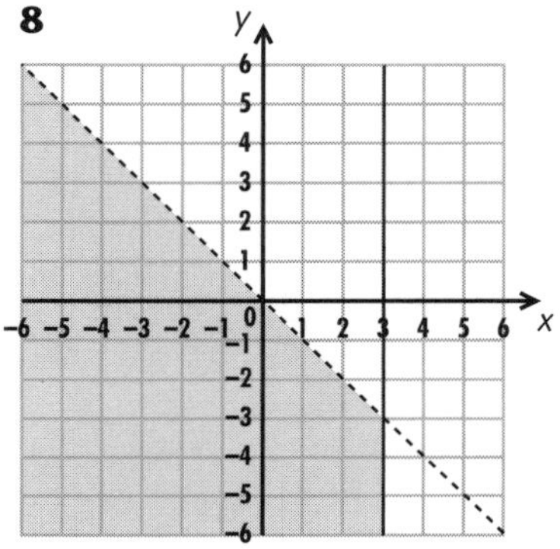

9

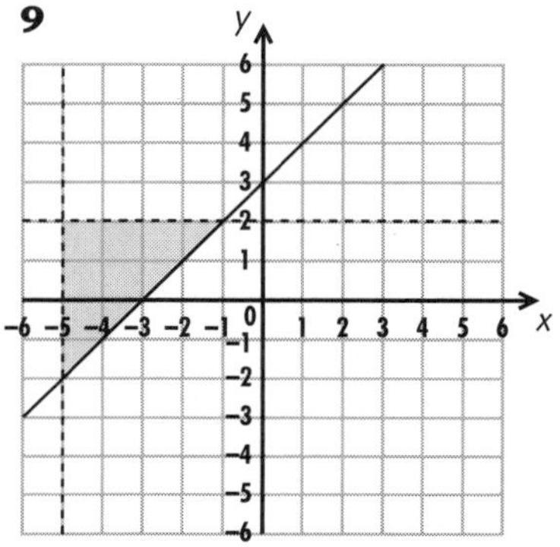

10

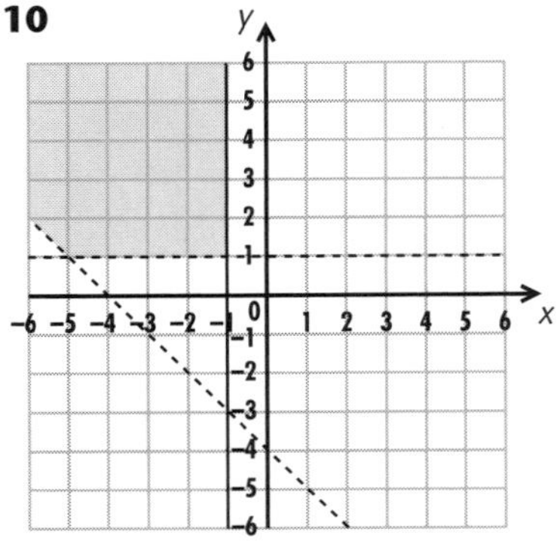

In each question use a grid, as in the previous diagrams, to shade the region which satisfies the inequalities.

11 $y \leq x + 3,\ y \geq -2,\ x \leq 2$

12 $y \geq 2x - 4,\ y > 3,\ x > 1$

13 $y \leq \frac{1}{2}x + 1,\ x \leq 1,\ y \geq -1$

14 $y < 3,\ x \geq -4,\ y > x + 1$

15 $y > x - 3,\ y > -5,\ x < 5$

16 $y \leq -x,\ x < -3$

17 $y \geq \frac{1}{2}x - 2,\ y \leq -1,\ x \leq 5$

18 $y < 4 - x,\ x > -4,\ y \leq 2$

19 $y > x,\ y < 5,\ x > 2$

20 $y < 2x + 1,\ y \leq 4,\ x \leq 5$

REVISION

Exercise D

1 Solve these equations.

(a) $10x - 1 = 89$ (b) $5 + 2t = 3$ (c) $2y + 3 = 4y + 5$

(d) $2(4x + 1) = 3x + 12$ (e) $6 - 5x = 21$ (f) $3(9x - 4) - (7x - 8) = 0$

2 Use 'trial and improvement' techniques to find the solutions to these equations. Give your answer correct to 2 decimal places.

(a) $x^2 - 4x = 8$ (b) $2x^2 + 6x + 3 = 0$ (c) $x^3 + 5x = 100$

3 Solve these simultaneous equations.

(a) $x + y = 10$, $x - y = 6$ (b) $6x + 2y = 5$, $2x + 2y = 3$ (c) $12x + 5y = 77$, $6x - y = 35$ (d) $5x + 3y = 6$, $7x + 4y = 9$

4 Write down the equations of the lines.

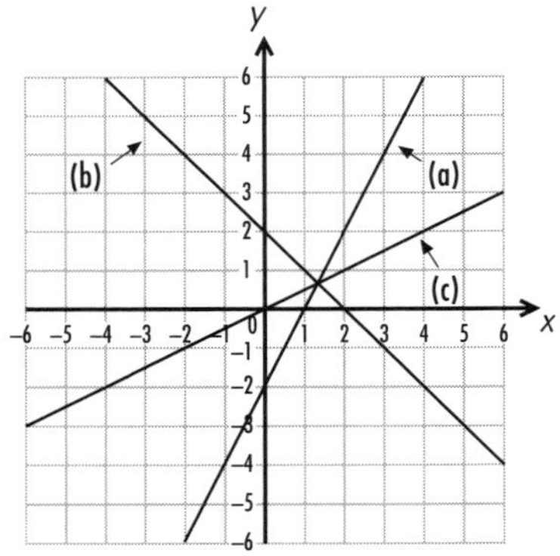

5 On a grid like the one in question 4, draw lines to represent these equations.

(a) $y = 3x - 5$ (b) $y = -2x + 1$ (c) $y = \frac{1}{3}x$

6 Use a graphical method to solve these simultaneous equations.

(a) $y = 2x - 3$
$y = -x + 3$

(b) $y = x - 3$
$y = -x - 2$

7 (a) Draw the graph of $y = x^2 - 3x - 6$ for $-2 \le x \le 5$.

(b) Write down the lowest value of $x^2 - 3x - 6$.

(c) Find the value of y when $x = 2.5$.

(d) Find the values of x when $y = 2$.

(e) Use the graph to find, correct to 2 d.p., the solution of the equation $x^2 - 3x - 6 = 0$.

(f) Use the graph to find, correct to 2 d.p., the solution of the equation $x^2 - 3x - 3 = 0$.

8 Draw the graph of $y = x^3 - x^2 - 5x$ for $-3 \le x \le 4$.

9 Draw the graph of $y = \dfrac{6}{x}$ for $-4 \le x \le 4$.

10 Write down the inequality shown on the following number lines.

(a)

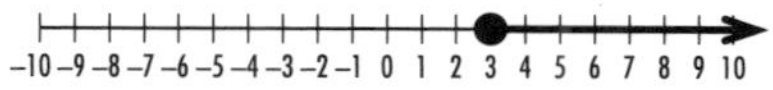

(b)

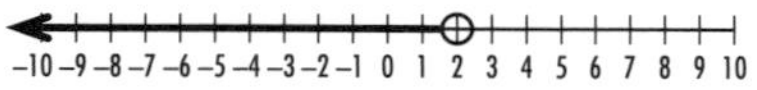

(c)

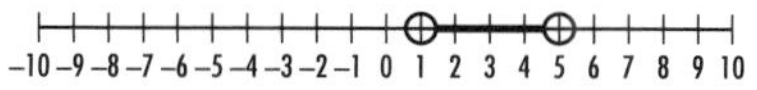

11 Draw a number line to show each of the following inequalities.

(a) $x \ge 3$ (b) $x > -1$ (c) $-8 < x \le 6$

12 Write down inequalities to describe each of the following regions.

(a)

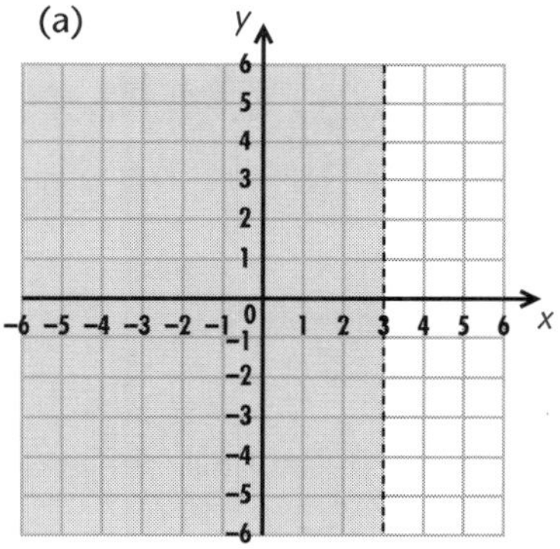

(b)

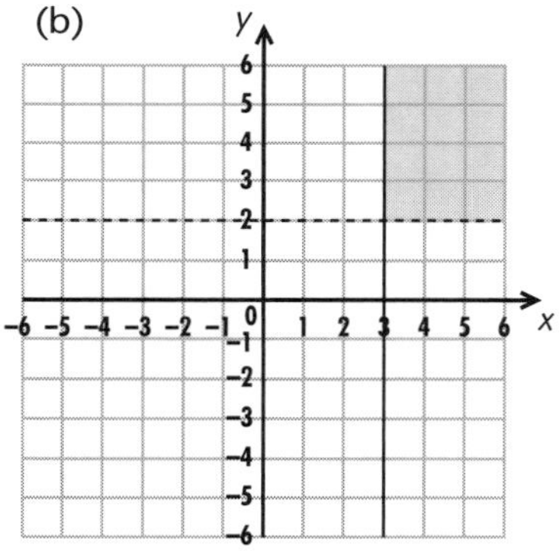

(c)

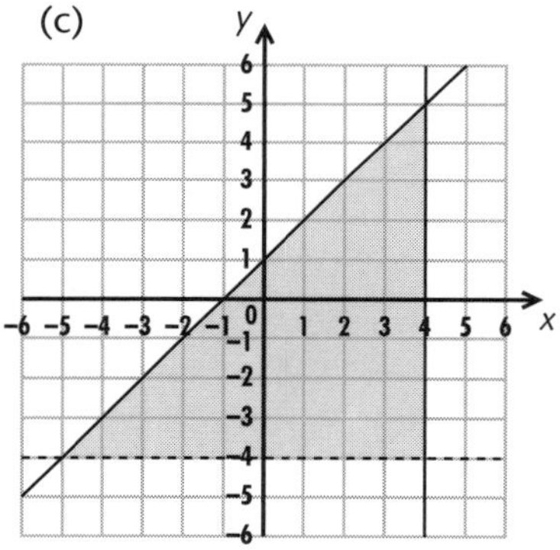

13 Use a grid for each question and shade the region which satisfies the inequalities.

(a) $y \ge -2$ (b) $y \le 3$, $x < 2$ (c) $y < 3 - x$, $x > 3$, $y > -2$

Exercise DD

1 Jan has £6.30 more than Jeremy. Together they have £21.10. How much do they each have?

2 James is one year younger than Sean. Their ages add up to 37 years. How old is Sean?

3 The perimeter of this triangle is 46 cm.

(a) Write an expression, using x, for the perimeter of the triangle.

(b) Write an equation, and solve it, to find the length of the rectangle.

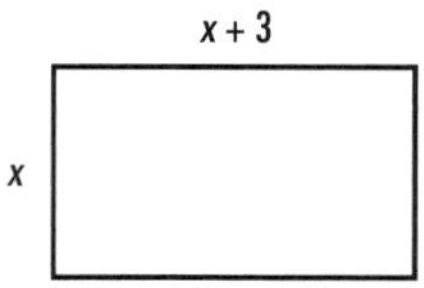

4 An apple weighs twice as much as a pear and an orange weighs 23 g more than a pear. If all three together weigh 143 g, how much does each weigh?

5 Five copies of book A and four copies of book B cost £46. Two copies of book A cost the same as three copies of book B. Find the cost of each book.

6 Three apples and two oranges cost 88p. One apple and three oranges cost 76p. Find the cost of (a) an apple (b) an orange.

7 The perimeter of a rectangle is 52 cm. The difference between the length and the width is 8 cm. Find the length and the width.

8 The graph shows the journey of a cyclist.

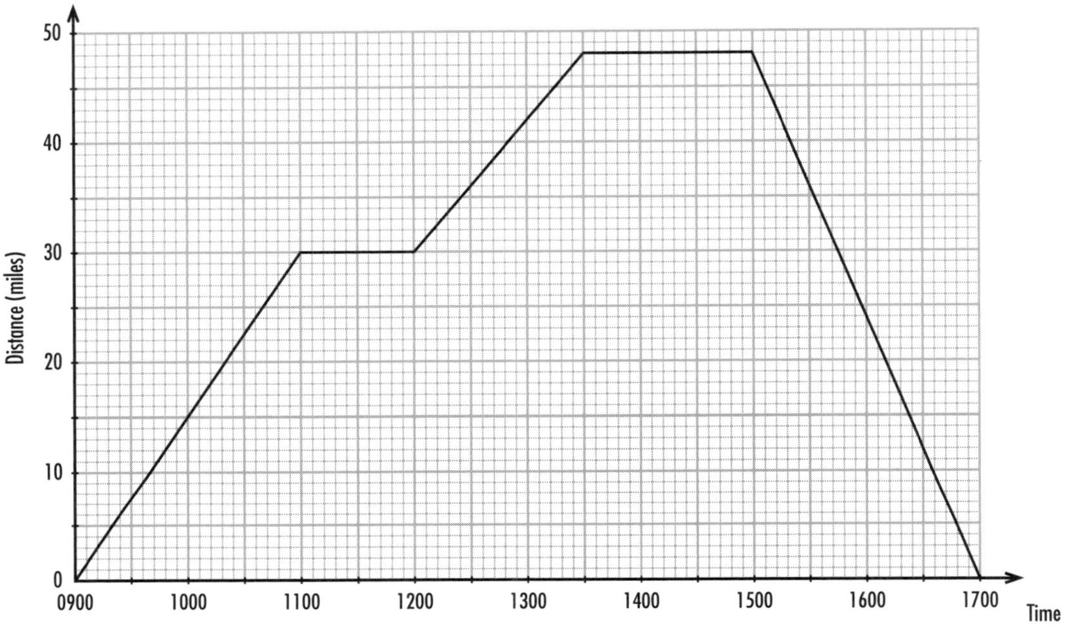

(a) At what time did the cyclist first stop?
(b) What was the average speed of the cyclist during the first part of the journey?
(c) For how long did the cyclist stop at 1330?
(d) At what time did the cyclist head for home?
(e) What was the average speed of the homeward journey?
(f) What was the total length of the journey?

Shape, space and measures

41/ BEARINGS

- **Bearings** are measured from the north.
- North is the bearing 000°.
- Three digits are used to state the angle.
- The angle for the required direction is found by moving **clockwise** from the north.

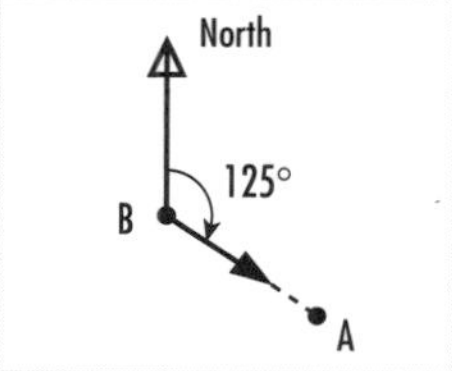

The word 'from' is particularly important to the understanding of bearings. In the diagram the bearing of A *from* B is found by going to B and looking towards A. The required bearing is 125°.

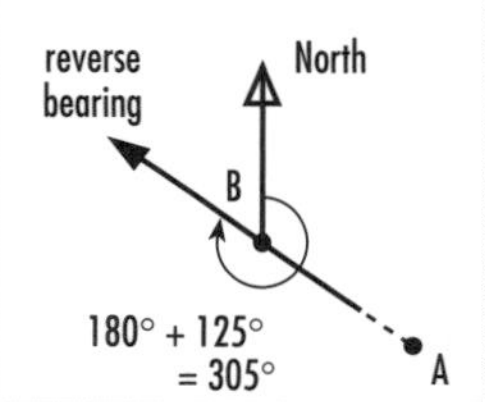

The **reverse bearing** of the above is the bearing of B from A. Again, to find the bearing, look for the word 'from'. Since the required direction is *from* A, go to A and look towards B. There is 180° difference in the direction for the reverse bearing compared with the original direction.
Reverse bearing = 125° + 180° = 305°

EXAMPLE

► State (i) the bearing of A from B (ii) the reverse bearing in each diagram.

(a)
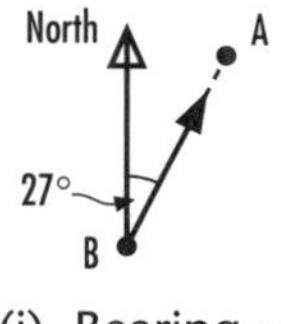

(b)
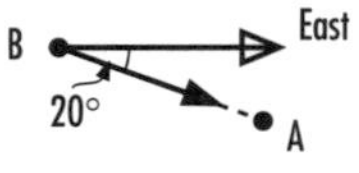

(c)
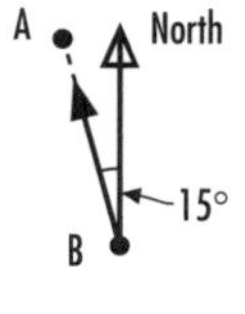

(a) (i) Bearing = 027° (ii) Reverse bearing = 180° + 27° = 207°

(b) (i) The angle from north is 90° + 20°, so the bearing is 110°.
(ii) Reverse bearing = 180° + 110° = 290°

(c) (i) Moving in a clockwise direction from north it is necessary to move through 360° – 15°; so the bearing is 345°.
(ii) The difference is still 180° but this would take the angle beyond 360°, so it makes more sense to subtract 180°.
Reverse bearing = 345° – 180° = 165°

Note: There is always a difference of 180° between a bearing and its reverse bearing. However, the reverse bearing can sometimes be obtained by addition of 180° and sometimes by subtraction of 180°.

Exercise 41A

1 State the bearing for each of the following compass directions.
(a) South (b) North-east (c) West (d) South-west

2 State the bearing of A from B in each diagram.

(a)
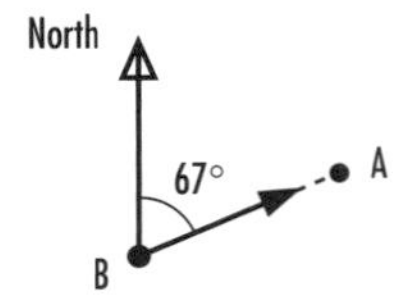

(b)
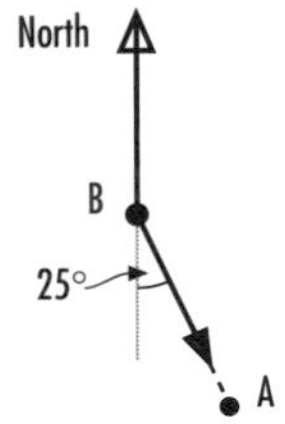

(c)
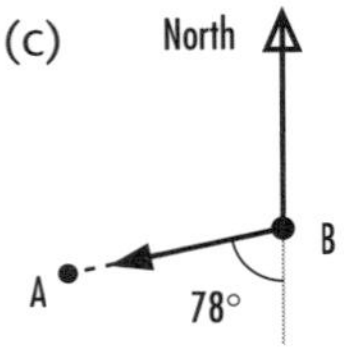

(d)
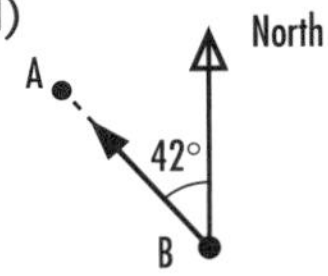

(e)
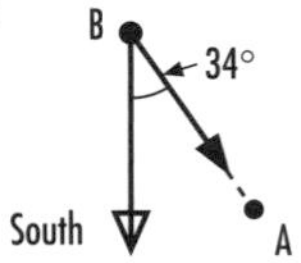

(f)
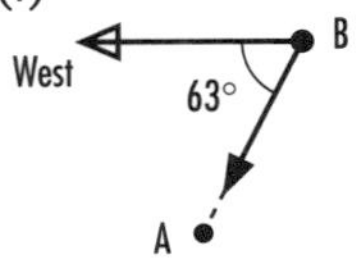

(g)
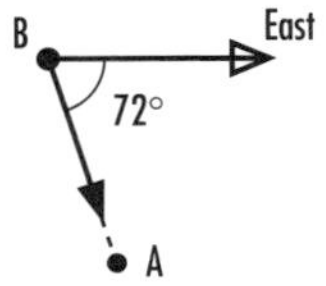

(h)
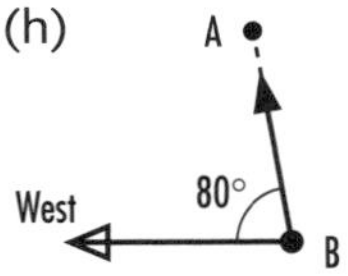

3 State the reverse bearing for each direction in question 2.

4 State the reverse bearing for each of the following bearings.
(a) 050° (b) 115° (c) 282° (d) 173° (e) 300° (f) 145°

5
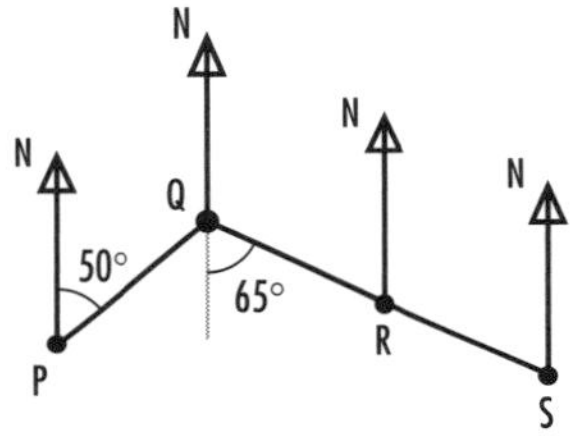

State the bearing of each of the following.
(a) Q from P
(b) R from Q
(c) P from Q
(d) S from R

Exercise 41B

1 State the bearing for each of the following compass directions.
(a) East (b) South-east (c) North-west (d) North

2 State the bearing of B from A in each diagram.

(a)
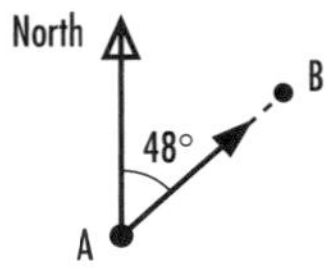

(b)
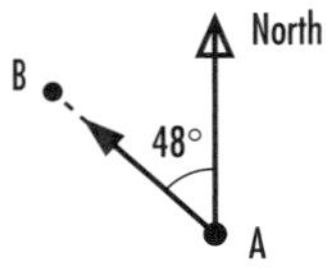

(c)
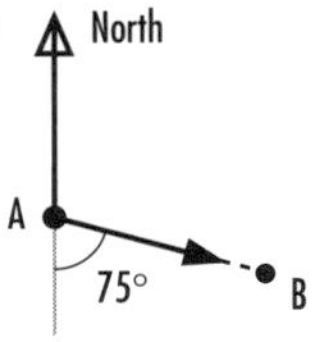

(d)
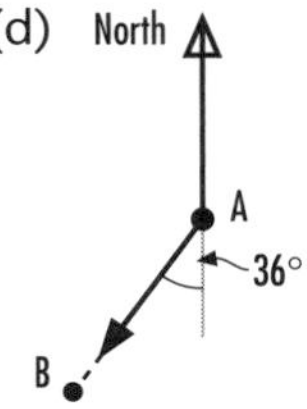

(e)
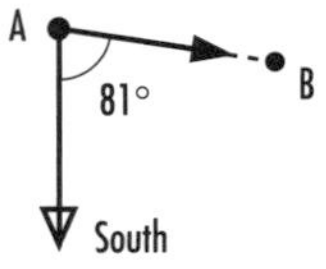

(f)
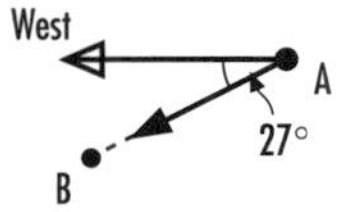

(g)
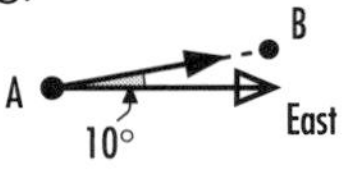

(h)
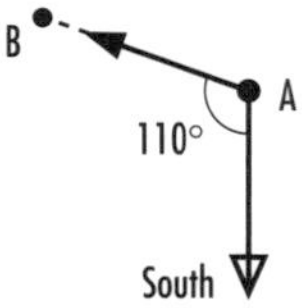

3 State the reverse bearing for each direction in question 2.

4 State the reverse bearing for each of the following bearings.
(a) 290° (b) 021° (c) 168° (d) 309° (e) 002° (f) 257°

5

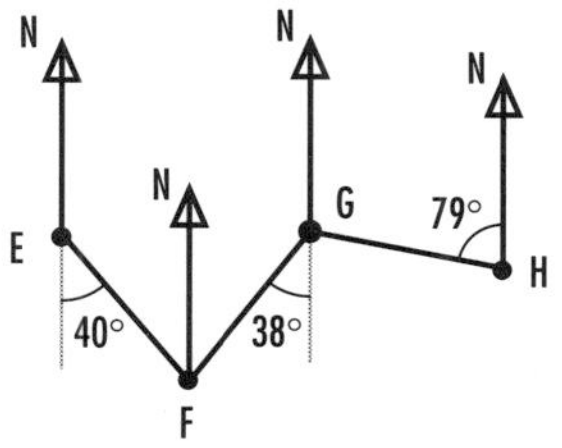

State the bearing of each of the following.

(a) F from E
(b) F from G
(c) G from H
(d) H from G

42/ PYTHAGORAS' THEOREM: FINDING THE HYPOTENUSE

The **hypotenuse** is the side opposite the right angle in a right-angled triangle.

The length of the hypotenuse, h, of a right-angled triangle is given by the formula:

$$h^2 = a^2 + b^2$$

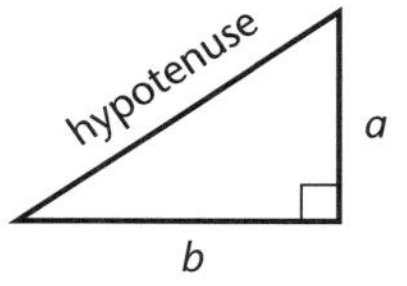

EXAMPLE

► Find the hypotenuse, h, in each of the diagrams.

(a)

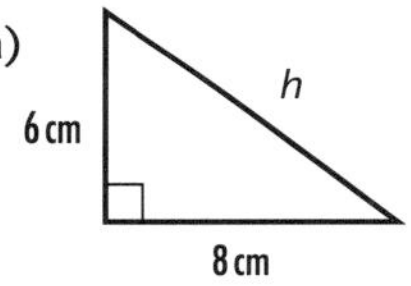

(b)

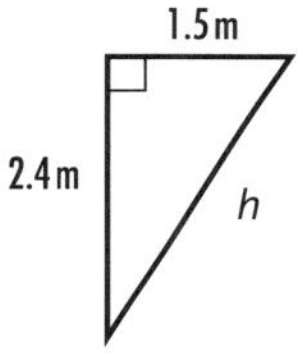

(a) $h^2 = a^2 + b^2$
$= 6^2 + 8^2$
$= 36 + 64$
$= 100$
$h = \sqrt{100} = 10\text{ cm}$

(b) $h^2 = a^2 + b^2$
$= 2.4^2 + 1.5^2$
$= 5.76 + 2.25$
$= 8.01$
$h = \sqrt{8.01} = 2.83\text{ m}$ (to 3 s.f.)

Exercise 42A

In each question find the hypotenuse given the other two sides, a and b, of a right-angled triangle. Give your answer to 3 significant figures where necessary.

1 $a = 12\text{ cm}, b = 16\text{ cm}$
2 $a = 5\text{ m}, b = 12\text{ m}$
3 $a = 7\text{ cm}, b = 10\text{ cm}$
4 $a = 14\text{ cm}, b = 48\text{ cm}$
5 $a = 1.8\text{ m}, b = 0.9\text{ m}$
6 $a = 56\text{ mm}, b = 42\text{ mm}$
7 $a = 2.8\text{ m}, b = 2.1\text{ m}$

Find the length of the hypotenuse in each of the right-angled triangles.

8

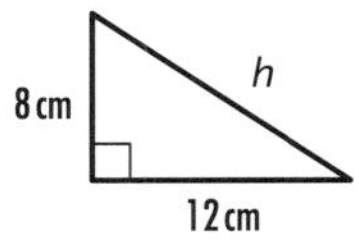

9

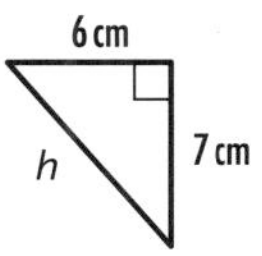

10

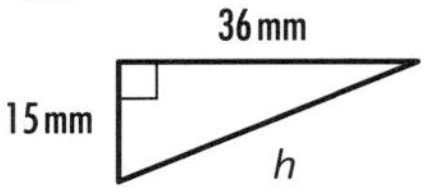

11

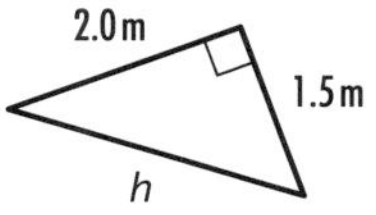

12

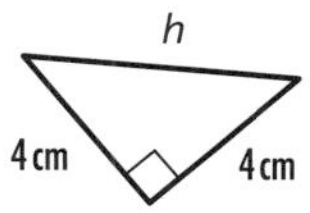

13

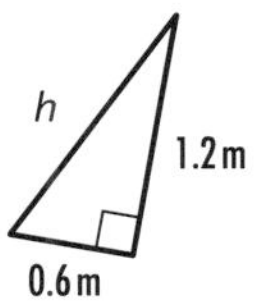

14

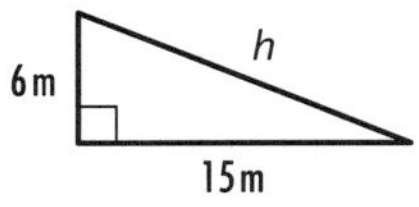

15

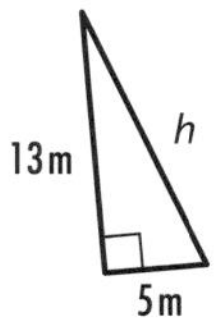

16 Calculate the length of a diagonal of a square which has sides of length 44 mm.

17 Calculate the length marked x in the diagram.

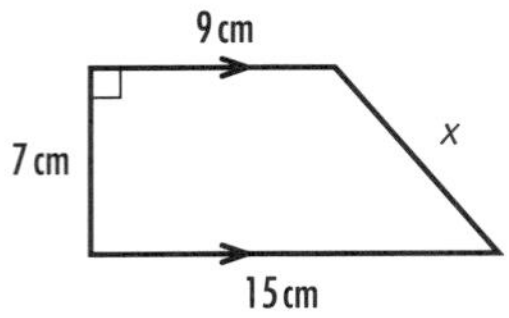

18 A pirate walks 20 paces north and then 36 paces east. How many paces is he from his starting point, to the nearest pace?

19 A ladder rests on horizontal ground against a vertical wall. The foot of the ladder is 3.2 m away from the base of the wall. If the ladder reaches a point 7.8 m from the ground, calculate the length of the ladder.

20 The diagram shows the plan of a room. Calculate the length of the longer diagonal.

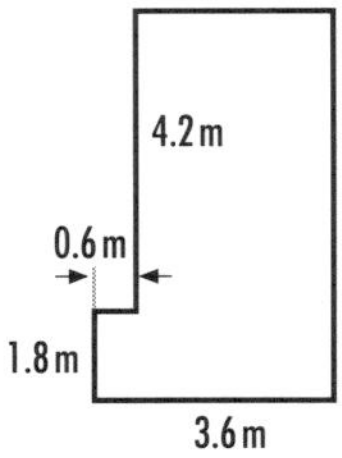

21

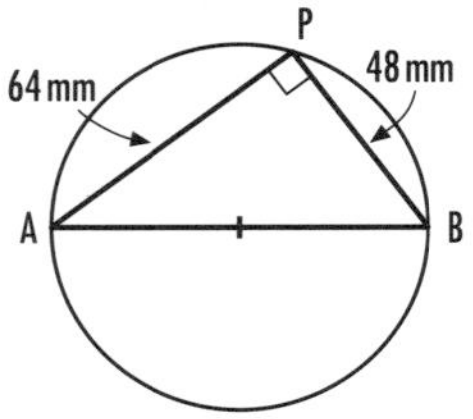

In the diagram AP = 64 mm and BP = 48 mm. Calculate the length of the diameter AB.

22 On a graph the distance between (0, 0) and (0, 1) is 2 cm. Calculate the distance between the points (1, 2) and (3, 5).

23 Calculate the length of a wire which has one end fixed to a point on horizontal ground 12 m from the base of a vertical pole. The other end of the wire is fixed to the top of the 5 m pole.

24 Calculate the greatest length of a knitting needle that will fit in a 20 cm × 30 cm flat tray.

Exercise 42B

In each question find the hypotenuse given the other two sides, a and b, of a right-angled triangle. Give your answer to 3 significant figures where necessary.

1 a = 24 cm, b = 10 cm
2 a = 7 m, b = 24 m
3 a = 15 cm, b = 8 cm
4 a = 9 cm, b = 9 cm
5 a = 35 mm, b = 60 mm
6 a = 0.75 m, b = 0.95 m
7 a = 172 mm, b = 105 mm

Find the length of the hypotenuse in each of the right-angled triangles.

8

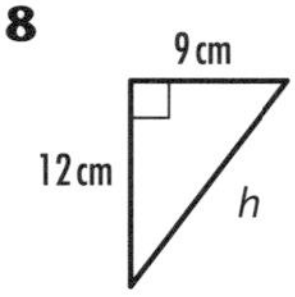

9

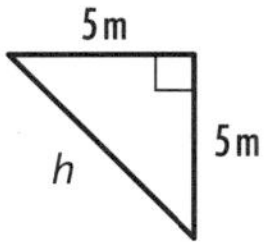

10

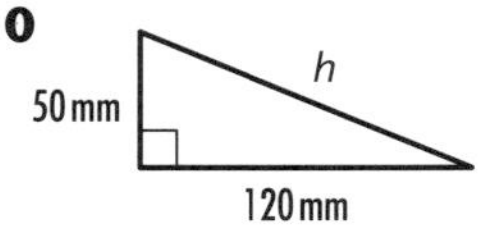

11

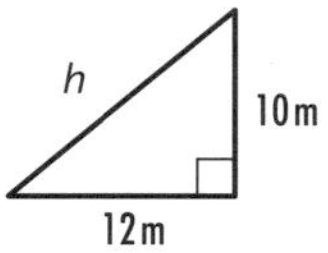

12

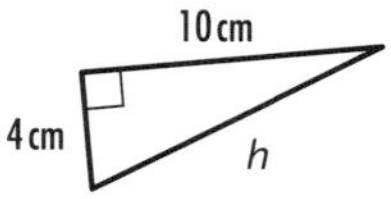

13

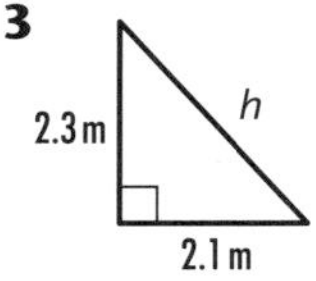

14

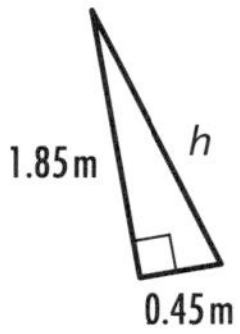

15

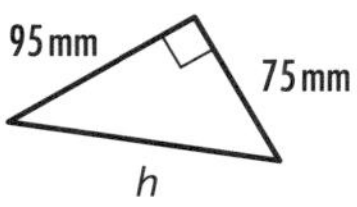

16 Calculate the diagonal of a rectangle with sides of length 20 mm and 48 mm.

17 A pilot flies 4 km due west and then 8 km due south. How far is she from her starting point?

18 In the diagram the radius OP = 5 cm. The length of the tangent TP = 12 cm. Calculate the length of OT.

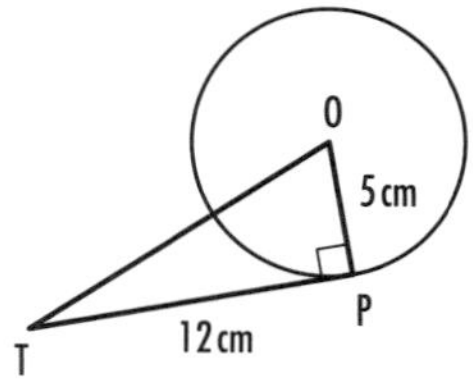

19 Paper of size A4 measures 21 cm by 29.7 cm. Calculate the length of a diagonal of a sheet of A4 paper.

20 Calculate the length of the sides of a rhombus which has diagonals of length 90 mm and 120 mm.

21 Calculate the length of a diagonal of a square which has sides of length 10 cm.

22 The diagram shows the end of a shed. The width is 2 m and the walls are 2.2 m and 2.5 m. Calculate the length, *d*, of the sloping roof.

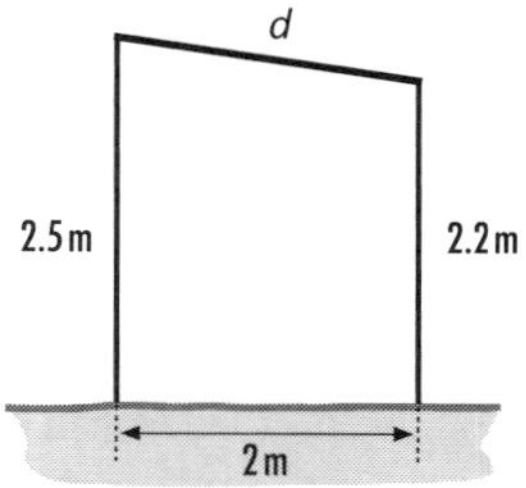

23 If the distance between the points (1, 0) and (1, 1) is 1 cm, calculate the distance between the points (1, 1) and (3, 3).

24

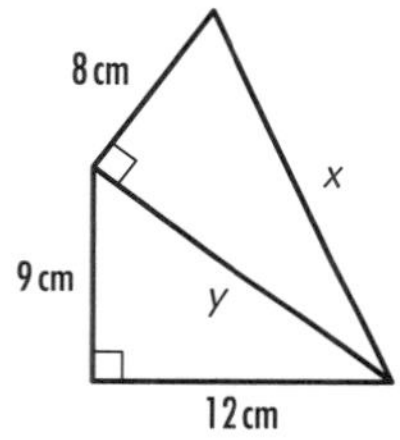

Calculate the length marked x in the diagram.
(Hint: Calculate the length y first.)

43/ PYTHAGORAS' THEOREM: FINDING A LENGTH GIVEN THE HYPOTENUSE

The hypotenuse is the longest side of a right-angled triangle and can be found using the formula:

$$h^2 = a^2 + b^2$$

If you know h and one of the other sides, use the alternative formula:

$$a^2 = h^2 - b^2$$

Note: Here you must *subtract from* h^2. This makes sense, since h is the longest side.

EXAMPLE

► Find the length of AB in the diagram.

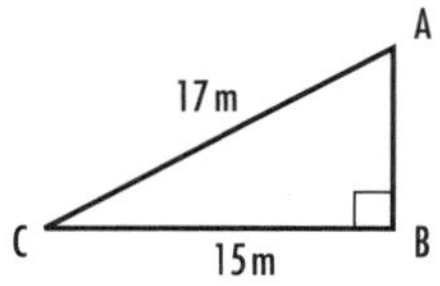

$$a^2 = h^2 - b^2$$
$$AB^2 = 17^2 - 15^2$$
$$= 289 - 225$$
$$= 64$$
$$AB = \sqrt{64} = 8 \text{ cm}$$

Exercise 43A

In each question find the unknown length in the right-angled triangle. Give your answer to 3 significant figures where necessary.

1 $h = 25$ cm, $a = 15$ cm
2 $a = 5$ m, $h = 13$ m
3 $h = 20$ cm, $b = 10$ cm
4 $h = 8$ cm, $a = 7$ cm
5 $a = 18$ mm, $h = 23$ mm
6 $h = 0.95$ m, $b = 0.75$ m
7 $h = 1.6$ m, $a = 1.3$ m

Find the unknown length, marked *a*, in each of the right-angled triangles.

8

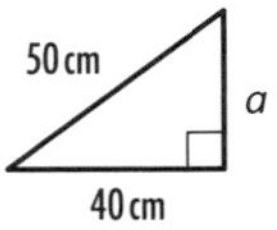

9

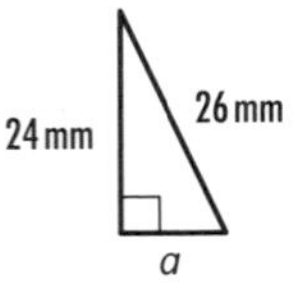

10

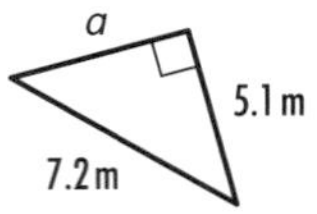

11

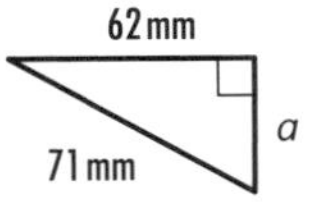

12

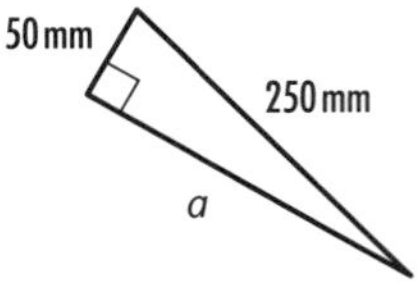

13

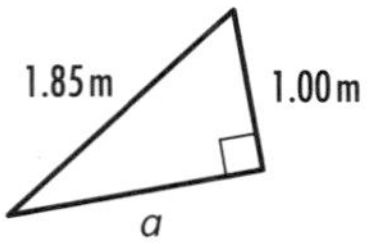

14

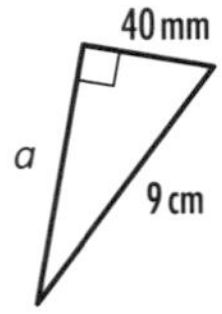

15

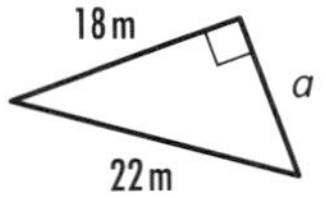

16 One side of a rectangle is 13 cm and the diagonals measure 20 cm. Calculate the length of the other side.

17 A picture frame has a diagonal of length 46.4 cm and one side of length 24.5 cm. Calculate the length of the other side.

18 A TV screen is advertised as having a diagonal of length 86 cm. Calculate the height of the screen, to the nearest centimetre, if the width is 70 cm.

19 The triangle ABC in the diagram is an isosceles triangle. Find its height, *h*.

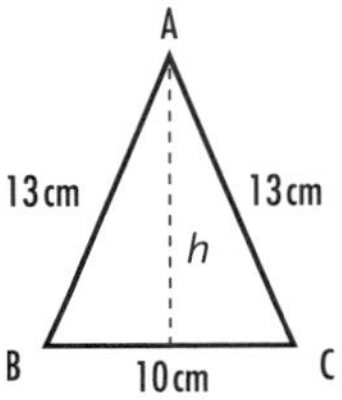

20 A rhombus of side length 41 cm has a diagonal 18 cm long. Calculate the length of the other diagonal.

21

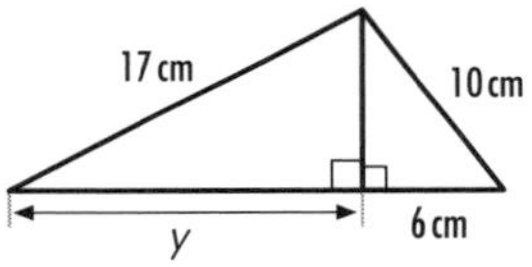

Find the length marked *y* in the diagram.
Hint: Find the height first.

22 A pilot is flying approximately south-west. When she has flown 50 km, she knows that she is 35 km west of her starting point. How far south of her starting point is she?

23 The diagram shows the net of a cuboid measuring 8 cm by 4 cm by *w* cm. The length QS = 25 cm. Calculate the length *w* cm.

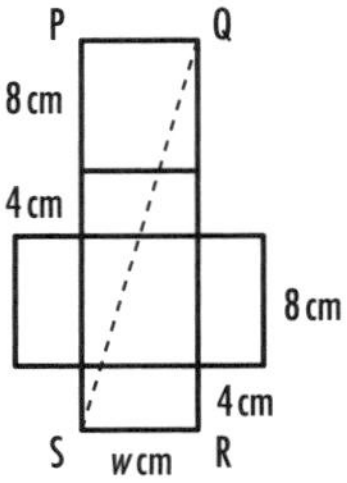

24 A square has diagonals of length 50 cm. Calculate the length of the sides of the square, to the nearest centimetre.

Exercise 43B

In each question find the unknown length in the right-angled triangle. Give your answer to 3 significant figures where necessary.

1 $h = 5$ m, $b = 3$ m
2 $a = 32$ cm, $h = 40$ cm
3 $h = 13$ cm, $a = 10$ cm
4 $a = 4$ m, $h = 6$ m
5 $h = 24$ mm, $b = 18$ mm
6 $a = 4.75$ m, $h = 6.50$ m
7 $h = 350$ mm, $a = 245$ mm

Find the unknown length, marked a, in each of the right-angled triangles.

8

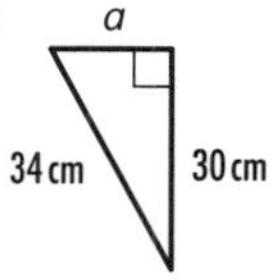

9

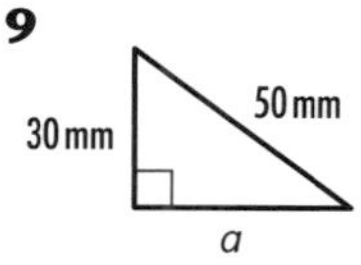

10

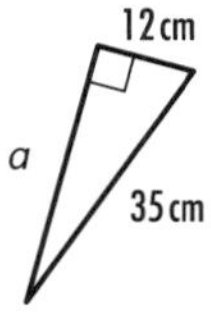

11

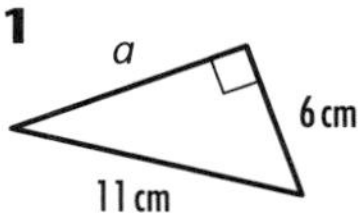

12

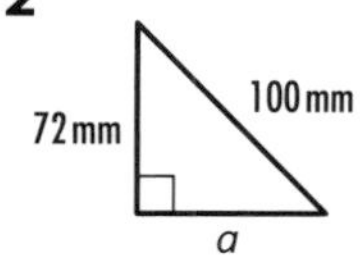

13

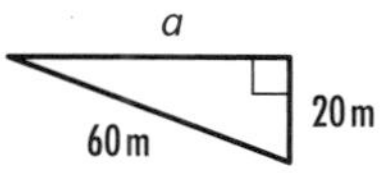

14

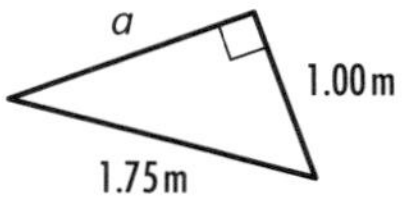

15

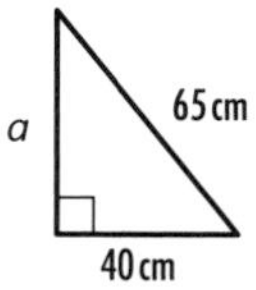

16 A picture frame has a diagonal of length 165 mm and one side of length 95 mm. Calculate the length of the other side (to the nearest millimetre).

17 A rectangle with diagonals of length 85 mm has a height of 60 mm. Calculate the length of the base.

18 A TV screen measures 20 cm in height and has a diagonal of length 35 cm. Calculate the width.

19 A pilot is flying approximately north-east. When he has flown 30 km, he knows that he is 20 km east of his starting point. How far north of his starting point is he?

20 The triangle PRQ in the diagram is an isosceles triangle. Find its height.

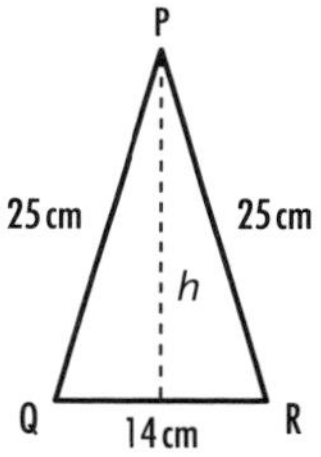

21 Tim is flying a kite on a string of length 50 m. The kite is directly above Sue who is 39 m from Tim. Calculate the height of the kite, to the nearest metre.

22

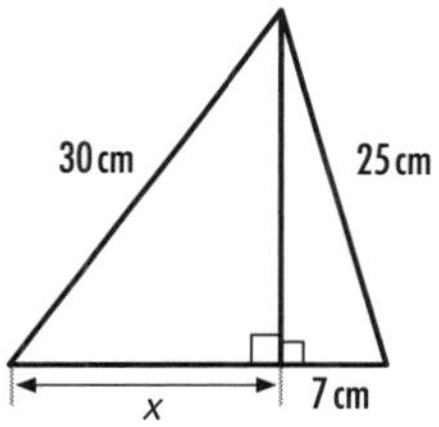

Find the length marked x in the diagram.
Hint: Find the height first.

23 A square has diagonals of length 95 cm. Calculate the length of the sides of the square, to the nearest centimetre.

24 A door-wedge is made by cutting a block of wood in half as shown in the diagram. Calculate the size of the original block of wood ignoring any loss during the cutting process.

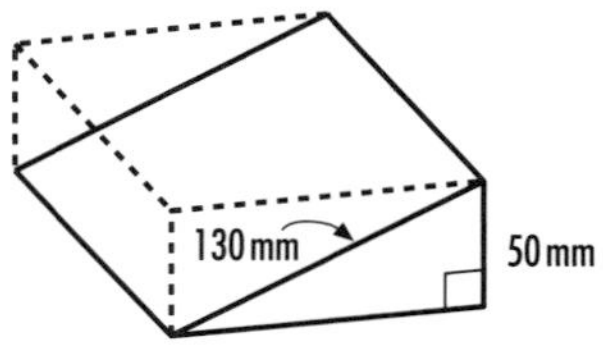

44/ PYTHAGORAS' THEOREM: MIXED EXAMPLES

Pythagoras' theorem is used to find the hypotenuse of a right-angled triangle using the formula:

$$h^2 = a^2 + b^2$$

Note: The squares are added when finding the hypotenuse (the hypotenuse is the longest side). When the hypotenuse is known, the square of one known side is *subtracted* from the square of the hypotenuse. The third side is found using the formula:

$$a^2 = h^2 - b^2$$

EXAMPLE

► Find the length of x and y in the diagram.

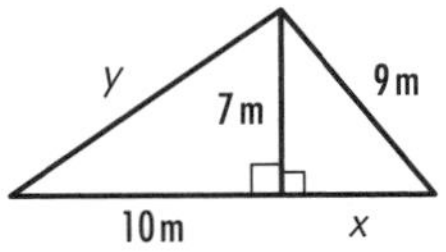

The length of x is found using subtraction since the hypotenuse is already known to be 9 m.

$x^2 = 9^2 - 7^2 = 81 - 49 = 32$

$x = \sqrt{32} = 5.66$ m (to 3 s.f.)

As y is the hypotenuse of the triangle, use the formula $h^2 = a^2 + b^2$.

$y^2 = 7^2 + 10^2 = 49 + 100 = 149$

$y = \sqrt{149} = 12.2$ m (to 3 s.f.)

In a right-angled triangle $h^2 = a^2 + b^2$. If a triangle has sides of length p, q and r and calculation shows that $p^2 = q^2 + r^2$, the triangle must be a right-angled triangle and p must be the hypotenuse.

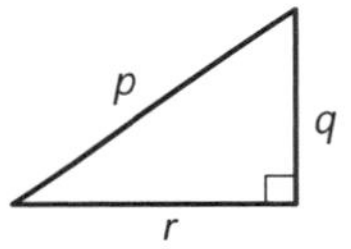

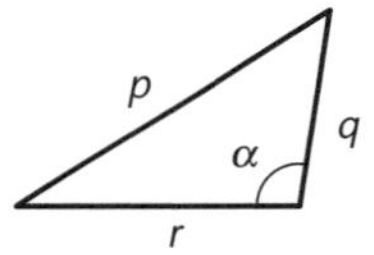

If $p^2 > q^2 + r^2$ then the triangle is NOT a right-angled triangle and the angle α is greater than a right angle (an obtuse angle).

If $p^2 < q^2 + r^2$ then the triangle is NOT a right-angled triangle and the angle β is less than a right angle (an acute angle).

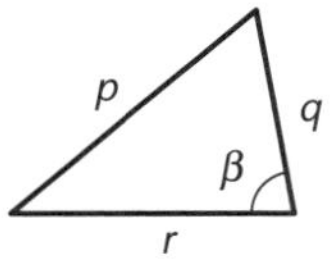

EXAMPLE

► Is angle STU a right angle?

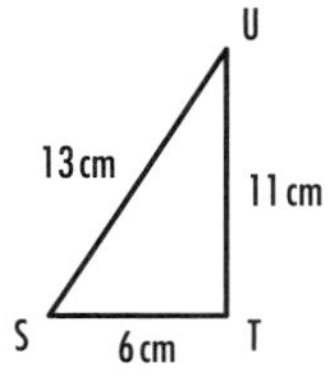

The side SU is the hypotenuse if angle STU is 90°.

$SU^2 = 13^2 = 169$

$ST^2 + TU^2 = 6^2 + 11^2 = 36 + 121 = 157$

$SU^2 \neq ST^2 + TU^2$ (Note: $\neq$ means 'is not equal to'.)

Angle STU $\neq 90°$

In fact $SU^2 > ST^2 + TU^2$ which means that angle STU is obtuse.

Exercise 44A

In each question find the unknown length in the right-angled triangle. Give your answer to 3 significant figures where necessary.

1
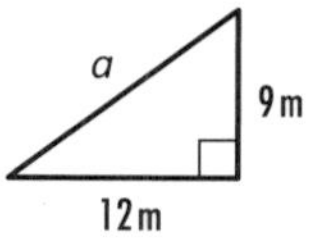

2
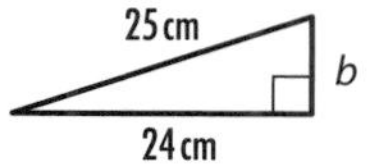

3
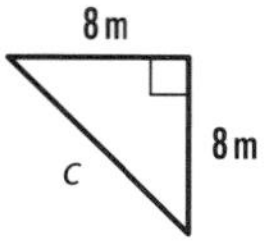

4
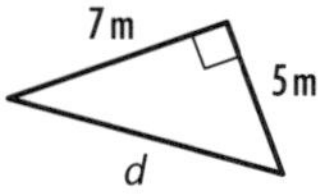

5
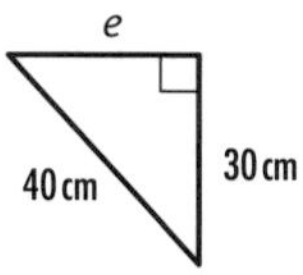

6
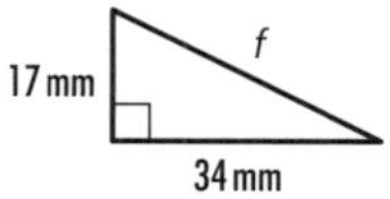

7
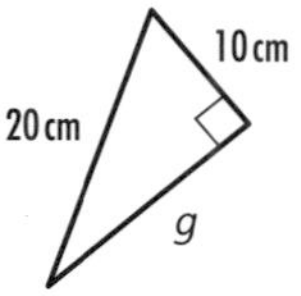

8
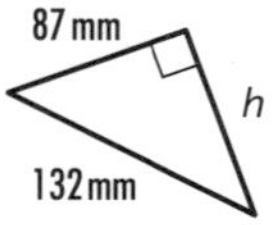

9
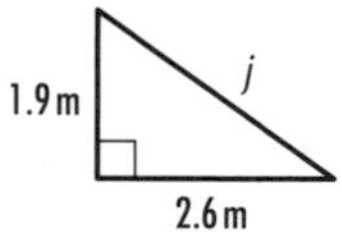

10
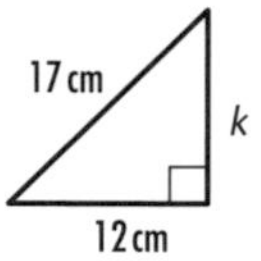

The following questions refer to the right-angled triangle PQR shown in the diagram.

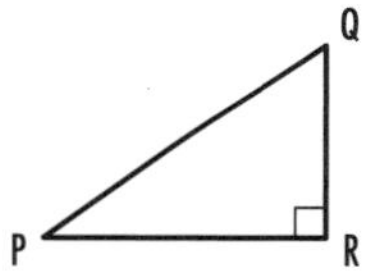

11 PQ = 45 mm, PR = 32 mm; calculate QR.
12 QR = 12 m, PR = 17 m; calculate PQ.
13 PR = 27 cm, PQ = 34 cm; calculate QR.
14 PQ = 8.5 cm, PR = 6.5 cm; calculate QR.
15 QR = 25 mm, PR = 23 mm; calculate PQ.
16 PQ = 100 mm, PR = 75 mm; calculate QR.
17 PQ = 3.25 m, QR = 3.15 m; calculate PR.
18 PR = 165 mm; QR = 207 mm; calculate PQ.

State whether the marked angle in each diagram is acute, obtuse or a right angle. Show your working.

19
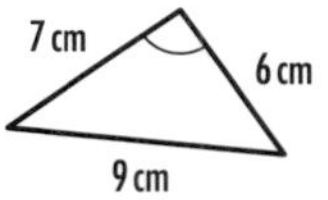

20
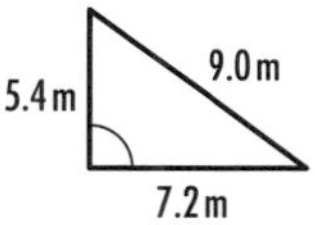

21
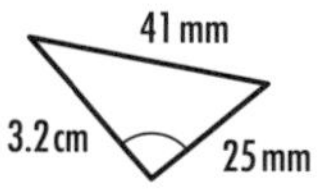

22
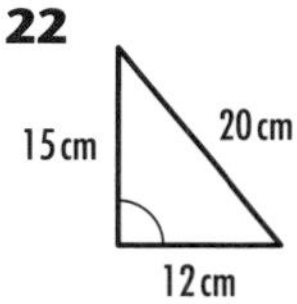

23
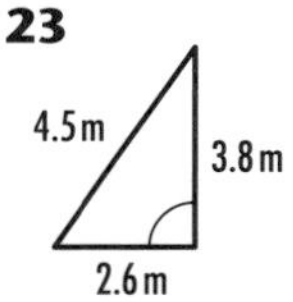

24
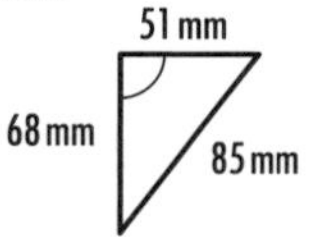

Exercise 44B

In each question find the unknown length in the right-angled triangle. Give your answer to 3 significant figures where necessary.

1
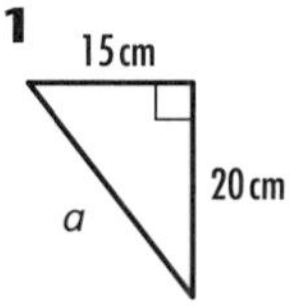

2
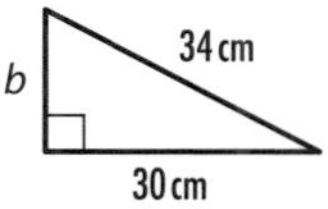

3
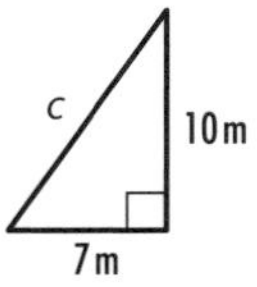

4
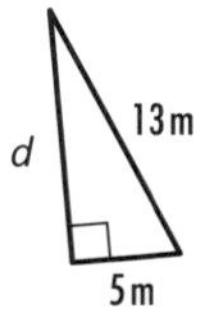

5
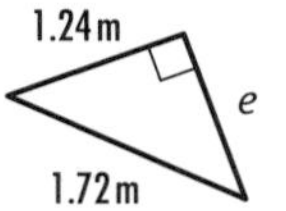

6
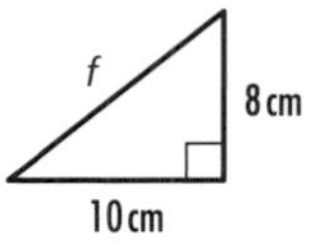

7
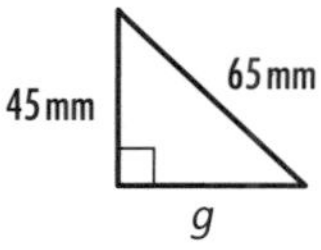

8
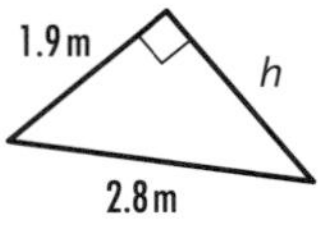

9
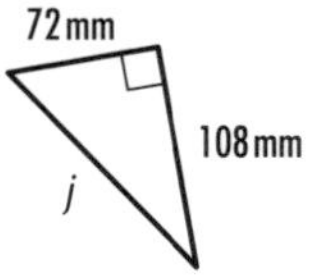

10
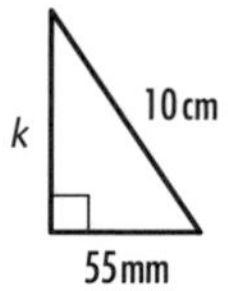

The following questions refer to the right-angled triangle STU shown in the diagram.

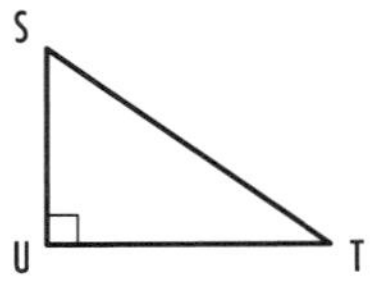

11 ST = 59 cm, TU = 39 cm; calculate SU.
12 ST = 10 cm, SU = 9 cm; calculate TU.
13 SU = 17 m, TU = 11 m; calculate ST.
14 ST = 44 cm, SU = 19 cm; calculate TU.
15 SU = 4.8 m, TU = 3.2 m; calculate ST.
16 TU = 72 mm, ST = 95 mm; calculate SU.
17 ST = 0.82 m, SU = 0.25 m; calculate TU.
18 SU = 48 cm, TU = 20 cm; calculate ST.

State whether the marked angle in each diagram is acute, obtuse or a right angle. Show your working.

19
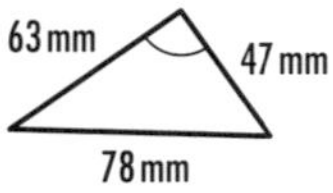

20
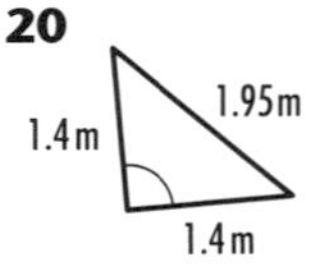

21
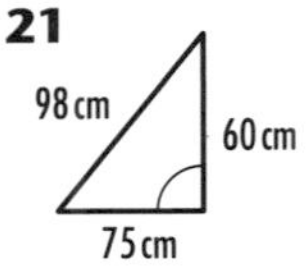

22
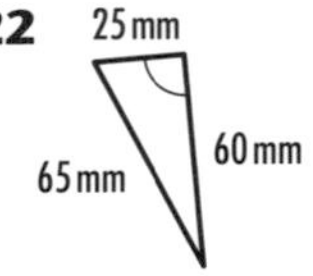

23
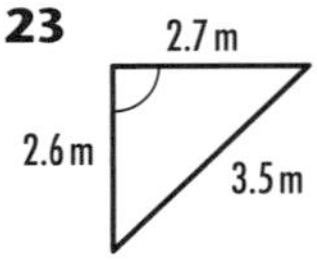

24
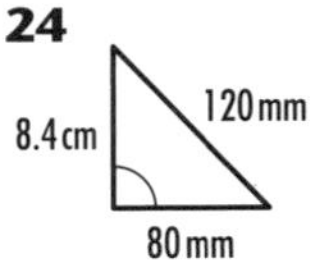

Exercise 44C

1 A rectangle measures 23 cm × 32 cm. Calculate the length of a diagonal.

2 Calculate the length of the diagonal of a 6-cm square.

3 A rectangle measures 55 mm × 45 mm. Calculate the length of a diagonal.

4 Calculate the lengths x and y in the diagram.

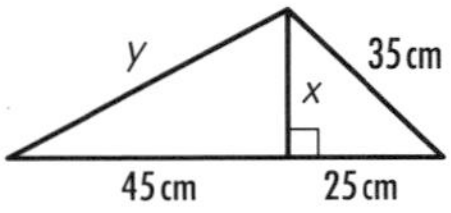

5 A rectangle has diagonals of length 18 cm and a side of length 11 cm. Calculate the length of the other side.

6 An angle in a semicircle as shown in the diagram is a right angle. If the diameter of the circle is 10 cm, calculate the length of the other side of the triangle.

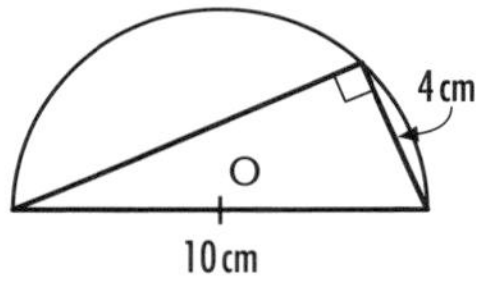

7

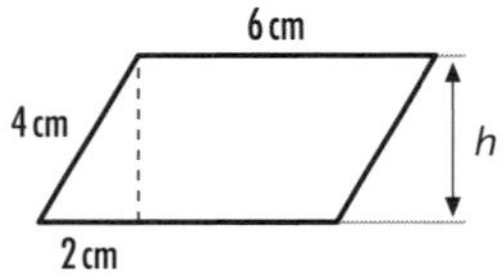

The diagram shows a parallelogram with sides of length 4 cm and 6 cm. Calculate the height, h.

8 Calculate the height, h, of the isosceles triangle shown in the diagram.

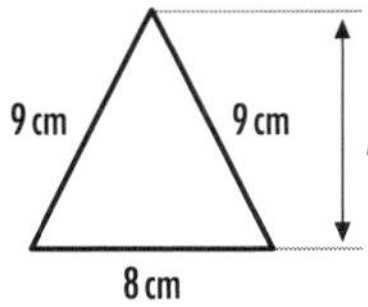

9 The distance between the points (0, 0) and (0, 1) on a graph is 2 cm. Calculate the distance between the points (0, 0) and (6, 8).

10 A driver in a car rally across a desert drives for 6 km in a straight line, which is approximately in the direction south-east. She knows that she is now 4 km south of her starting point. How far has she travelled east, to the nearest 0.1 km?

11 Calculate the length of the sides of a square that has a diagonal measuring 45 cm.

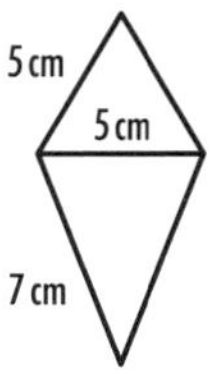

12 The diagram shows a kite with sides of length 5 cm and 7 cm. If one of its diagonals is 5 cm, calculate the length of the other diagonal.

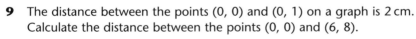

13 The distance between the points (0, 0) and (1, 0) on a graph is 2 cm. The distance between the points (0, 0) and (5, p) is known to be 26 cm. State the two possible values of p.

14 A rhombus has diagonals of length 12 cm and 16 cm. Calculate the length of each side.

15 The foot of a ladder is placed on horizontal ground at a distance of 1.5 metres from a vertical wall. Paul needs to reach a point 6 metres high on the wall. Calculate the length of the shortest ladder that he will need to buy if ladders are sold in lengths which are multiples of 1 metre.

Exercise 44D

1 Calculate the length of the diagonal of a 1-metre square.

2 A rectangular room measures 3.5 m by 3.6 m. Calculate the length of the diagonal.

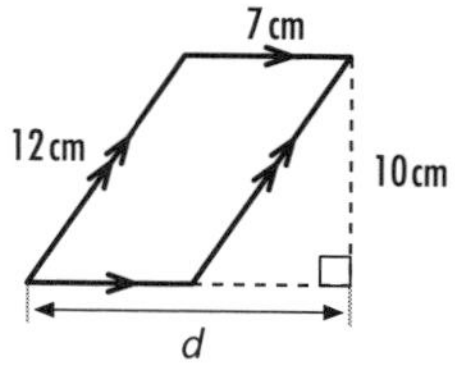

3 The diagram shows a parallelogram of height 10 cm and sides of length 7 cm and 12 cm. Calculate the distance *d*.

4 Calculate the shortest width (to the nearest centimetre) required for a rectangular piece of card of height 30 cm to have a diagonal greater than 45 cm.

5 A ship sails in a straight line in a direction that is approximately north-west. When it has sailed 11 nautical miles, it is 5 nautical miles west of its starting point. How far north of its starting point is it (to the nearest 0.1 nautical mile)?

6 Calculate the lengths *p* and *q* in the diagram.

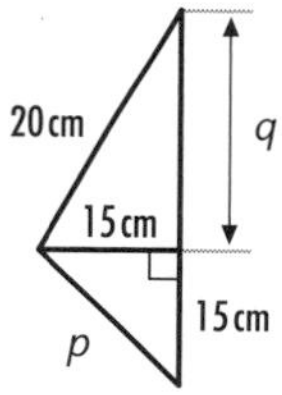

7 A rectangle has diagonals of length 100 mm and a side of length 64 mm.
Calculate the length of the other side.

8 Calculate the length of the sides of a square that has a diagonal measuring 150 mm.

9 The distance between the points (1, 1) and (1, 2) on a graph is 1 cm. Calculate the distance between the points (1, 1) and (6, 6).

10 Calculate the height, *h*, of the isosceles triangle shown in the diagram.

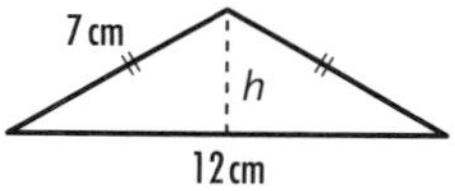

11 A rhombus of side length 70 mm has one diagonal of length 70 mm. Calculate the length of the other diagonal.

12 The distance between the points (0, 0) and (0, 1) on a graph is 1 cm. The distance between the points (0, 0) and (*k*, 6) is known to be $\sqrt{45}$ cm. State the two possible values of *k*.

13 The diagram shows two triangles each of which has a side that is also the side of a square.
Calculate the lengths *a* and *b*.

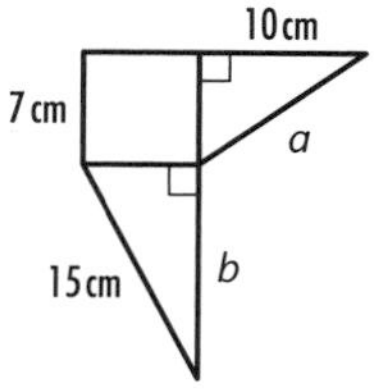

14 What is the greatest height that a ladder of length 7 metres can reach up a vertical wall if the foot of the ladder is placed 2 metres away from the wall on horizontal ground?

15

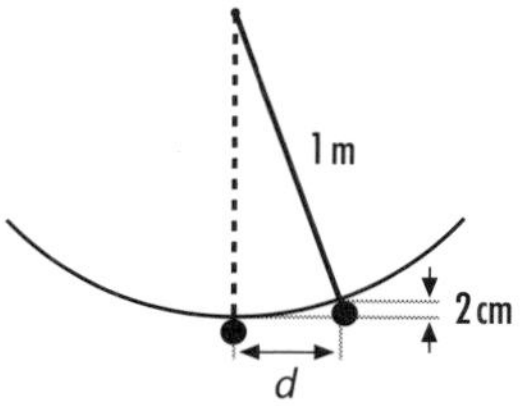

The simple pendulum shown in the diagram has a string of length 1 metre. Calculate the distance, *d*, to the nearest centimetre, when the 'bob' is 2 cm above its starting point.

45/ SIMILARITY (1)

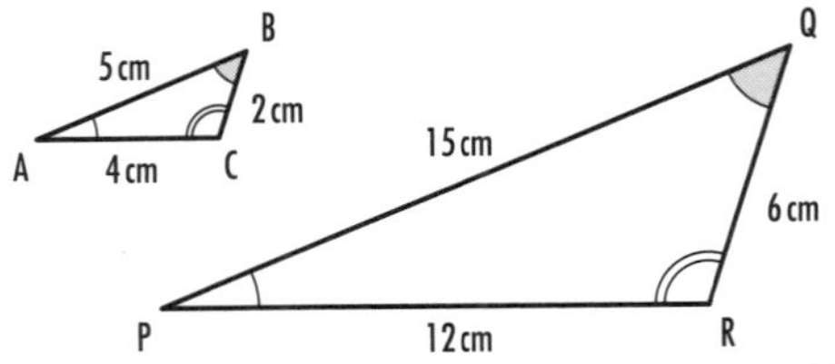

The diagram shows two **similar triangles**, ABC and PQR, drawn to the same scale. They are similar because they have exactly the *same shape* although the sizes are different.
It can be seen that:

- the corresponding angles are the same
- the corresponding sides are in a constant ratio, 1 : 3
- $\frac{AB}{PQ} = \frac{BC}{QR} = \frac{AC}{PR} = \frac{1}{3}$

PQR is an enlargement of ABC with a scale factor of 3.

EXAMPLE

▶ Are the triangles ABC and PQR similar?

(a) In triangle ABC, AB = 3 cm, BC = 4.5 cm and AC = 5 cm. In triangle PQR, PQ = 9 cm, QR = 13 cm and PR = 15 cm.

(b) In triangle ABC, angle A = 47°, angle B = 65°. In triangle PQR, angle Q = 65°, angle R = 68°.

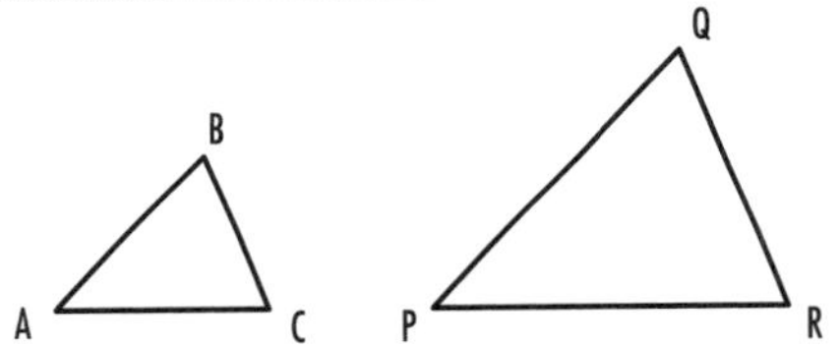

(a) AB : PQ = AC : PR = 1 : 3 but BC : QR does not equal 1 : 3 because 4.5 cm × 3 = 13.5 cm.
Therefore, triangles ABC and PQR are *not* similar.

(b) Angle C = 68° (sum of angles of a triangle = 180°) and angle P = 47°.
Therefore, triangles ABC and PQR *are* similar because corresponding angles are equal.

EXAMPLE

▶ The two triangles have equal angles as marked.

(a) State the ratio of the lengths of corresponding sides.

(b) Calculate the lengths a and b

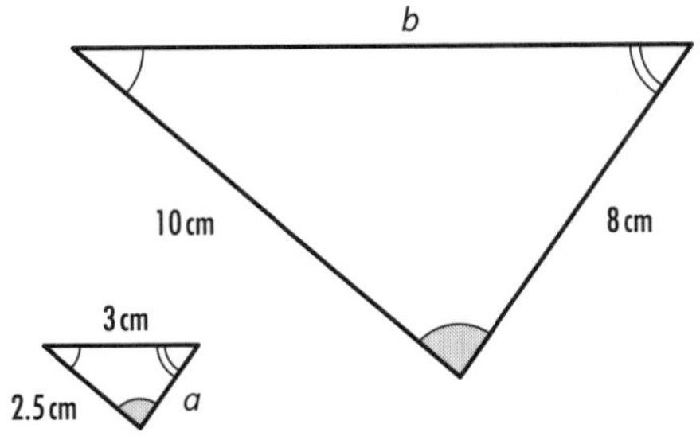

(a) Ratio = 2.5 cm : 10 cm = 1 : 4

(b) $\frac{a}{8} = \frac{1}{4}$ $\qquad a = 2$ cm

$\frac{3}{b} = \frac{1}{4}$ $\qquad b = 12$ cm

Exercise 45A

In questions 1–6, state whether the two triangles are similar. *If they are similar,* calculate the lengths marked x and y.

1

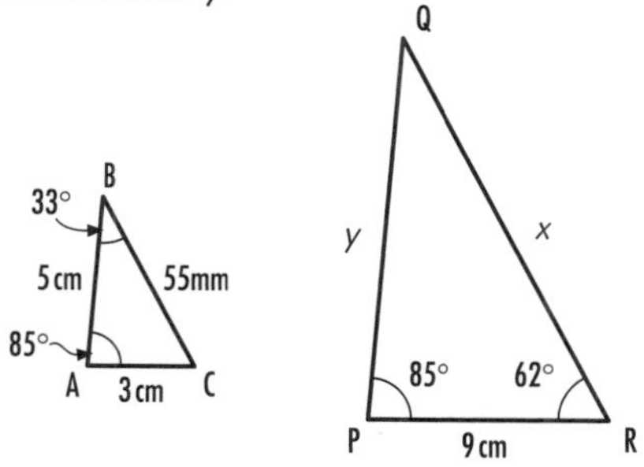

2

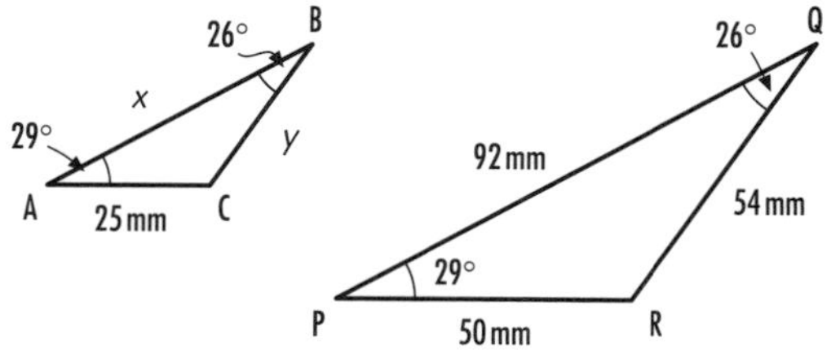

3

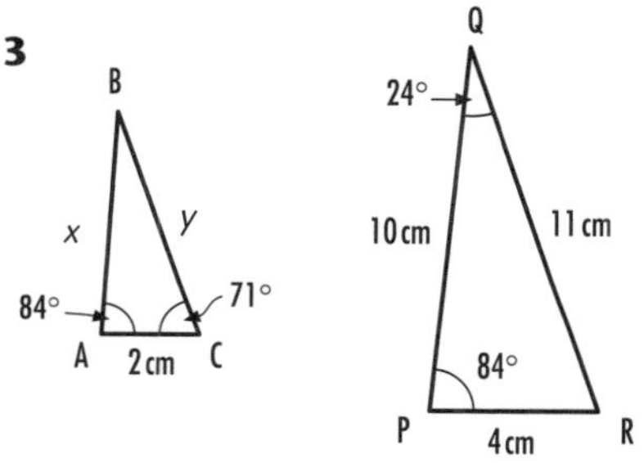

4

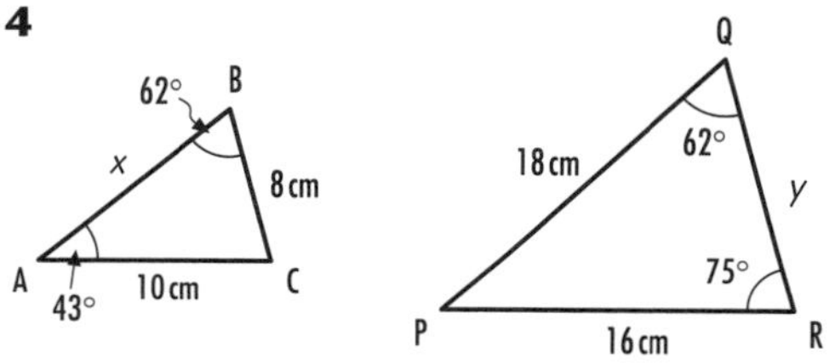

5

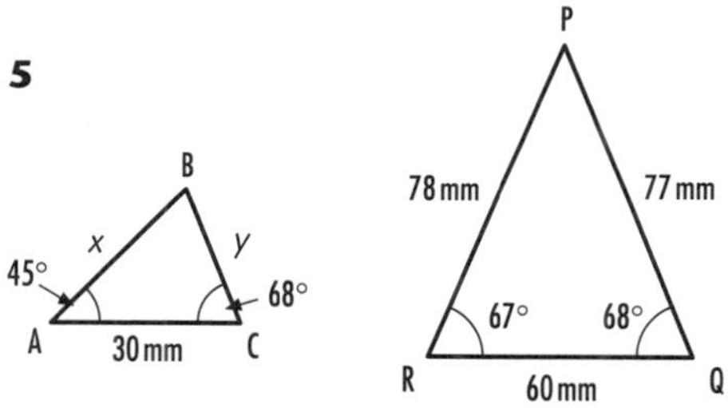

6

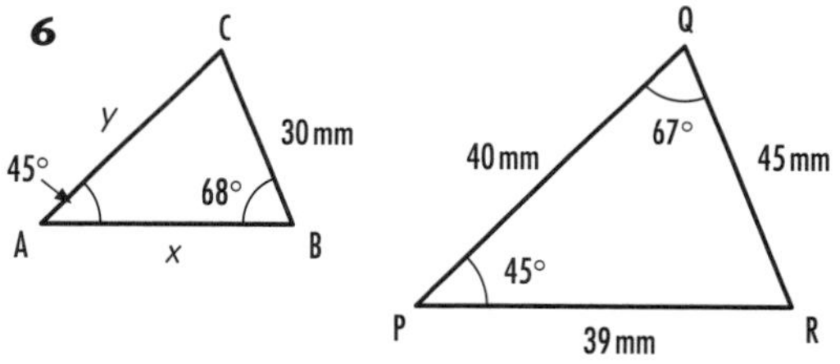

In questions 7–12, state whether triangles ABC and PQR are similar by considering the information given in each question. You are advised to draw the diagram in each case and write in the values given.

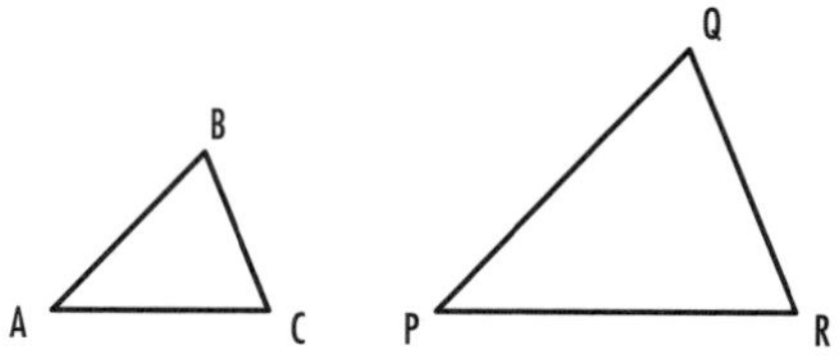

7 In triangle ABC, angle B = 25° and angle C = 50°.
In triangle PQR, angle P = 50° and angle Q = 105°.

8 In triangle ABC, AB = 3.5 cm, BC = 2.5 cm and AC = 5.5 cm.
In triangle PQR, PQ = 7 cm , QR = 5 cm and PR = 11 cm.

9 In triangle ABC, angle A = 63° and angle C = 78°.
In triangle PQR, angle Q = 63° and angle R = 49°.

10 In triangle ABC, AB = 49 mm, BC = 95 mm and AC = 65 mm.
In triangle PQR, PQ = 147 mm, QR = 275 mm and PR = 195 mm.

11 In triangle ABC, angle A = 71° and angle B = 74°.
In triangle PQR, angle P = 25° and angle R = 74°.

12 In triangle ABC, AB = 8 cm, BC = 6 cm and AC = 6 cm.
In triangle PQR, PQ = 12 cm, QR = 12 cm and PR = 16 cm.

In questions 13–18, triangles ABC and PQR in each diagram are similar, with angle A = angle P, angle B = angle Q and angle C = angle R.

13 AB = 5 cm, PQ = 10 cm, BC = 6 cm and AC = 7 cm. Calculate PR and QR.

14 AB = 45 mm, PQ = 90 mm, BC = 34 mm and AC = 58 mm. Calculate PR and QR.

15 PQ = 80 mm, PR = 64 mm, BC = 72 mm and QR = 36 mm. Calculate AB and AC.

16 AB = 18 cm, QR = 28 cm, BC = 21 cm and AC = 24 cm. Calculate PR and PQ.

17 PR = 54 mm, PQ = 42 mm, AC = 162 mm and QR = 25 mm. Calculate AB and BC.

18 BC = 2.5 cm, AC = 3.2 cm, AB = 4.2 cm and QR = 75 mm. Calculate PR and PQ.

Exercise 45B

In questions 1–6, state whether the two triangles are similar. *If they are similar*, calculate the lengths marked x and y.

1

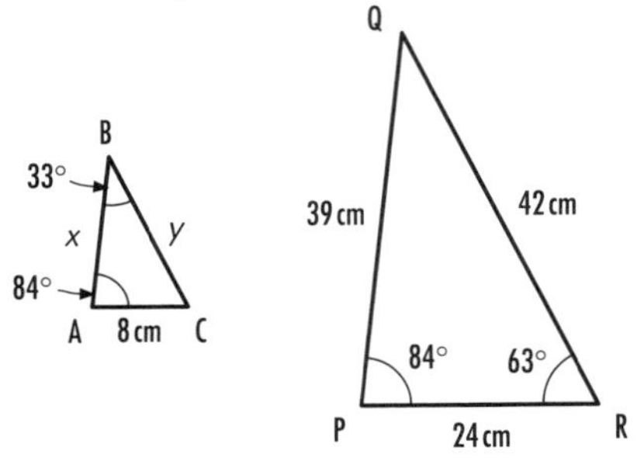

2

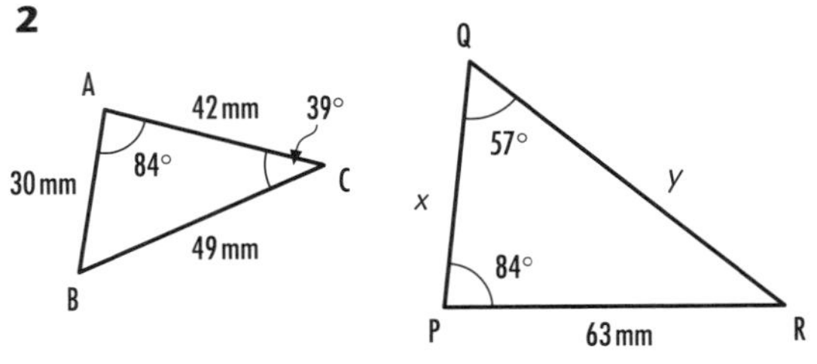

3

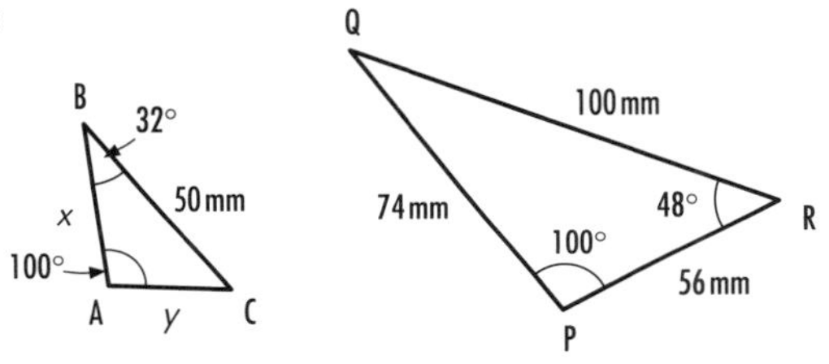

4

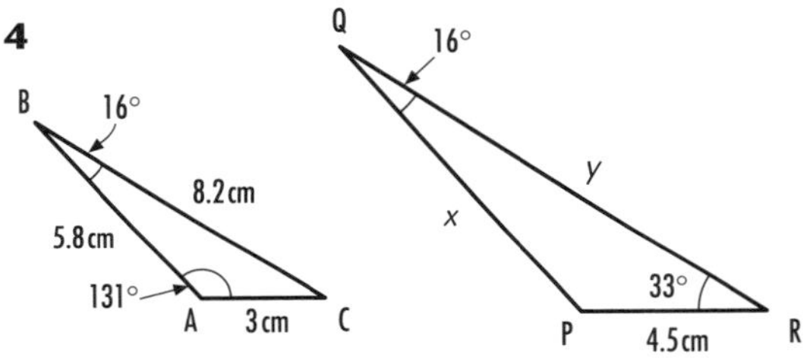

5

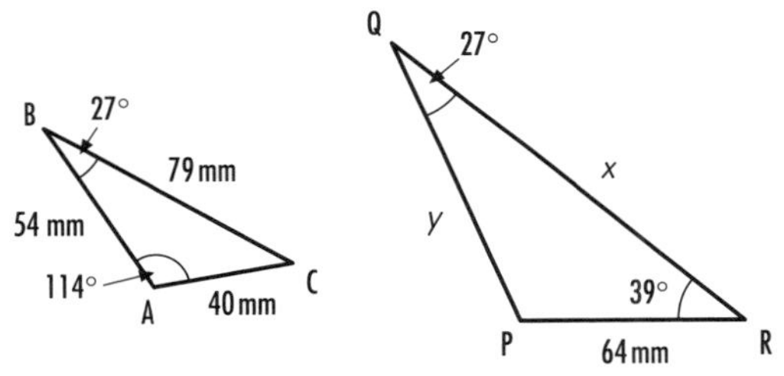

6

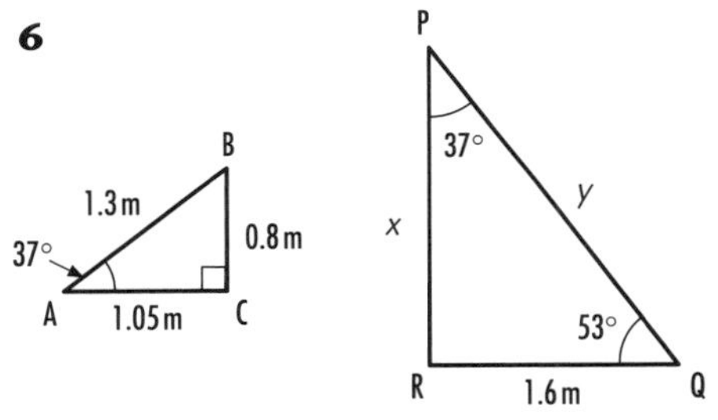

In questions 7–12, state whether triangles ABC and PQR are similar by considering the information given in each question. You are advised to draw the diagram in each case and write in the values given.

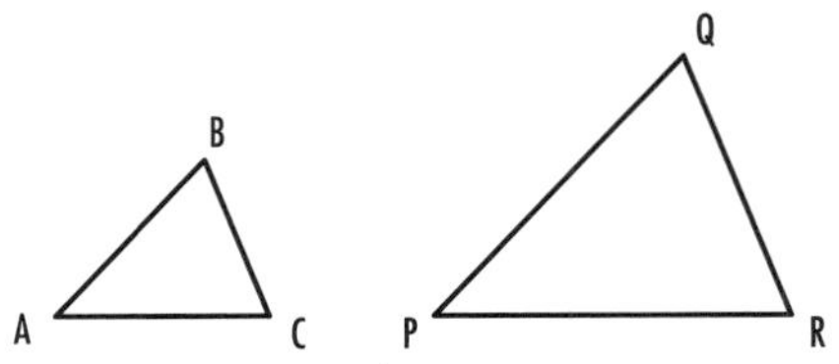

7 In triangle ABC, AB = 13 cm, BC = 15 cm and AC = 12 cm.
In triangle PQR, PQ = 65 mm, QR = 75 mm and PR = 6 cm.

8 In triangle ABC, angle C = 82° and angle B = 47°.
In triangle PQR, angle P = 47° and angle Q = 51°.

9 In triangle ABC, AB = 27 cm, BC = 36 cm and AC = 54 cm.
In triangle PQR, PQ = 9 cm, QR = 5 cm and PR = 6 cm.

10 In triangle ABC, angle B = 98° and angle C = 43°.
In triangle PQR, angle Q = 43° and angle R = 29°.

11 In triangle ABC, angle A = 49° and angle B = 61°.
In triangle PQR, angle Q = 49° and angle R = 70°.

12 In triangle ABC, AB = 3 cm, BC = 4 cm and AC = 5 cm.
In triangle PQR, PQ = 12.6 cm, QR = 16.8 cm and PR = 21 cm.

In questions 13–18, triangles ABC and PQR in each diagram are similar with angle A = angle P, angle B = angle Q and angle C = angle R.

13 AC = 7 cm, BC = 4 cm, AB = 6 cm and PQ = 9 cm. Calculate PR and QR.

14 PQ = 9 cm, PR = 15 cm, QR = 12 cm and AC = 10 cm. Calculate AB and BC.

15 AB = 3 cm, BC = 4 cm, AC = 5 cm and QR = 5 cm. Calculate PR and PQ.

16 AC = 36 mm, AB = 48 mm, BC = 30 mm and QR = 20 mm. Calculate PR and PQ.

17 AB = 12 cm, PQ = 6 cm, BC = 10 cm and AC = 9 cm. Calculate PR and QR.

18 AB = 5 cm, QR = 3.25 cm, BC = 6.5 cm and AC = 8 cm. Calculate PR and PQ.

46/ **SIMILARITY (2)**

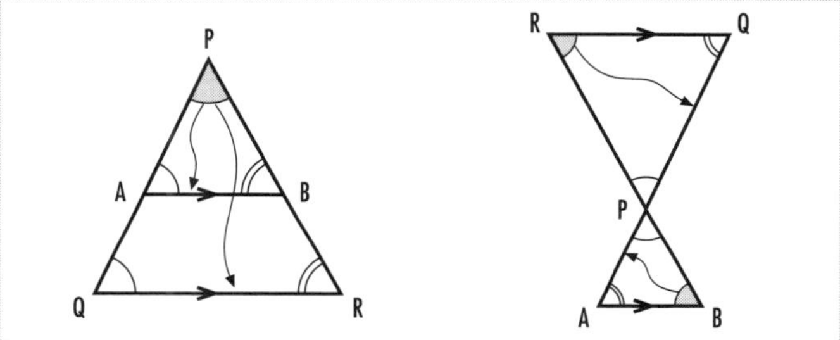

Similar triangles can be hidden within a diagram; look for the angles that are equal.
In both examples, triangle PAB and triangle PQR are similar, and

$$\frac{PA}{PQ} = \frac{PB}{PR} = \frac{AB}{QR}$$

It can be difficult to decide which sides are corresponding. A reliable method is to find two equal angles. Look at the sides *opposite* these equal angles; these sides are corresponding.
For example, in the diagrams, AB and QR are corresponding sides. (The other corresponding sides are AP and PQ, and PB and PR.)

EXAMPLE

▶ In the diagram QR is parallel to ST.

(a) State the side in triangle PST that corresponds to PQ in triangle PQR.

(b) State the ratio between the sides of triangle PQR and triangle PST.

(c) Calculate the lengths (i) ST (ii) PT and (iii) RT.

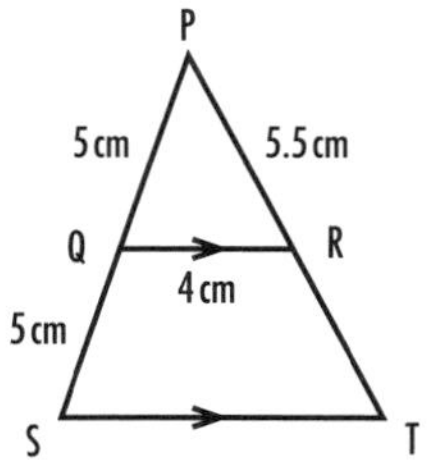

(a) PS corresponds to PQ.

(b) Since PQ corresponds to PS, the ratio is 5 : 10 = 1 : 2.

(c) (i) ST = 4 cm × 2 = 8 cm

(ii) PT = 5.5 cm × 2 = 11 cm

(iii) RT = 11 cm – 5.5 cm = 5.5 cm

EXAMPLE

▶ In the diagram AB is parallel to CD.

(a) State the side in triangle ABO that corresponds to AO in triangle CDO.

(b) State the ratio between the sides of triangle ABO and triangle CDO.

(c) Calculate the lengths (i) CO (ii) CD and (iii) BC.

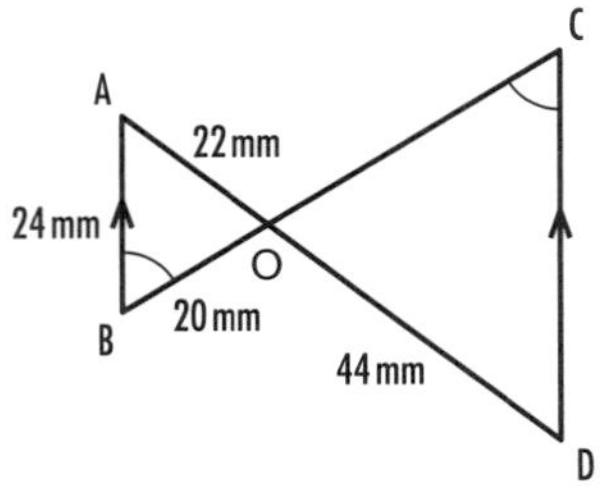

(a) Angle ABO = angle DCO (alternate angles)
AO is opposite angle ABO and DO is opposite angle DCO; so DO corresponds to AO.

(b) AO : DO = 22 : 44 = 1 : 2

(c) (i) CO = 20 mm × 2 = 40 mm
(ii) CD = 24 mm × 2 = 48 mm
(iii) BC = BO + CO = 20 mm + 40 mm = 60 mm

Exercise 46A

In each question:

(a) State the two similar triangles.

(b) State the ratio between the sides of the two similar triangles.

(c) Calculate the lengths stated (to 3 significant figures if necessary).

1 Calculate AE, CE and AD.

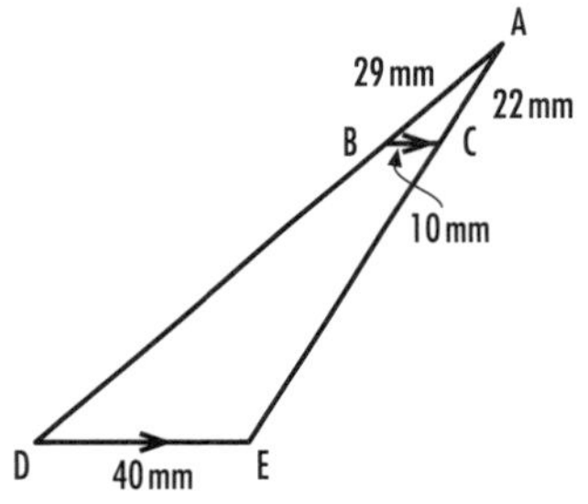

2 Calculate OW, OX and XY.

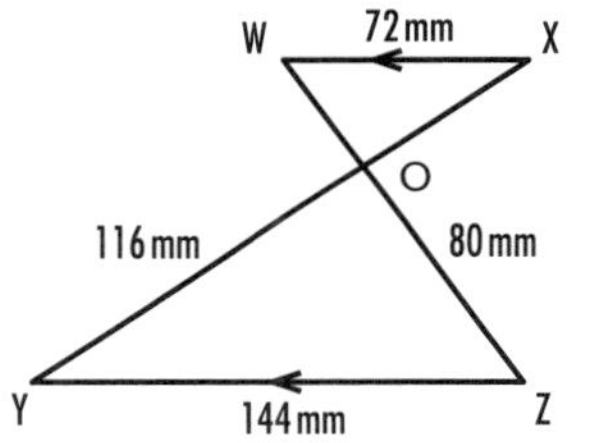

3 Calculate HI, EF and EH.

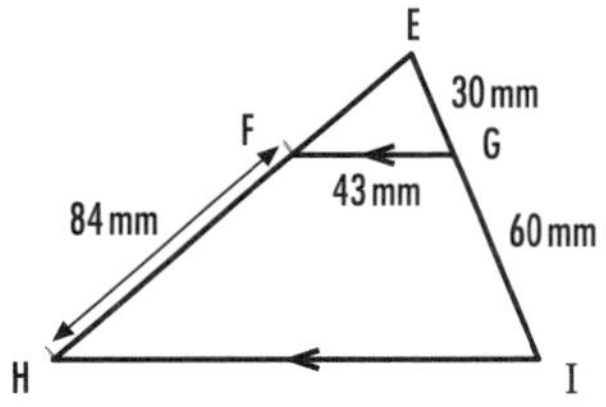

4 Calculate LM, JO and JM.

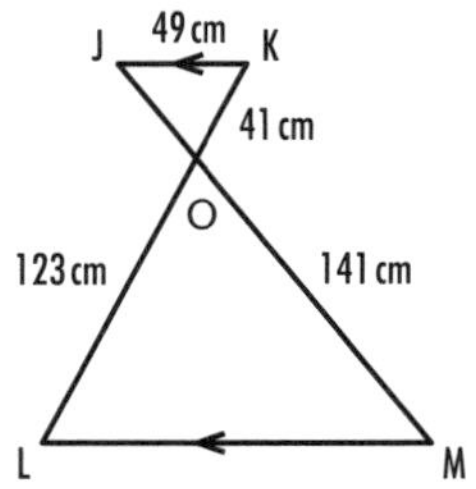

5 Calculate OS, OT and PT.

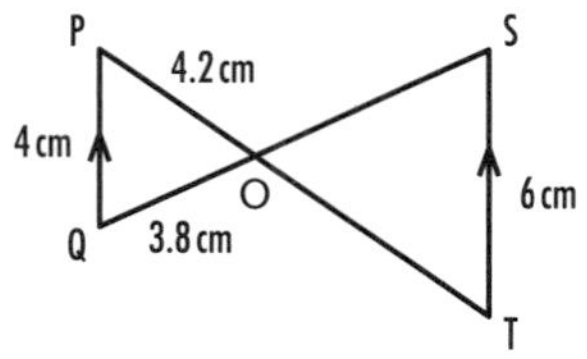

6 Calculate AC, AD and BC.

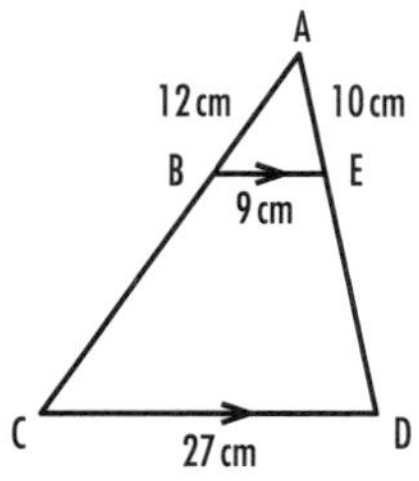

7 Calculate OQ, NP and MQ.

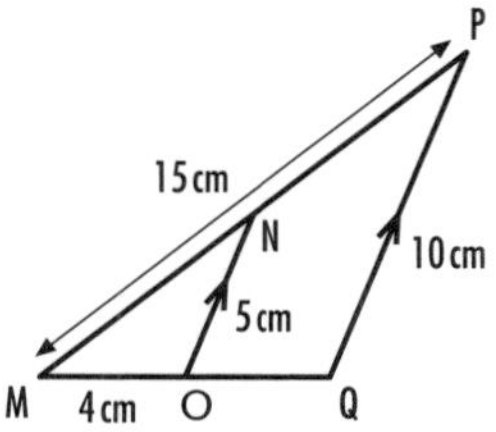

8 Calculate FO, GO and FI.

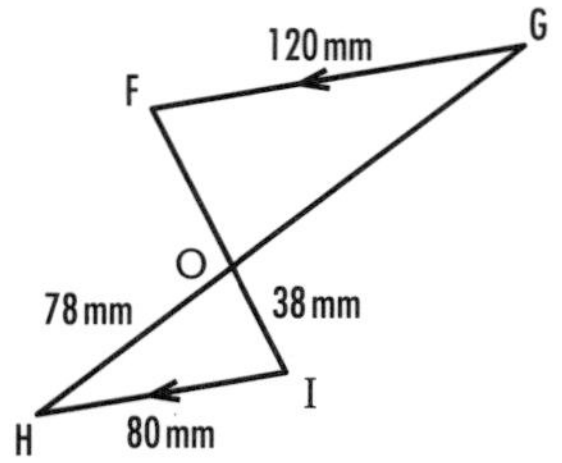

Exercise 46B

In each question:
(a) State the two similar triangles.
(b) State the ratio between the sides of the two similar triangles.
(c) Calculate the lengths stated (to 3 significant figures if necessary).

1 Calculate FI, HI and FJ.

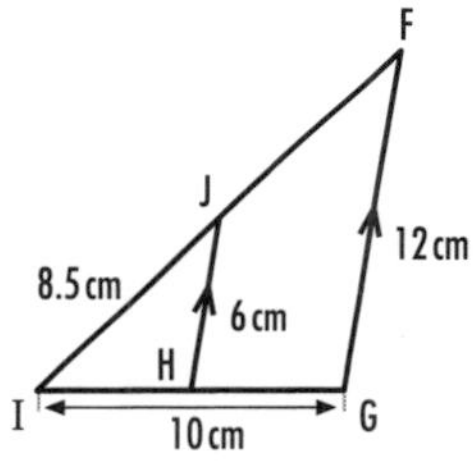

2 Calculate CD, BO and AD.

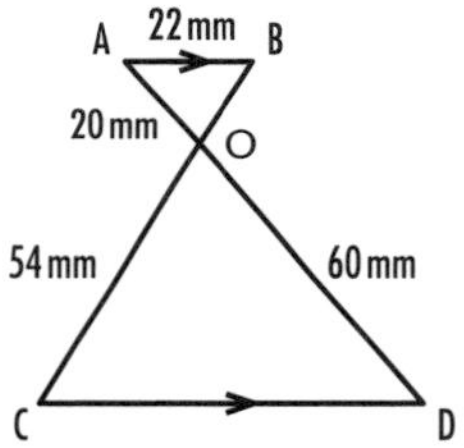

3 Calculate EF, ED and EO.

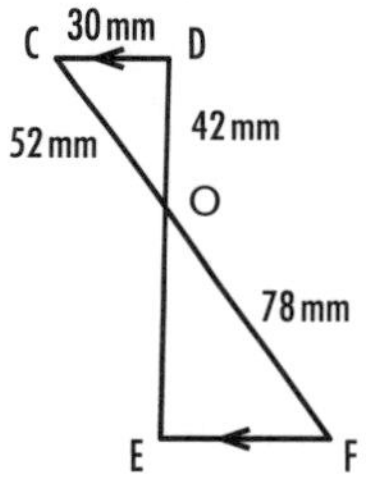

4 Calculate AD, DE and BE.

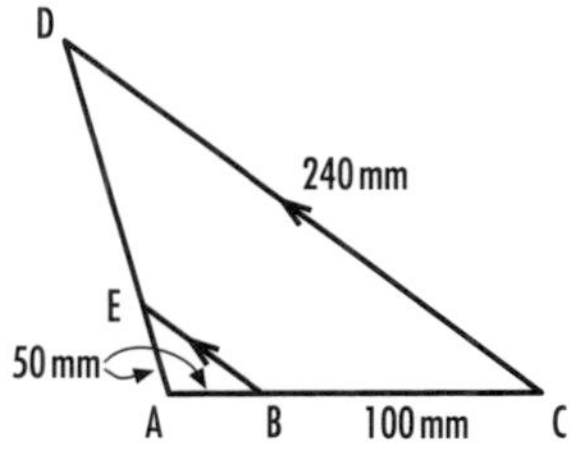

5 Calculate AO, AB and AY.

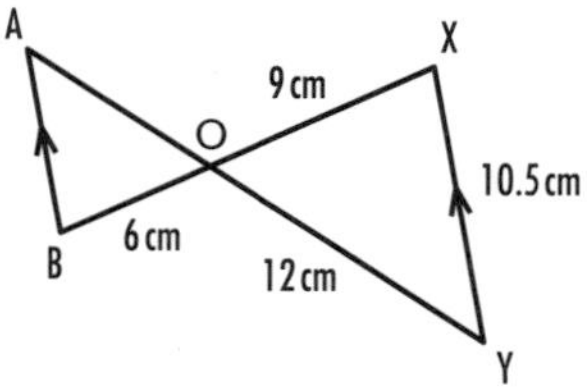

6 Calculate SX, TU and SV.

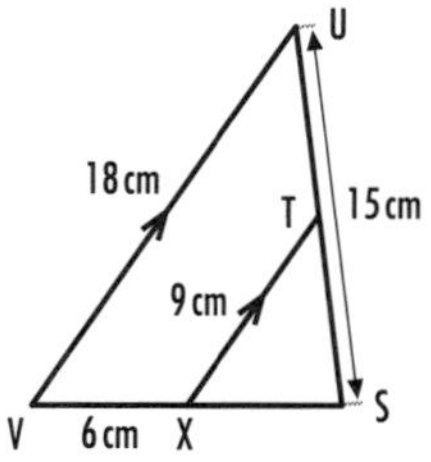

7 Calculate PT, PS and QS.

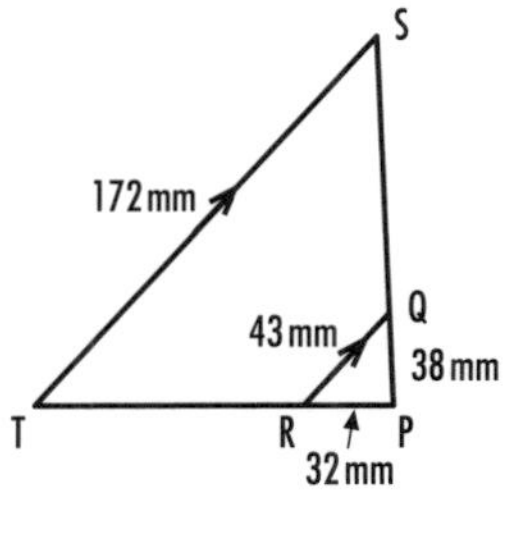

8 Calculate FO, DO and GO.

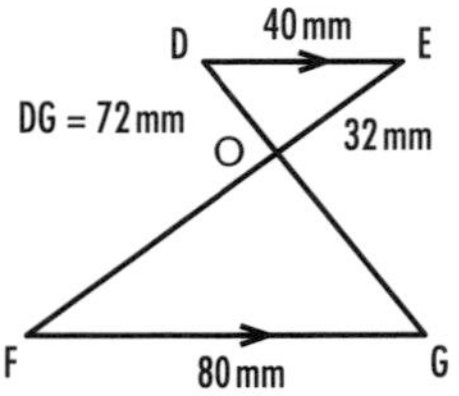

47/ TRIGONOMETRY: NAMING SIDES AND STATING TRIGONOMETRIC RATIOS

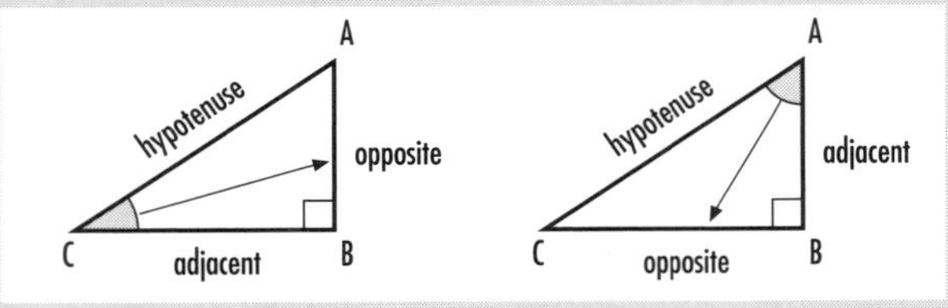

The longest length in a right-angled triangle is the **hypotenuse**.
There are two other sides, the **opposite** and the **adjacent**.
The naming of these depends upon which angle is involved.
The opposite is the side opposite the angle involved.
The adjacent is the side next to the angle involved (but not the hypotenuse).

Sin *A* means the **sine** of the angle *A*. $\text{Sin } A = \dfrac{\text{opposite}}{\text{hypotenuse}}$

Cos *A* means the **cosine** of the angle *A*. $\text{Cos } A = \dfrac{\text{adjacent}}{\text{hypotenuse}}$

Tan *A* means the **tangent** of the angle *A*. $\text{Tan } A = \dfrac{\text{opposite}}{\text{adjacent}}$

EXAMPLE

► State the three trigonometric ratios (as ratios of the sides involved) for each of the angles *C* and *A* shown in the diagram.

The first task is to write opp, adj and hyp on the diagram. This is done already.

$\text{Sin } C = \dfrac{\text{opp}}{\text{hyp}} = \dfrac{AB}{AC}$ $\text{Cos } C = \dfrac{\text{adj}}{\text{hyp}} = \dfrac{BC}{AC}$ $\text{Tan } C = \dfrac{\text{opp}}{\text{adj}} = \dfrac{AB}{BC}$

$\text{Sin } A = \dfrac{\text{opp}}{\text{hyp}} = \dfrac{BC}{AC}$ $\text{Cos } A = \dfrac{\text{adj}}{\text{hyp}} = \dfrac{AB}{AC}$ $\text{Tan } A = \dfrac{\text{opp}}{\text{adj}} = \dfrac{BC}{AB}$

EXAMPLE

► State the three trigonometric ratios for each of the two angles in the triangle that are not right angles.

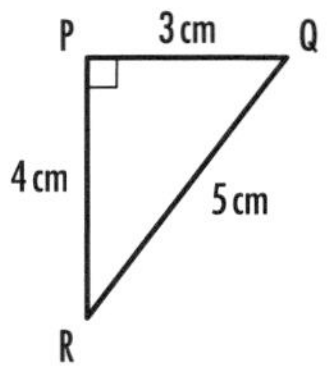

The first task is to write on opp, adj and hyp for each of the angles.

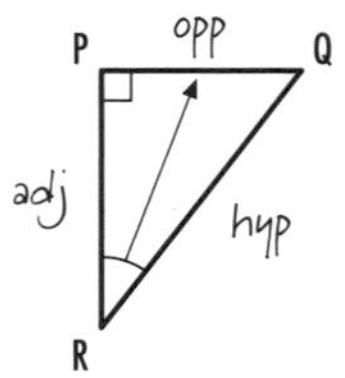

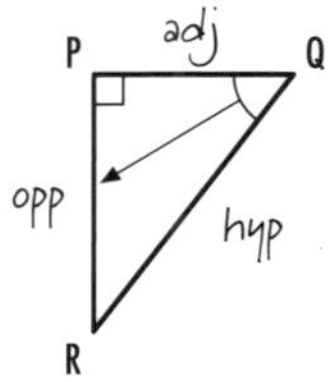

$\text{Sin } R = \frac{3}{5}$ $\text{Cos } R = \frac{4}{5}$ $\text{Tan } R = \frac{3}{4}$

$\text{Sin } Q = \frac{4}{5}$ $\text{Cos } Q = \frac{3}{5}$ $\text{Tan } Q = \frac{4}{3}$

EXAMPLE

► (a) Name the trigonometric ratio involving the marked lengths for each of the angles X and Y.
(b) Calculate the value of the ratios to 3 significant figures.

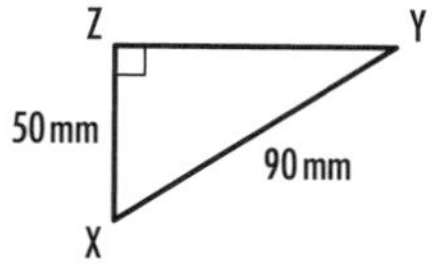

(a) For the angle X, adjacent = 50 mm and hypotenuse = 90 mm.

So, $\cos X = \frac{5}{9}$

For the angle Y, opposite = 50 mm and hypotenuse = 90 mm.

So, $\sin Y = \frac{5}{9}$

(b) $\text{Cos } X = \frac{5}{9} = 0.556$ (to 3 s.f.)

$\text{Sin } Y = \frac{5}{9} = 0.556$ (to 3 s.f.)

Exercise 47A

In each of the diagrams, state the three trigonometric ratios (as ratios of the sides involved) for each of the angles (except the right angle).

1

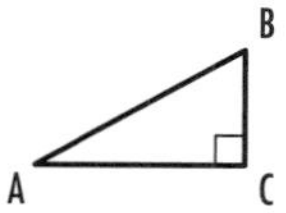

2

3

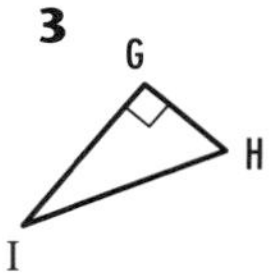

4

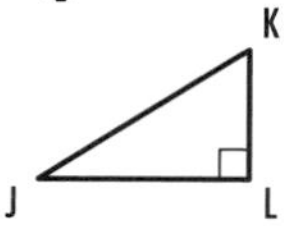

5

6

In each triangle, state the three trigonometric ratios for each of the two angles that are not right angles.

7

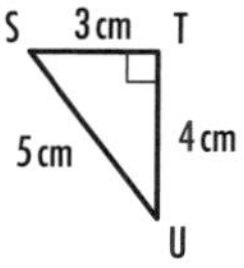

8

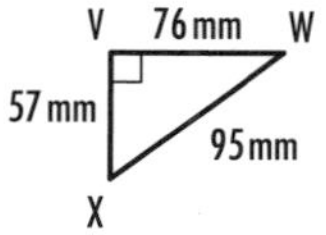

9

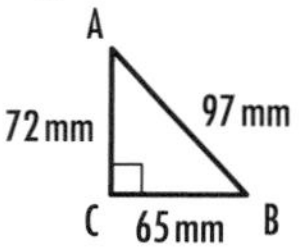

10

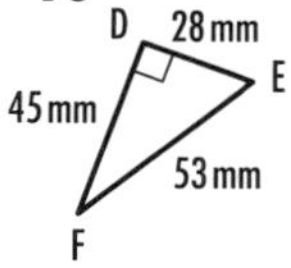

11

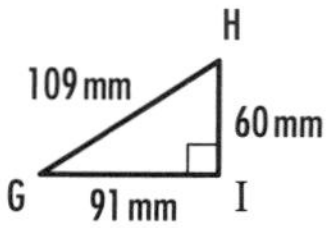

12

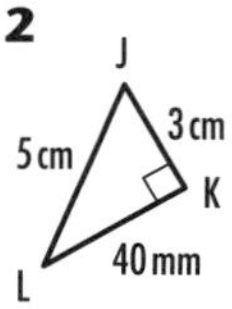

In each of the following questions:
(a) Name the trigonometric ratio involving the marked lengths for each of the angles.
(b) Calculate the value of each ratio (to 3 significant figures if necessary).

13

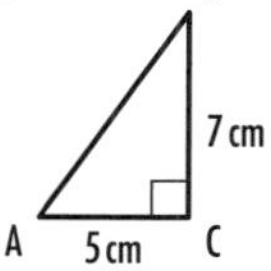

14

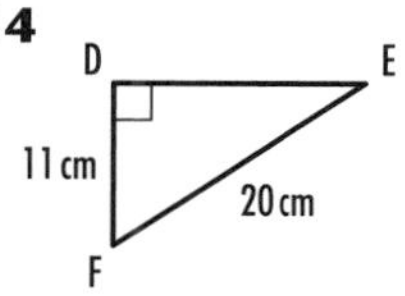

15

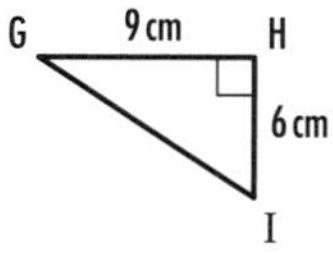

16

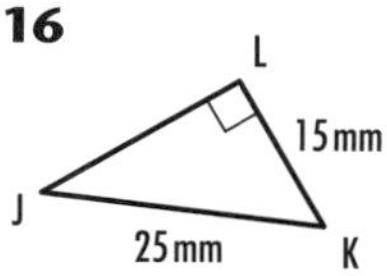

17

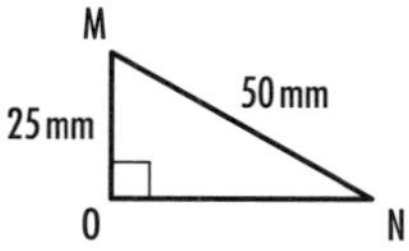

18

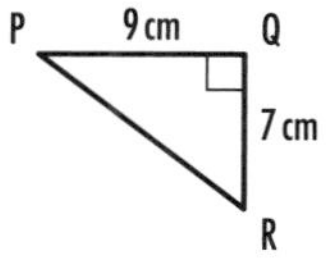

19

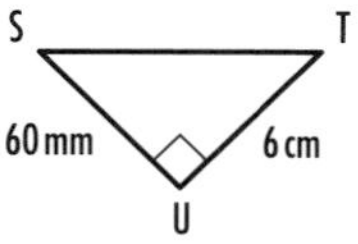

20

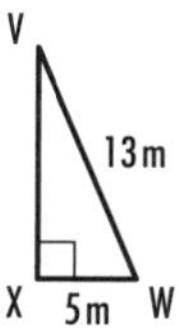

Exercise 47B

In each of the diagrams, state the three trigonometric ratios (as ratios of the sides involved) for each of the angles (except the right angle).

1

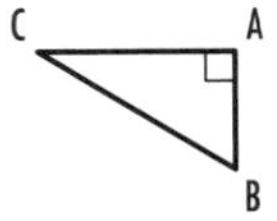

2

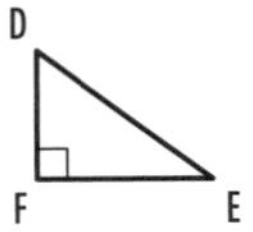

3

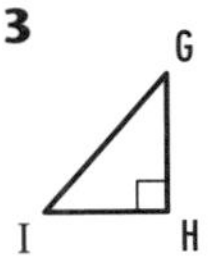

4

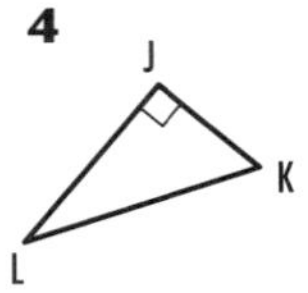

5

6

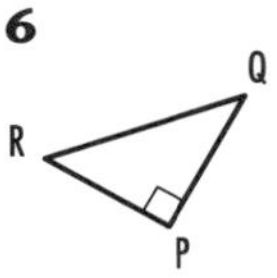

In each triangle, state the three trigonometric ratios for each of the two angles that are not right angles.

7

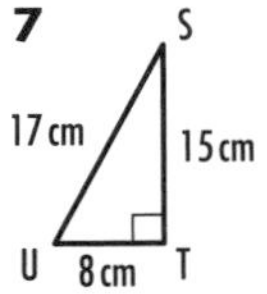

8

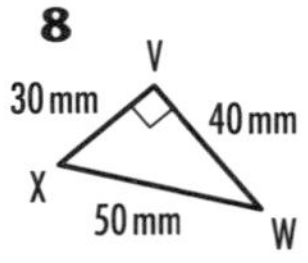

9

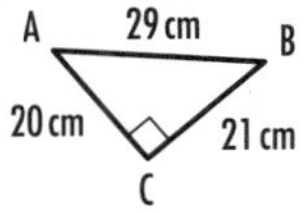

10

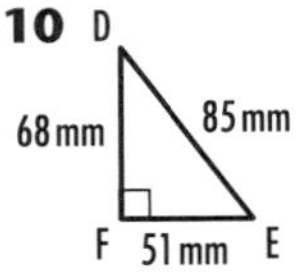

11

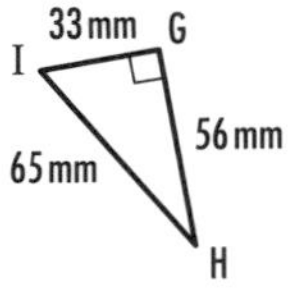

12

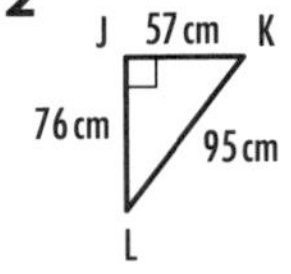

In each of the following questions:

(a) Name the trigonometric ratio involving the marked lengths for each of the angles.

(b) Calculate the value of each ratio (to 3 significant figures if necessary).

13

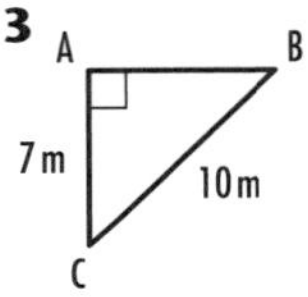

14

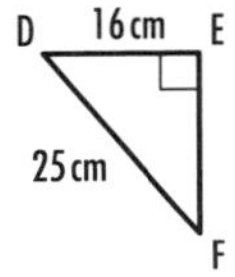

15

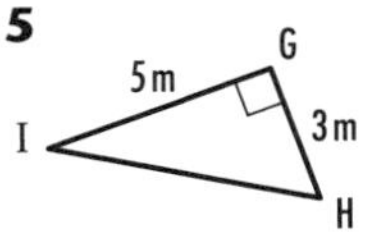

16

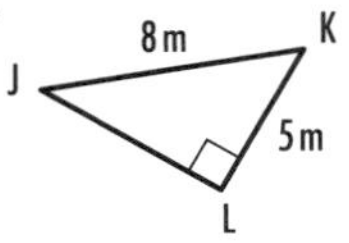

17

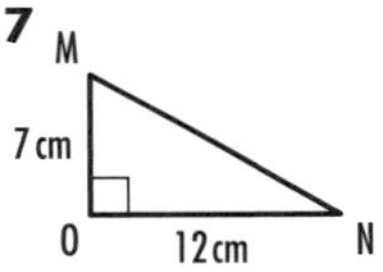

18

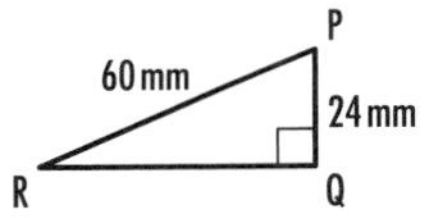

19

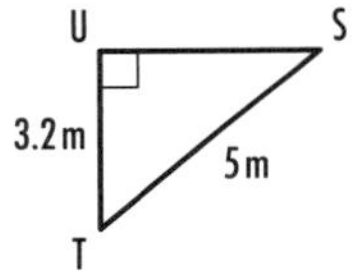

20

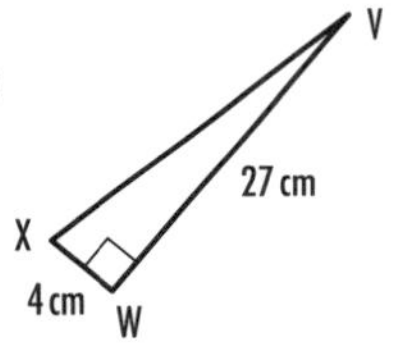

48/ TRIGONOMETRY: FINDING UNKNOWN ANGLES

$\sin^{-1}(x)$ means 'the angle whose sine has the value x'.

If $\cos A = \frac{4}{5}$, then $A = \cos^{-1}(\frac{4}{5}) = \cos^{-1}(0.8) = 36.9°$ (to nearest 0.1°).

EXAMPLE

► Calculate the angles P and Q in the diagram.

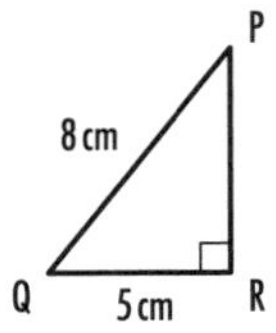

The trigonometric equation is:

$\text{Sin } P = \frac{5}{8}$

$P = \sin^{-1}(\frac{5}{8}) = 38.7°$ (to the nearest 0.1°)

$Q = 90° - 38.7° = 51.3°$

Note: There is no need to calculate Q using $\cos^{-1}(\frac{5}{8})$.

Exercise 48A

There are two unknown angles in each of questions 1–8.
(a) State a trigonometric equation including the value of the ratio.
(b) Calculate the size of each angle, to the nearest 0.1°.

1
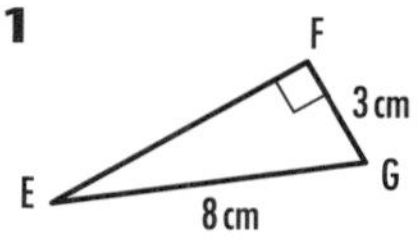

2
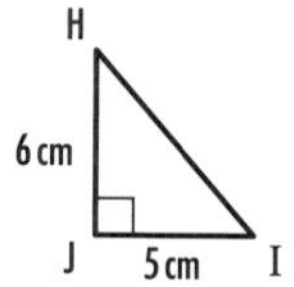

3
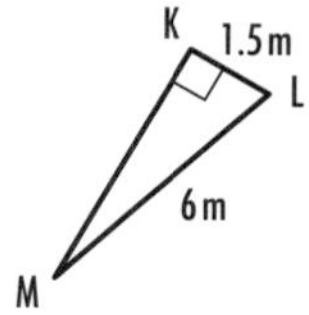

4
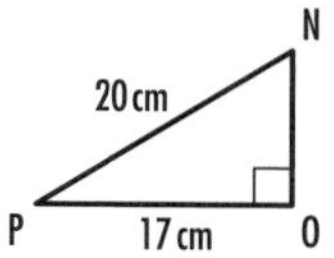

5
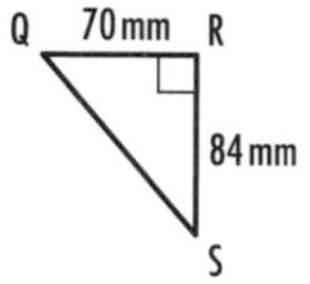

6
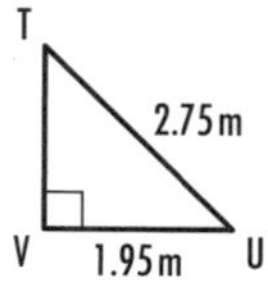

7
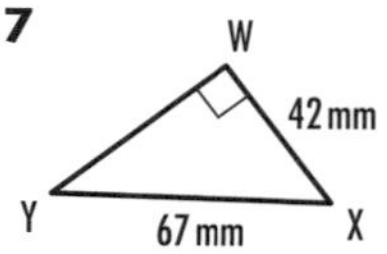

8
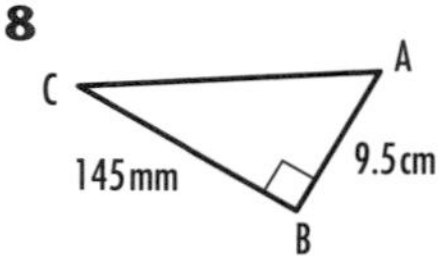

Each of the following questions refers to the angles P and Q in the diagram.
(a) State a trigonometric equation including the value of the ratio.
(b) Calculate the size of each angle, to the nearest 0.1°.

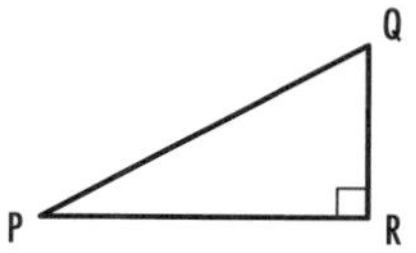

9 PQ = 10 cm and QR = 3 cm
10 PR = 55 mm and PQ = 12 cm
11 QR = 8 cm and PR = 4 cm
12 PR = 25 cm and QR = 20 cm
13 PQ = 25 mm and PR = 16 mm
14 QR = 27 mm and PR = 50 mm
15 PR = 125 mm and QR = 18 cm
16 QR = 13 cm and PQ = 29 cm

Exercise 48B

There are two unknown angles in each of questions 1–8.
(a) State a trigonometric equation including the value of the ratio.
(b) Calculate the size of each angle, to the nearest 0.1°.

1
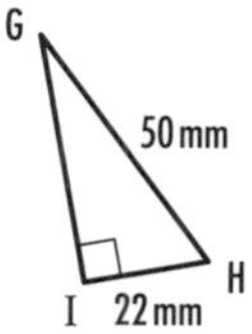

2
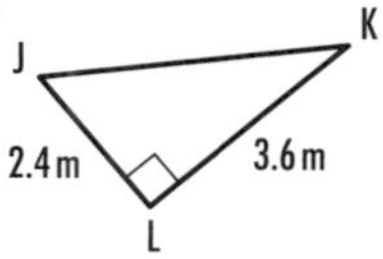

3
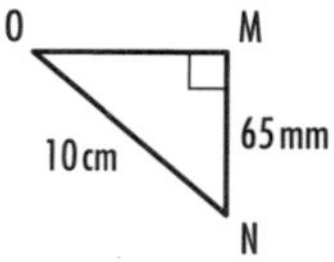

4
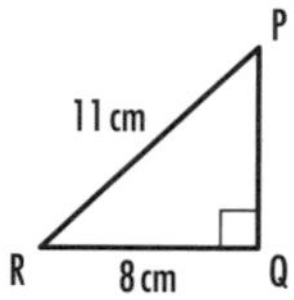

5
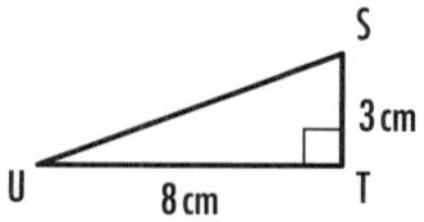

6
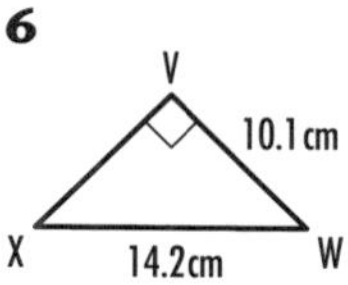

7
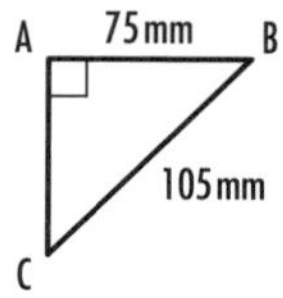

8
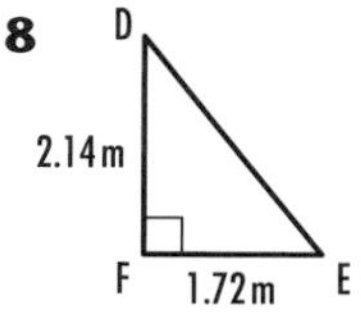

Each of the following questions refers to the angles P and Q in the diagram:
(a) State a trigonometric equation including the value of the ratio.
(b) Calculate the size of each angle, to the nearest 0.1°.

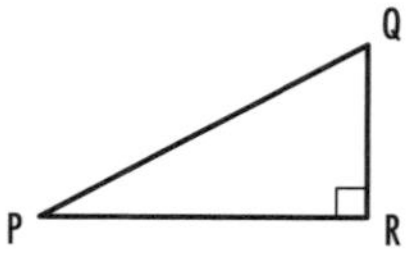

9 PR = 32 mm and QR = 40 mm
10 PR = 45 mm and PQ = 5 cm
11 QR = 8 cm and PQ = 25 cm
12 PR = 8 m and QR = 18 m
13 PQ = 80 mm and PR = 23 mm
14 QR = 75 cm and PQ = 95 cm
15 PR = 6.5 m and QR = 3.4 m
16 QR = 4.5 cm and PQ = 8.5 cm

49/ TRIGONOMETRY: FINDING UNKNOWN LENGTHS

EXAMPLE

▶ Calculate the length marked *a* in the diagram.

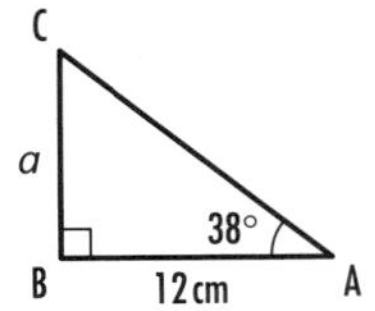

Always start with a trigonometric equation: $\tan 38° = \frac{a}{12}$

Multiply both sides of the equation by 12: $12 \times \tan 38° = 12 \times \frac{a}{12}$

$a = 12 \times \tan 38° = 9.38$ cm (to 3 s.f.)

EXAMPLE

▶ Calculate the length marked *q* in the diagram.

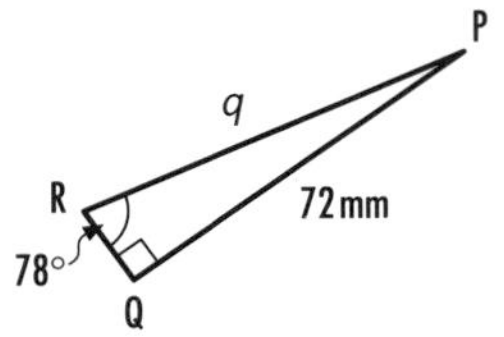

$\sin 78° = \frac{72}{q}$

Multiply both sides by *q*: $q \times \sin 78° = 72 \times \frac{q}{q}$ or $q \times \sin 78° = 72$

Divide by sin 78°: $q = \frac{72}{\sin 78°} = 73.6$ mm (to 3 s.f.)

Exercise 49A

Give your answers to 3 significant figures.

In questions 1–8, calculate the length of each of the unknown sides marked with a letter. In each question state the trigonometric equation used and show *all* your working.

1

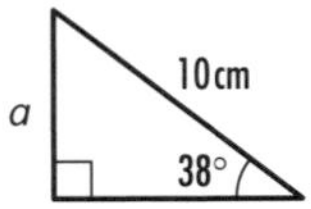

2

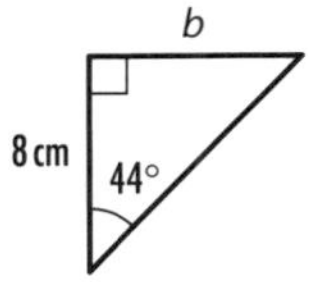

3

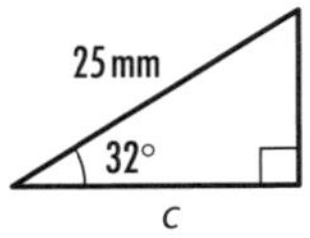

4

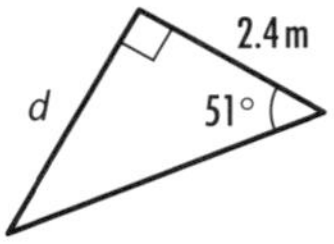

5

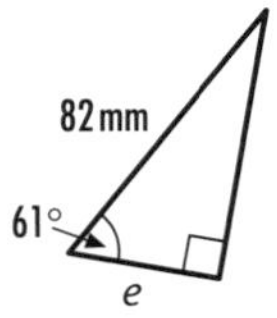

6

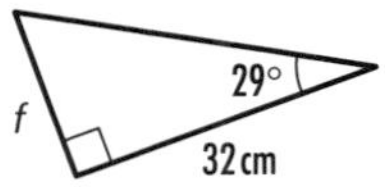

7

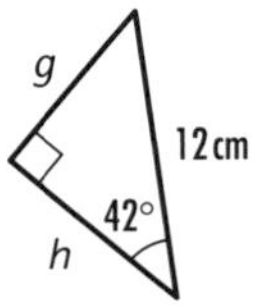

8

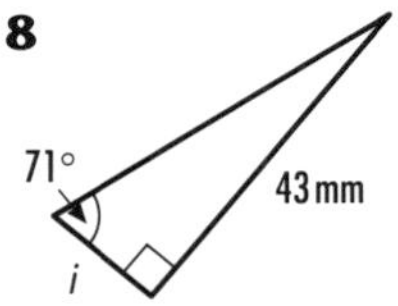

Each of the following questions refer to the diagram of the triangle ABC.
In each question state the trigonometric equation used and show *all* your working.

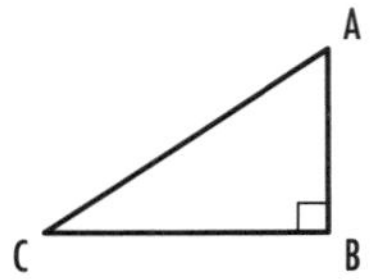

9 Angle C = 30°, AC = 7 cm. Calculate AB.
10 Angle C = 44°, BC = 20 cm. Calculate AB.
11 Angle A = 29.4°, AC = 100 mm. Calculate AB and BC.
12 Angle C = 12.7°, AB = 7.5 cm. Calculate BC.

13 Angle C = 60°, BC = 95 mm. Calculate AB and AC.
14 Angle A = 44°, AB = 25 cm. Calculate BC.
15 Angle A = 58.5°, BC = 2.8 m. Calculate AC and AB.
16 Angle C = 72.8°, AC = 112 mm. Calculate AB and BC.

Exercise 49B

Give your answers to 3 significant figures.

In questions 1–8, calculate the length of each of the unknown sides marked with a letter.
In each question state the trigonometric equation used and show *all* your working.

1

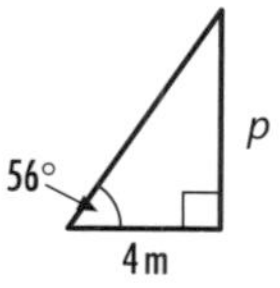

2

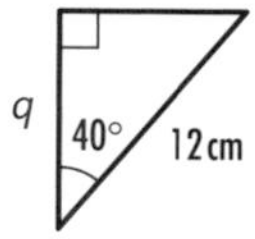

3

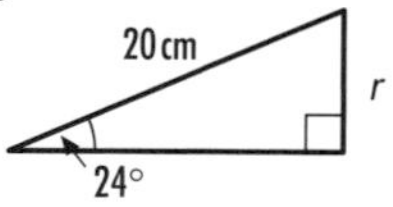

4

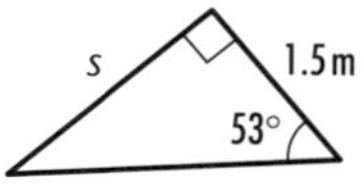

5

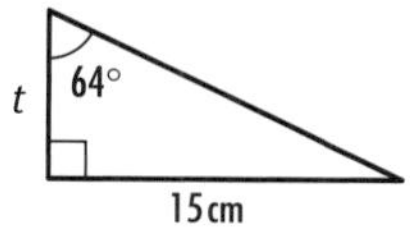

6

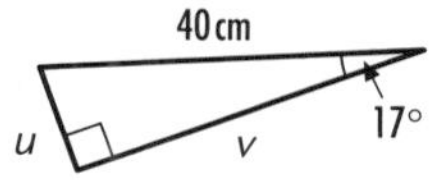

7

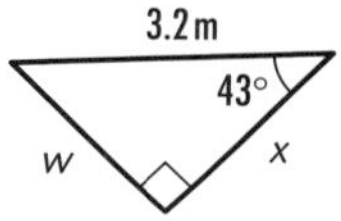

8

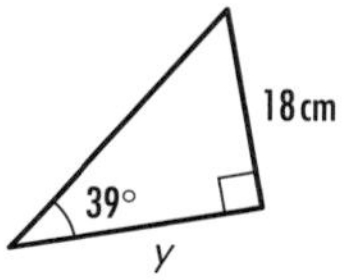

Each of the following questions refer to the diagram of the triangle ABC.
In each question state the trigonometric equation used and show *all* your working.

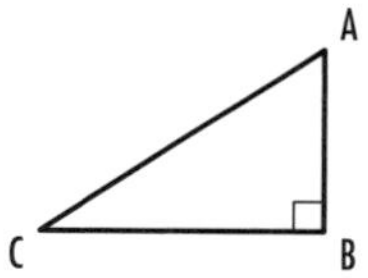

9 Angle A = 60°, AB = 12 cm. Calculate BC.
10 Angle C = 25°, AC = 30 cm. Calculate BC and AB.
11 Angle A = 50°, AC = 45 mm. Calculate BC.
12 Angle C= 42.5°, AB = 5.4 m. Calculate BC.
13 Angle C = 7.5°, AC = 75 mm. Calculate AB and BC.
14 Angle A = 82°, AB = 3.95 m. Calculate AC and BC.
15 Angle C = 38.6°, BC = 22 cm. Calculate AB and AC.
16 Angle A = 40°, AC = 157 mm. Calculate AB and BC.

50/ TRIGONOMETRY: MISCELLANEOUS PROBLEMS

Exercise 50A

Give your answers to 3 significant figures for lengths and to the nearest 0.1° for angles unless the question states otherwise.

1 Calculate each of the angles that the diagonal makes with the two edges of a sheet of A4 paper (21.0 cm by 29.7 cm).

2 A ladder of length 6 m has its foot on horizontal ground and is placed against a vertical wall. If the ladder reaches 5 m up the wall, calculate the angle that the ladder makes with the wall.

3 Peter is flying his kite. He uses all of the 50-m spool of line that came with the kite. He measures the angle that the string makes with the horizontal as being 58°. Calculate the height of the kite assuming that the string is straight.

4 A straight road on a steep hill rises 1 m for every 10 m along the surface. Calculate the angle that the road makes with the horizontal.

5 A door-wedge is to be cut from a piece of wood which is 12 cm wide (see diagram). It needs to have a height of at least 4 cm. Calculate the angle of the cut, α, to the nearest 0.5°.

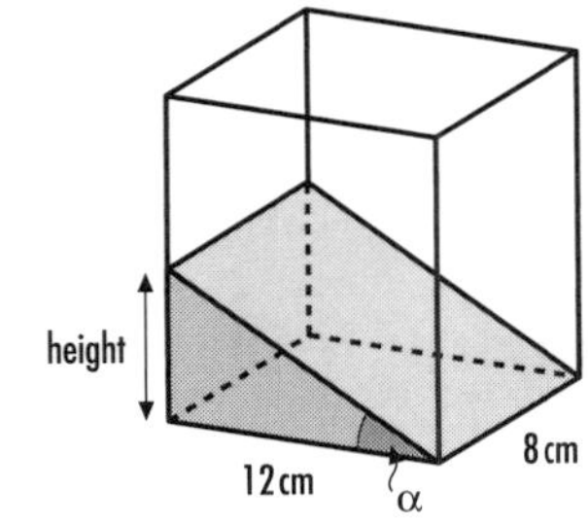

6 Ahsan measures the angle of inclination of the top of a vertical building as 17.5°. If he is 50 metres from the base of the building, calculate the height to the nearest metre. You should take into account the fact that Ahsan made his measurement from a height of 1.2 m.

7 A flat roof (see diagram) needs to be at an angle of at least 3° to the horizontal so that rain water will run off. Calculate the minimum height, h, to the nearest centimetre, by which the end of a 8.4 m roof-section must be raised.

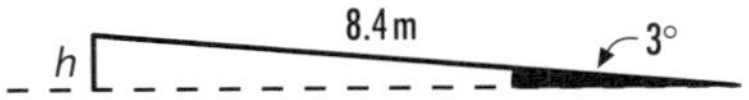

8 An isosceles triangle has a base of 7 cm and a height of 6 cm. Calculate the three angles of the triangle.

9 A rhombus has sides of 9 cm and one of its angles is 66°.
(a) Draw a diagram showing these details and also the diagonals of the rhombus.
(b) Calculate the length of each diagonal.

10 Sarah drives 8 km along a straight road on a bearing of 150°. Calculate how far she has travelled (a) south (b) east.

11 A vertical pole of length 3.4 m is held in place by ropes of length 5 m tied to the top of the pole and to pegs in the horizontal ground. Calculate the angle that each rope makes with the horizontal.

12 The diagram shows the triangle ABP where P is a point on the circumference of a circle and AB is a diameter of length 12 cm. The angle PAB is 53.5°.
(a) State the size of the angle APB.
(b) Calculate the length of (i) AP and (ii) BP.

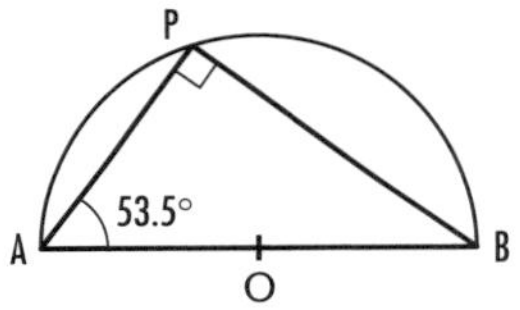

13 The point A is at (2, 4), the point B is at (3, 7) and the point C is at (5, 4). Calculate the angle CAB. Note: A unit on the x-axis is the same length as a unit on the y-axis.

14 Dianne sails 5 nautical miles east and then 2 nautical miles north. How far is she and what is her bearing (to the nearest degree) from her starting point?

15 A circle, centre O, is drawn so it passes through the corners of a rectangle as shown in the diagram. Calculate the radius of the circle.

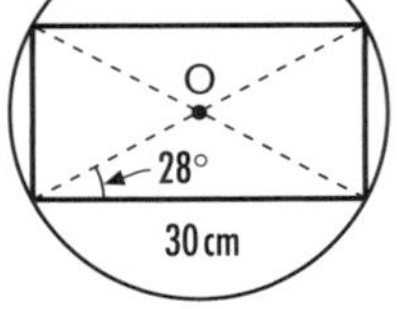

16 A man in the desert walks 8 km south-east and 5 km south-west.
(a) What is his bearing (to the nearest degree) now from his starting point?
(b) How far is he from his starting point?

Exercise 50B

Give your answers to 3 significant figures for lengths and to the nearest 0.1° for angles unless the question states otherwise.

1 The diagram shows the end of a shed. If the angle between the roof-sections is 130°, calculate the width of each roof-section, to the nearest 10 cm.

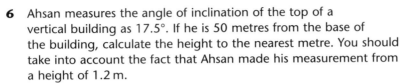

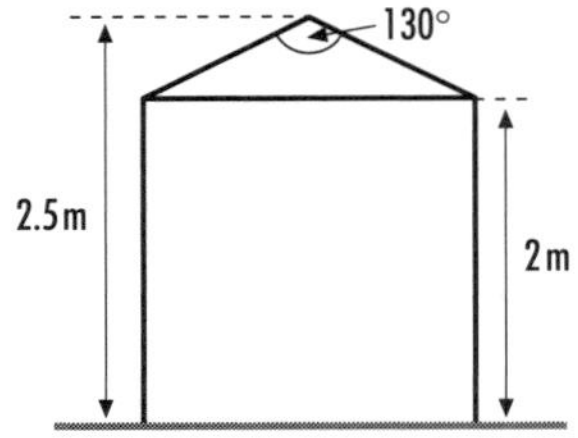

2 Syeda is flying a kite with a string of length 60 m. What angle (to the nearest degree) will the kite string make with the horizontal ground if the height of the kite is 40 m?

3 An aeroplane takes off at an angle of 7.8°. Assuming the path of the plane continues to rise at this rate, calculate its height, to the nearest 100 m, as it passes over a point 5 km from its take-off point.

4 Calculate each of the angles that the diagonal makes with the two sides of a rectangle measuring 12 cm by 16 cm.

5 Jaffar drives 12 km along a straight road on a bearing of 340°. Calculate how far he has travelled (a) north (b) west.

6 Rachel stands on horizontal ground and measures the angle of inclination of the top of a tree as 11°. Rachel makes her measurements from a height of 1.2 m. If she is 30 metres from the base of the tree and assuming the tree to be vertical, calculate its height to the nearest metre.

7 A ladder of length 7.5 m has its foot on horizontal ground against a vertical wall. If the ladder makes an angle of 72° with the ground, calculate the greatest distance that it can reach up the wall.

8 A pendulum of length 12 m is fixed at the point O and swings from P to Q as shown in the diagram. If the length of the straight line PQ is 1 m, calculate the angle α.

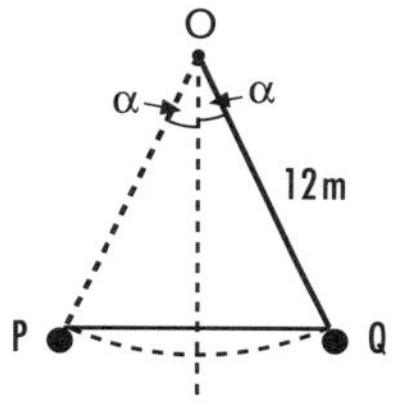

9 The point O is at (0, 0) and the point P is at (2, 3). Calculate the angle that OP makes with the *x*-axis. Note: A unit on the *x*-axis is the same length as a unit on the *y*-axis.

10

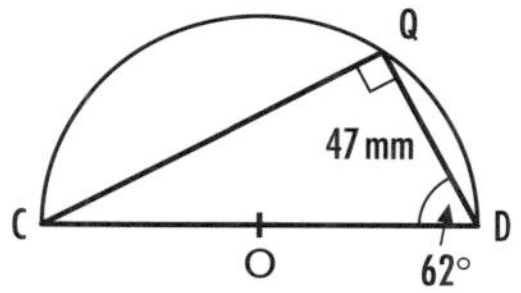

The diagram shows a point, Q, on the circumference of a circle with diameter CD. The chord DQ is 47 mm and the angle CDQ is 62°.
(a) State the size of the angle CQD.
(b) Calculate the radius of the circle to the nearest millimetre.

11 A vertical mast of length 12.6 m is held in place by wires of length 14.5 m fixed to the top of the mast and to points on the horizontal ground. Calculate the angle (to the nearest degree) that each wire makes with the vertical.

12 An isosceles triangle has a base of 96 mm and two other sides of 85 mm. Calculate the three angles of the triangle.

13 A pendulum of length 1.5 m is fixed at the point O and swings through an angle of 10° as shown in the diagram.
(a) Calculate the distance AB, to the nearest centimetre.
(b) Calculate the difference in height between the points B and C, to the nearest millimetre.

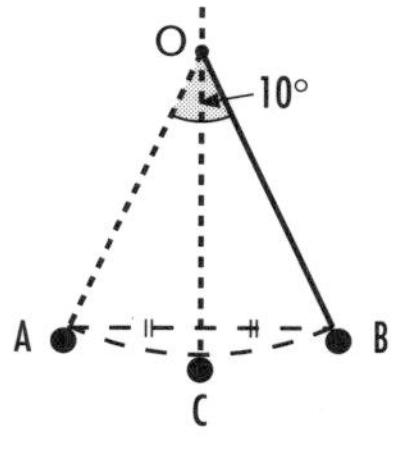

14 Nathan sails 3 nautical miles north and then 1.5 nautical miles east. How far is he and what is his bearing from his starting point?

15 A rhombus has sides of 120 mm and one of its angles is 130°.
(a) Draw a diagram showing these details and also the diagonals of the rhombus.
(b) Calculate the length of each diagonal.

16 A woman in the desert drives 12 km west and 10 km north.
(a) What is her bearing now (to the nearest degree) from her starting point?
(b) How far is she from her starting point?

51/ ENLARGEMENT: FRACTIONAL SCALE FACTORS

An **object** can be enlarged by a **scale factor** that is a fraction; this gives an **image** that is reduced in size.
Corresponding points on the object and image can be joined and then extended to pass through the **centre of enlargement**.

EXAMPLE

► Show the centre of enlargement, O, and state the scale factor for the object and image shown in the diagram.

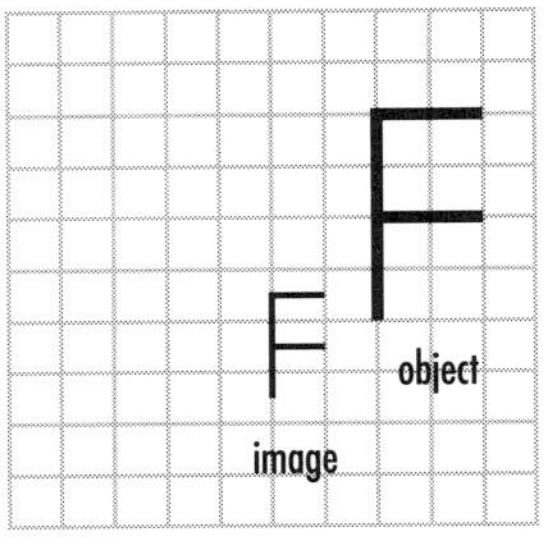

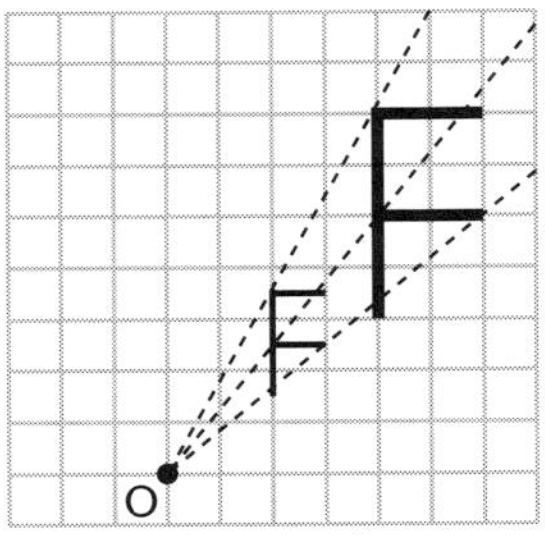

Scale factor = $\frac{1}{2}$

EXAMPLE

► Draw the image of the object after it has been enlarged by a scale factor of $\frac{2}{3}$ with the point (1, 2) as the centre of enlargement.

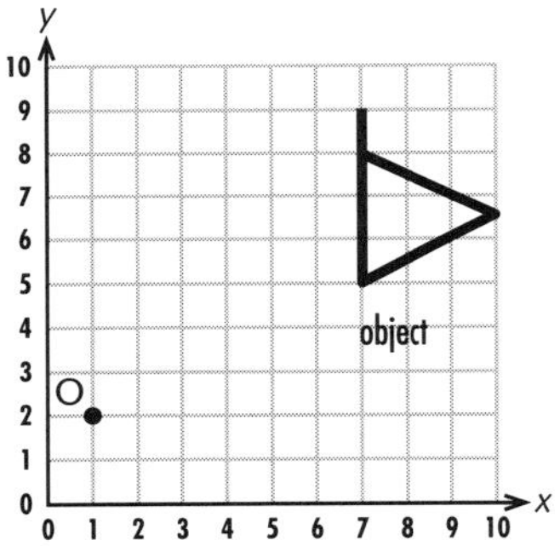

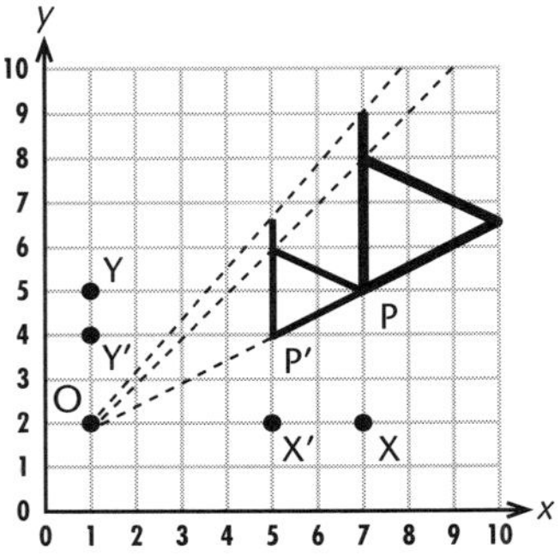

OX = 6 and so OX′ = $\frac{2}{3}$OX = 4

OY = 3 and so OY′ = $\frac{2}{3}$OY = 2

The point P′ is drawn in line with the points X′ and Y′ and it can be seen that OP′ = $\frac{2}{3}$OP. Other points of the image are drawn in the same way.

Exercise 51A

Each of the diagrams in questions 1–6 shows an object with two images, A and B. Copy each diagram onto squared paper and show clearly, by joining corresponding points on the object and the image, the centre of enlargement for each of the images shown. State the scale factor in each case.

1

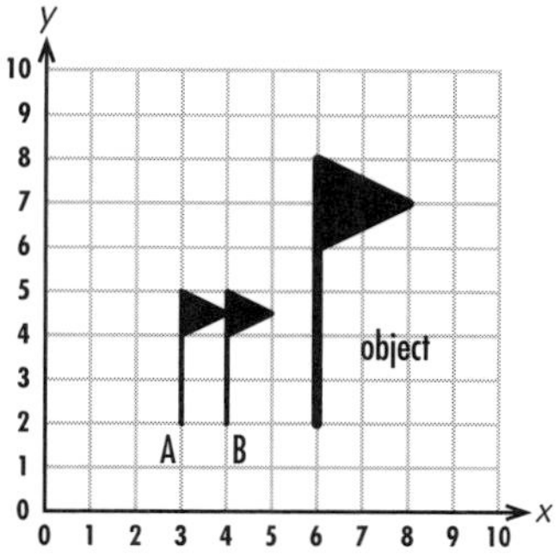

2

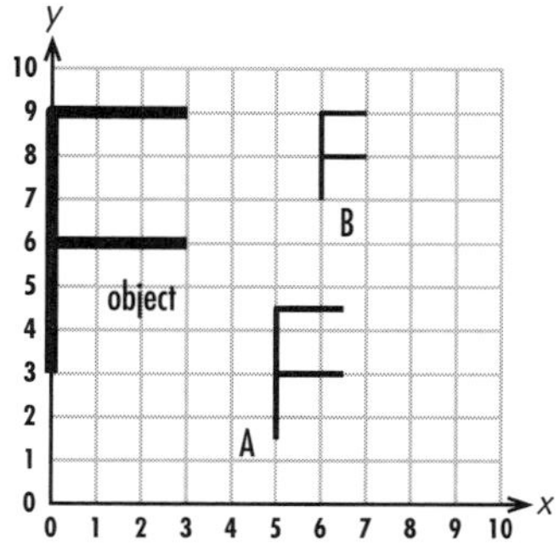

3

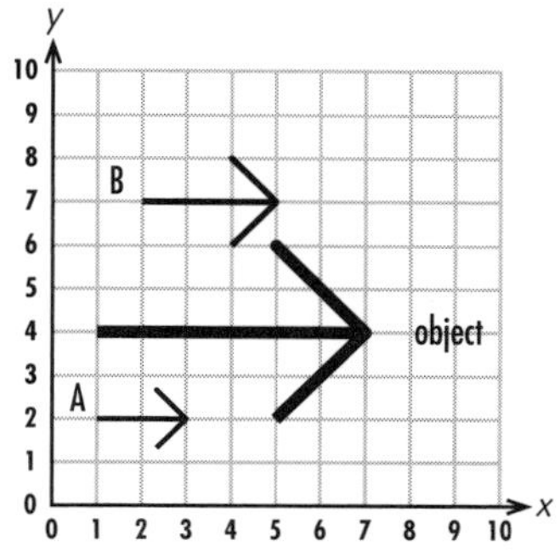

4

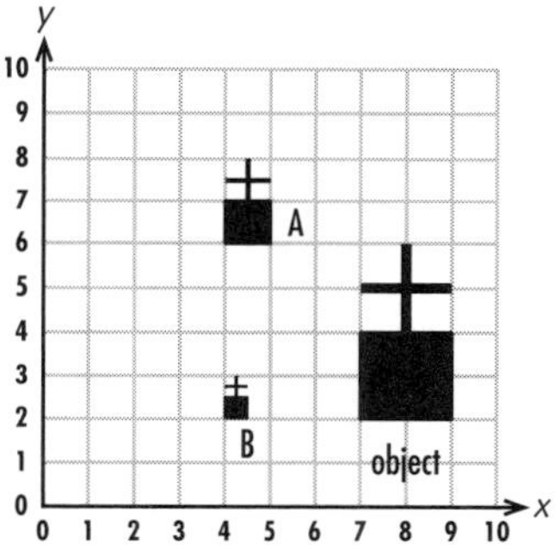

5

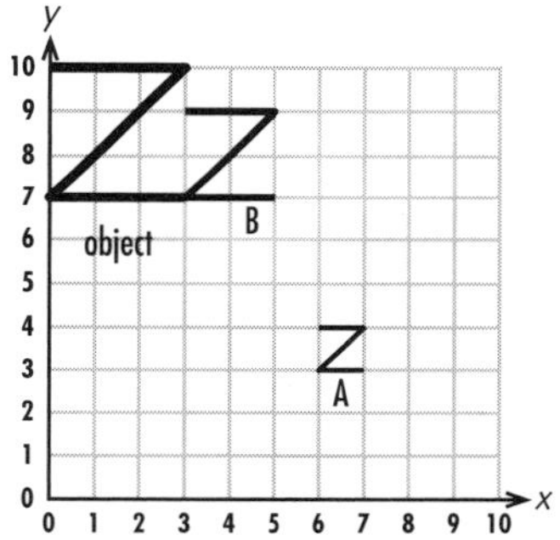

6

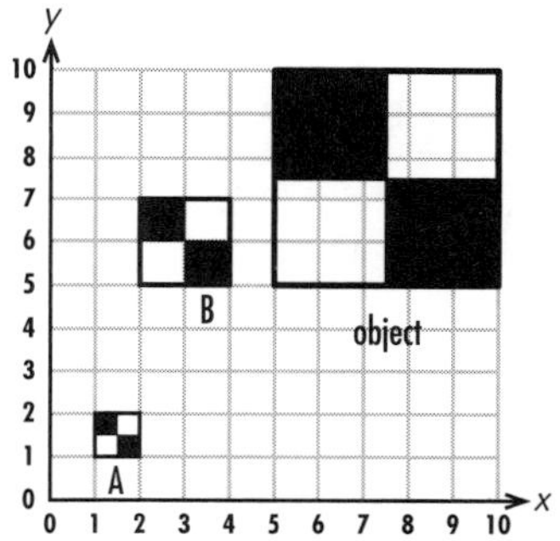

In questions 7–9, copy the diagrams as many times as is necessary onto squared paper and draw the images required using the scale factor and centre of enlargement given for each. Label each image A, B etc. as appropriate.

7

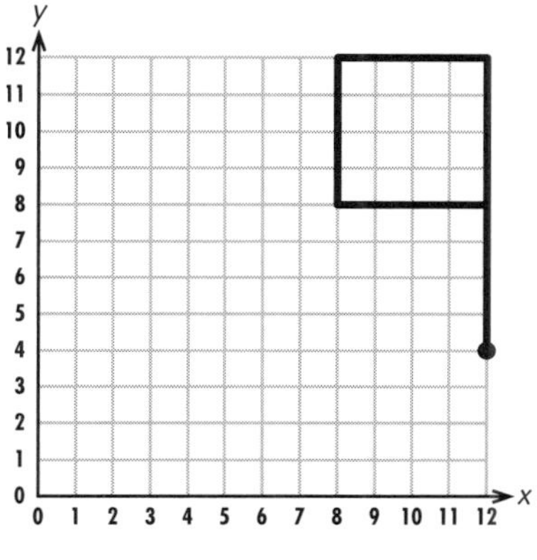

Image **A**: Scale factor = $\frac{1}{2}$, centre of enlargement = (0, 4)

Image **B**: Scale factor = $\frac{1}{2}$, centre of enlargement = (0, 12)

Image **C**: Scale factor = $\frac{1}{2}$, centre of enlargement = (4, 0)

Image **D**: Scale factor = $\frac{1}{2}$, centre of enlargement = (10, 4)

Image **E** Scale factor = $\frac{1}{2}$, centre of enlargement = (4, 4)

8

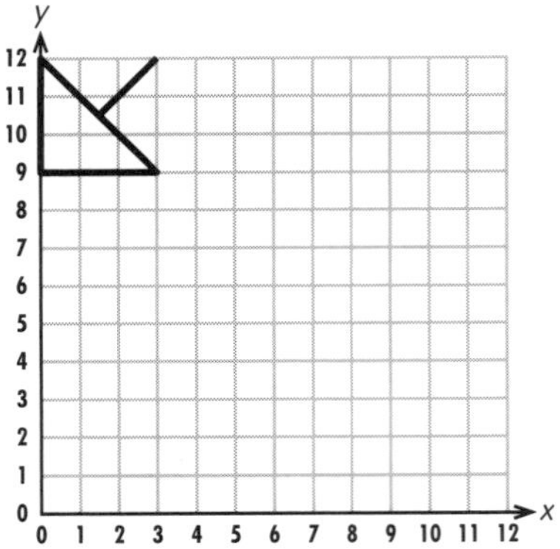

Image **F**: Scale factor = $\frac{1}{3}$, centre of enlargement = (9, 3)

Image **G**: Scale factor = $\frac{1}{3}$, centre of enlargement = (9, 9)

Image **H**: Scale factor = $\frac{2}{3}$, centre of enlargement = (9, 9)

Image **I**: Scale factor = $\frac{1}{3}$, centre of enlargement = (0, 3)

Image **J**: Scale factor = $\frac{2}{3}$, centre of enlargement = (6, 0)

9

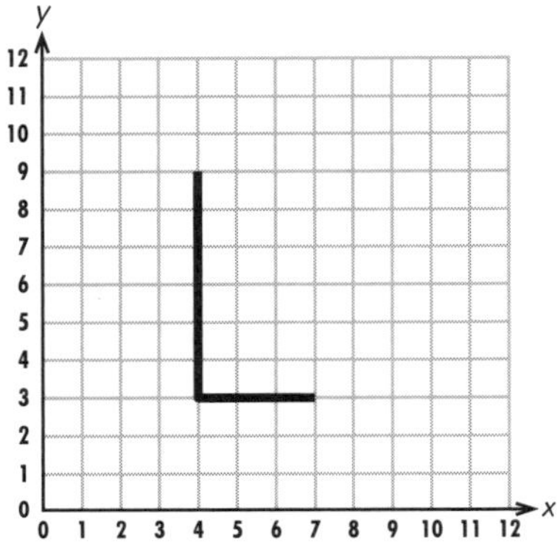

Image **K**: Scale factor = $\frac{1}{2}$, centre of enlargement = (0, 0)

Image **L**: Scale factor = $\frac{1}{2}$, centre of enlargement = (0, 12)

Image **M**: Scale factor = $\frac{1}{4}$, centre of enlargement = (12, 11)

Image **N**: Scale factor = $\frac{3}{4}$, centre of enlargement = (12, 11)

Image **P**: Scale factor = $\frac{2}{3}$, centre of enlargement = (5, 6)

Exercise 51B

Each of the diagrams in questions 1–6 shows an object with two images, A and B. Copy each diagram onto squared paper and show clearly, by joining corresponding points on the object and the image, the centre of enlargement for each of the images shown. State the scale factor in each case.

1

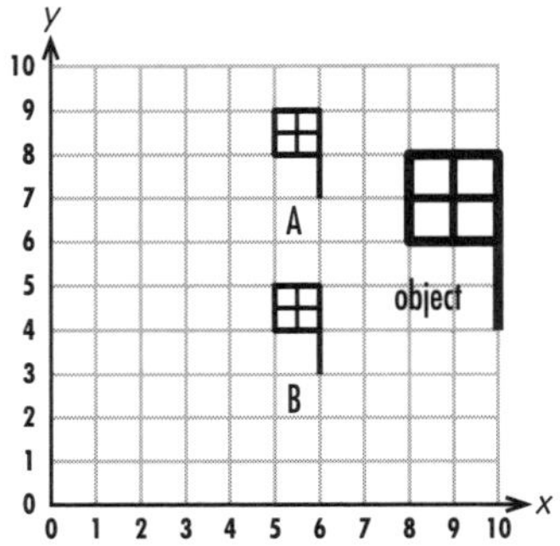

2

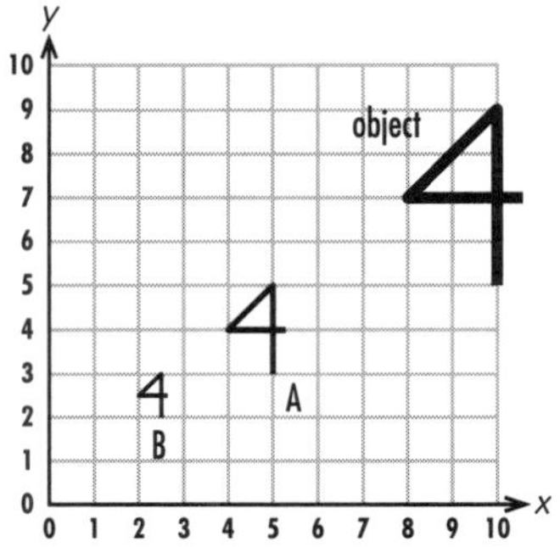

3

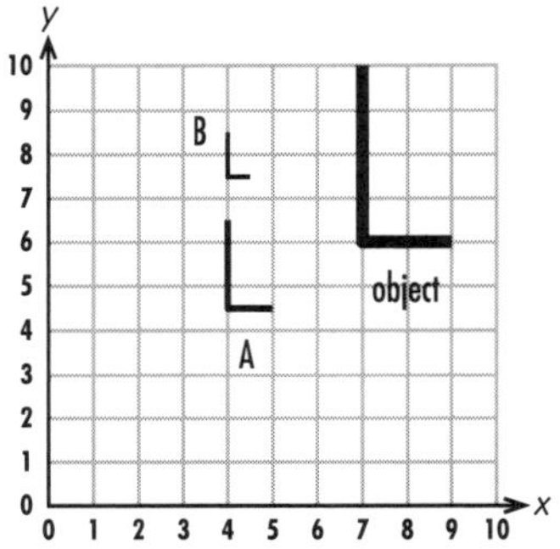

4

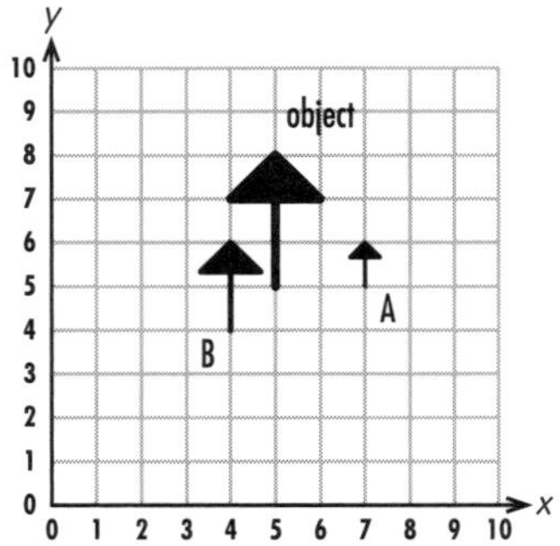

5

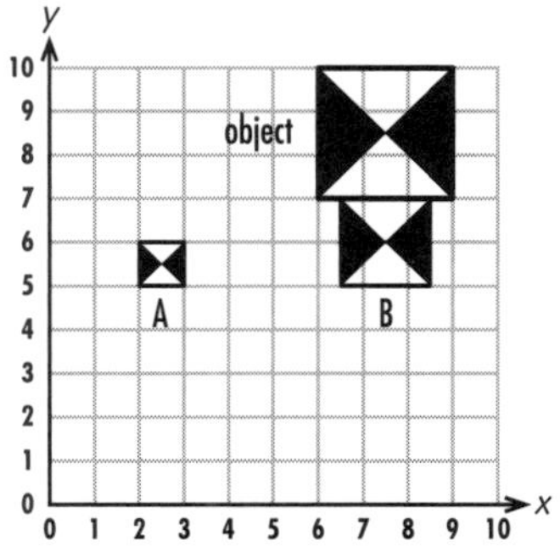

6

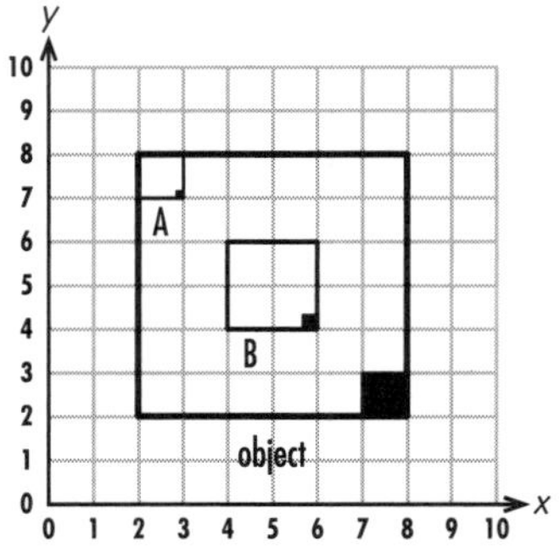

In questions 7–9, copy the diagrams as many times as is necessary onto squared paper and draw the images required using the scale factor and centre of enlargement given for each. Label each image A, B etc. as appropriate.

7

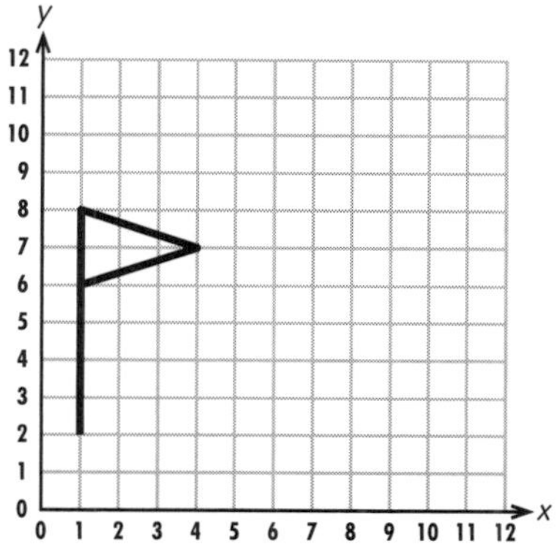

Image **A**: Scale factor = $\frac{1}{3}$, centre of enlargement = (10, 2)

Image **B**: Scale factor = $\frac{1}{2}$, centre of enlargement = (9, 8)

Image **C**: Scale factor = $\frac{1}{3}$, centre of enlargement = (1, 11)

Image **D**: Scale factor = $\frac{1}{2}$, centre of enlargement = (9, 2)

Image **E**: Scale factor = $\frac{2}{3}$, centre of enlargement = (10, 11)

8

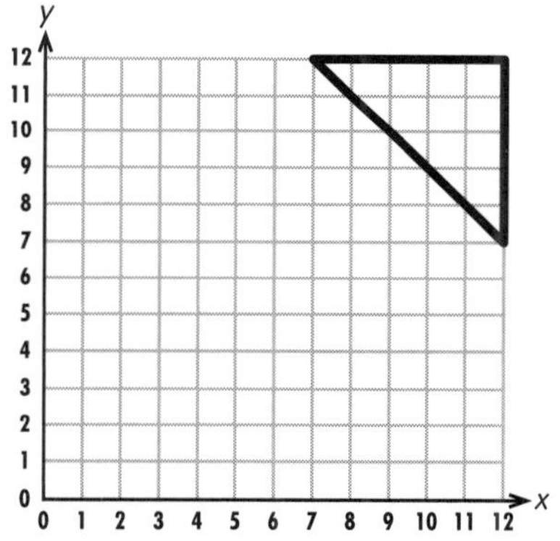

Image **F**: Scale factor = $\frac{1}{5}$, centre of enlargement = (2, 12)

Image **G**: Scale factor = $\frac{1}{5}$, centre of enlargement = (2, 2)

Image **H**: Scale factor = $\frac{2}{5}$, centre of enlargement = (2, 2)

Image **I**: Scale factor = $\frac{3}{5}$, centre of enlargement = (2, 2)

Image **J**: Scale factor = $\frac{4}{5}$, centre of enlargement = (2, 2)

9

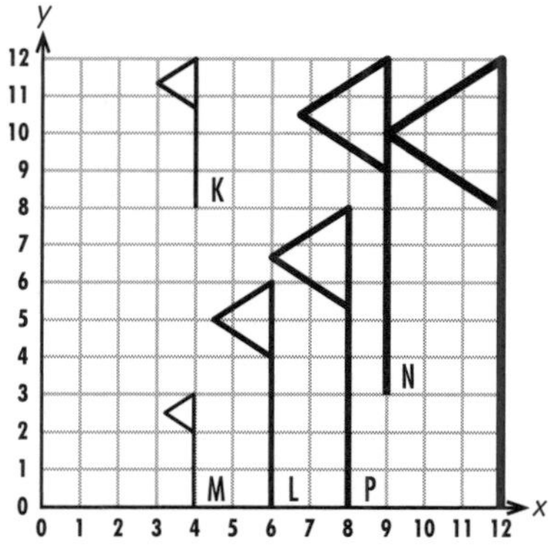

Image **K**: Scale factor = $\frac{1}{3}$, centre of enlargement = (0, 12)

Image **L**: Scale factor = $\frac{1}{2}$, centre of enlargement = (0, 0)

Image **M**: Scale factor = $\frac{1}{4}$, centre of enlargement = (0, 0)

Image **N**: Scale factor = $\frac{3}{4}$, centre of enlargement = (0, 12)

Image **P**: Scale factor = $\frac{2}{3}$, centre of enlargement = (0, 0)

52/ THE LOCUS OF A POINT

The **locus** of a point is the path traced out by a point when it moves according to a given rule.
Note: The plural of locus is loci.

EXAMPLE

▶ A security light has a sensor that can detect movement at a distance of 15 metres or less. The angle of detection is 110°. Draw a labelled diagram to show the maximum area that it can scan.

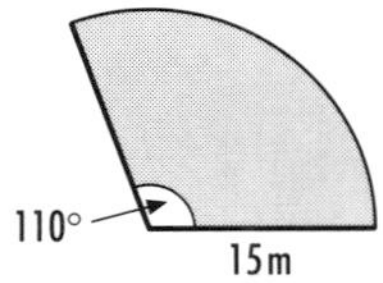

EXAMPLE

▶ AB = 6 cm. Draw a diagram to show the locus of a point which is equidistant from two points A and B.

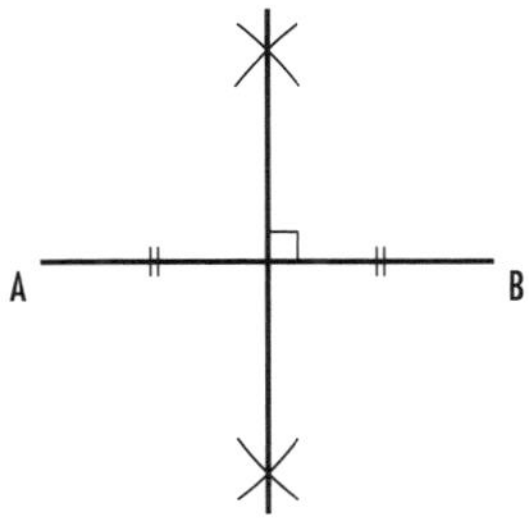

The locus is the line that bisects AB at right angles to AB. This is called the **perpendicular bisector** of AB.
Note: Compasses can be used to draw the perpendicular bisector, using A and B as centres.

EXAMPLE

▶ The angle between the two lines PR and QR is 58°. Draw the locus of the point that moves so as to be equidistant from PR and QR.

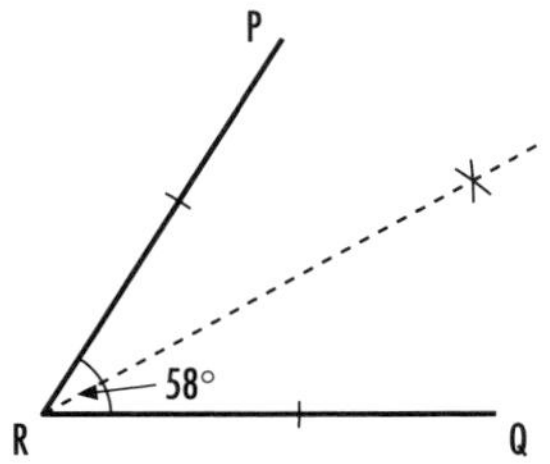

The locus is the angle bisector of angle PRQ and this can be drawn using compasses as shown.

Exercise 52A

1 Neil has damaged his compasses (see diagram). Despite this he decides to attempt to draw a circle. Draw the shape you think he will manage, indicating any lengths that you think are involved.

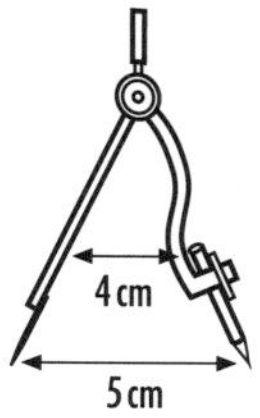

2 Mark a point on the circumference of a coin. Use the coin to draw the locus of this point as the coin is rolled along a straight line on a flat surface.

3

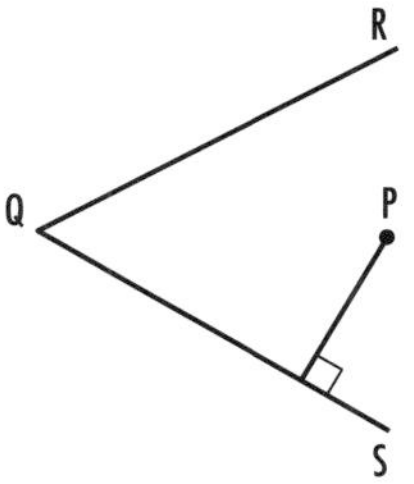

The point P in the diagram is equidistant from the lines QR and QS. Copy the diagram and show the distances of P from QR and QS. Show the locus of all the points that are equidistant from QR and QS.

4 Draw a line of length 4 cm and sketch the locus of a point that moves so it is 3 cm from the line.

5 A goat is tied to the middle of one wall of a shed in the middle of a field. The shed measures 8 m × 4 m.

Draw diagrams to show the area of grass that can be eaten by the goat when the rope has a length of (a) 2 m (b) 4 m (c) 8 m.

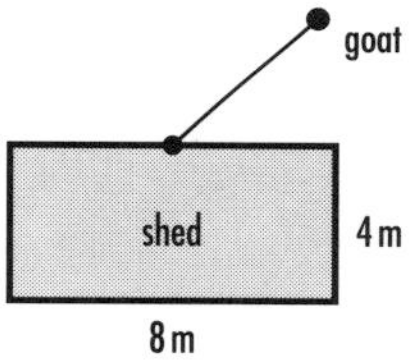

6

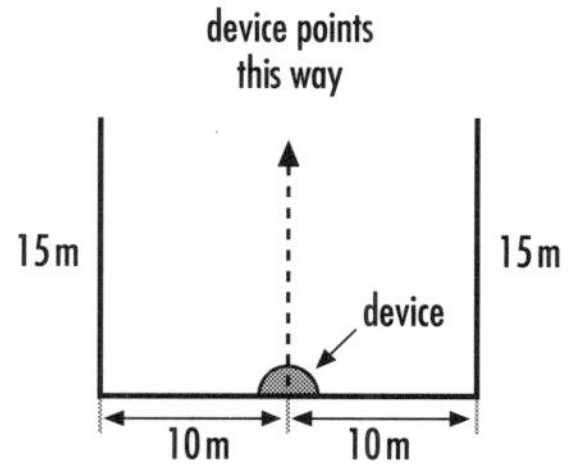

A security device has a sensor that can detect movement at a distance of 15 metres or less. The angle of detection is 110°. The device is placed on the wall of a garden as shown. Copy the diagram and show the area that is scanned by the device.

7 A gardener plants two plants 30 cm apart. This is the minimum distance that can be allowed between plants. Draw a diagram to show the area in which a third plant *cannot* be planted.

8 A lamp is fixed to the wall of a house as shown in the diagram. It gives sufficient light at distances of 20 m or less. Copy the diagram and show the areas that will not be lit by the lamp.

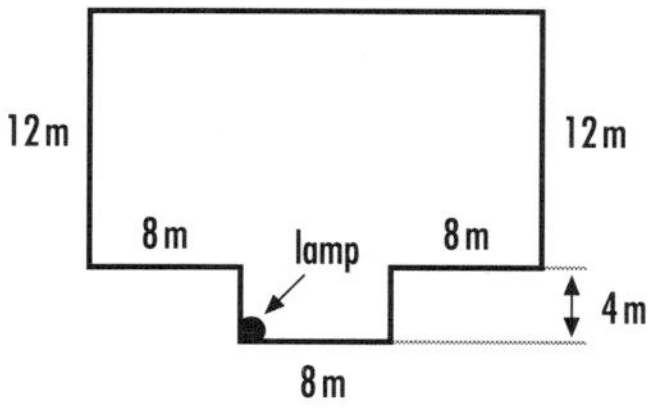

9

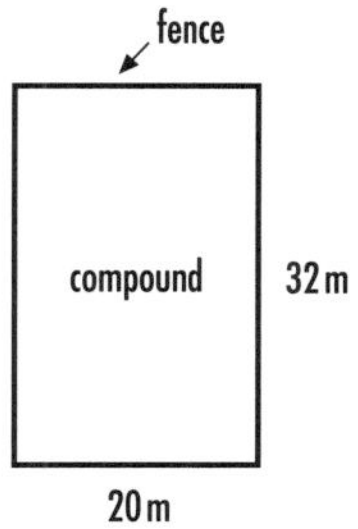

(a) A security guard walks around the outside of the compound shown in the diagram at a distance of 3 metres from the fence. Draw a diagram to show the path taken by the security guard.

(b) Another guard walks around the inside of the compound at a distance of 2 metres from the fence. Show the path taken by this guard.

10 Draw the triangle ABC accurately given that AB = 48 mm, BC = 40 mm and AC = 45 mm.
(a) Draw the locus of the point that is equidistant from the points A and B.
(b) Draw the locus of the point that is equidistant from the points A and C.
(c) Draw the locus of the point that is equidistant from the points B and C.
If you have completed (a), (b) and (c) correctly, the three loci should pass through a single point; label this O. With centre O and radius of length OA, draw a circle that passes through the points A, B and C.

Exercise 52B

1 Sketch the locus of a point that moves so as to be 45 mm or more from the point A.

2

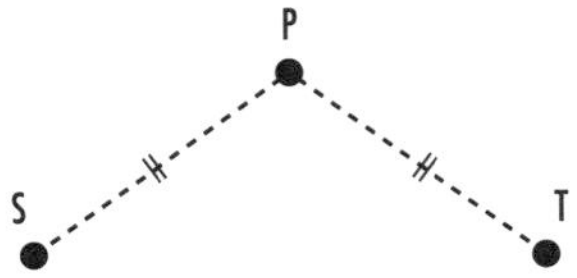

The point P is equidistant from the points S and T.
(a) Copy the diagram and draw in the distances from P to S and T.
(b) Draw the locus of the point that moves so it is equidistant from S and T.

3 The point P is equidistant from the lines AB and AC.
(a) Copy the diagram and draw in two lines that show the distances from P to AB and to AC.
(b) Draw the locus of the point that moves so it is equidistant from AB and AC.

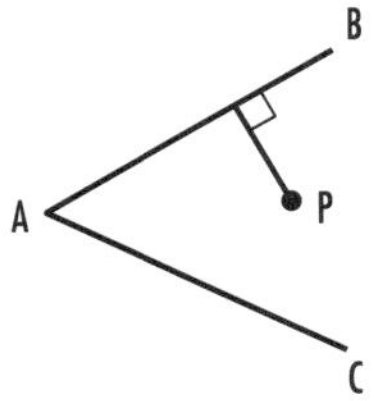

4

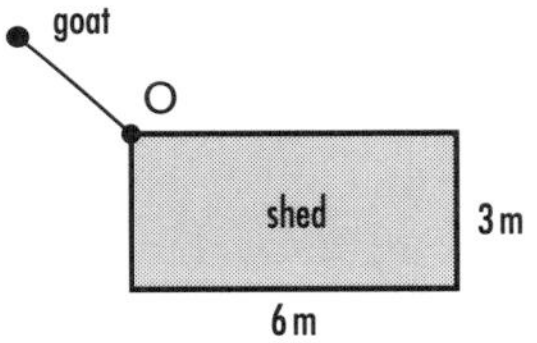

A goat is tied to a rope fixed at the point O on the corner of a 6 m × 3 m shed.
Draw diagram(s) to show the area of grass that can be eaten by the goat when the rope has a length of (a) 2 m (b) 3 m (c) 6 m.

5 Sketch the locus of point P that moves so that the angle SPT is always 90°.

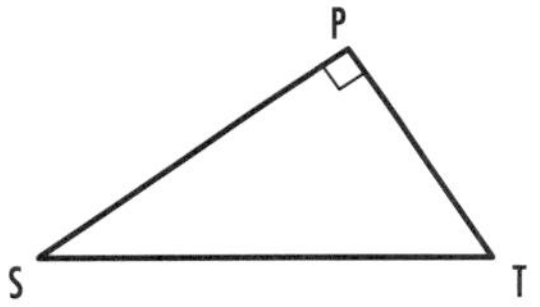

6 A security light has a sensor that can detect movement at a distance of 18 metres or less. The angle of detection is 100°. Draw a labelled diagram to show the maximum area that it can scan.

7 A television cable is to be laid so as to run between the house belonging to the Jones family and the house belonging to the Smith family. Both families insist that the cable must be as far from their house as is possible. The houses are 24 metres apart. Draw a diagram to show where the cable should be laid so that both families are happy.

8 A lamp is fixed to the corner of a house as shown in the diagram. It lights to a distance of 20 m. Copy the diagram and indicate the areas that will be in darkness.

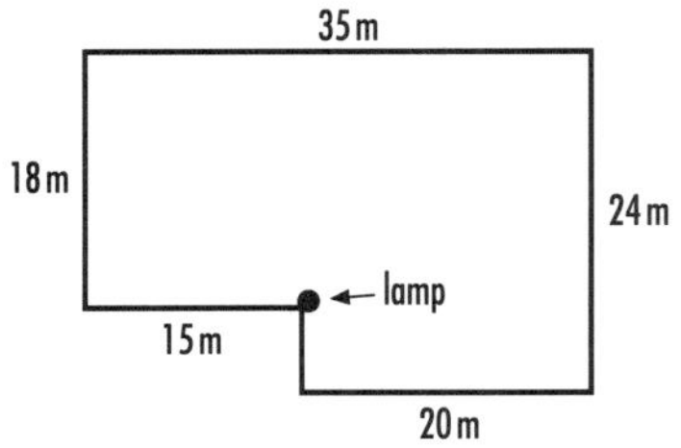

9 A horse can lean over a low fence to reach grass to a maximum distance of 2 metres from the fence. The field and the low fence are shown in the diagram. Copy the diagram and show the area that the horse can reach outside the field.

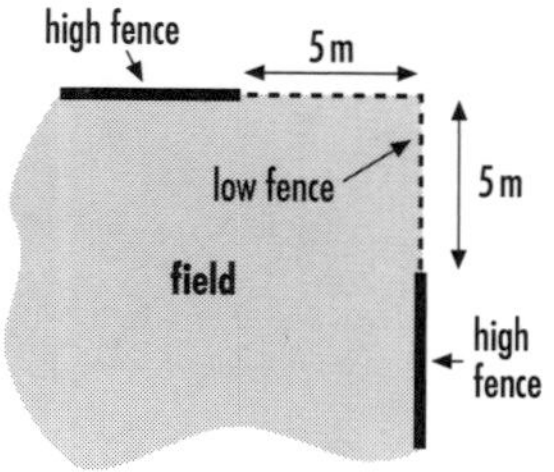

10 Draw an accurate drawing of the triangle QRS where QR = 4 cm, RS = 5 cm and QS = 4 cm.
(a) Draw the locus of the point that is equidistant from the lines QR and QS.
(b) Repeat this for the line QS and RS and also for the lines QR and RS.
(c) If you have completed (a) and (b) correctly, all three loci should meet at a point, O. With centre at O, draw a circle which just *touches* each of the sides of the triangle.

REVISION

Exercise E

1 State the bearing of A from B in each diagram.

(a)
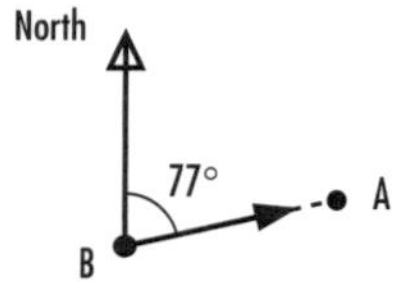

(b)
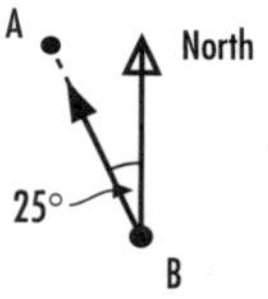

(c)
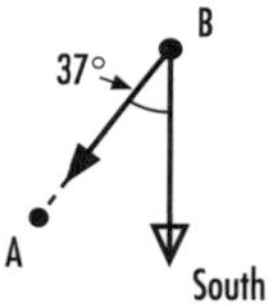

(d)
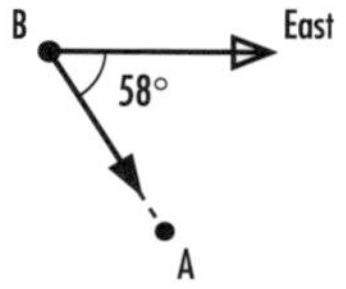

2 State the bearing of B from A in each of the examples in question 1.

3 Calculate the lengths of the sides marked with letters.

(a)
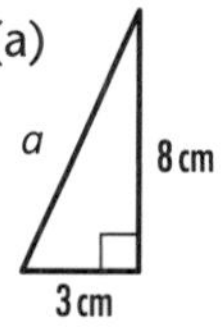

(b)
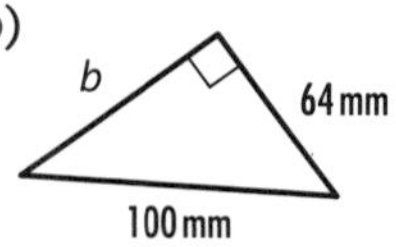

(c)
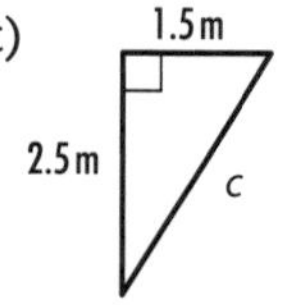

4 For each pair of triangles, ABC and PQR, state whether the two triangles are similar. If they are similar, calculate the two unknown lengths.

(a)
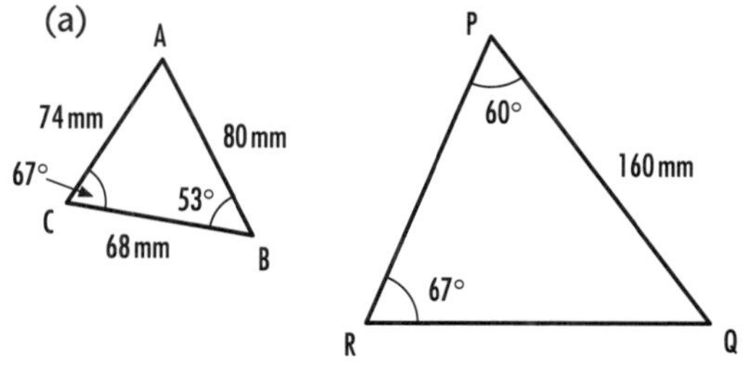

(b)
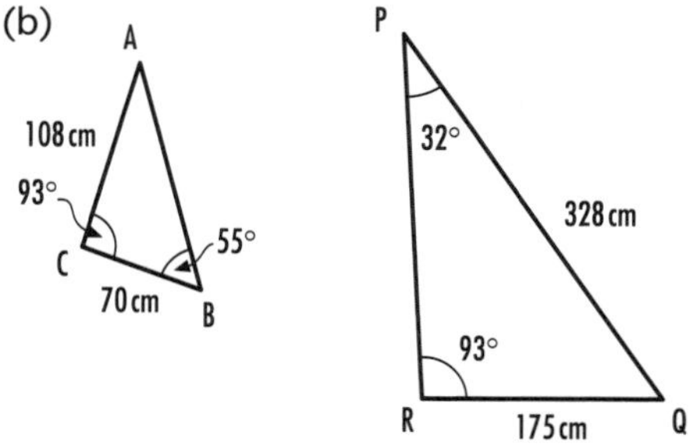

(c)
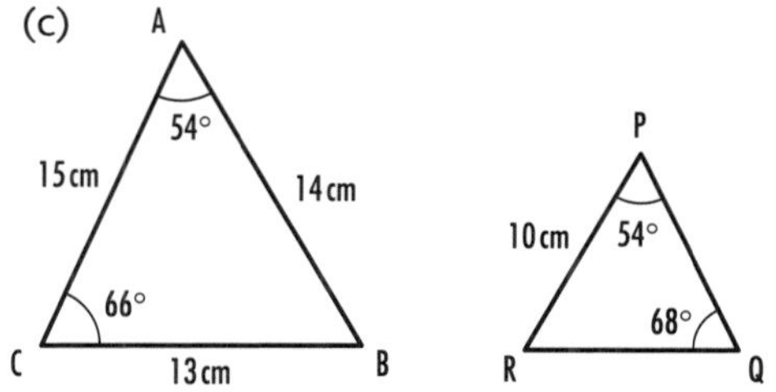

5 Calculate the unknown lengths or angles marked with letters in the diagrams.

(a)

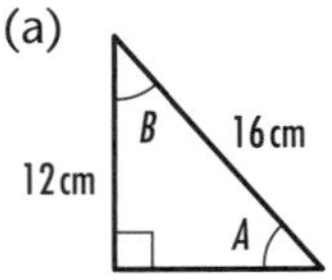

(b)

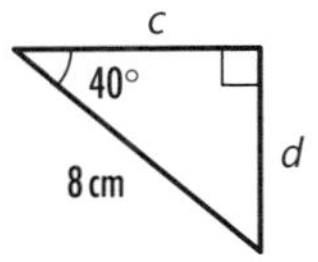

(c)

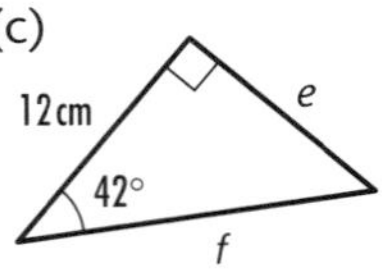

(d)

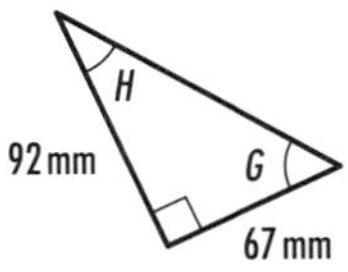

6 In each case, copy the diagram and find the centre of enlargement by drawing methods. State the coordinates of the centre of enlargement and the scale factor.

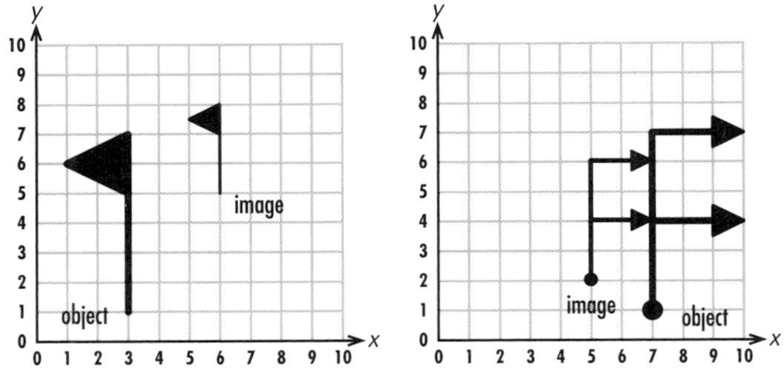

7 Draw the line AB = 45 mm, the line AC = 60 mm and angle BAC = 58°. Draw the locus of the point P that moves so it is equidistant from AB and AC.

8 Draw the line ST = 78 mm. Draw the locus of the point P that moves so it is equidistant from S and T.

Exercise EE

1

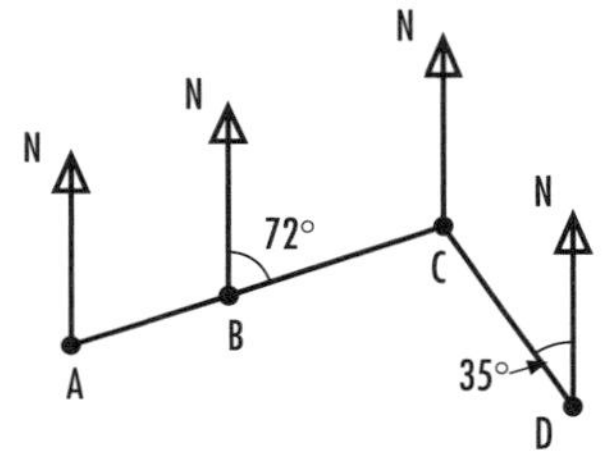

State the bearing of each of the following.

(a) C from B (b) B from C

(c) C from A (d) C from D

2 Copy each of the two diagrams onto squared paper. Draw the image of each object using the centre of enlargement, O, and the scale factor given.

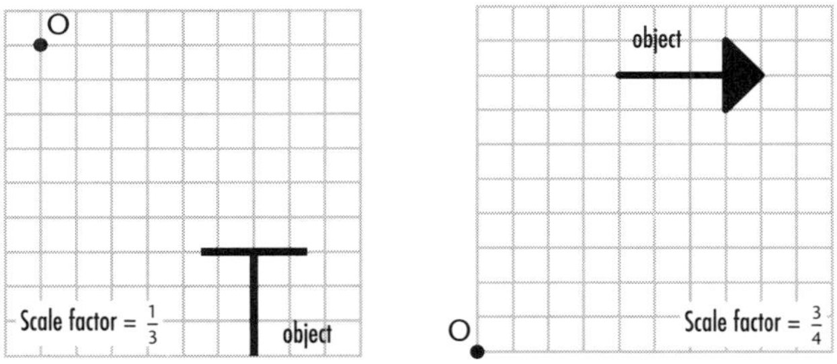

3

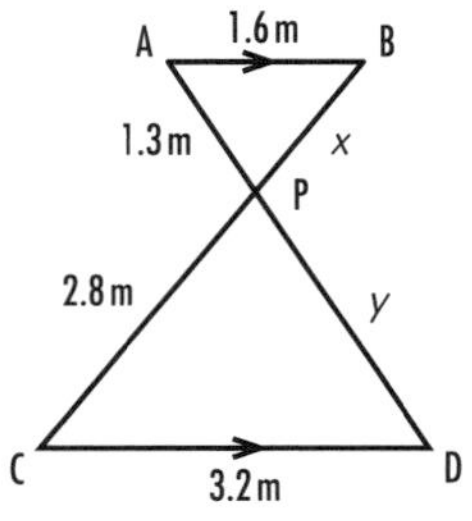

In the diagram AB is parallel to CD. Calculate the lengths x and y to 3 significant figures.

4

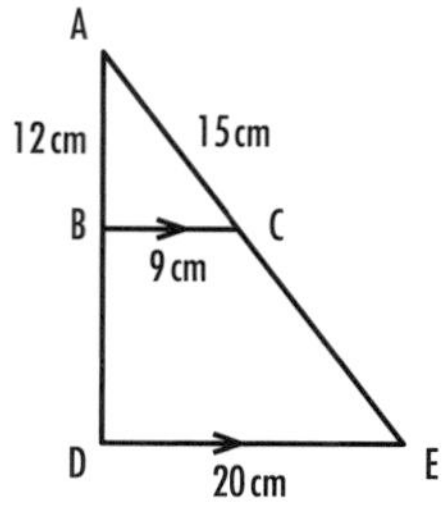

In the diagram BC is parallel to DE.

(a) State the two similar triangles.

(b) Calculate AD.

(c) Calculate AE and hence CE.

5 A5 paper measures 14.8 cm × 21 cm.

(a) Calculate the length of the diagonal.

(b) Calculate the angle that the diagonal makes with the 21-cm side.

6 A ship sails 4 nautical miles south and then 7 nautical miles east. Calculate its bearing (to the nearest degree) and its distance from the starting point.

7 A square has diagonals of length 21 cm. Calculate the length of the sides of the square.

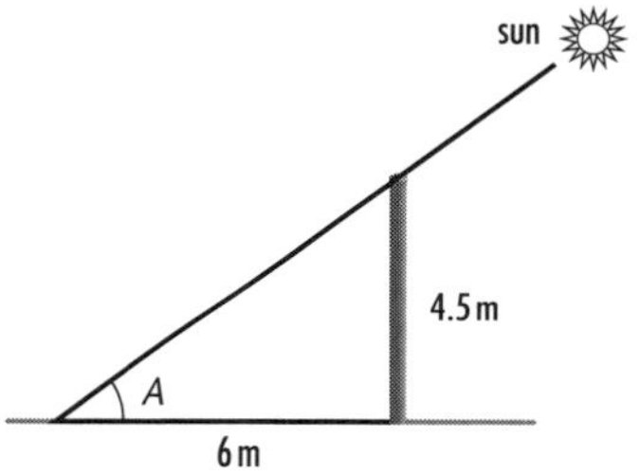

8 A vertical flag pole of height 4.5 m makes a shadow of length 6 m on horizontal ground. Calculate the angle of elevation of the sun (angle *A* in the diagram).

9 A kite string of length 40 m makes an angle of 63° with the horizontal ground. Calculate its height to the nearest metre.

10 A plane flies 25.4 km on a bearing of 074°. Calculate how far north it is from its starting point.

11 A farmer places a fence, in the form of a circle of radius 4 m, around a tree to protect it from the cows in a field. The tree is at the centre of the circle. The cows are able to reach grass inside the circle which is 1.5 m and less from the fence. Draw a diagram to show the grass available to the cows.

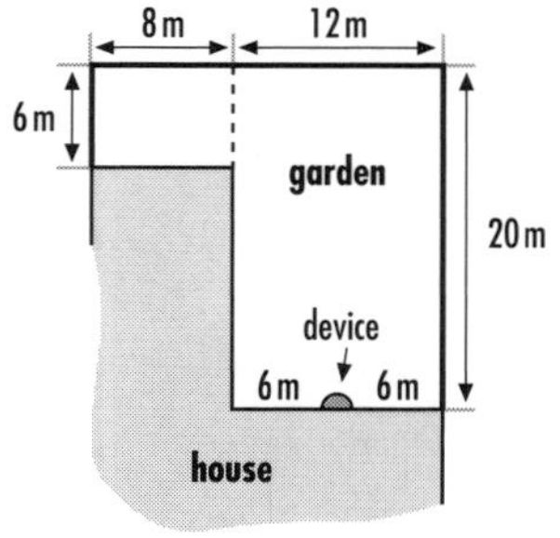

12 A security device can detect movement at distance of 20 metres within an angle of 120°. It is placed on the wall of a house as shown in the diagram. Copy the diagram and show the area that is not covered by the device.

13 Construct the triangle WXY accurately given that WX = 35 mm, WY = 42 mm and XY = 46 mm.

(a) Draw the locus of the point that is equidistant from the points W and Y.

(b) Draw the locus of the point that is equidistant from the points W and X.

(c) Draw the locus of the point that is equidistant from the points X and Y.

If you have completed (a), (b) and (c) correctly, the three loci should pass through a single point; label this O. With centre O and radius of length OX, draw a circle that passes through the points W, X and Y.

53/ COMPOUND MEASURES

Density is normally measured in g/cm^3 (or g cm^{-3}) or grams **per** cubic centimetre.
For example: The density of copper is 8.9 g/cm^3. This means that 1 cm^3 of copper weighs 8.9 grams.

Consumption is measured in compound units such as litres per mile (l/mile), litres per kilometre (l/km) etc.
For example: A certain car is said to have a fuel consumption of 0.11 l/km. This means that it uses 0.11 l for each kilometre travelled.

Economy is measured in units such as miles per gallon (m.p.g. or miles/gallon), kilometres per litre (km/l or km l^{-1}) etc.
For example: A car with an economy of 13 km/l will be able to travel 13 km for each litre of fuel used.

Speed is measured in units that combine distance and time such as kilometres per hour (km/h or km h^{-1}), metres per second (m/s or m s^{-1}), miles per hour (m.p.h.) etc.
For example: A runner who completes a race at an average speed of 8 km/h will cover 8 km in 1 hour at this rate.

EXAMPLE

► The density of gold is 19.3 g/cm^3. What is the weight of 5.6 cm^3 of gold?

1 cm^3 of gold weighs 19.3 g.
So 5.6 cm^3 of gold weigh $19.3 \times 5.6 = 108$ g.

EXAMPLE

► A car uses 18 litres whilst travelling 250 km. Calculate the average fuel consumption per kilometre.

$$\text{Consumption} = \frac{18}{250}$$
$$= 0.072\ l/\text{km}$$

Exercise 53A

1 Pete drives 125 miles in $2\frac{1}{2}$ hours. Calculate his average speed.

2 If 45 kg rests on an area of 9 cm^2, calculate the pressure in kg/cm^2.

3 Water flows through a pipe at the rate of 2.5 litres/second. Calculate the volume of water that flows in a minute.

4 A car is quoted as having a fuel consumption of 0.025 gallon/mile. Calculate the quantity of petrol required to travel 50 miles.

5 Zinc has a density of 7 g/cm^3. Calculate the volume of zinc that weighs 1.4 kg.

6 A lorry has a fuel economy of 11 km/l. How many litres of fuel will be needed to drive 350 km?

7 Don travels for 48 minutes at 110 km/h. Calculate the distance travelled.

8 In an experiment a trolley travels 1 metre in 0.62 second. Calculate the average speed of the trolley in m/s.

9 How many minutes will it take Kate to walk $2\frac{1}{2}$ miles at a steady speed of 3 m.p.h.?

10 Calculate the fuel economy, in m.p.g., if a car can travel 126 miles using 3 gallons of petrol.

11 Wes drives 210 miles and uses 5 gallons of fuel. Calculate the fuel consumption in gallons/mile.

12 Mercury has a density of 13.5 g/cm^3. Calculate the volume of mercury that weighs 2 g.

13 Oil is flowing at the rate of 0.05 litres/second. Calculate the flow in litres/hour.

14 A car is advertised as having a fuel economy of 45 m.p.g. How far can it travel at this rate on 5 gallons of fuel?

15 Fatima drives 100 miles at 50 m.p.h. and then 105 miles at 70 m.p.h. Calculate her average speed for the whole journey.

16 Sally cycles 6 km in 40 minutes. Calculate her average speed in km/h.

Exercise 53B

1 Floyd drives for 3 hours. If he travels 207 miles, calculate his average speed.

2 Calculate the fuel economy, in km/*l*, if a car can travel 132 km using 6 litres of petrol.

3 A car is quoted as having a fuel consumption of 0.075 *l*/km. How far will the car travel on 2 litres of fuel?

4 Calculate its density if 2.7 cm^3 of a substance has a weight of 10 grams.

5 Calculate the flow, in litres/hour, if 250 litres flow in 12 minutes.

6 A car has a fuel economy of 38 m.p.g. How many gallons of fuel will be needed (to the nearest gallon) for a journey of 220 miles?

7 Nathan runs at a steady speed of 15 km/h. How long will it take him to run 5 km?

8 A car is advertised as having a fuel economy of 58 m.p.g. How far can it travel at this rate on 4.5 gallons of fuel?

9 Gold has a density of 19.3 g/cm^3. Calculate the weight of a small bar with a volume of 24 cm^3.

10 Flora drives 140 km and uses 7 litres of fuel. Calculate the fuel consumption in *l*/km.

11 Rajesh travels for 2 hours at 64 m.p.h. Calculate the distance travelled.

12 Calculate the density of a substance if 5 cm^3 of the substance weighs 14.8 grams.

13 Water is flowing through a pipe at the rate of 120 cm^3/s. Calculate the time needed (to the nearest second) to fill a 5-litre can.

14 Tin has a density of 7.3 g/cm^3. Calculate the weight of 75 cm^3 of tin.

15 Chris drives 90 km at 60 km/h but then travels 120 km at 90 km/h.

(a) For how long does he travel at 90 km/h?

(b) Calculate his average speed for the whole journey.

16 A mass of 80 grams presses on an area of 0.5 cm^2. Calculate the pressure in g/cm^2.

54/ AREA AND PERIMETER (1)

Perimeter

The **perimeter** of a shape is the distance around the outside.

For example:

The perimeter of a rectangle of base, *b*, and height, *h*, is $2b + 2h$ or $2(b + h)$.

The perimeter of a circle is called the **circumference**, and $C = \pi d$, where *d* is the diameter of the circle.

Area

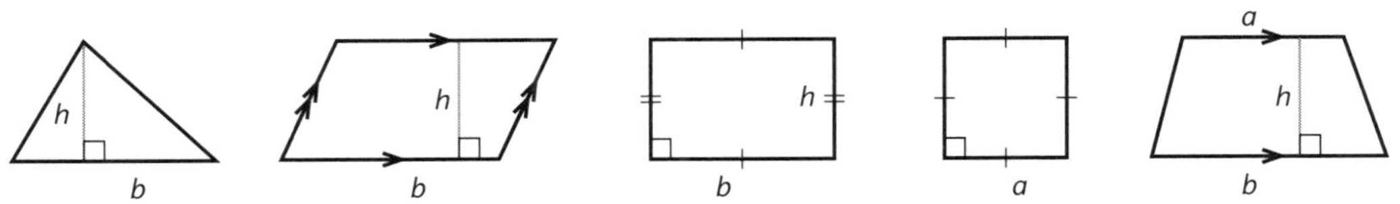

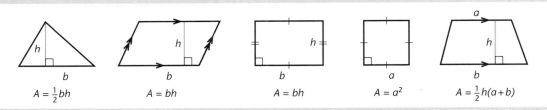

$A = \frac{1}{2}bh$ | $A = bh$ | $A = bh$ | $A = a^2$ | $A = \frac{1}{2}h(a+b)$

Area of a circle $= \pi r^2$, where *r* is the radius of the circle.

Exercise 54A

Give your answers to 3 significant figures if necessary.

Calculate the area of each of the following.

1 Triangle with height 6.2 cm and base 5.4 cm
2 Rectangle with sides of 12 cm and 8 cm
3 Parallelogram with height 1.5 m and base 1.2 m
4 Triangle with base 8.5 cm and height 4.2 cm
5 Square of sides 35 mm
6 Circle of radius 8 cm
7 Trapezium with parallel sides of 5 cm and 3 cm, and the distance between the parallel sides 4 cm
8 Circle of diameter 1.8 m

Calculate the perimeter of each of the following.

9 Circle of diameter 12 cm
10 Square with sides of 1.2 m
11 Rectangle with sides of 15 cm and 21 cm
12 Circle of radius 25 mm

For each shape calculate (a) the area (b) the perimeter.

13

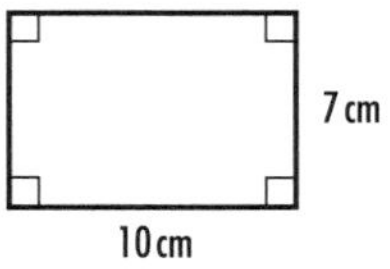

14

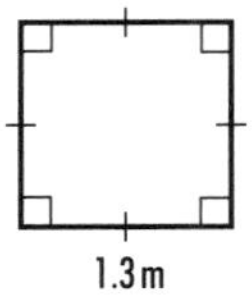

15

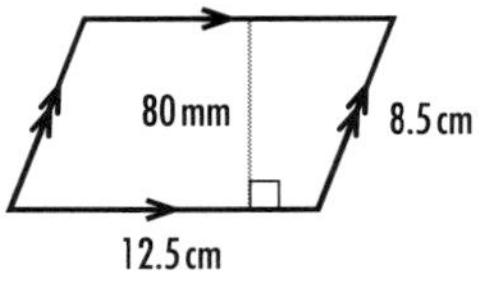

16

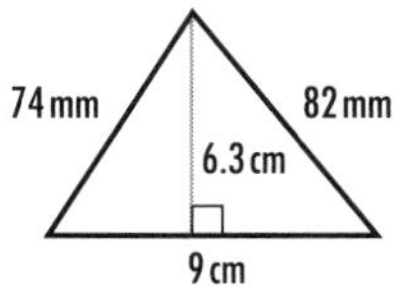

17

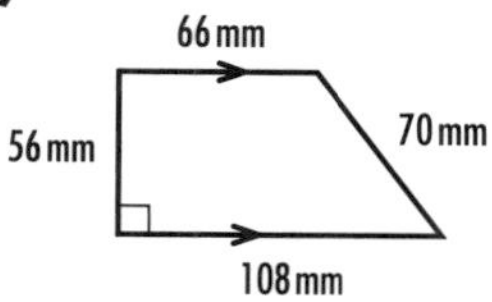

18

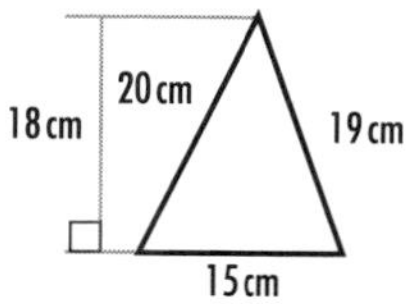

19

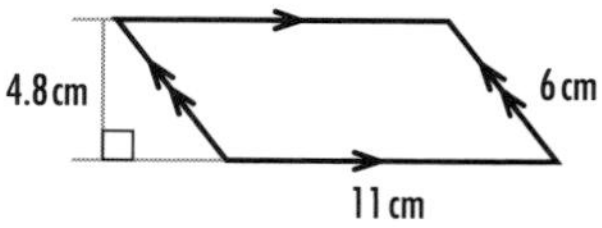

20

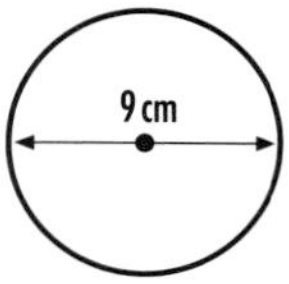

Exercise 54B

Give your answers to 3 significant figures if necessary.

Calculate the area of each of the following.

1 Rectangle with sides of 1.4 m and 0.8 m

2 Triangle with height 1.1 m and base 0.9 m

3 Parallelogram with base 48 mm and height 34 mm (answer in cm^2)

4 Square with side of 7.6 cm

5 Triangle with base 56 mm and height 4 cm

6 Circle of diameter 10 cm

7 Circle of radius 45 mm

8 Trapezium with parallel sides of 12 cm and 10 cm, and the distance between the parallel sides 9 cm

Calculate the perimeter of each of the following.

9 Square with sides of 32 mm

10 Rectangle with sides of 78 mm and 52 mm

11 Circle of diameter 45 mm

12 Circle of radius 8.5 cm

For each shape calculate (a) the area (b) the perimeter.

13

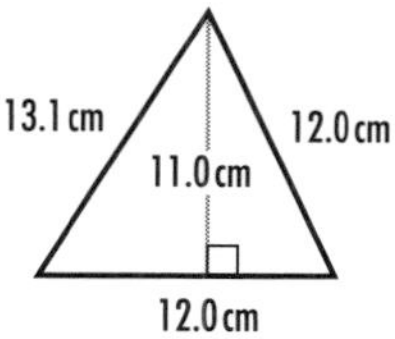

14

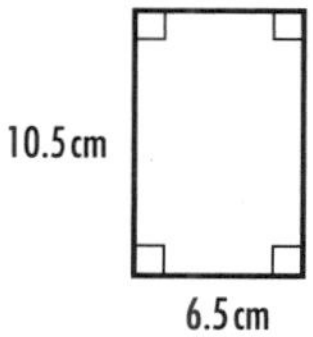

15

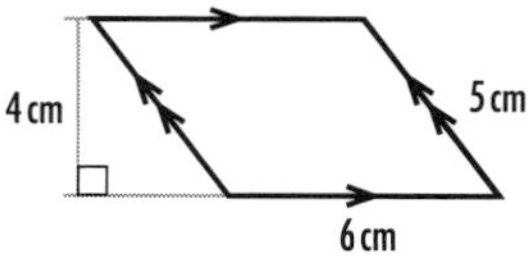

16

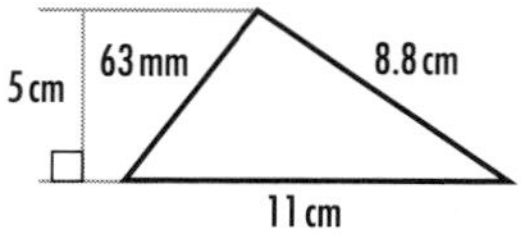

17

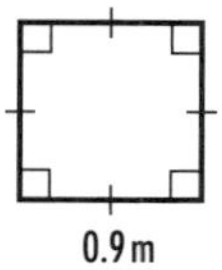

18

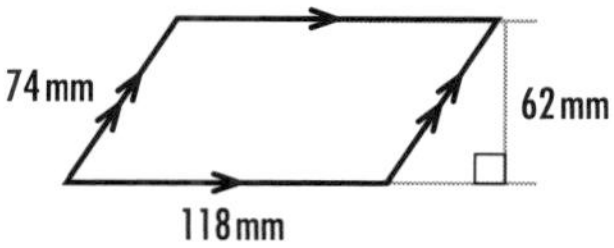

19

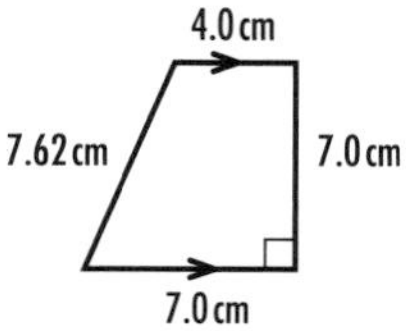

20

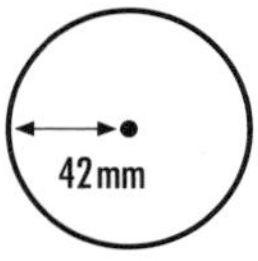

Semicircles and quadrants

Note: A **quadrant** is a quarter of a circle.

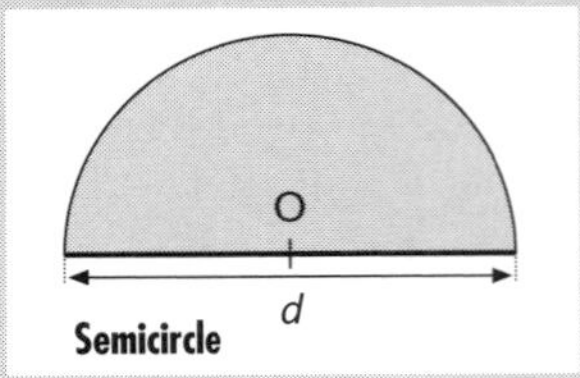

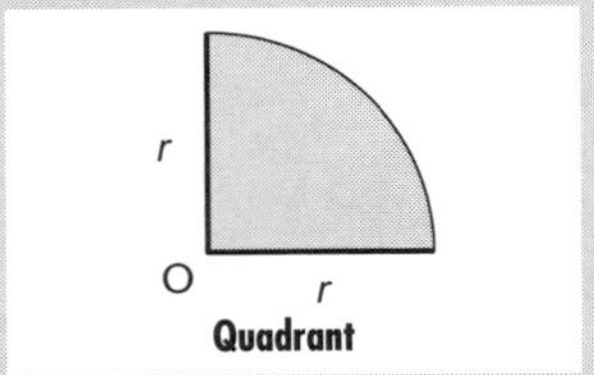

Area = $\frac{1}{2}\pi r^2$

Perimeter = $\frac{1}{2}$ × circumference + diameter

= $\frac{1}{2}\pi d + d$

Area = $\frac{1}{4}\pi r^2$

Perimeter = $\frac{1}{4}$ × circumference + 2 × radius

= $\frac{1}{4}\pi d + 2r$

Combined areas

EXAMPLE

► Calculate the total area of the shape.

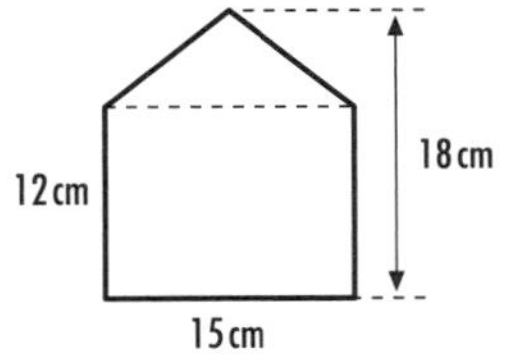

The area can be broken down into a rectangle and a triangle.

Area of rectangle $= bh = 15 \times 12 = 180\text{ cm}^2$

Area of triangle $= \frac{1}{2}bh = \frac{1}{2} \times 15 \times 6 = 45\text{ cm}^2$

Total area $= 180 + 45 = 225\text{ cm}^2$

Subtraction of areas

Sometimes it is much quicker to subtract one area from another or, as in the example that follows, it can be the only way of finding an area.

EXAMPLE

► Calculate the shaded area in the diagram.

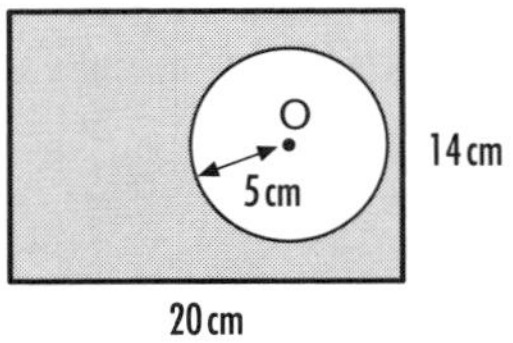

Area of rectangle $= bh = 20 \times 14 = 280\text{ cm}^2$

Area of circle $= \pi r^2 = \pi \times 5 \times 5 = 78.5\text{ cm}^2$

Shaded area = area of rectangle – area of circle

$= 280 - 78.5 = 201.5\text{ cm}^2$

Exercise 55A

Give your answers to 3 significant figures where necessary.

Calculate the shaded area in each of the following.

1

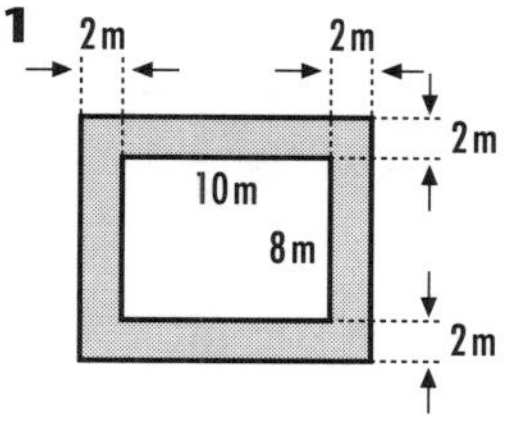

2

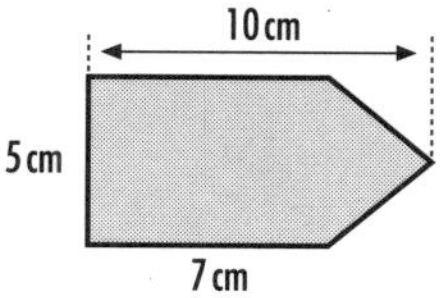

3

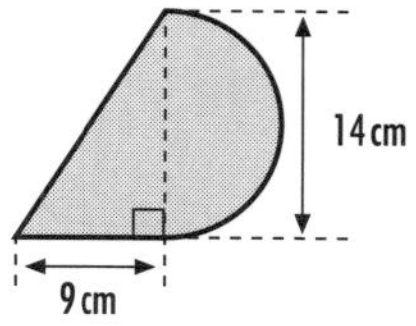

4

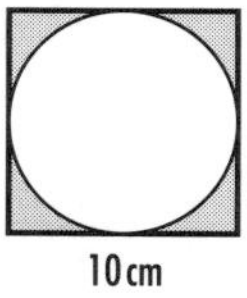

Calculate the area and perimeter in each of the following.

5

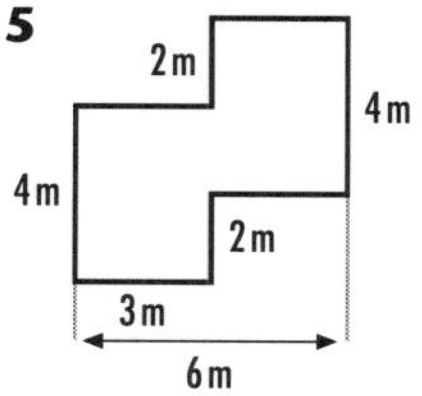

6

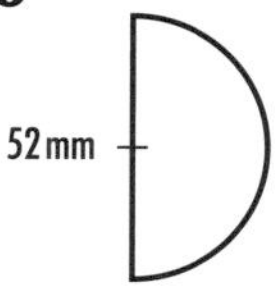

7

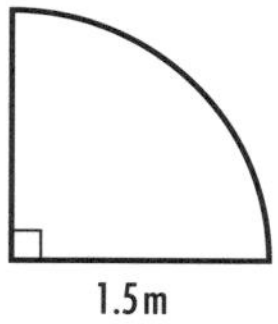

8

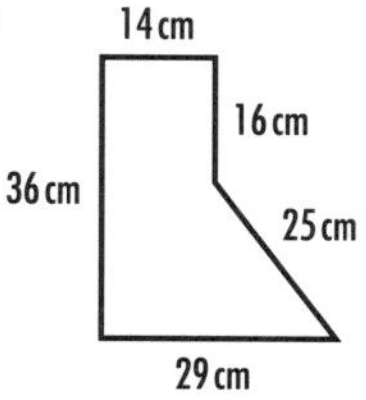

9 A room, which measures 3.5 m by 2.8 m, has a wood floor. A circular rug with a diameter of 2.1 m is placed on the floor. What area of wood flooring remains uncovered?

10 A copper pipe with a circular cross-section has an external diameter of 63 mm and an internal diameter of 60 mm. Calculate the area of copper in the cross-section.

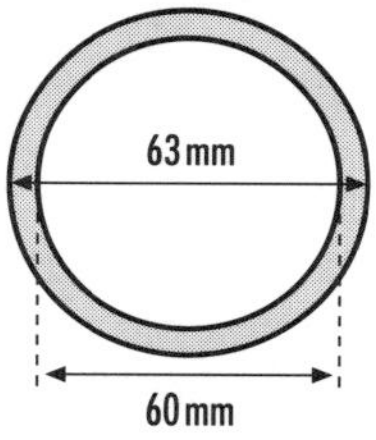

11 A rectangular piece of card measures 42 cm by 30 cm. A rectangular hole is cut in the card so that there is a 4 cm surround for a rectangular picture.
(a) State the measurements of the picture.
(b) Calculate the area of card that remains.

12 A square pond has a paved section around the outside. If the pond has sides of 2.4 m and the paved section is 1.2 m wide, calculate (a) the distance around the outer edge of the paved section (b) the area of the paved section.

13 The diagram shows a running track with a straight of 105 m and two semicircular ends of diameter 57.3 m. Calculate the total distance around the track.

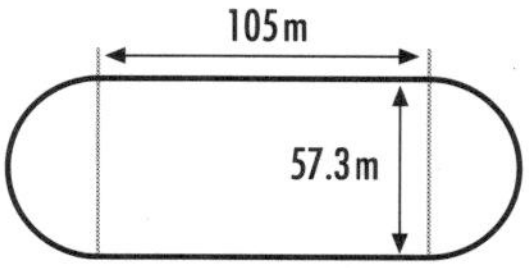

14 A section of a wall in a bathroom is tiled so there is a rectangular area measuring 126 cm by 66 cm in white tiles with a surrounding border of square green tiles of side length 6 cm. The border is one tile wide all the way round.
(a) How many green tiles are needed?
(b) What is the area of white tiles?
(c) What is the area of green tiles used?

15 A right-angled triangle has sides of 6 cm, 8 cm and 10 cm as shown in the diagram. Semicircles are drawn using the sides of the triangle as diameters. Calculate
(a) the area of the semicircle on the hypotenuse,
(b) the total area of the semicircles on the other two sides.
(c) What do you notice about the answers to (a) and (b)?
(d) Calculate the perimeter of the curved outer edge of the shape.

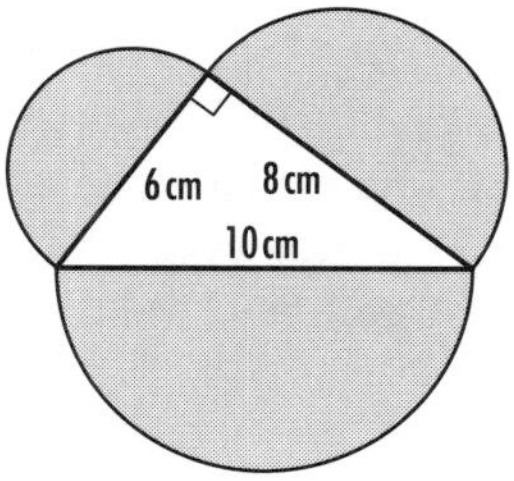

Exercise 55B

Give your answers to 3 significant figures where necessary.

Calculate the shaded area in each of the following.

1

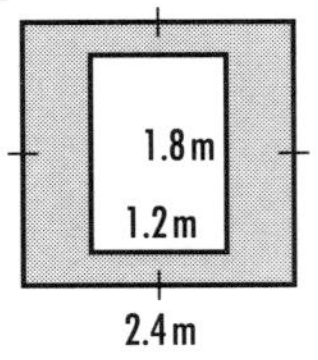

2

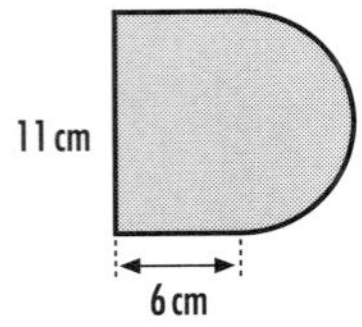

3

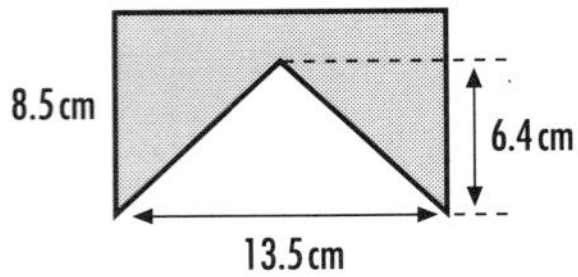

4

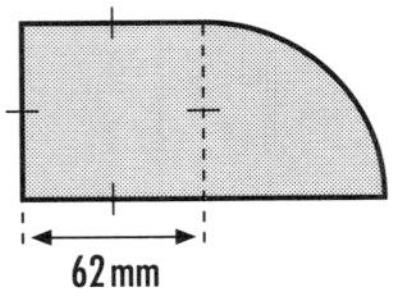

Calculate the area and perimeter in each of the following.

5

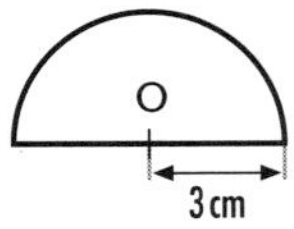

6

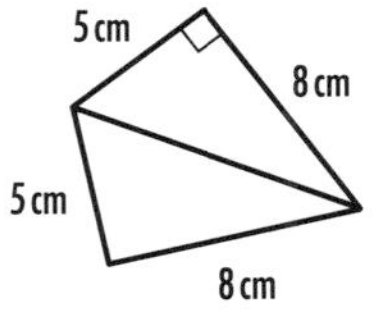

7

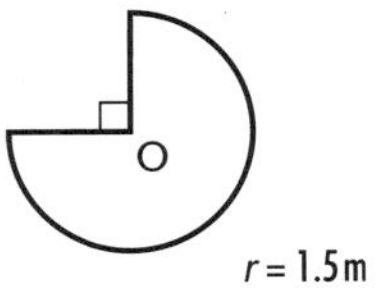

8

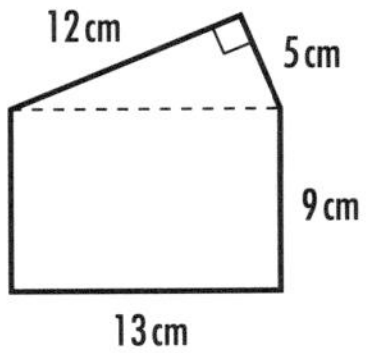

9 A rectangular flower bed measures 2.5 m by 4.2 m and is surrounded by a paved area which is 1.5 m wide. Calculate (a) the area of the paving (b) the perimeter of the flower bed.

10 Some lengths of wood-framing have a cross-section that is a quadrant. Calculate the area of the cross-section if the straight lengths in the cross-section measure 12 mm.

11 A plastic pipe has a square cross-section. The external square has an edge length of 8.1 cm and the plastic walls are 2 mm thick. Calculate (a) the difference between the outside and inside perimeters of the plastic in the cross-section (b) the area of plastic in the cross-section.

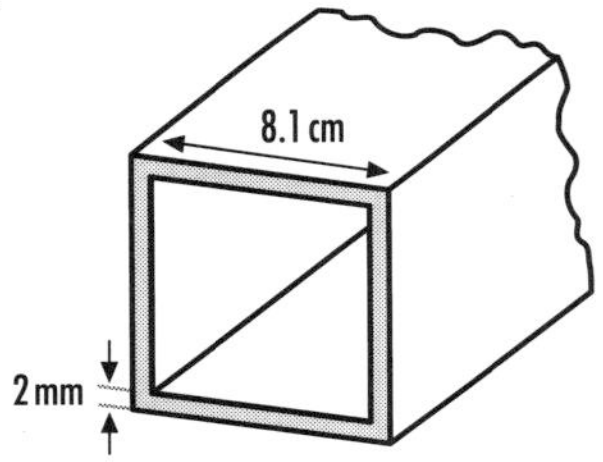

12 A carpet is made in the shape of a quadrant where each straight length measures 135 cm. The edge of the carpet needs tape. Calculate the length of tape required, to the nearest 10 cm.

13 Some edging strip has a cross-section that is a square with a quadrant removed as shown in the diagram. Calculate the area and perimeter of the cross-section.

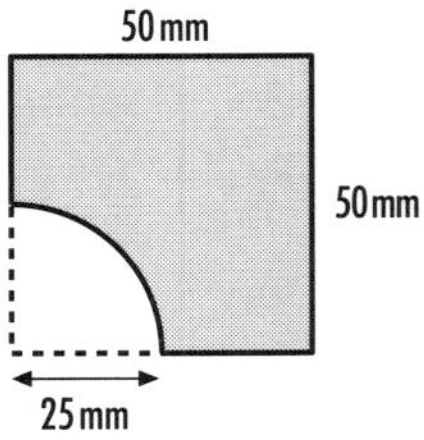

14

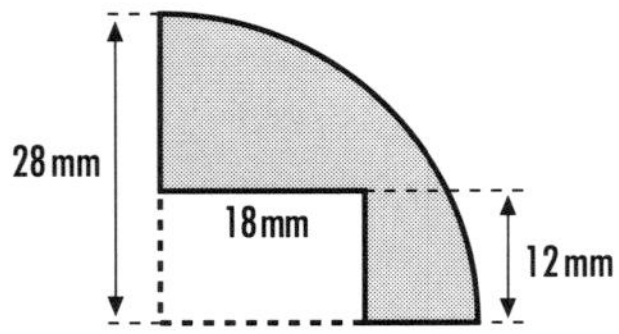

Lengths of wood used for framing pictures have a cross-section which is a quadrant with a rectangular section removed as shown in the diagram. Calculate the area of the cross-section.

15 A circular pond of radius 3.7 m has a concrete path around it. The path is 1.1 m wide. Calculate (a) the area of the path (b) the difference between the distance around the outside of the path and the distance around the outside of the pond.

56/ VOLUME: CUBES AND CUBOIDS

EXAMPLE

▶ Calculate the volume of water in a tank whose base measures 45 cm by 60 cm when the height of the water is 40 cm. Give your answer in cubic centimetres and also in litres.

$V = l \times w \times h$
$= 45 \times 60 \times 40 = 108\,000\text{ cm}^3$
$= 108\,000 \div 1000 = 108$ litres

Note: 1 litre = 1000 ml or 1000 cm^3
$1\text{ m}^3 = 1\,000\,000\text{ cm}^3 = 1000$ litres

EXAMPLE

▶ The volume of a cube of metal is 10 cm^3. Calculate the length of an edge.

$V = l^3 = 10$

So $l = \sqrt[3]{10} = 2.15$ cm (to 3 s.f.)

EXAMPLE

▶ Calculate how many cubes of edge length 9 cm can be fitted into a cube of edge 1 metre (a) by division of volumes (b) by considering how the cubes could be packed in practice.

(a) Volume of 9-cm cube = $9^3 = 729\text{ cm}^3$
Volume of $1\text{ m}^3 = 1\,000\,000\text{ cm}^3$
Number of small cubes that will fit into $1\text{ m}^3 = 1\,000\,000 \div 729$
$= 1\,371.74 \approx 1371$ cubes

(b) Number of 9-cm lengths that can be placed in 1 m = $100 \div 9 = 11$
(with 1 cm remaining wasted)
So the number of cubes = $11 \times 11 \times 11 = 1331$ cubes

Note: The number that *actually* can be packed into the space is less than the theoretical number obtained by dividing the smaller volume into the larger.

Exercise 56A

Give your answers to 3 significant figures where necessary.

1 Calculate the volume of each of the following.
(a) A cuboid measuring 12 cm by 15 cm by 20 cm
(b) A cube with an edge length of 15 cm
(c) A cuboid measuring 40 cm by 25 cm by 30 cm
(d) A cuboid measuring 1.5 m by 2.1 m by 1.8 m
(e) A cube with an edge length of 32 mm
(f) A cuboid measuring 16 cm by 18 cm by 15 cm

2 Calculate the volume of each of the cubes and cuboids shown in the diagrams.

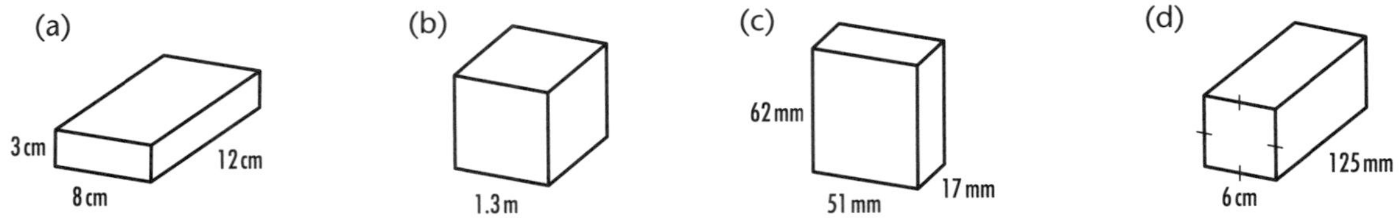

3 The volume of each of the cuboids in the diagram is shown together with two of the edge lengths. Calculate the length of the third edge in each case.

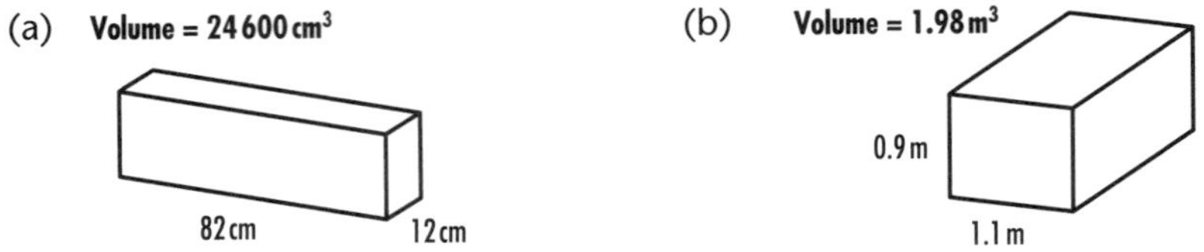

4 A tank holds 100 litres. If the base of the tank measures 50 cm by 40 cm, calculate the height of the tank.

5 A cube has a volume of 512 cm^3. Calculate the length of each edge.

6 The rectangular base of a water tank measures 75 cm by 60 cm. How far will the level of the water in the tank rise when 50 litres are added?

7 A cuboid has a volume of 720 cm^3. If two of the edge lengths are 12 cm and 6 cm, calculate the other edge length.

8 A cube has a volume of 800 cm^3. Calculate the length of each edge.

9 Water flows into a tank at the rate of 2.5 litres/second. Calculate the time it would take to fill a tank with a rectangular base measuring 80 cm by 100 cm to a height of 60 cm.

10 Assuming that there is no change in volume, what volume of water is required to make 48 ice-cubes if each measures 35 mm by 35 mm by 40 mm. Give your answer in millilitres.

11 A cube of side 12 cm is melted down and reshaped into a block of width 15 cm and length 18 cm. How high is the block?

12 What is the volume, in cm^3, of a piece of cardboard that measures 1.5 m by 1.6 m and is 4 mm thick?

13 Some cardboard boxes measure 32 cm by 18 cm by 16 cm.
(a) State the dimensions of a stack if the boxes are arranged 10 boxes by 10 boxes per layer and 6 boxes high.
(b) How many boxes are there in the stack?
(c) Calculate the volume of the stack in m^3.

14 A 1.2 m^3 block of metal is rolled out into a strip 60 cm wide and 2 mm thick. How many metres long is the strip?

15 Water flows from a tank with a rectangular base measuring 80 cm by 70 cm into a tank with a square base of side 60 cm. If the water in the first tank is 50 cm deep, how deep will it be when it is in the second tank?

Exercise 56B

Give your answers to 3 significant figures where necessary.

1 Calculate the volume of each of the following.
(a) A cuboid measuring 35 cm by 30 cm by 25 cm
(b) A cuboid measuring 65 mm by 75 mm by 50 mm
(c) A cube with an edge length of 2.6 cm
(d) A cube with an edge length of 75 mm
(e) A cuboid measuring 2.5 m by 2.2 m by 1.8 m
(f) A cuboid measuring 21 cm by 16 cm by 12 cm

2 Calculate the volume of each of the cubes and cuboids shown in the diagrams.

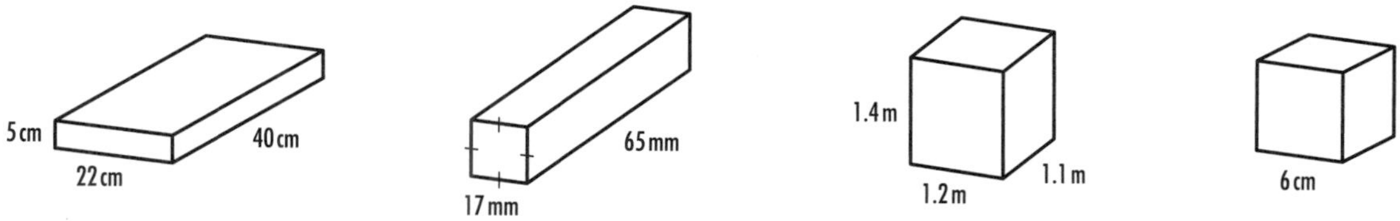

3 The volume of each of the cuboids in the diagrams is shown together with two of the edge lengths. Calculate the length of the third edge in each case.

(a) **Volume = 604.8 cm^3**

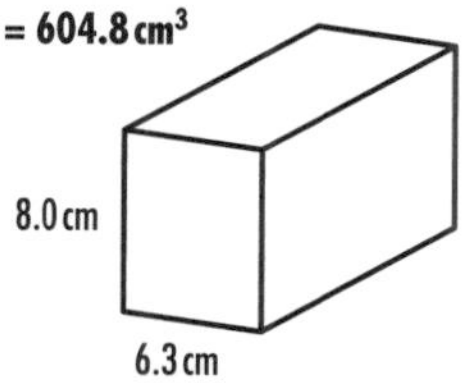

(b) **Volume = 2 cm^3**

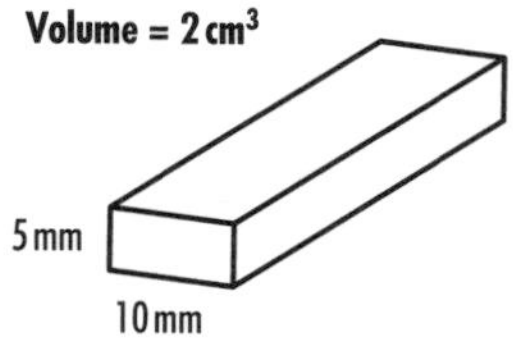

4 A tank holds 125 litres. If the base of the tank measures 60 cm by 75 cm, calculate the height of the tank.

5 A cube has a volume of 729 cm^3. Calculate the length of each edge.

6 The square base of a water tank has sides which are 75 cm in length. How far will the level of the water in the tank rise when 450 litres are added?

7 Oil flows into a tank at the rate of 0.05 litres/second. Calculate the time it would take to fill a tank with a square base of side length 25 cm to a height of 40 cm.

8 A cuboid has a volume of 560 cm^3. If two of the edge lengths are 8 cm and 5 cm, calculate the other edge length.

9 A cube has a volume of 500 cm^3. Calculate the length of each edge.

10 A wall is made using 2400 bricks that are 21 cm long, 9 cm wide and 6 cm high.
Calculate (a) the volume of each brick, in cm^3 (b) the total volume of the bricks used, in m^3.

11 A block measuring 15 cm by 12 cm by 20 cm is melted down and reshaped into a cube. Calculate the edge length of the cube.

12 A block of metal measuring 50 cm $\times$ 50 cm $\times$ 60 cm is rolled into a thin strip 600 m long and 1 mm thick.

(a) What is the volume of the block, in cm^3?
(b) What is the volume of the block, in m^3?
(c) What is the width of the strip, in cm?

13 A chemical flows from a tank with a square base of side 45 cm into a second tank with a rectangular base measuring 40 cm by 56 cm. If the depth of the chemical in the first tank is 52 cm, how deep will it be after it has flowed into the second tank?

14 What is the volume of a sheet of plasterboard measuring 2.4 m by 1.2 m and 18 mm thick? Give your answer in m^3.

15 Some boxes measure 12 cm by 15 cm by 10 cm high.

(a) How many boxes occupy a space of 2.5 m^3, to the nearest 100 boxes?
(b) If the 2.5 m^3 used is in the form of a container measuring 1.8 m by 2 m, how high is the container?
(c) What is the maximum number of boxes that can be stacked on the floor in a single layer if all the boxes are the correct way up and all in the same direction?
(d) What is the maximum number of boxes that can be stacked in the container if all the boxes are the correct way up and all in the same direction?

57/ VOLUME OF A PRISM

The volume of a prism is given by the formula

$$V = Al$$

where A is the area of the cross-section of the prism and l is the length or height of the prism. Some examples of the use of this formula are:

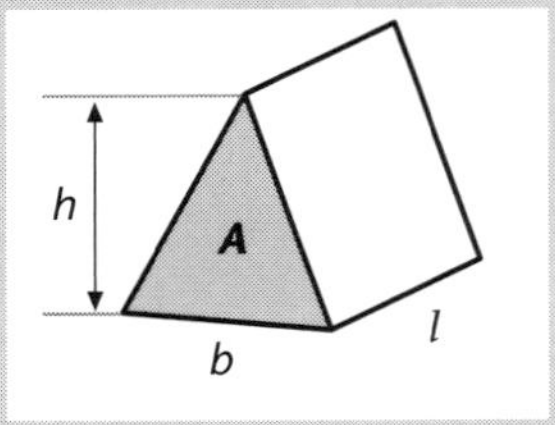

Triangular prism

$A = \frac{1}{2}bh$

$V = \frac{1}{2}bhl$

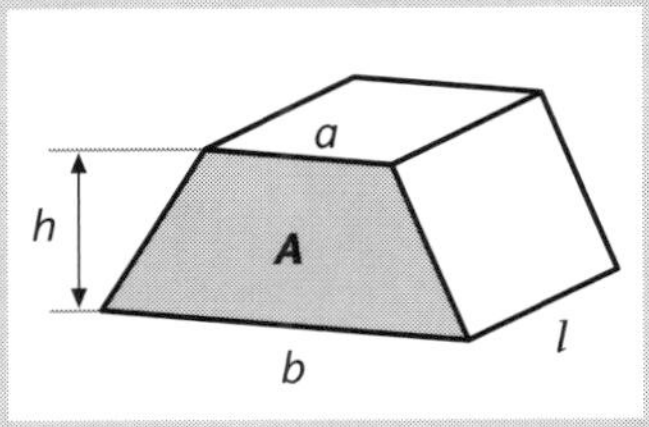

Trapezoidal prism

$A = \frac{1}{2}h(a + b)$

$V = \frac{1}{2}h(a + b)l$

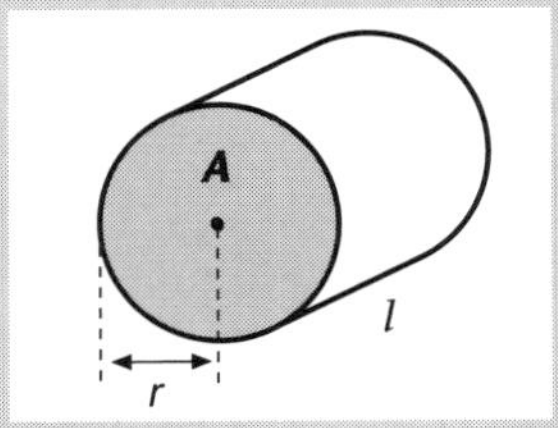

Cylinder

$A = \pi r^2$

$V = \pi r^2 l$ or $\pi r^2 h$

EXAMPLE

▶ A cylinder has a diameter of 9 cm and a height of 11 cm. Calculate its volume.

$V = Al = \pi r^2 h$
$= \pi \times 4.5^2 \times 11 = 699.7914 = 700 \text{ cm}^3$ (to 3 s.f.)

EXAMPLE

▶ A triangular prism has a volume of 50 cm^3. If the base of the triangle is 8 cm and the length of the prism is 5 cm, calculate the height of the triangle.

$V = Al = 50$
$5 \times A = 50$ and so $A = 10 \text{ cm}^2$

But $A = \frac{1}{2}bh$ and so $10 = \frac{1}{2} \times 8 \times h$

Therefore $h = 2.5$ cm

Exercise 57A

Give your answers to 3 significant figures where necessary.

1 Calculate the volume of each of the following prisms.

(a)

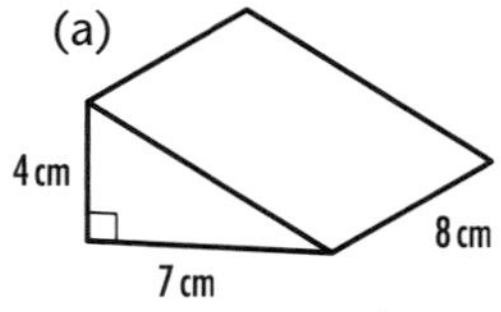

(b)

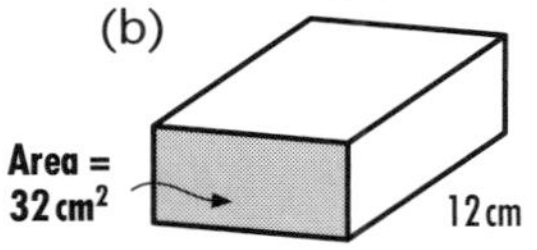

(c)

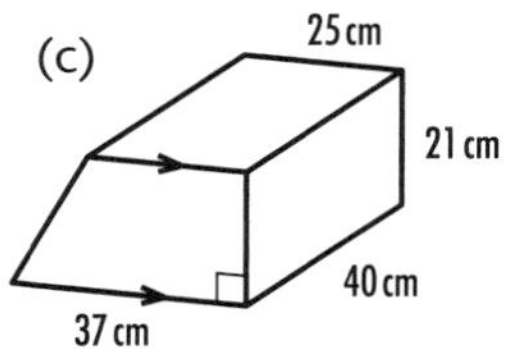

(d)

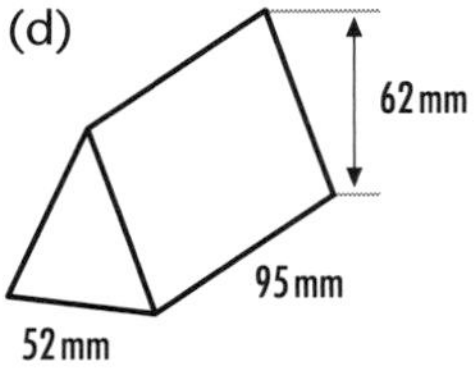

(e)

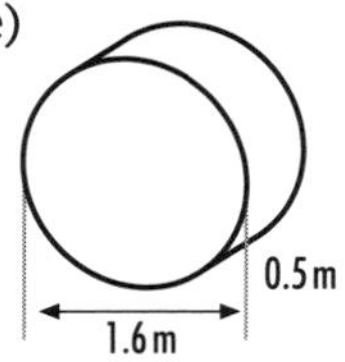

(f)

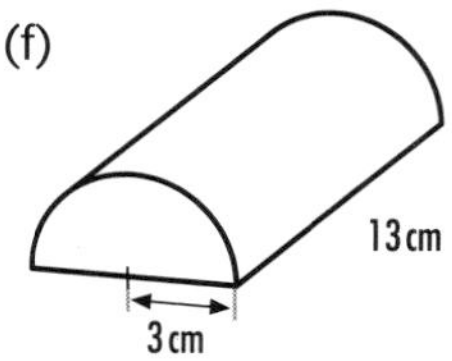

2 Given the volume of each prism, calculate the required quantity.

(a) Volume = 108 cm^3; find the area, A.

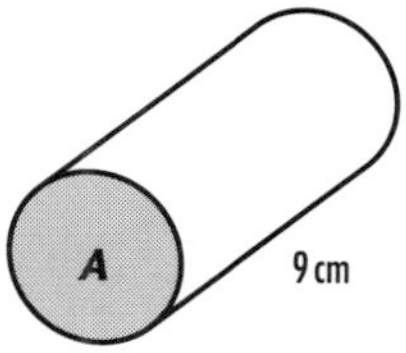

(b) Volume = 135 cm^3; find the height, h.

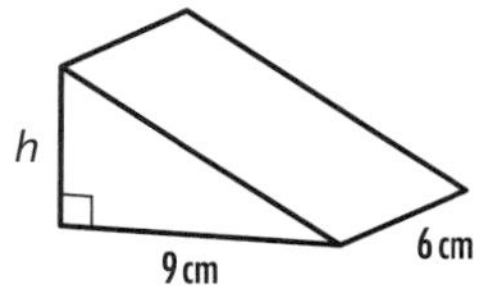

(c) Volume = 42 cm^3; find the height, h.

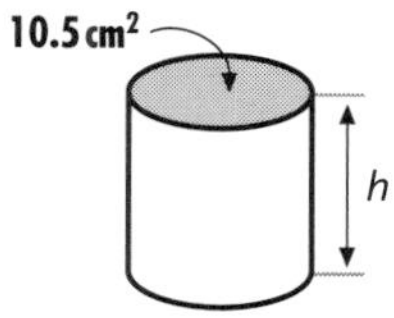

(d) Volume = 225 cm^3; find the shaded area, A.

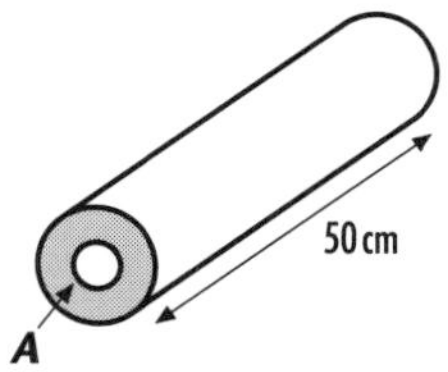

3 A prism of length 6 cm has a triangular cross-section of height 2.5 cm and base 4 cm. Calculate its volume.

4 Calculate the volume of a cylinder of diameter 42 mm and height 90 mm. Give your answer in cm^3.

5 The cross-section of a prism is a trapezium with parallel sides of length 6 cm and 10 cm; the distance between these parallel lines is 5 cm. Calculate the volume of the prism if its length is 9 cm.

6 Calculate the volume of a cylinder of diameter 3.8 cm and length 10.2 cm.

7 A container is in the shape of a prism of height 12 cm. If the container holds a litre, calculate the area of the cross-section of the prism.

8 Calculate the volume of a cylinder of diameter 4.2 cm and height 4.5 cm.

9 The volume of a cylinder, of radius 6 cm, is 826 cm^3. Calculate the length of the cylinder, to the nearest mm.

10 A prism has a volume of 360 cm^3. The cross-section is a parallelogram of height 45 mm. If the length of the prism is 10 cm, calculate the length of the base of the parallelogram.

11 A prism has a cross-section that is a triangle of base 34 mm and height 19 mm. If the volume of the prism is 64.6 cm^3, calculate its length.

12 Calculate the volume of a prism of length 12 cm if the cross-section is a rhombus with diagonals of length 10 cm and 8 cm.

13 Calculate the volume of a 40-cm long prism which has a cross-section that is a semicircle of diameter 2.5 cm.

14 The cross-section of a prism is a right-angled triangle with sides of length 50 mm, 12 cm and 13 cm. The length of the prism is 205 mm. Calculate (a) the area of the cross-section (b) the volume of the prism.

Exercise 57B

Give your answers to 3 significant figures where necessary.

1 Calculate the volume of each of the following prisms.

(a)

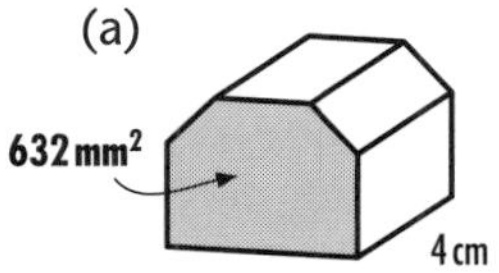

(b)

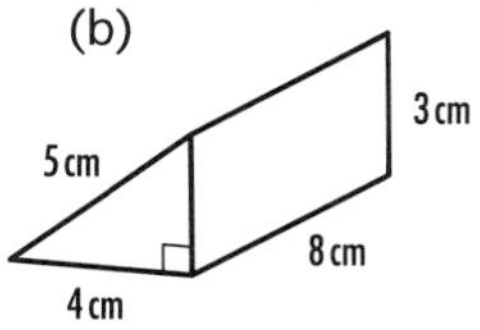

(c)

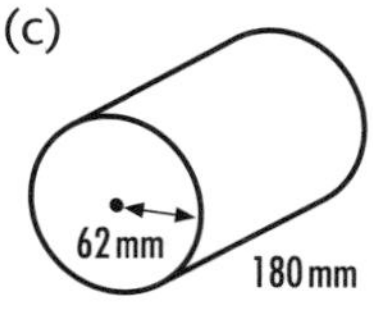

(d)

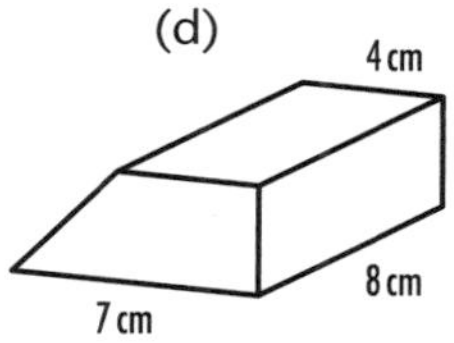

(e)

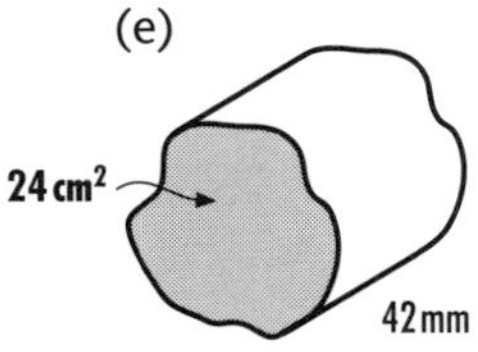

(f)

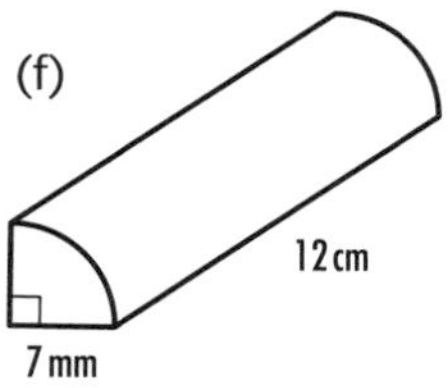

2 Given the volume of each prism, calculate the required quantity:

(a) Volume = 21 cm^3;
find the area, A.

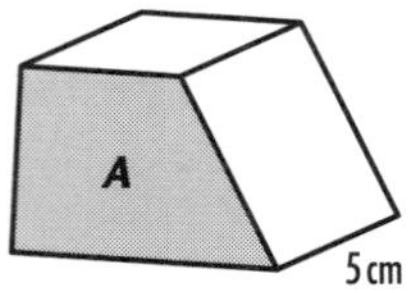

(b) Volume = 3 cm^3;
find the length, l, in cm.

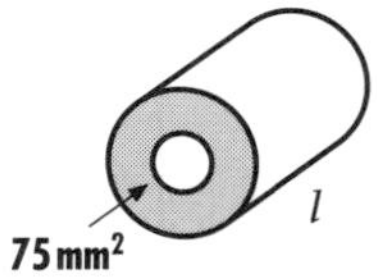

(c) Volume = 5376 mm^3;
find the height, h.

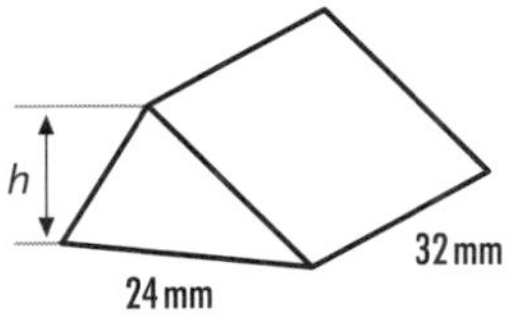

(d) Volume = 560 cm^3;
find the area, A.

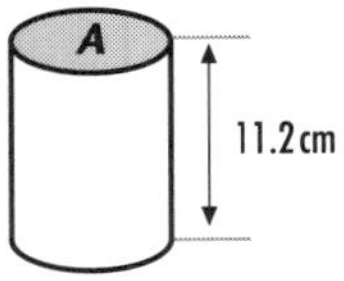

3 Calculate the volume of a prism of length 9 cm if the cross-section is a triangle of height 7 cm and base 8 cm.

4 The volume of a prism is 10 cm^3 and the cross-section has an area of 250 mm^2. Calculate the length of the prism.

5 Calculate the volume, to the nearest 10 mm^3, of a cylinder of radius 7 mm and height 12 mm.

6 A container is in the shape of a prism of height 13 cm. If the container holds 500 ml, calculate the area of the cross-section of the prism.

7 Calculate the volume of a 50 cm length of quadrant beading if the cross-section is a quadrant of radius 25 mm. Give your answer in cm^3.

8 The volume of a cylinder is 650 cm^3. If the radius is 5.1 cm, calculate the length of the cylinder, to the nearest mm.

9 Calculate the volume of a prism of length 10 cm if the cross-section is a kite with diagonals of length 6 cm and 12 cm.

10 Calculate the volume of a 1-metre length of beading that has a cross-section in the shape of a semicircle of diameter 44 mm. Give your answer in cm^3.

11 A prism has a cross-section that is a trapezium with parallel sides of length 5 cm and 7 cm. The length of the prism is 14 cm and its volume is 588 cm^3. Calculate the distance between the parallel lines.

12 A prism of length 56 cm has a cross-section which is a parallelogram. If the base of the parallelogram is 34 mm and the height 27 mm, calculate the volume of the prism.

13 Calculate the volume of a cylinder of radius 5 cm and height 12 cm.

14 A prism has a cross-section which is a trapezium with parallel sides of length 34 mm and 48 mm. The distance between the parallel sides is 30 mm.

(a) Calculate the area of the cross-section (i) in mm^2 (ii) in cm^2.

(b) Calculate the volume of the prism, in cm^3, if its length is 62 mm.

58/ SURFACE AREA

On straight-forward examples it is possible to identify the number of faces and the size of each.

EXAMPLE

► Calculate the total surface area of a cuboid measuring 7 cm, 8 cm and 12 cm.

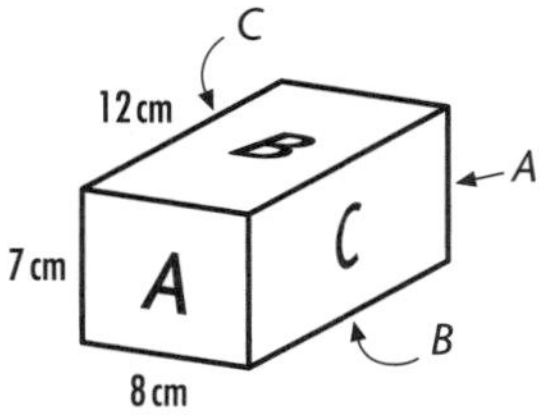

There are three sizes of faces and each occurs twice.

Area $A = 7 \times 8 = 56\ \text{cm}^2$

Area $B = 8 \times 12 = 96\ \text{cm}^2$

Area $C = 7 \times 12 = 84\ \text{cm}^2$

Total area $= 2A + 2B + 2C$ or $2(A + B + C)$

$= 2 \times (56 + 96 + 84)$

$= 472\ \text{cm}^2$

At other times it can be helpful to draw a sketch of the net of the shape. This can be used to break the total area down into its separate faces.

EXAMPLE

► Calculate the total surface area of the triangular prism shown in the diagram.

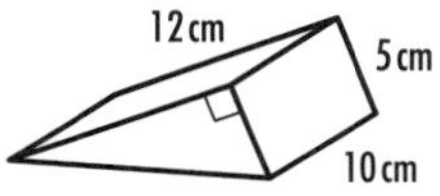

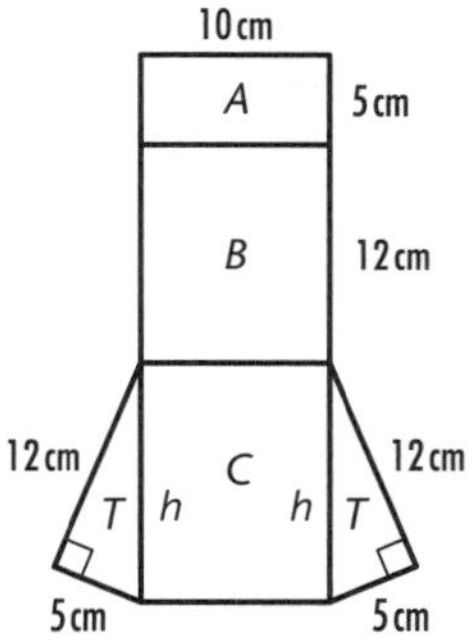

Area $A = 5 \times 10 = 50\ \text{cm}^2$

Area $B = 12 \times 10 = 120\ \text{cm}^2$

Area $T = \frac{1}{2} \times 5 \times 12 = 30\ \text{cm}^2$

In order to find area C, it is necessary to find h using Pythagoras' theorem.

$h^2 = 5^2 + 12^2 = 169$ and so $h = 13$ cm

Area $C = 13 \times 10 = 130\ \text{cm}^2$

Total area $= A + B + C + 2T$

$= 50 + 120 + 130 + (2 \times 30)$

$= 360\ \text{cm}^2$

Exercise 58A

Give your answers to 3 significant figures where necessary.

1 Calculate the total surface area of each of the shapes in the diagrams.

(a)

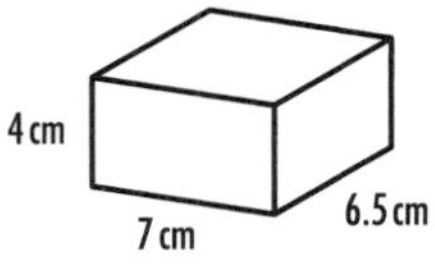

(b)

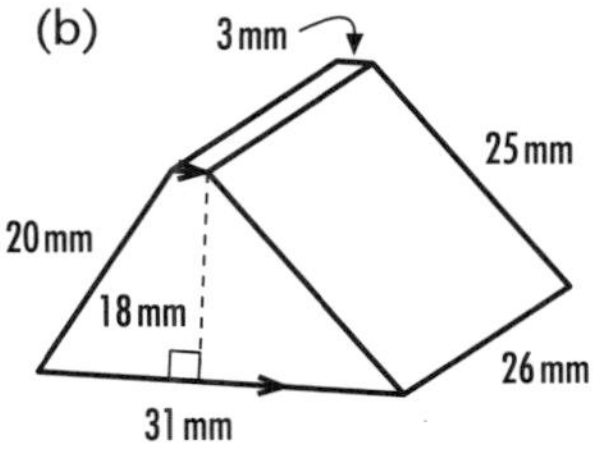

(c)

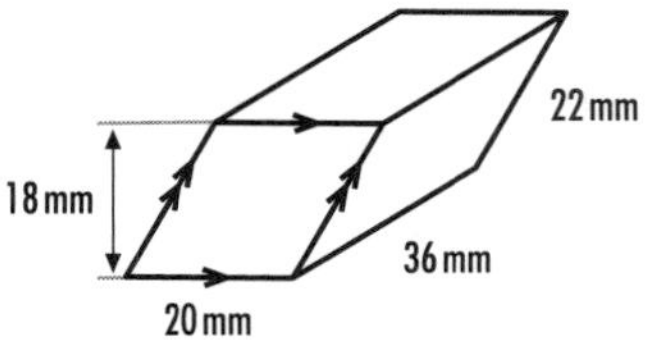

(d)

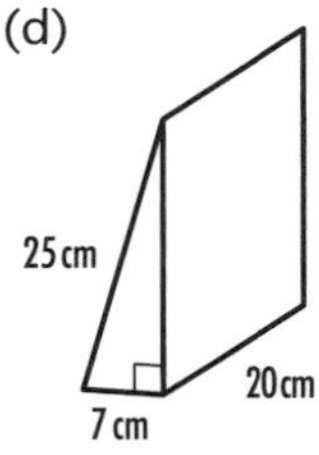

2 Calculate the total surface area of a cuboid measuring 4 cm by 6 cm by 9 cm.

3 The window-box in the diagram needs to be painted inside and out. Ignoring the thickness of the wood used calculate the area to be painted, to the nearest 100 cm^2, (a) in cm^2 (b) in m^2.

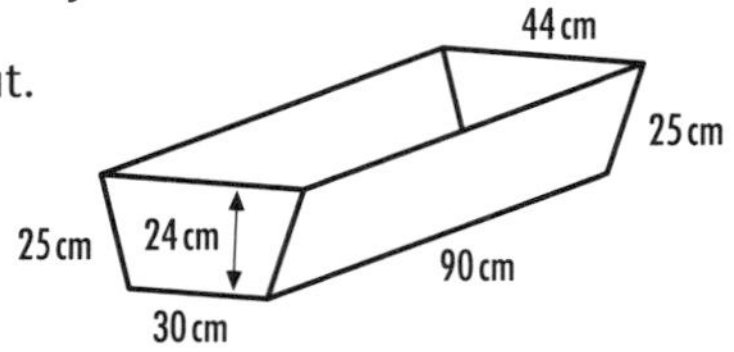

4 Calculate the total surface area of a cube of edge length 5 cm.

5 Calculate the total surface area of a prism with a cross-section that is a parallelogram. The sides of the parallelogram are 8 cm (base) and 6 cm. The height of the parallelogram is 5 cm. The length of the prism is 11 cm.

6 Calculate the total surface area of the outside of an open box (without a lid) which has a base measuring 4 cm by 8 cm and has a height of 5 cm.

7 Calculate the total surface area of a cuboid measuring 24 mm by 36 mm by 5 cm.

8 Calculate the total surface area of a cube of edge length 1.2 m.

9 Calculate the total surface area of a prism with a cross-section that is a square of area 2.25 m^2 if the length of the prism is 0.6 m.

10 Calculate the total surface area of the outside of an open box (without a lid) which has a base measuring 11.5 cm by 8.2 cm and has a height of 6.5 cm.

11 A rectangular room measuring 3.2 m by 2.8 m has a height of 2.4 m. The *walls* of the room are to be painted. Calculate the total area of the walls of the room.

12 Calculate the total surface area of each of the shapes shown.

(a)

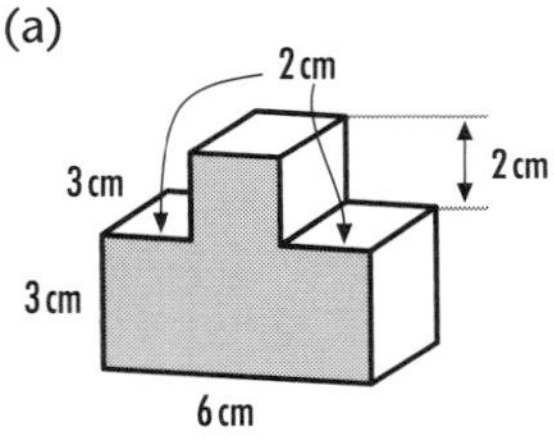

(b)

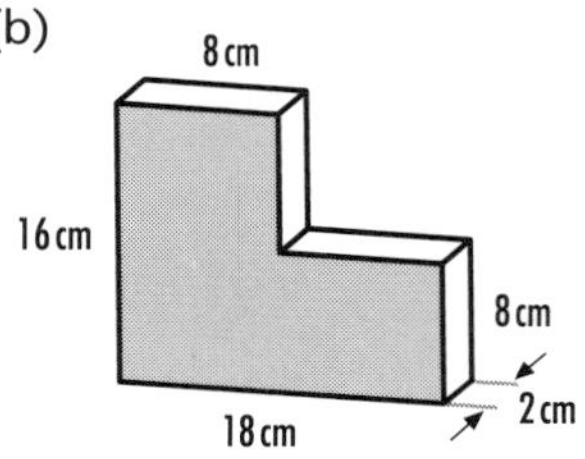

Exercise 58B

Give your answers to 3 significant figures where necessary.

1 Calculate the total surface area of each of the shapes in the diagrams.

(a)

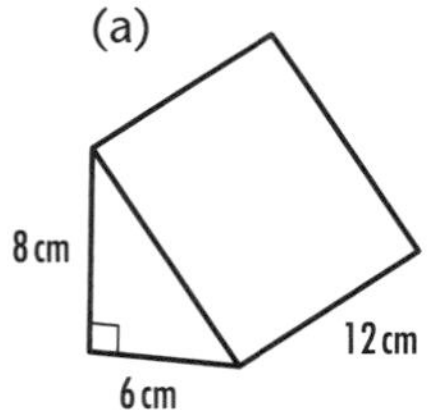

(b)

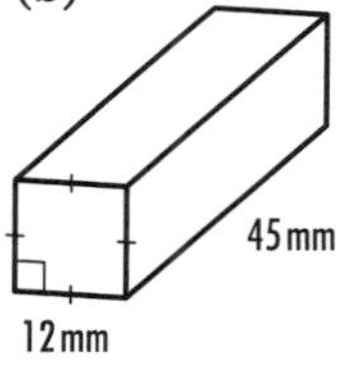

(c)

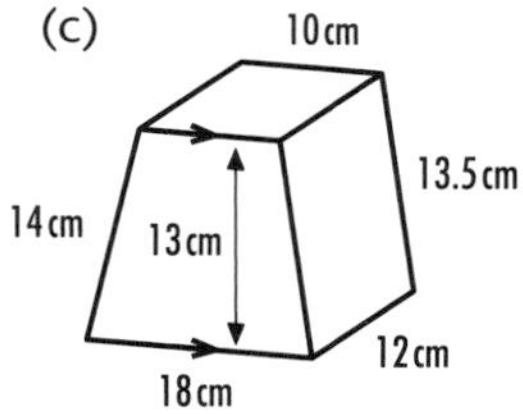

(d)

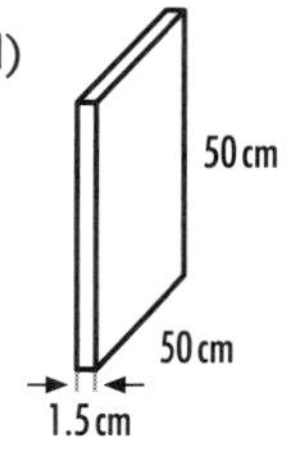

2 Calculate the total surface area of a cuboid measuring 5 cm by 6 cm by 8 cm.

3 Calculate the total surface area of the outside of an open box (without a lid) which has a base measuring 1.0 m by 0.8 m and has a height of 0.5 m.

4 A prism has a cross-section that is a rhombus of side length 7 cm and area 12 cm^2. Calculate the total surface area of the prism if its length is 11 cm.

5 Calculate the total surface area of a cube of edge length 25 mm.

6 The shape of the floor of a room is shown in the diagram. The height of the room is 2.6 m. The ceiling and the walls are to be painted. Calculate the area to be painted, to the nearest m^2.

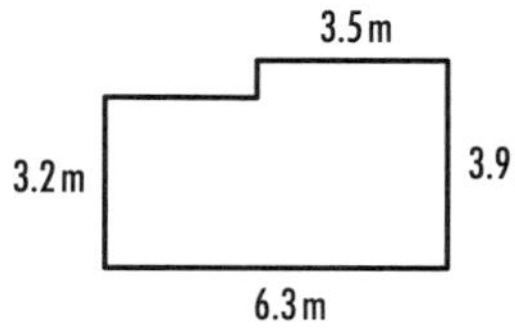

7 Calculate the total surface area of a cuboid measuring 0.8 m by 0.6 m by 1.6 m.

8 Calculate the total surface area of the outside of an open box (without a lid) which has a base measuring 11.5 cm by 8.2 cm and has a height of 6.5 cm.

9 Calculate the total surface area of a cuboid measuring 14 mm by 2 cm by 25 mm. Give your answer in cm^2.

10 Calculate the total surface area of a cube of edge length 0.8 m.

11 An open box (as in the diagram) is made of wood that is 1 cm thick. The whole of the inside and outside is to be painted. Calculate the area to be painted.

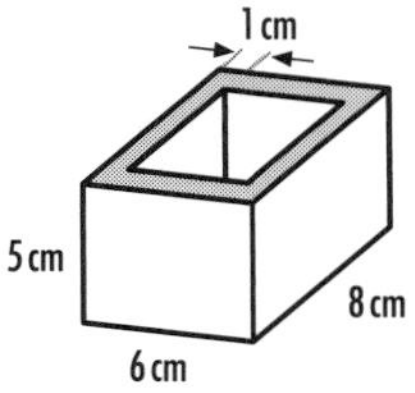

12 Calculate the total surface area of each of the shapes shown.

(a)

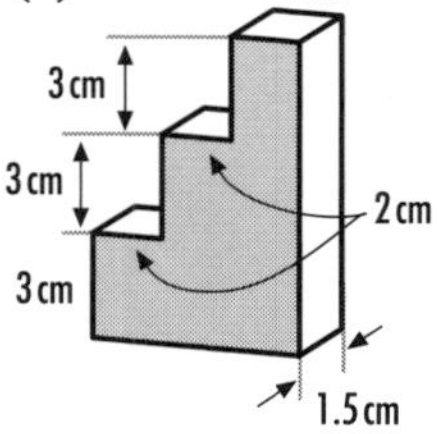

(b)

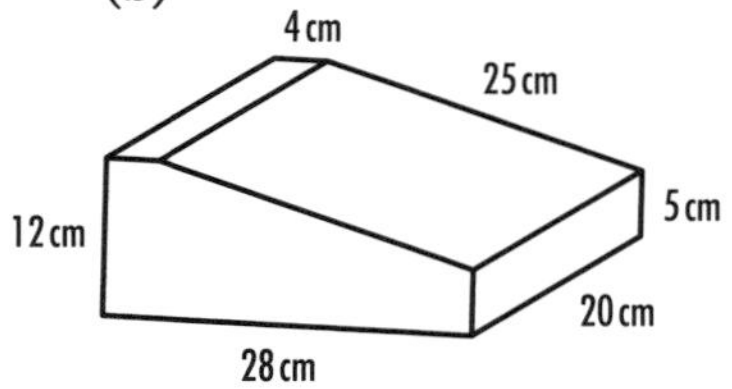

REVISION

Exercise F

1 The density of iron is 7.8 g cm^{-3}. What is the weight of 24 cm^3 of iron?

2 Pete travels for 45 minutes at 120 km/h. Calculate the distance travelled.

3 A car is quoted as having a fuel consumption of 0.02 gallon/mile. Calculate the quantity of petrol required to travel 60 miles.

4 Calculate (i) the area (ii) the perimeter of each of the shapes.

(a)

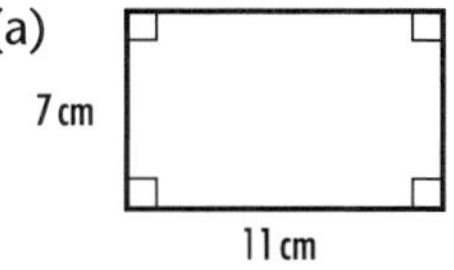

(b)

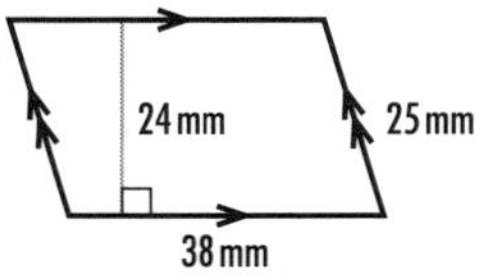

(c)

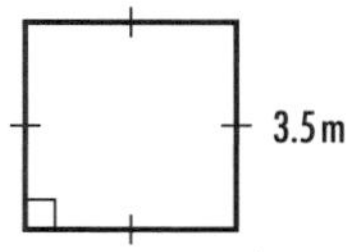

(d)

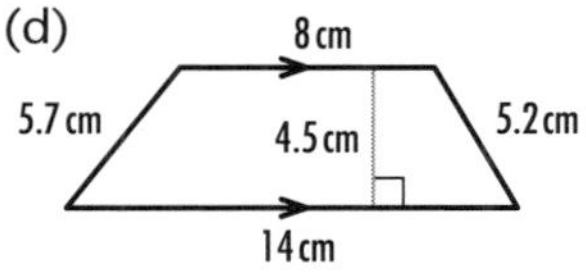

(e)

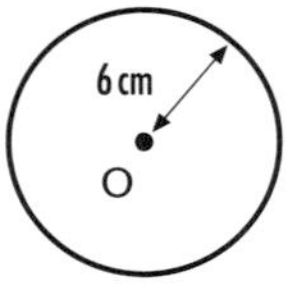

(f)

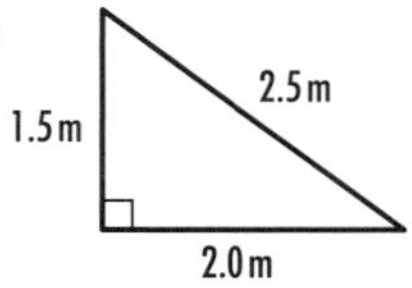

5 Calculate the area and perimeter of each of the shapes.

(a)

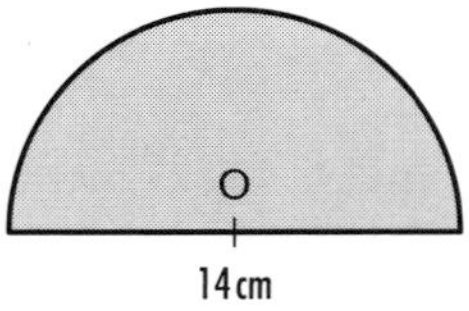

(b)

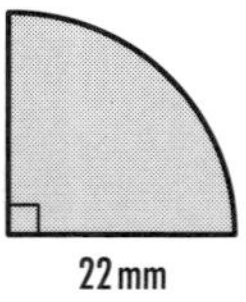

6 Calculate the shaded area in each diagram.

(a)

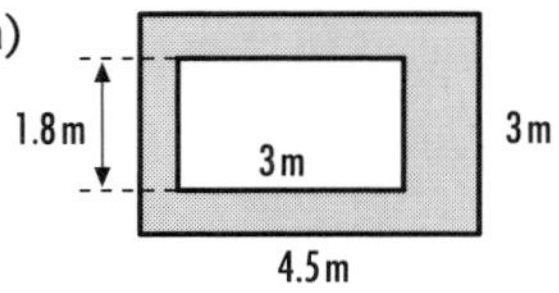

(b)

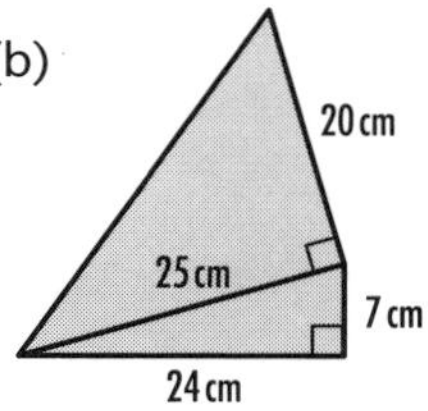

7 A cuboid measures 4 cm by 6 cm by 10 cm. Calculate (a) the surface area (b) the volume.

8 Calculate the surface area and volume of a cube of side length 7 cm.

9 For each of the shapes calculate (i) the surface area (ii) the volume.

(a)

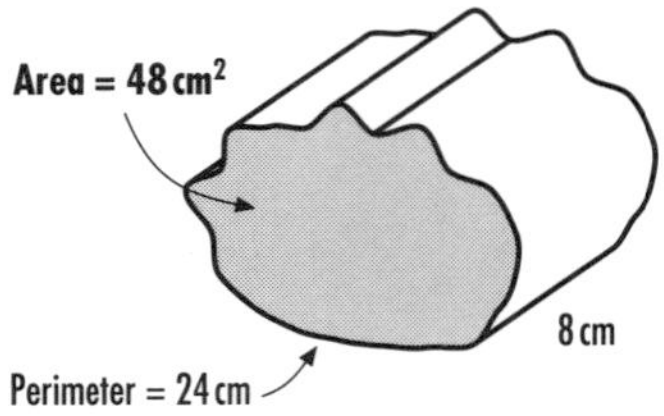

(b)

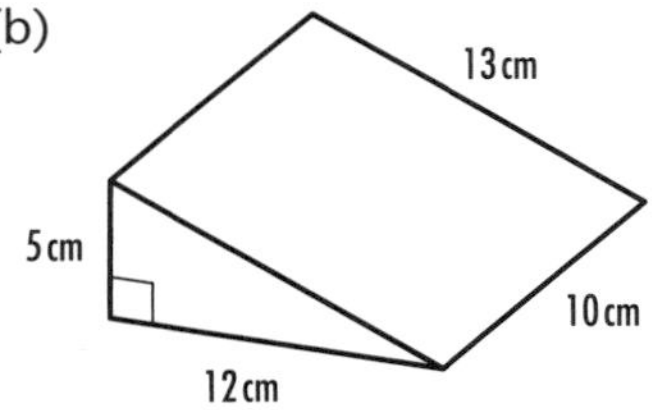

Exercise FF

1 Sarah drives 120 miles at 40 m.p.h. and then 80 miles at 60 m.p.h. Calculate her average speed for the whole journey.

2 Zinc has a density of 7 g/cm^3. Calculate the volume of zinc that weighs 1.4 kg.

3 Water is flowing through a pipe at the rate of 85 cm^3/s. Calculate the time needed (to the nearest second) to fill a 4.5 litre can.

4 A flower bed is in the shape of a semicircle with a diameter of 4.2 m.
(a) The flower bed is to be edged with lawn-edging. How many packs of lawn-edging are required if each pack contains 5 m?
(b) Calculate the area of the flower bed.
(c) Fertiliser is to be applied to the flower bed at the rate of 75 g/m^2. How many 500 g boxes of fertiliser will be required?

5 The density of ice is 0.92 g/cm^3 but, when it melts, the water has a density of 1.0 g/cm^3. There is 500 kg of water in a rectangular tank with a base area of 4550 cm^2 which then freezes.
(a) Calculate the volume of the water.
(b) Calculate the depth of water in the tank.
(c) Calculate the volume of ice when the water freezes.
(d) Calculate the increase in the depth when the water freezes.

6 A right-angled triangle ABC has lengths AB = 20 cm and AC = 10 cm. The angle ACB = 90°. Calculate the perimeter and area of the triangle.

7 Plastic coving is made in the shape of a prism with a cross-section that is a quadrant of radius 48 mm. The density of the plastic is 0.1 g/cm^3.
Calculate (a) the volume of a 1-metre length of the coving
(b) its weight, to the nearest gram.

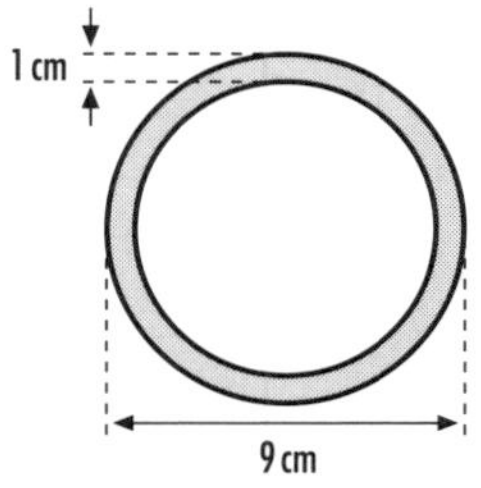

8 The diagram shows the cross-section of a pipe. Calculate (a) the area of the cross-section (b) the volume of a 60 cm length of the pipe.

9 A block of copper measures 40 cm by 40 cm by 60 cm.
(a) What is the volume of the block?
(b) If copper has a density of 8.9 g/cm^3, what is the weight of the block?
The block of copper is made into wire with a circular cross-section of diameter 2 mm.
(c) Calculate the area of the cross-section of the wire, in mm^2.
(d) How many mm^2 are there in 1 cm^2?
(e) What length of wire, to the nearest 1000 m, can be made from the block of copper?

10 A covering for plants is made using wire bent to the shape shown in the diagram which is a semi-circle and two straight sections. The wire is pushed into the ground to a depth of 12 cm as shown.

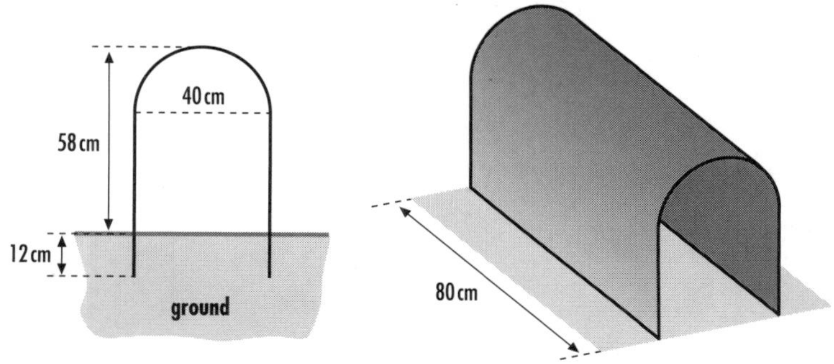

(a) Calculate the length of wire required for one hoop, to the nearest centimetre.

Plastic sheeting that is 80 cm wide is fixed to the hoops as shown.

(b) Calculate the area of plastic sheet required for the frame.

(c) Calculate the volume enclosed by the covering.

Handling data

59/ MEAN, MODE, MEDIAN AND RANGE FOR GROUPED DATA

EXAMPLE

► As part of a survey Brian notes the number of people in each car that passes in a period of 15 minutes. He includes in his survey vehicles that carry up to eight people. He writes his results in the form of a table:

Number of people	1	2	3	4	5	6	7	8
Frequency	35	41	22	19	9	2	0	3

(a) Calculate the mean, mode, median and range of these results.
(b) If Brian decides not to include vehicles with more than five occupants, which of the above are changed and which remain the same?

(a)

Number of people, x	Frequency, f	$f \times x$
1	35	35
2	41	82
3	22	66
4	19	76
5	9	45
6	2	12
7	0	0
8	3	24

Total number of people = 35 + 82 + 66 + 76 + 45 + 12 + 0 + 24 = 340
Total number of cars = 35 + 41 + 22 + 19 + 9 + 2 + 0 + 3 = 131

Mean = $\frac{340}{131}$ = 2.60 (to 3 s.f.)

Mode = 2 people (since this occurs most frequently)

There are 131 vehicles so the middle ranked is $\frac{131 + 1}{2}$ = 66th vehicle
There are 35 vehicles with one occupant.
There are 35 + 41 = 76 vehicles with 1 or 2 occupants.
Therefore the 66th vehicle contains 2 people.

Median = 2 people

Range = 8 − 1 = 7 people

(b) The mode and median remain the same.
The mean and range are changed.

EXAMPLE

► A research scientist is developing a new plant. She measures the height of each of a sample of 100 plants. She groups the heights as follows:

Height, h (cm)	Frequency
$6 \le h < 8$	3
$8 \le h < 10$	4
$10 \le h < 12$	11
$12 \le h < 14$	22
$14 \le h < 16$	49
$16 \le h < 18$	8
$18 \le h < 20$	3

(a) Calculate an estimated mean.
(b) State the modal class.
(c) In which class is the median value?
(d) State the maximum value for the range.
(e) What do the mode and mean values tell you about the plants?

(a) In order to calculate a mean value, replace each group by its mid-point.

Height, h (cm)	Frequency, f	Mid-point, m	$m \times f$
$6 \le h < 8$	3	7	21
$8 \le h < 10$	4	9	36
$10 \le h < 12$	11	11	121
$12 \le h < 14$	22	13	286
$14 \le h < 16$	49	15	735
$16 \le h < 18$	8	17	136
$18 \le h < 20$	3	19	57

$$\text{Mean} = \frac{21 + 36 + 121 + 286 + 735 + 136 + 57}{100} = 13.9\text{ cm (to 3 s.f.)}$$

(b) Modal class = $14 \le h < 16$ cm

(c) The middle rank of 100 is the 50.5th. This occurs in the class $14 \le h < 16$ cm because there are 40 plants up to 14 cm (3 + 4 + 11 + 22) and there are 49 in the class interval $14 \le h < 16$ cm; so the median value (50.5th) must be in this class.

(d) Lowest value could be 6 cm and the highest possible value is 20 cm.
Range = 20 – 6 = 14 cm

(e) The modal value tells you that a height of 14 to 16 cm is typical of these plants.
The mean value of 13.9 cm is a single figure that acts as an average value having taken all the plants into consideration.

Exercise 59A

1 As part of an experiment in probability a dice is thrown many times and each score is noted. The results are shown in the frequency table.

Score	1	2	3	4	5	6
Frequency	23	20	18	32	23	10

(a) Calculate the mean, median, mode and range of the data.
(b) What does the value of the mode and the frequency of the mode tell you about the dice?

2 A group of students receive a test on mental arithmetic. The maximum score is 10. The marks received by the group are as follows.

Score	0	1	2	3	4	5	6	7	8	9	10
Frequency	0	1	1	1	2	3	4	6	9	4	2

(a) Calculate the mean, mode, median and range.
(b) If one of the students who scored 10 cheated and a re-mark gave a score of 6, what is the effect on the statistical values in (a)?

3 The marks of the candidates in an examination are grouped as follows:

Marks, m	Frequency
$20 \le m < 30$	28
$30 \le m < 40$	33
$40 \le m < 50$	41
$50 \le m < 60$	67
$60 \le m < 70$	185
$70 \le m < 80$	75
$80 \le m < 90$	30
$90 \le m < 100$	8

(a) How many candidates are there?
(b) Calculate estimated values for the mean, median and range.
(c) State the modal class and comment on what this tells you.

4 The weight of each sack from a sample of sacks taken from a machine that is meant to deliver 25 kg is noted.

Weight, W (kg)	Frequency
$15 \le W < 20$	6
$20 \le W < 25$	7
$25 \le W < 30$	67
$30 \le W < 35$	15
$35 \le W < 40$	5

(a) State the mid-point of the class interval $15 \le W < 20$ kg.
(b) Calculate an estimated value of the (i) mean (ii) median.
(c) State (i) the modal class (ii) the maximum range of the data.
(d) Comment on the modal value.
(e) If the sacks that weigh less than 25 kg are removed, calculate an estimated value for the new mean.

5 Twenty-one competitors in a strong-man competition are required to hold a heavy sack at arms' length for as long as possible. The times (in seconds) are listed.

23	34	18	42	35	37	25	15	41	37	32
26	28	24	25	31	26	37	19	27	33	

(a) Calculate the actual mean value of these times.

(b) Copy and complete the table showing these times grouped together with class widths of 5 seconds.

Time, T, (s)	Frequency
$15 \le T < 20$	
$20 \le T < 25$	
$25 \le T < 30$	
$30 \le T < 35$	
$35 \le T < 40$	
$40 \le T < 45$	

(c) Use this table to calculate an estimated value of the mean time.

(d) State the mode of the actual times. Does this value have any real meaning? Explain why the modal class tells us more.

6 Before an examination a teacher predicted that half her class would gain a C grade and half would gain a D grade.
When the results were received, the examination board also sent the marks awarded for each grade. The grouped frequency table shows the results for the pupils:

Grade awarded	Marks, m (%)	Frequency
E	$52 \le m < 60$	6
D	$60 \le m < 67$	9
C	$67 \le m < 75$	12
B	$75 \le m < 82$	5

(a) State the mid-point of the marks for each grade.
(b) Calculate an estimate for the mean mark of the results.
(c) Use the marks for which the grades C and D were awarded to calculate the mean mark for the teacher's prediction.
(d) Comment on the results compared with the teacher's prediction.
(e) Comment on the median of the actual results and the estimated grades.

Exercise 59B

1 An experiment in probability involves tossing five coins and counting the number of heads. This is repeated many times and the results are put into a frequency table.

Number of heads	0	1	2	3	4	5
Frequency	1	11	23	25	13	2

(a) Calculate an estimate of the mean and median.
(b) State the mode.
(c) Is it sensible to quote just one mode in the circumstances? Comment on this.

2 Roy is taking part in a sponsored run. He manages to persuade people to pledge money that they will pay if he completes the distance. He records these in a frequency table.

Pledge, £P	1	2	3	4	5	10
Frequency	16	12	5	3	17	2

(a) Calculate the mean, mode, median and range.
(b) Comment on the value of the mode.
(c) The two people who have pledged £10 change their minds. One decides not to sponsor Roy; the other decides to pledge only £5. State the new values for the mean, mode, median and range. Which one(s) have not changed?

3 The price of a loaf of bread was surveyed in a particular town. The results are shown in the grouped frequency table:

Price of loaf, C (pence)	Frequency
$20 \le C < 30$	3
$30 \le C < 40$	11
$40 \le C < 50$	11
$50 \le C < 60$	8
$60 \le C < 70$	5
$70 \le C < 80$	2
$80 \le C < 90$	1
$90 \le C < 100$	1

(a) Estimate the total price of the loaves.
(b) Calculate an estimate for the mean price of a loaf.
(c) Calculate the median and range.
(d) Comment on the modal price.

4 Jacquie works for a firm that services photocopiers. She needs to survey the distance to each customer. She decides to list them in a grouped frequency table.

Distance, M (miles)	Frequency
$10 \le M < 20$	1
$20 \le M < 30$	2
$30 \le M < 40$	7
$40 \le M < 50$	45
$50 \le M < 60$	22
$60 \le M < 70$	2

(a) Calculate an estimated value of (i) the mean (ii) the median.
(b) State the modal class.
(c) State the maximum range of the data.
(d) The firm decides to cancel contracts with customers who are 50 miles or more away. Calculate the mean of the distances from the remaining customers.

5 A group of students sit two examination papers in science. The marks are grouped together for each examination as follows:

Marks, m	Frequency: Paper 1	Frequency: Paper 2
$0 \le m < 10$	3	7
$10 \le m < 20$	6	15
$20 \le m < 30$	11	30
$30 \le m < 40$	35	5
$40 \le m < 50$	5	3

(a) Calculate an estimated mean for each paper.
(b) Use the mean and the modal class to compare the two papers.

6 The length of time for each phone call, *rounded up* to the nearest minute, is noted.

2	3	2	5	7	5	1	3	2	4	5	1
1	1	2	3	5	3	2	6	5	9	14	7
3	6	5	3	2	1	2	1	3	4	8	6
1	1	2	4	2	1	13	652				

The call of 652 minutes occurred when the phone was not disconnected from the Internet overnight!
(a) Calculate the mean of the actual values listed.
(b) Calculate the mean without the *rogue value* of 652 minutes being included.
(c) Copy and complete the grouped frequency table for these times.

Times, T (min)	Frequency
$1 \le T < 5$	
$5 \le T < 10$	
$11 \le T < 15$	
$651 \le T < 655$	

(d) State the mid-point of each class (or group).
(e) Calculate an estimate for the mean using the grouped frequency table (i) including the rogue value (ii) without the rogue value.
(f) Compare the means calculated using the grouped frequency table and the mean values calculated by using the actual times. How close are the estimates to the actual mean times?
(g) What is the range of the actual times (i) with the rogue value (ii) without the rogue value?

60/ INTERPRETING AND COMPARING FREQUENCY POLYGONS

EXAMPLE

► The frequency polygons show the distribution of ages in two villages, one in the UK and one in The Gambia. The ages are put into class intervals of $0 \le \text{age} < 10$ years, etc.

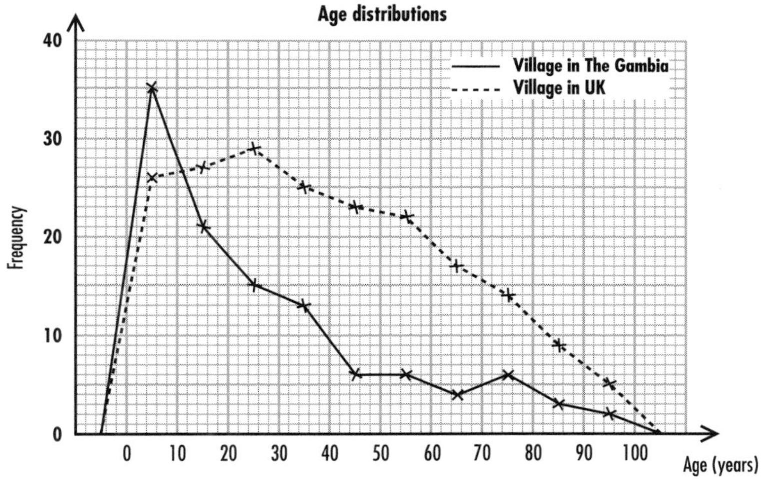

State whether the following statements about the two frequency polygons are true or false. If you think that a statement is false, state your reason for thinking that it is false.

(a) The total populations of the two villages are approximately the same.
(b) The Gambian village has a lower percentage in the 10–20 years age group than the UK village.
(c) Most people live far longer in the UK village.
(d) There are approximately 18 people aged 20 years in the Gambian village.

(a) Untrue – Village populations are UK 197, The Gambia 111.

(b) Untrue – Percentages are UK = $100 \times \frac{27}{197} = 13.7\%$;

The Gambia = $100 \times \frac{21}{111} = 18.9\%$

(c) True
(d) Untrue – The graph has no meaning between points.

Exercise 60A

In each of questions 1–4 study the frequency polygons and say whether the statements about them are *true* or *false*. If you think that a statement is false, state your reason for thinking that it is false.

1 Gary spins five coins many times and notes the number of heads that occur. He records his results in a frequency polygon. Gary also draws what should happen in theory.

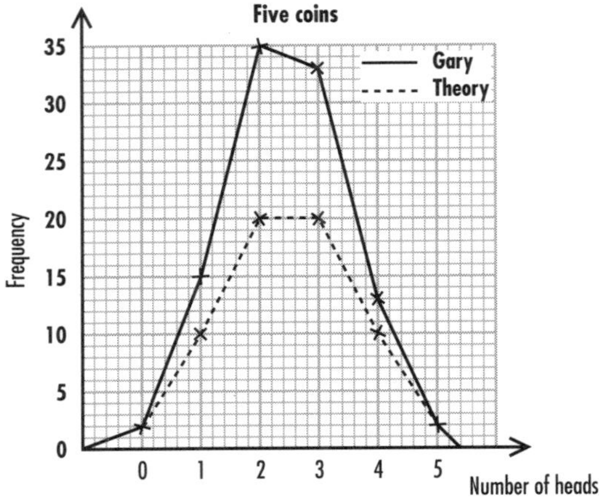

(a) Gary spins the coins 110 times.
(b) The theoretical results are for half the number of spins compared with Gary's experiment.
(c) Gary needed three more results that had three heads in order to make his graph symmetrical.
(d) 'All five coins showed the same' occurred four times in Gary's experiment.

2 The management of a factory conduct a survey of the number of absentees per day over a period of time during the winter and also a period of time in summer.

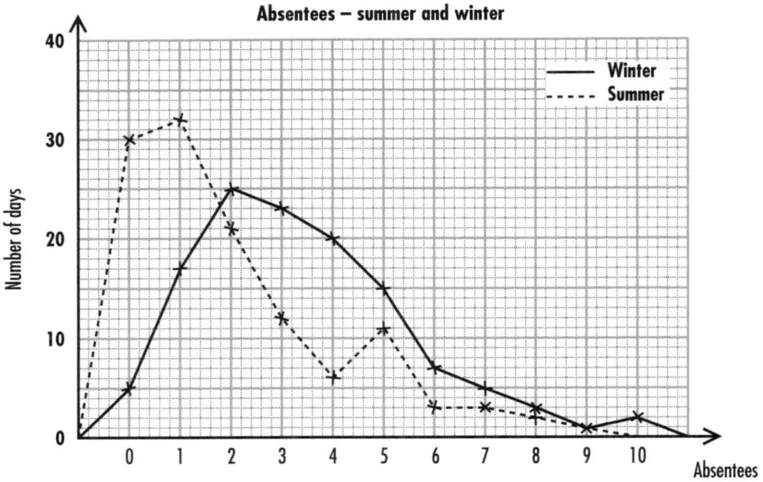

(a) There are more days in the period surveyed in the summer than in the period surveyed in winter.
(b) There were more days of absence in the winter.
(c) There were 11 days in the summer when there were five absentees.
(d) There were 50 days or more in winter when there were two or less absentees.

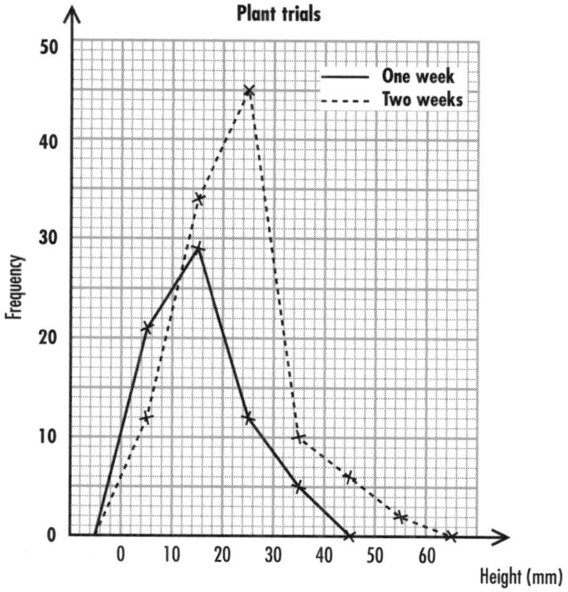

3 As part of some trials of a new variety of plant the height of each of a batch of seedlings is measured one week after the first seedling appears and then again after another week. The heights are grouped into class intervals of 0 mm ≤ height < 10 mm, etc.

(a) There are more plants after two weeks than after one week.
(b) At one week there are 10 plants just appearing (0 mm high).
(c) The modal class has changed by 10 mm over the week between measurements.
(d) After two weeks the highest plant measures 65 mm.

4 Omar and Mary are drivers for a firm that delivers goods to their area. They group their delivery distances for a particular week into class intervals 0 km ≤ distance < 5 km, etc. (The distance includes the return journey.)

(a) Omar makes more deliveries than Mary.
(b) A good estimate for the total distance for Omar's deliveries in the 0 ≤ distance < 5 km class is 30 km.
(c) Omar travels further in the week than Mary.
(d) Omar makes more journeys of 5 km than Mary.

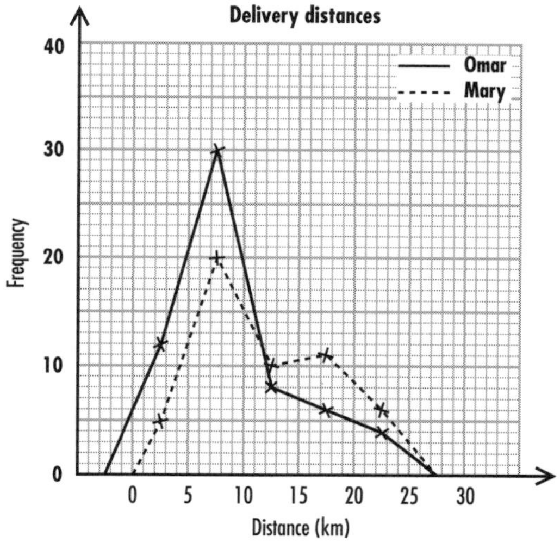

5 Two resorts are analysed for the hours of sunshine (to the nearest hour) over a period of two months.

Number of hours	0	1	2	3	4	5	6	7	8	9	10
Resort P	0	2	4	8	5	6	3	15	5	8	6
Resort Q	0	4	6	4	3	4	6	8	8	11	8

Show this information as two frequency polygons on the same pair of axes.

Use these polygons to state whether each of the following is true or false. If you consider a statement to be false, give your reason for this.

(a) There were no days at either resort when there was less than 1 hour of sunshine.
(b) The period of time covered 62 days for each resort.
(c) Resort Q had more days when there were 8 hours of sunshine or more.
(d) The number of days that Resort P had 7 hours of sunshine was 25% of the period of the survey.

6 A group of students sit two different examination papers in science. The marks for each paper are grouped into class intervals of 0% ≤ marks < 10%, etc. for Paper 1 and 0% ≤ marks < 20%, etc. for Paper 2.

Marks, m (%)	$0 \le m < 10$	$10 \le m < 20$	$20 \le m < 30$	$30 \le m < 40$	$40 \le m < 50$	$50 \le m < 60$
Paper 1	5	10	18	16	8	4
Marks, M (%)	$0 \le M < 20$	$20 \le M < 40$	$40 \le M < 60$	$60 \le M < 80$	$80 \le M < 100$	
Paper 2	5	10	20	23	3	

Show this information as two frequency polygons on the same pair of axes.
Remember: The points are plotted at the mid-point of each class interval.
Use these polygons to state whether each of the following is true or false. If you consider a statement to be false, give your reason for this.

(a) There are more students sitting Paper 2 than Paper 1.
(b) Students performed better in Paper 2 than in Paper 1.
(c) Some students in Paper 2 scored 100%.
(d) A good estimate for the total score of students is 3000–3500 marks.

Exercise 60B

In each of questions 1–4 study the frequency polygons and say whether the statements about them are *true* or *false*. If you think that a statement is false, state your reason for thinking that it is false.

1 The number of goals scored by a team per match for the 1994 and 1995 seasons is shown.

(a) The team played the same number of games in 1994 and 1995.
(b) The team scored 84 goals in 1995.
(c) The team scored more goals in 1994 than in 1995.
(d) There were more games in 1995 than in 1994 where three goals or less were scored.

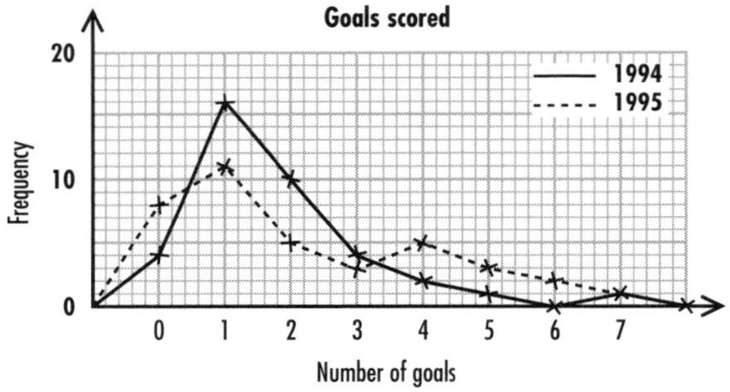

2 As part of her statistics assignment Rachel counts the number of letters in the words in two pieces of text, text A and text B.

(a) There are more than 100 words in each piece of text.
(b) There are the same number of words in each piece of text.
(c) Text B contains a higher percentage of long words than text A.
(d) Words that contain three letters or more have a total of more than 170 letters.

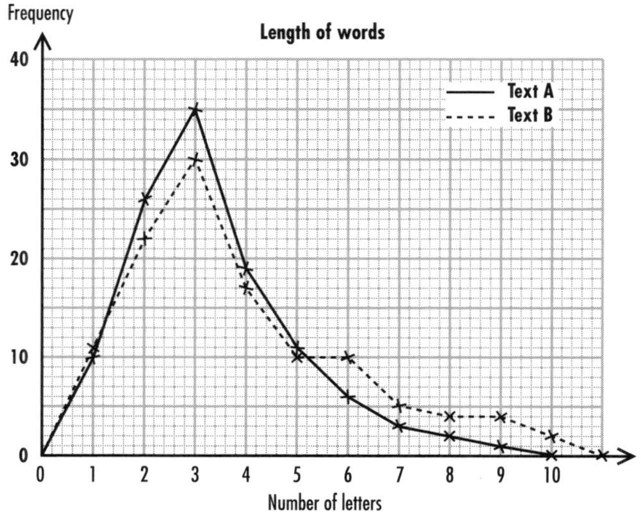

3 Stacey and Geoffrey take turns at throwing three darts at a dart board. They record the total score for each set of three darts and group the scores in class intervals of $0 \le$ score <30, etc.

(a) Stacey throws more sets of three darts.
(b) Stacey scores 105 thirty-four times.
(c) A good estimate for Stacey's total score is about 8000.
(d) Geoffrey must have scored more than Stacey.

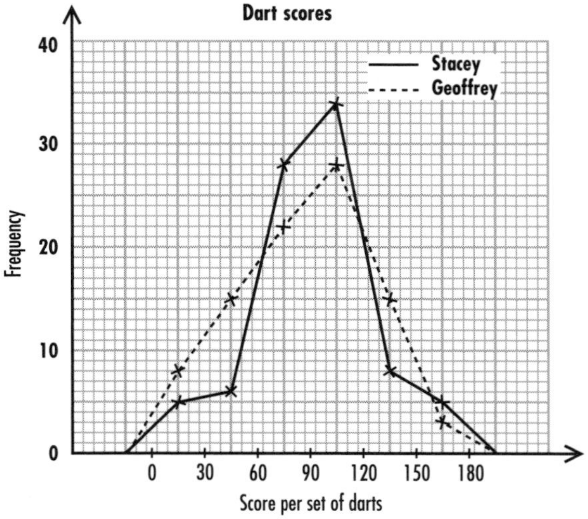

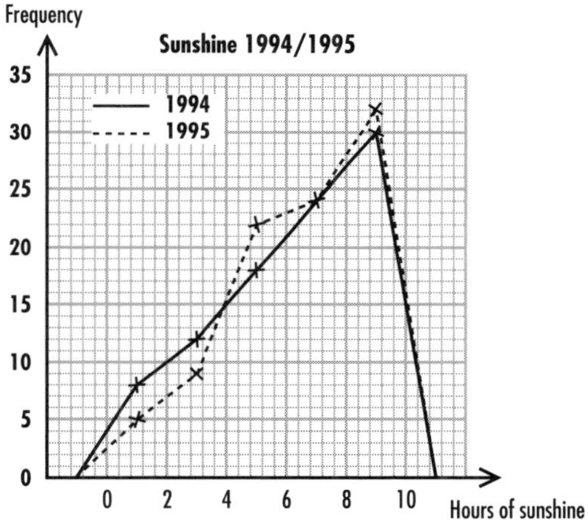

4 The hours of sunshine in 1994 and 1995 are analysed for a seaside resort. The results are grouped in class intervals of $0 \le$ hours of sunshine < 2, etc.

(a) There was the same number of days surveyed in 1994 as in 1995.
(b) There were more sunny days in the survey in 1995.
(c) There were ten days in 1995 during the survey with 2 hours of sunshine.
(d) There was the same number of days in 1994 and in 1995 during the survey with 6–8 hours of sunshine per day.

5 The data shows the results of two tests, Test 1 and Test 2.

Marks	0	1	2	3	4	5	6	7	8	9	10
Test 1	2	3	5	8	8	6	5	5	3	2	1
Test 2	1	1	2	14	12	6	4	2	1	0	0

Show this information as two frequency polygons on the same pair of axes.
Use these polygons to state whether each of the following is true or false. If you consider a statement to be false, give your reason for this.

(a) The same number of students sat each test.
(b) Test 2 must have been marked out of 8.
(c) More than 2% of the students who sat Test 1 gained 10 marks.
(d) The students who gained less than 5 marks in Test 2 gained a total of 95 marks between them.

6 The times for runners in a Fun Run are noted in class intervals of width 10 minutes. The race is divided into under 50s and over 50s.

Time, T (min)	$40 \le T < 50$	$50 \le T < 60$	$60 \le T < 70$	$70 \le T < 80$	$80 \le T < 90$
Under 50s	22	32	24	15	4
Over 50s	3	25	36	19	6

Show this information as two frequency polygons on the same pair of axes.
Remember: The points are plotted at the mid-point of each class interval.

Use these polygons to state whether each of the following is true or false. If you consider a statement to be false, give your reason for this.

(a) There are less than 200 runners in total.
(b) There are less Under 50s than Over 50s.
(c) There are 15 Over 50s who completed the course in 50 minutes.
(d) The modal classes differ by 10 minutes.

61/ SCATTER DIAGRAMS: LINES OF BEST FIT

A scatter diagram is a graph where the points compare the value of each of two variables, for example the weight and the height of one person.
The points are not joined directly to form a line but a **line of best fit** can be drawn which indicates the trend of the points. It does not need to pass through any of the points but *must* pass through the point which plots the mean of each variable.

EXAMPLE

► A group of men at a fitness club are weighed and also have their height measured.

Name	Tim	Zak	Wes	Mike	Asif	Alan	Ray	Nick	Sam	Ali
Weight (kg)	74	78	81	82	87	89	94	96	100	112
Height (cm)	168	165	173	180	178	175	180	181	179	185

(a) Draw the scatter graph of height against weight.
(b) Label the points that represent the height and weight of (i) Sam (ii) Zak.
(c) Calculate the mean value for (i) the heights (ii) the weights.
(d) Plot the point for these mean values.
(e) Draw a line of best fit for the points.
(f) Use your line of best fit to estimate the height of a man with a weight of 70 kg.
(g) Use your line of best fit to estimate the weight of a man of height 170 cm.
(h) State the type of correlation, if any, between height and weight.

(a), (b) and (d)

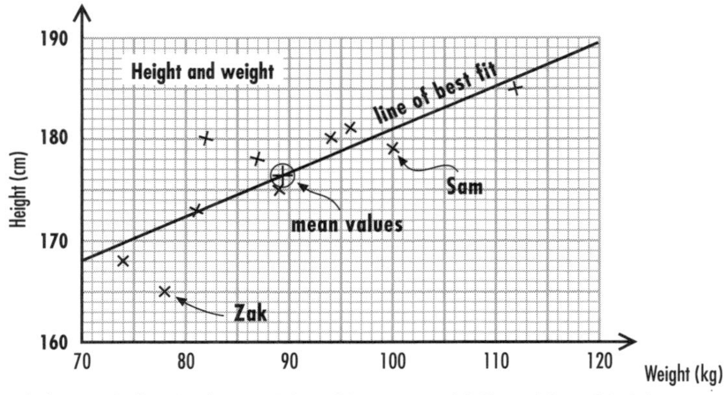

(c) (i) The mean of the weights is (74 + 78 + 81 + … + 112) ÷ 10 = 89.3 kg
(ii) The mean of the heights is (168 + 165 + 173 + … + 185) ÷ 10 = 176.4 cm
(e) The line of best fit is a matter of your judgement. It *must* pass through the mean values point and every point must be taken into account.
(f) 168 cm
(g) 75 kg
(h) Positive correlation

Exercise 61A

For each question:
(a) Plot the points on the scatter diagram.
(b) Calculate the mean values for each variable.
(c) Plot and label the point that represents these mean values.
(d) Draw the line of best fit.
(e), (f) and (g) Answer the additional questions.

1 An examiner compares the scores in Paper 1 and Paper 2 for eight candidates.

Candidate number	2034	2037	2057	2089	2091	2105	2123	2131
Paper 1 (% marks)	26	37	50	59	66	78	94	99
Paper 2 (% marks)	28	47	40	49	62	65	74	67

Use 1 cm to represent 10% for Paper 1 marks between 20% and 100%.
Use 1 cm to represent 10% for Paper 2 marks between 20% and 80%.

(e) Label the points that represent candidates 2037 and 2089.
(f) Use your line of best fit to estimate (i) the mark in Paper 2 for a candidate who scored 80% in Paper 1 (ii) the mark in Paper 1 for a candidate who scored 50% in Paper 2.
(g) State the type of correlation (if any) between Paper 1 and Paper 2.

2 The owner of a drinks stall in a market notes the approximate number of cups of hot soup sold against the average temperature for that day.

Date	12 Nov.	19 Nov.	26 Nov.	3 Dec.	10 Dec.	17 Dec.	24 Dec.
Ave. temp. (°C)	4	12	10	0	5	8	–2
Cups of soup	50	20	25	70	45	35	95

Use 2 cm to represent 5°C between temperatures of –5°C and 15°C.
Use 1 cm to represent 25 cups of soup between 0 and 100 cups of soup.

(e) Label the points that represent 3 Dec. and 17 Dec.
(f) Use your line of best fit to estimate (i) the temperature when sales reach zero (ii) sales at –5°C.
(g) State the type of correlation (if any) between soup sales and temperature.

3 An engineer tests the economy of a car at various speeds. He drives at constant speeds and records the fuel used for 50 miles.

Speed (m.p.h.)	30	40	50	60	70	80
Fuel (gallons)	0.92	0.98	1.01	1.05	1.08	1.10

Use 2 cm to represent 10 m.p.h. between speeds of 30 and 80 m.p.h.
Use 2 cm to represent 0.1 gallon between 0.9 and 1.1 gallon.

(e) Label the points that show the test at 50 m.p.h. and the test that used 1.08 gallons.
(f) Use your line of best fit to estimate (i) the fuel used at 65 m.p.h (ii) the speed if 1.00 gallons are used.
(g) State the type of correlation (if any) between speed and fuel used.

4 A doctor records the age and blood pressure readings for ten patients.

Patient	A	B	C	D	E	F	G	H	I	J
Age (years)	84	73	70	68	64	61	58	55	51	49
Blood pressure (mm)	179	165	154	164	162	158	148	150	146	144

Use 2 cm to represent 10 years between ages of 40 and 80 years.
Use 2 cm to represent 10 mm between blood pressures of 140 mm to 180 mm.

(e) Label the points that represent patients A and C.
(f) Use your line of best fit to estimate (i) the blood pressure for a person aged 80 years (ii) the age of a person with a blood pressure of 140 mm.
(g) State the type of correlation (if any) between age and blood pressure.

5 A house owner notes the number of units of electricity used on eight different days and also the average temperature for each day.

Date	1 Nov.	12 Nov.	23 Nov.	30 Nov.	3 Dec.	10 Dec.	24 Dec.	30 Dec.
Ave. temp. (°C)	10	8	2	6	12	9	5	0
Units of electricity	22	25	38	34	20	23	31	41

Use 1 cm to represent 5 °C between 0°C and 15°C.
Use 1 cm to represent 5 units of electricity between 15 units and 45 units.

(e) Label the points that represent 30 Nov. and 10 Dec.
(f) Use your line of best fit to estimate (i) the average temperature if 35 units are used (ii) the number of units used if the average temperature is 10°C.
(g) State the type of correlation (if any) between the average temperature and units of electricity used.

6 The prices of seven cars are noted at a car auction together with the engine size. The cars are in similar condition and are all approximately the same age.

Car number	1	2	3	4	5	6	7
Price (£)	2800	2900	3100	3200	3300	3700	3900
Engine size (litres)	2.3	2.8	2.0	2.3	1.8	1.6	1.6

Use 2 cm to represent £500 between prices of £2500 and £4000.
Use 2 cm to represent 1 litre between engine sizes of 1 litre and 3 litres.

(e) Label the points that represent car number 4 and car number 6.
(f) Use your line of best fit to estimate (i) the likely engine size of a car with a price of £2500 (ii) the price of a car with an engine size of 1.5 litres.
(g) State the type of correlation (if any) between the price and the engine size of the cars.

Exercise 61B

For each question:
(a) Plot the points on the scatter diagram.
(b) Calculate the mean values for each variable.
(c) Plot and label the point that represents these mean values.
(d) Draw the line of best fit.
(e), (f) and (g) Answer the additional questions.

1 Kim is researching the number of hours of sunshine and the temperature at 1800 during an eight-day period in June.

Day	2 Jun.	3 Jun.	4 Jun.	5 Jun.	6 Jun.	7 Jun.	8 Jun.	9 Jun.
Hours of sunshine	5	5	6	8	6	10	7	9
Temperature (°C)	16	15	18	20	19	23	20	21

Use 2 cm to represent 2 hours between times of 4 hours and 10 hours.
Use 2 cm to represent 5°C between temperatures of 15°C and 25°C.

(e) Label the points that represent the values for 3 June and 8 June.
(f) Use your line of best fit to estimate (i) the temperature on a day with 10 hours sunshine (ii) the number of hours of sunshine if the temperature is 15°C.
(g) State the type of correlation (if any) between the temperature and the number of hours of sunshine.

2 Kim is researching the connection between temperature at night and the amount of cloud cover. She measures the temperature at dawn for eight days in December. She also notes the number of hours that the sky was mainly clear of clouds.

Date	7 Dec.	8 Dec.	9 Dec.	10 Dec.	11 Dec.	12 Dec.	13 Dec.	14 Dec.
Hours of clear sky	1	0	8	11	10	5	7	2
Temperature (°C)	4	6	–3	–6	–5	–1	0	5

Use 2 cm to represent 5 hours between 0 and 15 hours of clear sky.
Use 2 cm to represent 5°C between temperatures of –10°C and +10°C.

(e) Label the points that represent the values for 10 Dec. and 14 Dec.
(f) Use your line of best fit to estimate (i) the temperature on a night with 12 hours of clear sky (ii) the number of hours of clear sky if the temperature is –2°C.
(g) State the type of correlation (if any) between the temperature and the number of hours of clear sky.

3 A small group of students are examined in English and PE.

Name	Bob	Doug	Roy	Sue	Kath	Ben	Cilla	Ahmed	Wes	Nazir
English (%)	8	17	36	48	50	64	68	75	84	95
PE (%)	64	54	44	44	34	38	26	37	27	22

Use 1 cm to represent 10% between marks of 0 and 100% in English.
Use 1 cm to represent 10% between marks of 0 and 80% for PE.

(e) Label the points that represent the marks for Doug and Wes.
(f) Use your line of best fit to estimate (i) the mark in PE for a student who scores 74% in English (ii) the mark in English for a student who scores 54% in PE.
(g) State the type of correlation (if any) between the marks in English and PE.

4 Akpata lists her results for examinations this year and also last year.

Subject	English	Maths	Science	History	French	Art	Tech.
This year (%)	72	84	75	69	65	86	81
Last year (%)	65	77	72	66	60	81	76

Use 2 cm to represent 10% between 60% and 90% for both axes.

(e) Label the points that show the marks for history and maths.
(f) Use your line of best fit to estimate (i) the mark this year for a subject with 60% last year (ii) the mark last year for a subject with 90% this year.
(g) State the type of correlation (if any) between the marks in the two years.

5 Eight athletes take part in 100 m and 200 m races. They record their times to 0.1 of a second.

Athletes	Julia	Dave	John	Lyn	Noah	Roger	Bill	Fiona
Time (100 m)	13.7	12.4	12.6	13.6	11.8	12.9	12.2	14.0
Time (200 m)	24.6	22.4	23.6	25.2	22.2	22.9	22.0	25.9

Use 2 cm to represent 1 s between times of 11 and 15 s.
Use 2 cm to represent 1 s between times of 22 and 26 s.

(e) Label the points that show the times for Roger and Lyn.
(f) Use your line of best fit to estimate (i) the 100 m race time for an athlete with a time in the 200 m race of 25 s (ii) the 200 m race time for an athlete with a time in the 100 m race of 13 s.
(g) State the type of correlation (if any) between the times in the two races.

6 The marks in a French examination are noted for the reading paper and the writing paper for a small group of students.

Student	Neil	Rose	Paul	Morag	Tarik	Don	Gill
Reading paper (%)	28	35	45	50	59	64	72
Writing paper (%)	35	42	50	56	58	68	75

Use 2 cm to represent 20% between 20% and 80% for both axes.

(e) Label the points that show the marks for Morag and Don.

(f) Use your line of best fit to estimate (i) the mark in the reading paper for a student who scores 60% on the writing paper (ii) the mark in the writing paper for a student who scores 40% on the reading paper.

(g) State the type of correlation (if any) between the marks in the two papers.

62/ CUMULATIVE FREQUENCY: TABLES AND CURVES

The **cumulative frequency** is the 'running total' of the frequencies up to and including a particular value. When dealing with grouped data, it is usual to consider the cumulative frequency up to the **upper limit** of each class interval.

EXAMPLE

► A machine is designed to deliver 80 grams of chemical. One hundred, randomly selected samples from the machine are weighed accurately and these are grouped as follows.

Mass, m (g)	Frequency
$78 < m \leq 79$	2
$79 < m \leq 80$	7
$80 < m \leq 81$	32
$81 < m \leq 82$	31
$82 < m \leq 83$	21
$83 < m \leq 84$	6
$84 < m \leq 85$	1

Create a cumulative frequency table for these results.

Mass, m (g)	Cumulative frequency
$m \leq 79$	2
$m \leq 80$	$2 + 7 = 9$
$m \leq 81$	$9 + 32 = 41$
$m \leq 82$	$41 + 31 = 72$
$m \leq 83$	$72 + 21 = 93$
$m \leq 84$	$93 + 6 = 99$
$m \leq 85$	$99 + 1 = 100$

Cumulative frequencies can be plotted and the points joined with a smooth curve called a **cumulative frequency curve**. This curve is normally 'S' shaped. (This happens so often that the shape has its own name, **ogive**.)

EXAMPLE

► Draw a cumulative frequency curve for the data in the previous example.
Use your cumulative frequency curve to answer the following.
(a) If ten of the samples are rejected, what is the upper limit for the weight of acceptable samples?
(b) If the limit is reduced to 81.5 g, how many samples fail?

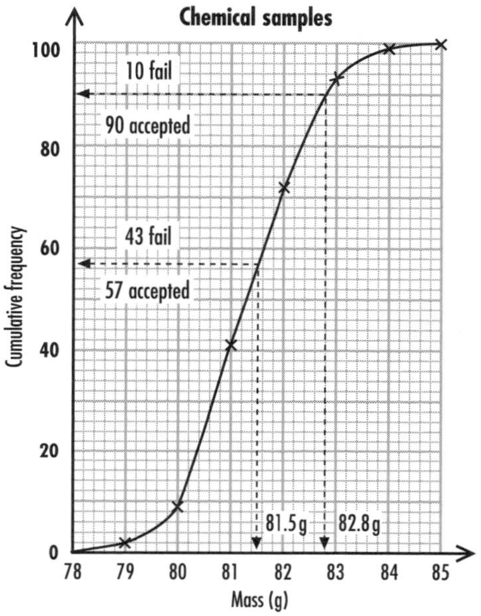

(a) If 10 fail, 90 are accepted. The upper limit is read off as 82.8 g.
(b) Reading off the graph at 81.5 g, the number accepted is 57, so 43 fail.

Exercise 62A

In each of the following create a cumulative frequency table, draw the cumulative frequency curve and use the curve to answer the questions.

1 The number of absences during a year are recorded for the members of a class and this information is shown as a frequency table

Absences (days)	Frequency (No. of students)
$0 < n \leq 5$	4
$5 < n \leq 10$	5
$10 < n \leq 15$	5
$15 < n \leq 20$	4
$20 < n \leq 25$	4
$25 < n \leq 30$	3
$30 < n \leq 35$	2
$35 < n \leq 40$	1
$40 < n \leq 45$	1

Use 2 cm to represent 10 days on the horizontal axis and 2 cm to represent 10 on the cumulative frequency axis.

(a) A quarter of a term is 16 days. How many students are absent for 16 days or less?
(b) How many students are absent for more than half of the term?

2 Students at a boarding school conduct a survey of how much pocket money each receives.

Pocket money	Frequency
$0 < P \leq £1$	3
$£1 < P \leq £2$	5
$£2 < P \leq £3$	8
$£3 < P \leq £4$	16
$£4 < P \leq £5$	15
$£5 < P \leq £6$	10
$£6 < P \leq £7$	8
$£7 < P \leq £8$	4
$£8 < P \leq £9$	3
$£9 < P \leq £10$	2

Use 1 cm to represent £1 on the horizontal axis and 1 cm to represent 10 on the cumulative frequency axis.

(a) How much pocket money, to the nearest 10p, do the top 20 students receive?
(b) What fraction of the students receive £4.60 or less?

3 A bus company is worried about complaints from customers that buses are late. The company asks 250 customers to state how long they had waited.

Time (min)	Frequency
$0 < T \leq 2$	8
$2 < T \leq 4$	18
$4 < T \leq 6$	34
$6 < T \leq 8$	48
$8 < T \leq 10$	45
$10 < T \leq 12$	34
$12 < T \leq 14$	25
$14 < T \leq 16$	17
$16 < T \leq 18$	10
$18 < T \leq 20$	7
$20 < T \leq 22$	3
$22 < T \leq 24$	1

Use 2 cm to represent 5 min on the horizontal axis and 2 cm to represent 50 on the cumulative frequency axis.

(a) How many customers had waited a quarter of an hour or less?
(b) How long was the waiting time (to the nearest minute) of each of the 125 customers who had waited the least time?

4 A survey of expense accounts is conducted for a sales team.

Account (£)	Frequency
$0 < A \leq 100$	2
$100 < A \leq 200$	3
$200 < A \leq 300$	5
$300 < A \leq 400$	7
$400 < A \leq 500$	8
$500 < A \leq 600$	6
$600 < A \leq 700$	4
$700 < A \leq 800$	3
$800 < A \leq 900$	2
$900 < A \leq 1000$	1

Use 1 cm to represent £100 on the horizontal axis and 2 cm to represent 10 on the cumulative frequency axis.

(a) How many people are surveyed?
(b) How many people have an account of more than £640?

5 As part of a cost-saving exercise at an engineering works the length of each of 100 pieces of wasted brass rod is recorded.

Length (mm)	Frequency
$50 < L \leq 51$	3
$51 < L \leq 52$	6
$52 < L \leq 53$	14
$53 < L \leq 54$	17
$54 < L \leq 55$	22
$55 < L \leq 56$	16
$56 < L \leq 57$	10
$57 < L \leq 58$	7
$58 < L \leq 59$	4
$59 < L \leq 60$	1

Use 1 cm to represent 1 mm on the horizontal axis and 1 cm to represent 10 on the cumulative frequency axis.

(a) What is the length (to the nearest 0.2 mm) of each of the shortest 50 pieces?
(b) The acceptable limit for waste is set at 56.4 mm or less. How many pieces fail this?

6 The weight of each of a sample of one hundred sacks is recorded. Each sack should weigh 50 kg.

Weight (kg)	Frequency
$48.0 < D \leq 48.5$	4
$48.5 < D \leq 49.0$	6
$49.0 < D \leq 49.5$	9
$49.5 < D \leq 50.0$	14
$50.0 < D \leq 50.5$	18
$50.5 < D \leq 51.0$	17
$51.0 < D \leq 51.5$	15
$51.5 < D \leq 52.0$	10
$52.0 < D \leq 52.5$	5
$52.5 < D \leq 53.0$	2

Use 2 cm to represent 1 kg on the horizontal axis and 1 cm to represent 10 on the cumulative frequency axis.

(a) The lowest acceptable weight is 49.9 kg or less. How many sacks are rejected?
(b) Fifty sacks are accepted as not being too heavy or too light. What is the weight of the heaviest acceptable sack (to the nearest 0.2 kg)?

Exercise 62B

In each of the following create a cumulative frequency table, draw the cumulative frequency curve and use the curve to answer the questions.

1 The score of each competitor at a shooting competition is recorded and the results are shown as a frequency table.

Score	Frequency
$60 < A \leq 70$	2
$70 < A \leq 80$	5
$80 < A \leq 90$	7
$90 < A \leq 100$	8
$100 < A \leq 110$	4
$110 < A \leq 120$	2

Use 1 cm to represent 10 on the horizontal axis and 2 cm to represent 10 on the cumulative frequency axis.

(a) How many competitors are there?
(b) How many competitors scored 85 or less?

2 A shop owner surveys the length of each of 100 nails in a pack of mixed nails.

Length (mm)	Frequency
$0 < L \leq 25$	3
$25 < L \leq 50$	6
$50 < L \leq 75$	14
$75 < L \leq 100$	41
$100 < L \leq 125$	20
$125 < L \leq 150$	8
$150 < L \leq 175$	5
$175 < L \leq 200$	3

Use 2 cm to represent 50 mm on the horizontal axis and 2 cm to represent 20 on the cumulative frequency axis.

(a) What is the length of the 50th nail, to the nearest 10 mm?

(b) How many nails are 110 mm or less in length?

3 The paper bills per week for each house on an estate are analysed.

Bill (£)	Frequency
$0 < B \leq 1$	2
$1 < B \leq 2$	4
$2 < B \leq 3$	7
$3 < B \leq 4$	8
$4 < B \leq 5$	11
$5 < B \leq 6$	8
$6 < B \leq 7$	5
$7 < B \leq 8$	2
$8 < B \leq 9$	2
$9 < B \leq 10$	1

Use 1 cm to represent £1 on the horizontal axis and 2 cm to represent 10 on the cumulative frequency axis.

(a) How many houses are there in the analysis?

(b) How many houses have a bill of £2.50 or less?

4 The distances travelled by salespersons each week are listed.

Distance (miles)	Frequency
$0 < D \leq 100$	4
$100 < D \leq 200$	6
$200 < D \leq 300$	9
$300 < D \leq 400$	12
$400 < D \leq 500$	14
$500 < D \leq 600$	10
$600 < D \leq 700$	5
$700 < D \leq 800$	2

Use 1 cm to represent 100 miles on the horizontal axis and 1 cm to represent 10 on the cumulative frequency axis.

(a) How many salespersons were surveyed?

(b) How many salespersons drove 450 miles or more per week?

5 A supermarket manager is concerned about the waiting times at the check-outs. She conducts a survey and times how long each of 100 customers (chosen at random during the day) have to wait.

Time (s)	Frequency
$0 < T \leq 20$	6
$20 < T \leq 40$	6
$40 < T \leq 60$	13
$60 < T \leq 80$	21
$80 < T \leq 100$	22
$100 < T \leq 120$	14
$120 < T \leq 140$	10
$140 < T \leq 160$	6
$160 < T \leq 180$	2

Use 2 cm to represent 50 s on the horizontal axis and 1 cm to represent 10 on the cumulative frequency axis.

(a) The company policy is that 60% of customers shall wait $1\frac{1}{2}$ minutes or less. What percentage of the customers in the survey waited $1\frac{1}{2}$ minutes or less?

(b) How many customers had to wait $2\frac{1}{2}$ minutes or more?

6 The marks for students in a science examination are as follows.

Mark (%)	Frequency
$0 < m \leq 10$	2
$10 < m \leq 20$	4
$20 < m \leq 30$	8
$60 < m \leq 40$	14
$40 < m \leq 50$	16
$50 < m \leq 60$	23
$60 < m \leq 70$	12
$70 < m \leq 80$	8
$80 < m \leq 90$	6
$90 < m \leq 100$	2

Use 1 cm to represent 10% on the horizontal axis and 1 cm to represent 10 on the cumulative frequency axis.

(a) How many students took the exam?

(b) If 40% of the students pass the examination, estimate the pass mark.

63/ CUMULATIVE FREQUENCY: MEDIAN AND INTERQUARTILE RANGE

The **median** is the middle term in a set of data. This value can be read off the cumulative frequency curve. If there are 240 items of data, the median is read off at a cumulative frequency of 120.
The **interquartile range** is a measure of the spread of the data.
Interquartile range = $Q_3 - Q_1$,
where Q_3 is the **upper quartile** and Q_1 is the **lower quartile**.

If there are 240 items of data, the lower quartile, Q_1, is read off at a cumulative frequency of $\frac{1}{4} \times 240 = 60$. The upper quartile, Q_3, is read off at a cumulative frequency of $\frac{3}{4} \times 240 = 180$.

EXAMPLE

► Two groups of students sit the same examination. The graph shows the cumulative frequency curve of the marks for each group.
Use the cumulative frequency curves to find
(a) the median
(b) the lower and upper quartiles for each group
(c) the interquartile range of each set of marks.
(d) Use these values to compare the two sets of marks.

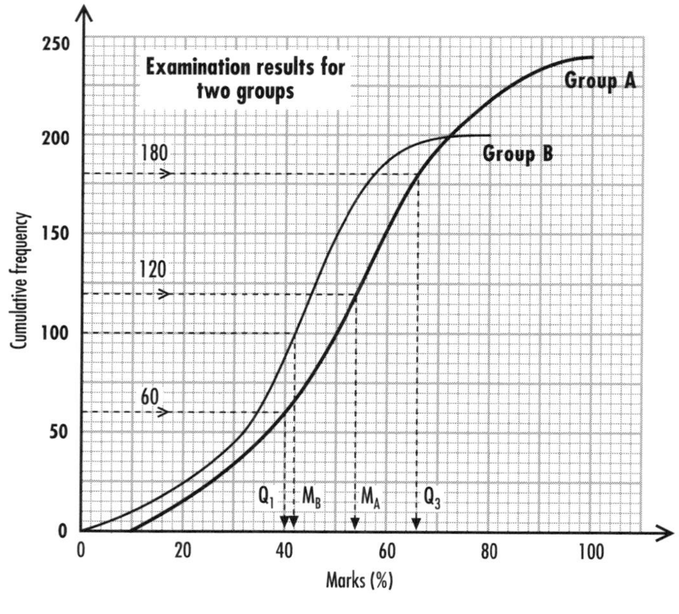

(a) There are 240 students in group A. The median of group A is read off at 120 on the cumulative frequency curve.
The median mark of group A (shown as M_A) is 54%.
There are 200 students in group B. The median is read off at a cumulative frequency of 100.
The median mark of group B (shown as M_B) is 42%.

	Group A	*Group B*
(b)	$\frac{1}{4}$ of 240 = 60 and so Q_1 = 40%	$\frac{1}{4}$ of 200 = 50 and so Q_1 = 32%
	$\frac{3}{4}$ of 240 = 180 and so Q_3 = 66%	$\frac{3}{4}$ of 200 = 150 and so Q_3 = 50%
(c)	IQR = 66 – 40 = 26%	IQR = 50 – 32 = 18%

(d) The median for A is 54% and the median for B is 42%. This indicates that group A performed better than group B.
The IQR for A is 26% and the IQR for group B is 18%. This indicates that the results for group A are more spread out than group B.

Exercise 63A

In each of the following questions:

(a) Create a cumulative frequency table.
(b) Draw the cumulative frequency curve.
(c) State the median value.
(d) State (i) the lower quartile, Q_1 (ii) the upper quartile, Q_3 (iii) the IQR.

1 The number of pupils with certain days of absence per year in a small school.

Absences (days)	No. of Pupils
$0 < n \leq 5$	12
$5 < n \leq 10$	15
$10 < n \leq 15$	18
$15 < n \leq 20$	14
$20 < n \leq 25$	14
$25 < n \leq 30$	12
$30 < n \leq 35$	10
$35 < n \leq 40$	8
$40 < n \leq 45$	4
$45 < n \leq 50$	1

2 The marks of students in a French examination.

Mark (%)	Frequency
$0 < m \leq 10$	1
$10 < m \leq 20$	2
$20 < m \leq 30$	5
$60 < m \leq 40$	9
$40 < m \leq 50$	14
$50 < m \leq 60$	14
$60 < m \leq 70$	8
$70 < m \leq 80$	4
$80 < m \leq 90$	2
$90 < m \leq 100$	1

3 The times for phone calls (up to 5 min).

Time (s)	Frequency
$0 < T \leq 30$	11
$30 < T \leq 60$	18
$60 < T \leq 90$	26
$90 < T \leq 120$	42
$120 < T \leq 150$	39
$150 < T \leq 180$	22
$180 < T \leq 210$	17
$210 < T \leq 240$	11
$240 < T \leq 270$	9
$270 < T \leq 300$	5

4 The weight for each of a sample of bags of chemical which should weigh 100 g.

Weight (kg)	Frequency
$95 < m \leq 96$	1
$96 < m \leq 97$	2
$97 < m \leq 98$	12
$98 < m \leq 99$	17
$99 < m \leq 100$	20
$100 < m \leq 101$	7
$101 < m \leq 102$	6
$102 < m \leq 103$	4
$103 < m \leq 104$	2
$104 < m \leq 105$	1

5 The marks of a group of students who sit examinations in French and German.

Mark (%)	Frequency (French)	Frequency (German)
$0 < m \le 10$	1	0
$10 < m \le 20$	2	2
$20 < m \le 30$	5	5
$30 < m \le 40$	9	9
$40 < m \le 50$	17	10
$50 < m \le 60$	15	11
$60 < m \le 70$	8	11
$70 < m \le 80$	4	9
$80 < m \le 90$	2	4
$90 < m \le 100$	1	3

The two cumulative frequency curves should be drawn on the same graph. Compare the medians and the IQRs for the two examinations.

6 The frequency table shows the distribution of the ages of the populations of two small villages (one in Egypt and one in Italy).

Age (years)	Frequency (Egypt)	Frequency (Italy)
$0 < A \le 10$	19	11
$10 < A \le 20$	17	12
$20 < A \le 30$	15	13
$60 < A \le 40$	12	13
$40 < A \le 50$	10	10
$50 < A \le 60$	5	10
$60 < A \le 70$	4	9
$70 < A \le 80$	4	8
$80 < A \le 90$	2	4
$90 < A \le 100$	0	2

The two cumulative frequency curves should be drawn on the same graph. Compare the medians and the IQRs for the populations of the two villages.

Exercise 63B

In each of the following questions:

(a) Create a cumulative frequency table.
(b) Draw the cumulative frequency curve.
(c) State the median value.
(d) State (i) the lower quartile, Q_1 (ii) the upper quartile, Q_3 (iii) the IQR.

1 The height of each of a group of students.

Height (cm)	Frequency
$150 < h \le 155$	2
$155 < h \le 160$	5
$160 < h \le 165$	13
$165 < h \le 170$	16
$170 < h \le 175$	20
$175 < h \le 180$	14
$180 < h \le 185$	7
$185 < h \le 190$	3

2 The marks for students in a mathematics examination.

Mark (%)	Frequency
$0 < m \le 10$	0
$10 < m \le 20$	1
$20 < m \le 30$	5
$60 < m \le 40$	8
$40 < m \le 50$	13
$50 < m \le 60$	15
$60 < m \le 70$	11
$70 < m \le 80$	9
$80 < m \le 90$	7
$90 < m \le 100$	3

3 A waiter records the tips he receives per day.

Tip (£)	Frequency
$0 < t \leq £1$	2
$£1 < t \leq £2$	3
$£2 < t \leq £3$	6
$£3 < t \leq £4$	8
$£4 < t \leq £5$	13
$£5 < t \leq £6$	11
$£6 < t \leq £7$	7
$£7 < t \leq £8$	5
$£8 < t \leq £9$	3
$£9 < t \leq £10$	2

4 The employees' pay in a department of a company.

Pay (× £1000)	Frequency
$8 < P \leq 10$	5
$10 < P \leq 12$	12
$12 < P \leq 14$	16
$14 < P \leq 16$	35
$16 < P \leq 18$	34
$18 < P \leq 20$	25
$20 < P \leq 22$	16
$22 < P \leq 24$	10
$24 < P \leq 26$	4
$26 < P \leq 28$	2
$28 < P \leq 30$	1

5 The times taken to complete a multiple-choice unit test by two groups (A and B).

Time (min)	Frequency (group A)	Frequency (group B)
$10 < T \leq 12$	4	5
$12 < T \leq 14$	6	8
$14 < T \leq 16$	9	11
$16 < T \leq 18$	14	16
$18 < T \leq 20$	16	17
$20 < T \leq 22$	11	18
$22 < T \leq 24$	7	8
$24 < T \leq 26$	5	4
$26 < T \leq 28$	3	1
$28 < T \leq 30$	1	0

The two cumulative frequency curves should be drawn on the same graph.
Compare the medians and the IQRs for the times taken by each of the two groups.

6 The ages of the populations in two small towns, one in the Philippines and one in the UK.

Age (years)	Frequency (× 100) (UK)	Frequency (× 100) (Philippines)
$0 < A \leq 10$	28	35
$10 < A \leq 20$	30	38
$20 < A \leq 30$	32	32
$30 < A \leq 40$	28	22
$40 < A \leq 50$	23	15
$50 < A \leq 60$	19	11
$60 < A \leq 70$	18	9
$70 < A \leq 80$	12	8
$80 < A \leq 90$	8	6
$90 < A \leq 100$	2	4

The two cumulative frequency curves should be drawn on the same graph.
Compare the medians and the IQRs for the two towns.

REVISION

Exercise G

1 A restaurant owner conducts a survey of the number of people in each group of customers that arrives at his restaurant. He writes his results in the form of a table.

Number of people	1	2	3	4	5	6	7	8
Frequency	7	11	24	18	9	5	3	2

(a) Calculate the mean, mode, median and range of these results.
(b) If the groups of seven and eight people do not eat at the restaurant because the tables can only seat six people, which of the above values are changed and which remain the same?

2 Two classes (X and Y) are given the same mental arithmetic test. The two frequency polygons each show the performance of a class.

Use the graphs to state which of the following are true and which are untrue. If you think that a statement is untrue, state your reason.

(a) There is the same number of students in each class.
(b) Every student scored 1 mark or more.
(c) Twelve students scored 4 marks.
(d) The modal mark for class Y is 5 marks.

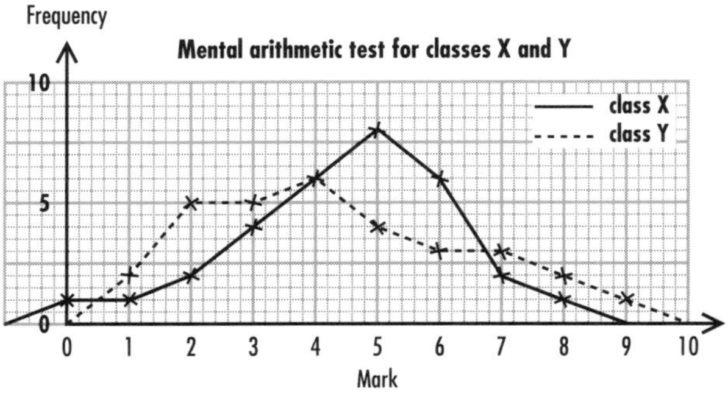

3 The scatter diagram shows the height and weight of each of a group of students. The line of best fit has been drawn.

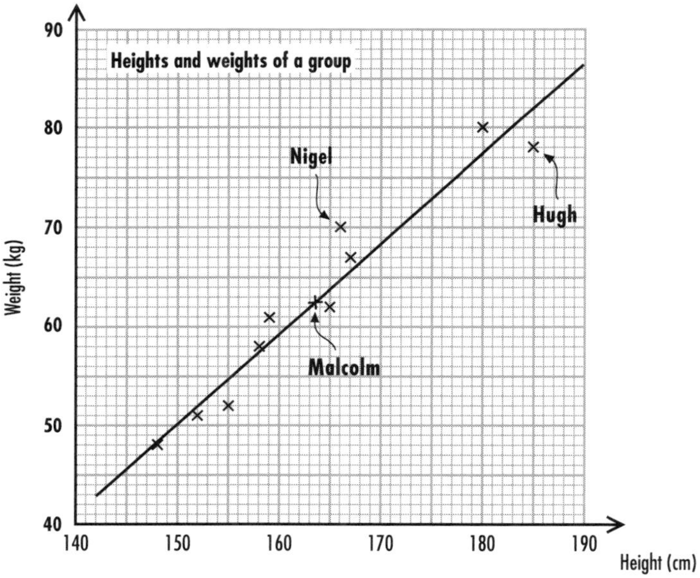

(a) Describe Hugh's height and weight compared with the rest of the group.
(b) Describe Nigel compared with the rest of the group.
(c) Describe Malcolm compared with the rest of the group.
(d) Use the line of best fit to estimate the likely weight of a student with a height of 175 cm.
(e) Use the line of best fit to estimate the likely height of a student with a weight of 50 kg.

4 Plants are measured to check on the progress of a new variety under test at a government research centre.

Height, h (mm)	Frequency	Upper limit (mm)	Cumulative frequency
$65 < h \leq 70$	3	70	3
$70 < h \leq 75$	8	75	11
$75 < h \leq 80$	41		
$80 < h \leq 85$	45		
$85 < h \leq 90$	11		
$90 < h \leq 95$	2		

(a) Copy and complete the table.
(b) Draw the cumulative frequency curve using 2 cm to represent 10 mm on the horizontal axis and 2 cm to represent 20 on the vertical axis.
(c) Use your cumulative frequency curve to answer the following.
   (i) If the 50 tallest plants are considered to be satisfactory, at what height are plants considered to be satisfactory?
   (ii) Plants are thrown away if their height is 78 mm or less. How many plants are thrown away?

Exercise GG

1 The hours of sunshine per day, over a period of 10 weeks, is noted at two seaside resorts, A and B:

Hours, H	Frequency (A)	Frequency (B)
$0 \leq H < 2$	4	1
$2 \leq H < 4$	6	7
$4 \leq H < 6$	14	20
$6 \leq H < 8$	18	14
$8 \leq H < 10$	23	16
$10 \leq H < 12$	5	12

(a) Calculate an estimated mean (to 1 d.p.) for (i) resort A (ii) resort B (iii) both resorts combined.
(b) State the modal class for each resort.
(c) State the median for each resort.
(d) State the modal class for both resorts combined.
(e) Which resort can claim to be sunniest and why?

2 The marks for a group of 32 students in a science examination and an English examination are noted and grouped into class intervals $0 \leq$ marks $< 10\%$, etc. The information is shown as two frequency polygons.

Use the graphs to state which of the following are true and which are untrue. If you think that a statement is untrue, state your reason.

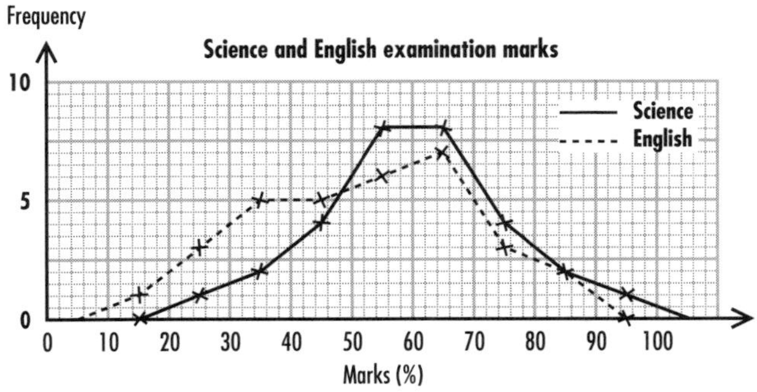

(a) The science marks are symmetrical about the mark of 50%.
(b) The top mark in science must be higher than the top mark in English.
(c) The total of the marks of the students in the $80 \leq$ marks $< 90\%$ group will be the same in English and in science.
(d) Two students had the same mark in English and science (48%).

3 A manufacturing company finds that the cost of producing a circuit board varies according to how many are produced in a week. The works manager decides to list the number produced and the calculated cost of each circuit board for a period of ten weeks.

Week number	1	2	3	4	5	6	7	8	9	10
Number of circuit boards produced	5100	5300	5500	6300	7000	5800	4200	3700	3200	3500
Cost per circuit board (£)	1.50	1.45	1.40	1.30	1.20	1.37	1.65	1.74	1.85	1.72

(a) Plot the price per circuit board against the number of circuit boards produced per week.
Use 2 cm to represent 1000 circuit boards between 3000 and 9000 boards.
Use 1 cm to represent 10p for the price of a circuit board between £1.00 and £2.20.

(b) Label the points that represent week 4 and week 8.

(c) Calculate the mean values for each variable.

(d) Plot and label the point that represents these mean values.

(e) Draw the line of best fit.

(f) Use your line of best fit to estimate:

(i) the number of boards, to the nearest 100, that would need to be produced to bring the cost down to £1,

(ii) the cost per board when 3000 are produced in a week.

4 A group of students sit an examination in maths and an examination in science. All students sit both examinations. The marks for each examination are grouped into class intervals of $0 < m \leq 10$, etc.

Marks (%)	Frequency (maths)	Frequency (science)
$0 < m \leq 10$	2	0
$10 < m \leq 20$	3	0
$20 < m \leq 30$	5	2
$30 < m \leq 40$	7	5
$40 < m \leq 50$	8	7
$50 < m \leq 60$	11	9
$60 < m \leq 70$	12	18
$70 < m \leq 80$	9	18
$80 < m \leq 90$	5	4
$90 < m \leq 100$	2	1

(a) Create a cumulative frequency table for each examination.

(b) Draw the cumulative frequency curves.

(c) State the median value for each examination.

(d) For each examination state (i) the lower quartile, Q_1 (ii) the upper quartile, Q_3 (iii) the IQR.

(e) Use these values to comment on the performance of the group in the two examinations.

64/ PROBABILITY: RELATIVE FREQUENCY USED TO MAKE ESTIMATES

The results of experiments and surveys can be used to predict what might happen in the future.

$$\textbf{Relative frequency} = \frac{\text{number of times a particular result happens}}{\text{total number of results}}$$

This is very similar to a **probability** and can be used as such but it only gives an **estimate** of what might happen if the experiment or survey is repeated.

EXAMPLE

▶ The colour of each of 100 cars passing a point is surveyed: 23 of the cars are white and 12 are blue.
Use this information to answer the following.
(a) What is the probability that the next car is white?
(b) Estimate how many of the next 50 cars are likely to be blue.

(a) P(white) = $\frac{23}{100}$ or 0.23

(b) Number of blue cars = $\frac{12}{100} \times 50 = 6$

It is important to remember that these are **predictions** based upon previous results. You should not expect that this is exactly what would happen.

Exercise 64A

In each of the following questions you are expected to use relative frequency as a method of predicting probability.

1 Adam takes 25 coins at random from a large bag of change. He finds that he has £2.10. Estimate the value of the bag of change if it holds 1000 coins.

2 In an experiment 220 out of 500 seeds germinate. Estimate the weight of seeds that would germinate in 5 kg of the seeds.

3 Six coins are tossed in an experiment in probability. The number of 'heads' are noted.

Number of heads	0	1	2	3	4	5	6
Frequency	2	8	22	35	20	9	1

(a) How many times are the coins tossed?
(b) If the coins had been thrown 1000 times, how many times would you expect '3 heads' to occur? Give your answer to the nearest 10.
(c) What is the probability of getting all the coins the same?
(d) Is '6 heads' really twice as likely as '6 tails'? Explain your answer.

4 In a shooting competition Bruce notes the frequencies of the scores of his shots.

Score	10	9	8	7	6	5
Frequency	33	25	16	10	4	2

(a) How many shots does Bruce make?
(b) What is the relative frequency of Bruce scoring 10?
(c) Estimate the number of times that Bruce is likely score 10 in 210 shots.
(d) Estimate the probability that his next shot will score less than 9.

5 As part of an experiment in probability John spins a hexagonal spinner and a pentagonal spinner. He notes the total of their scores.

Total score	2	3	4	5	6	7	8	9	10	11
Frequency	3	7	10	13	19	19	11	8	6	4

(a) How many times did John spin the spinners?
(b) What is the probability of a score of 10?
(c) What is the probability of obtaining a score of 6 or 7 with one spin of the spinners?
(d) If John invents a game that costs 10p a try with a prize of 10p and your money back for a score of 6 or 7, how much profit or loss would he make if 100 people have a try?

6 A sample of 100 out of the 56 000 voters in an election are asked for whom they would vote.

Candidate	Sue Norris	Neil Rose	John Minor	Jill Oxford	Do not know
Number of votes	21	16	27	11	25

(a) How many of the voters are likely to be in the group who 'Do not know'?
(b) What is likely to be the majority for John Minor (the number of votes that he gets compared with the number of votes of his nearest rival)? Give your answer to the nearest thousand.
(c) Neil Rose hopes to receive 10 000 votes. How many of the 'Do not know' voters will he need to convince in order to reach his target?
(d) If 10 000 of those who 'Do not know' vote for Sue Norris, is she likely to win? Explain the reasons for your answer.

Exercise 64B

In each of the following questions you are expected to use relative frequency as a method of predicting probability.

1 So far this season Mat has scored 15 goals, Ali 12 goals and Robin 13 goals. Estimate the probability that Mat will be the next of the three to score.

2 William Roberts is one of two candidates in a local election. A survey of 100 voters taken at random gives him 28 votes more than the other candidate. Estimate how many votes more than the other candidate he will receive if 2500 people vote.

3 A game at a school fair pays £5 every time that 11 is scored with two dice. Jane tries out the game before the fair starts. She has fifty goes and scores 11 three times.
(a) Estimate the probability of (i) winning (ii) losing at this game.
(b) How much will Jane have to charge per go at the game in order to cover the cost of the £5 wins?

4 250 light bulbs are taken at random from boxes at a factory. They are tested and the time that each lasts is noted.

Time (hours)	0 (broken)	up to 600	600–999	1000–1999	2000 and over
Frequency	5	12	60	168	5

(a) What is the probability that a light bulb taken at random is broken?
(b) What is the probability that a light bulb taken at random will last for 1000 hours or more?
(c) Boxes contain 100 bulbs. How many light bulbs per box are likely to last 2000 hours or more?
(d) In a batch of 10 000 bulbs, how many are likely to be unacceptable if acceptable bulbs last 600 hours or more?

5 There is a game at a fête that has three outcomes, 'WIN 50p', 'WIN £10' and 'LOSE'. The results of 100 attempts are noted and are listed.

Result	WIN 50p	WIN £10	LOSE
Frequency	14	2	84

(a) What is the probability of a win?
(b) What is the probability that one play will lead to a £10 win?
(c) If someone has a winner, what is the probability that it is a £10 win?
(d) Jenny buys £12.50 worth of 25p tickets. What sort of profit or loss is she likely to make?

6 There are three candidates in an election, Asif Singh, Floyd Parker and Kate John. There are 48 000 people who can vote in the election. Of those who voted, 200 are selected at random and asked for whom they voted.

Candidate	Asif Singh	Floyd Parker	Kate John	Will not say
Number of votes	36	84	50	30

(a) What percentage of those selected will not say how they voted?
(b) Using the number who said that they had voted for him, estimate the total number of the 48 000 who are likely to have voted for Floyd Parker, to the nearest thousand.
(c) Using the number who said that they had voted for him, estimate the total number of the 48 000 who are likely to have voted for Asif Singh, to the nearest thousand.
(d) If 80% of those who were in the category 'Will not say' voted for Kate John, is Floyd Parker likely to win? How many votes to the nearest thousand is Kate John likely to receive?

65/ PROBABILITY: ADDITION RULE FOR MUTUALLY EXCLUSIVE EVENTS

Events are **mutually exclusive** if it is impossible for the events to happen at the same time. If a dice is thrown and it comes up as a 2, then it cannot come up as 1, 3, 4, 5 or 6 as well. The fact that the score was 2 excludes the other scores.

The 'OR' rule

Probability of event *A* OR event *B* happening = probability of event *A* + probability of event *B*

$$P(A \text{ or } B) = P(A) + P(B)$$

EXAMPLE

► What is the probability that a dice will have an even score?

$P(2) = P(4) = P(6) = \frac{1}{6}$ $\quad$ $P(2 \text{ or } 4 \text{ or } 6) = \frac{1}{6} + \frac{1}{6} + \frac{1}{6} = \frac{3}{6} = \frac{1}{2}$

EXAMPLE

► A bag contains coloured discs: five are red, eight are blue and seven are green. One disc is taken from the bag. State the probability of each of the following.
The disc is (a) red (b) blue (c) red or blue (d) blue or green.
There is a total of 20 discs.

(a) $P(\text{red}) = \frac{5}{20} = \frac{1}{4}$ $\quad$ (b) $P(\text{blue}) = \frac{8}{20} = \frac{2}{5}$

(c) $P(\text{red or blue}) = \frac{5}{20} + \frac{8}{20} = \frac{13}{20}$ $\quad$ (d) $P(\text{blue or green}) = \frac{8}{20} + \frac{7}{20} = \frac{15}{20} = \frac{3}{4}$

Exercise 65A

1 A bag contains coloured discs. Two are red, five are blue and seven are green. One disc is removed from the bag.
State the probability that the disc is (a) red (b) red or blue (c) red or green (d) not red.

2 A card is taken from a standard pack of 52 playing cards. State the probability that the card is (a) the 7 of diamonds (b) a red 7 (c) a black 7 (d) a 7.

3 A dice is rolled. State the probability that the score is (a) odd (b) even (c) 3 or more (d) 3 or less.

4 A box contains coloured discs. One is blue, three are yellow and four are red. One disc is removed from the box.
State the probability that the disc is (a) yellow (b) yellow or blue (c) red or blue (d) not blue.

5 A card is taken from a standard pack of 52 playing cards. State the probability that the card is (a) a 4 or a 5 (b) a picture card (Jack, Queen or King) (c) an Ace (d) a picture card or an Ace.

6 A bag contains a 5p-coin, two 50p-coins, three 10p-coins and a £1 coin. If one coin is taken from the bag, state the probability that it will be worth (a) 5p (b) 10p or 50p (c) 50p or more (d) 50p or less.

7 A box contains raffle tickets. Of these 150 are yellow, 200 are pink, 50 are white and 250 are red. One raffle ticket is taken from the box. State the probability that it will be (a) pink (b) red or pink (c) red or white (d) not white.

8 If four coins are tossed, the probabilities of the possible outcomes are as follows:
P(4 heads) = 0.0625 P(3 heads) = 0.25 P(2 heads) = 0.375
P(1 head) = 0.25 P(4 tails) = 0.0625
State the probability that (a) all coins come down the same (b) there are more than two heads (c) there are more than two tails (d) there are one or two heads.

9 If two dice are rolled, the probability for each total score on the two dice is as follows.

Score	2	3	4	5	6	7	8	9	10	11	12
Probability	$\frac{1}{36}$	$\frac{1}{18}$	$\frac{1}{12}$	$\frac{1}{9}$	$\frac{5}{36}$	$\frac{1}{6}$	$\frac{5}{36}$	$\frac{1}{9}$	$\frac{1}{12}$	$\frac{1}{18}$	$\frac{1}{36}$

(a) State the probability of each of the following scores.
(i) 11 or more (ii) A multiple of 3 (iii) 6 or 7 (iv) 4 or less
(b) State the probability of (i) an even score (ii) an odd score. Which is more likely?

10 If a pentagonal spinner and a hexagonal spinner are spun, the probability for each total score on the two spinners is as follows.

Score	2	3	4	5	6	7	8	9	10	11
Probability	$\frac{1}{30}$	$\frac{1}{15}$	$\frac{1}{10}$	$\frac{2}{15}$	$\frac{1}{6}$	$\frac{1}{6}$	$\frac{2}{15}$	$\frac{1}{10}$	$\frac{1}{15}$	$\frac{1}{30}$

(a) State the probability for each of the following scores.
(i) 6 or 7 (ii) A multiple of 5 (iii) Less than 6 (iv) More than 6
(b) State the probability of (i) an even score (ii) an odd score. Which is more likely?

Exercise 65B

1 A box contains coloured discs. Of these eight are green, ten are red and seven are yellow. One disc is removed from the box. State the probability that the disc is (a) red (b) red or yellow (c) red or green (d) not red.

2 State the probability of each of the following when the octagonal spinner shown in the diagram is spun once.
(a) A number (b) A letter
(c) An even number (d) An even number or a B

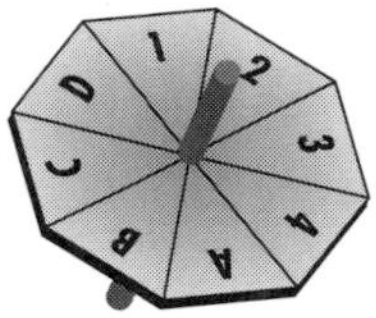

3 A card is taken from a standard pack of 52 playing cards. State the probability that the card is (a) a black 3 (b) the 3 of spades (c) a 4 (d) a 3 or a 4 or a 5.

4 A bag contains five 2p-coins, three 5p-coins, five 10p-coins and two 20p-coins. If one coin is taken from the bag, state the probability that it will be worth (a) 10p (b) 5p or 10p (c) 5p or more (d) 5p or less.

5 A box contains raffle tickets of which 125 are yellow, 150 are pink, 100 are white and 25 are red. One raffle ticket is taken from the box. State the probability that it will be (a) white (b) red or white (c) pink or yellow (d) not yellow.

6 A card is taken from a standard pack of 52 playing cards. State the probability that the card is (a) the Queen of hearts (b) a red Queen (c) a black Queen (d) any King.

7 A bag contains coloured discs. Of these three are red, two are blue and five are green. One disc is removed from the bag. State the probability that the disc is (a) blue (b) red or green (c) blue or green (d) not green.

8 If three coins are tossed, the probabilities of the possible outcomes are as follows.

P(3 heads) = $\frac{1}{8}$ P(2 heads) = $\frac{3}{8}$ P(1 head) = $\frac{3}{8}$ P(3 tails) = $\frac{1}{8}$

State the probability of the following.
(a) All coins come down the same.
(b) There is more than one head.
(c) There is one tail or more.
(d) There are one or two heads.

9

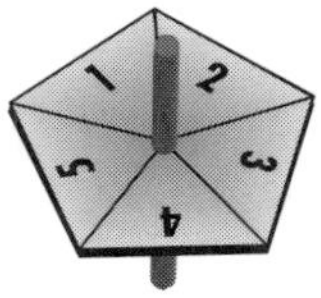

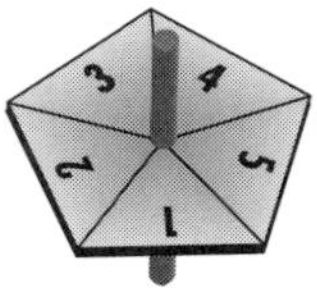

If two pentagonal spinners are spun, the probability for each total score on the two spinners is as follows.

Score	2	3	4	5	6	7	8	9	10
Probability	0.04	0.08	0.12	0.16	0.2	0.16	0.12	0.08	0.04

(a) State the probability of each of the following scores.
(i) 4 or less (ii) A multiple of 3 (iii) 5 or 6 (iv) 9 or 10
(b) State the probability of (i) an even score (ii) an odd score. Which is more likely?

10 If five coins are tossed, the probabilities of the possible outcomes are as follows.

P(5 heads) = $\frac{1}{32}$ P(4 heads) = $\frac{5}{32}$ P(3 heads) = $\frac{5}{16}$

P(2 heads) = $\frac{5}{16}$ P(1 head) = $\frac{5}{32}$ P(5 tails) = $\frac{1}{32}$

State the probability of the following.
(a) All coins come down the same.
(b) There are more than two heads.
(c) There are more than two tails.
(d) There are three or four heads.

66/ PROBABILITY: MULTIPLICATION RULE FOR TWO INDEPENDENT EVENTS

When two events are **independent**, the outcome in one event does not affect the outcome in the other event in any way, for example, the outcome of picking a card from a pack does not affect the outcome of tossing a coin.

The 'AND' rule

For two independent outcomes A and B,

P(A and B) = P(A) × P(B)

P(A and B) means 'the probability that *both* A and B will happen'.

EXAMPLE

► A bag contains three red discs and five blue discs. One disc is picked out at random and *is then replaced* before another disc is picked at random. State the probability of each of the following outcomes for the two discs.

(a) Two red discs (b) Two blue discs (c) One of each colour

The two events are independent because the first disc is replaced and thus has no effect on the second disc.

(a) P(2 red) = P(red) × P(red) = $\frac{3}{8} \times \frac{3}{8} = \frac{9}{64}$

or $= 0.375 \times 0.375 = 0.141$ (to 3 s.f.)

(b) P(2 blues) = P(blue) × P(blue) = $\frac{5}{8} \times \frac{5}{8} = \frac{25}{64}$ or 0.391 (to 3 s.f.)

(c) If the discs are not the same colour, there must be one of each colour.
So P(one of each colour) = 1 – P(2 red) – P(2 blue)

$= 1 - \frac{9}{64} - \frac{25}{64}$

$= \frac{30}{64}$

$= \frac{15}{32}$ or 0.469 (to 3 s.f.)

EXAMPLE

► A bag contains three red discs, two blue discs and five green discs. One disc is picked out at random and is *not replaced* before another disc is picked at random. State the probability of each of the following outcomes for the two discs.

(a) Two red discs (b) Two blue discs (c) One red and one green disc

The two events are not independent now as, when the first disc is removed, the number of discs available is changed.

(a) P(2 red) = P(1st red) × P(2nd red) = $\frac{3}{10} \times \frac{2}{9} = \frac{6}{90} = \frac{1}{15}$

(b) P(2 blue) = P(1st blue) × P(2nd blue) = $\frac{2}{10} \times \frac{1}{9} = \frac{2}{90} = \frac{1}{45}$

(c) There are two ways of obtaining one red and one green. This could be achieved with a red followed by a green or with a green followed by a red.
P(1 red and 1 green) = P(red then green) + P(green then red)

$= (\frac{3}{10} \times \frac{5}{9}) + (\frac{5}{10} \times \frac{3}{9})$

$= \frac{1}{6} + \frac{1}{6} = \frac{1}{3}$

Exercise 66A

1 A dice is rolled twice. State the probability of each of the following outcomes for the two scores.
(a) The total score is 2.
(b) The first score is even and the second is odd.
(c) The first score is odd and the second is even.
(d) The first is a 6 and the second odd.

2 A game involves spinning the pointer which has an equal probability of stopping in each of the three sections. The sections are marked WIN or LOSE as shown in the diagram. The game involves spinning the pointer twice. State the probability of each of the following.

(a) Both spins are WIN.
(b) Both spins are LOSE.
(c) The first spin is LOSE and the second is WIN.
(d) The first spin is WIN and the second is LOSE.

3 The pentagonal spinner in the diagram is spun twice. State the probability of each of the following outcomes.

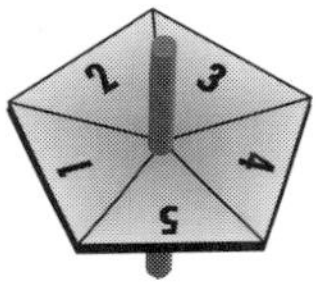

(a) Both scores are 5.
(b) Both scores are odd.
(c) The first score is 4 and the second score is not 4.
(d) The total score is 2.

4 A dice is rolled and a card is picked at random from a pack of playing cards. State the probability of each of the following outcomes.
(a) A score of 5 and a Queen.
(b) An even score and the Jack of clubs.
(c) A score of 1 and a picture card (Jack, Queen or King).
(d) A score of more than 2 and a picture card.

5 A card is taken from a standard pack of 52 cards. It is *not* replaced and a second card is taken. State the probability of the following.
(a) The first card is black and the second card is a diamond.
(b) The first card is a spade and the second card is a club.
(c) Both cards are black.
(d) Both cards are clubs.

6 A bag contains 20 tickets. One ticket is a winner and 19 are losers. A ticket is taken at random and *not* replaced. A second ticket is taken at random. State the probability of the following outcomes.
(a) Both tickets are losers.
(b) Both tickets are winners.
(c) The first ticket is a loser and the second ticket is a winner.
(d) The first ticket is a winner and the second ticket is a loser.

7 A dice is rolled twice. State the probability of each of the following outcomes for the two scores.
(a) Both scores are 5.
(b) Both scores are odd.
(c) The first score is a 6 and the second is a 1.
(d) The first is a 6 and the second is a 4 or a 5.

8 A card is taken from a standard pack of 52 cards. It is *not* replaced and a second card taken. State the probability of the following.
(a) Both cards are hearts.
(b) Both cards are red.
(c) Each card is a 7.
(d) The first card is a Queen and the second card is a King.

9 Each of two roadworks on a motorway is controlled by traffic lights. The probability of being delayed at traffic light A is 0.6 and at traffic light B the probability is 0.5. State the probability of the following.
(a) A driver is delayed at both lights.
(b) A driver is not delayed at either light.
(c) A driver is delayed at light A but not at light B.
(d) A driver is delayed at just one of the lights.

10 The probability of a team winning is calculated to be $\frac{5}{8}$, for losing $\frac{1}{8}$ and for drawing $\frac{1}{4}$.
Assuming that these probabilities do not change, state the probability of each of the following for the next two games.
(a) Both are won.
(b) Both are lost.
(c) The first is won and the second is drawn.
(d) One game or more is lost.

Exercise 66B

1 A bag contains six red discs and four white discs. A disc is picked at random and then returned to the bag. A second disc is picked at random. State the probability of the following outcomes.
(a) The first is red and the second is white.
(b) Both are red.
(c) Both are white.
(d) Both are the same colour. (Hint: Both are red *or* both are white.)

2 A dice is rolled twice. State the probability of each of the following outcomes for the two scores.
(a) The total score is 12.
(b) Both scores are greater than 4.
(c) The first score is a 4 and the second is a 3 or a 4.
(d) Both scores are 1 or 2.

3

A game involves spinning a pointer which has an equal probability of stopping in each of the five sections. The sections are marked WIN or LOSE as shown in the diagram. The game involves spinning the pointer twice.
State the probability of each of the following.
(a) Both spins are WIN.
(b) Both spins are LOSE.
(c) The first spin is WIN and the second is LOSE.
(d) The results of the two spins are different. (Hint: They are *not* the same.)

4 The hexagonal spinner in the diagram is spun twice. State the probability of each of the following outcomes.
(a) The first score is a 4 and the second score is a 3.
(b) Both scores are 4.
(c) Both scores are 3.
(d) Both scores are the same. (Hint: Both scores are 1 *or* both scores are 2 etc.)

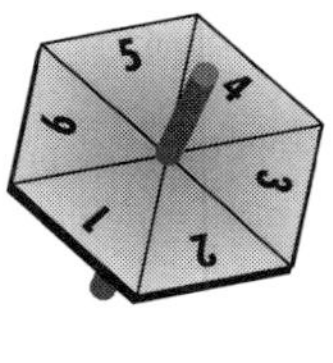

5 A card is taken from a standard pack of 52 cards. It is *not* replaced and a second card is taken. State the probability of the following.
(a) Both cards are spades.
(b) The first card is red and the second card is black.
(c) The first card is black and the second card is red.
(d) The cards are different colours. (Hint: Red then black *or* black then red.)

6

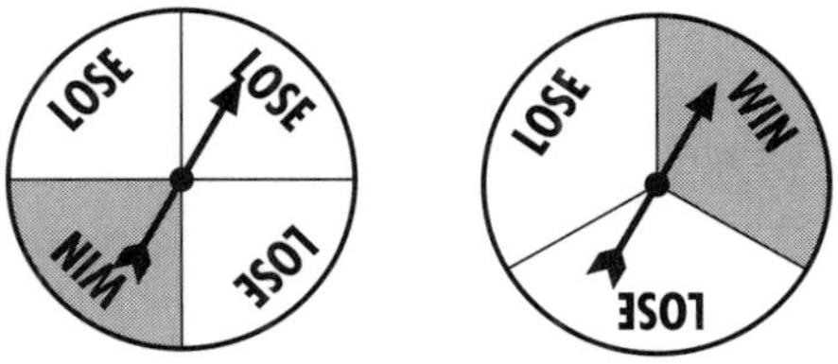

A game involves spinning the two pointers A and B as shown in the diagram. The game is won only if both pointers point to WIN. If only one pointer points to WIN, then the person playing is allowed to spin the pointers again. State the probability of each of the following outcomes.
(a) Both are LOSE.
(b) Both are WIN.
(c) A is WIN and B is LOSE.
(d) The person receives another go. (Hint: A is a WIN and B is a LOSE *or* B is a WIN and A is a LOSE).

7 A box contains 12 pencils of which four are black, three are blue and five are red. A pencil is taken at random and is *not* replaced before another pencil is taken at random. State the probability of the following.
(a) Both pencils are black.
(b) Both pencils are red..
(c) The first pencil is red and the second is blue.
(d) One of the pencils is red and the other is blue. (Hint: Red then blue or blue then red.)

8 A card is taken from a standard pack of 52 cards. It is *not* replaced and a second card taken. State the probability of the following.
(a) The first card is an Ace and the second card is a Jack.
(b) Both cards are Aces.
(c) Both cards are diamonds.
(d) Both cards are picture cards (Jack, Queen or King).

9 The probability of a team winning is calculated to be 0.3, for losing 0.6 and for drawing 0.1. Assuming that these probabilities do not change, state the probability of each of the following for the next two games.
(a) Both are won.
(b) Both are drawn.
(c) Both are lost.
(d) At least one game is won.

10 A spinner used in a game has three possible outcomes: 'win', 'lose' and 'blank'. The probability for each of the outcomes is as follows: win $\frac{1}{4}$, lose $\frac{1}{2}$ and blank $\frac{1}{4}$.
The spinner is spun until a 'lose' is obtained.
State the probability of each of the following.
(a) The first two spins both give wins.
(b) The first two spins are blanks.
(c) The first four spins are blanks.
(d) The game ends at the second spin.

67/ PROBABILITY: TREE DIAGRAMS

A **tree diagram** is a way of simplifying complicated probability situations. Each branch is an outcome. The probability for that outcome is written against the branch. The probability of getting to each end-point is found by multiplying the probabilities on each branch used.

EXAMPLE

► The two spinners in the diagram are used in a game. In order to win the player needs to get a WIN on both spinners.

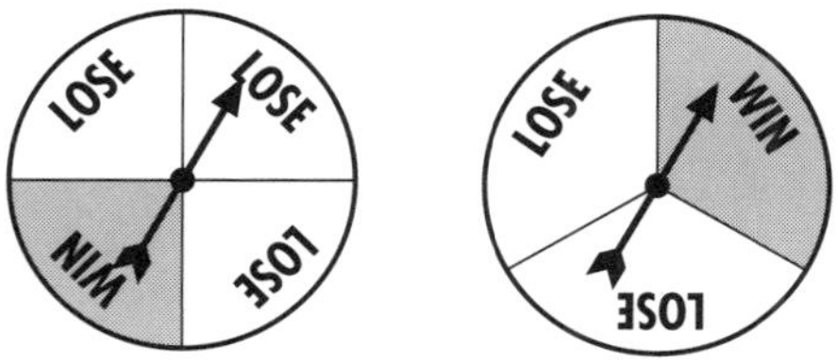

Draw a tree diagram for the outcomes of the two spinners. Use this to state the probability of each of the following outcomes.
(a) Both point to WIN.
(b) Both point to LOSE.
(c) There is a mixture of WIN and LOSE.

— WIN ···· LOSE

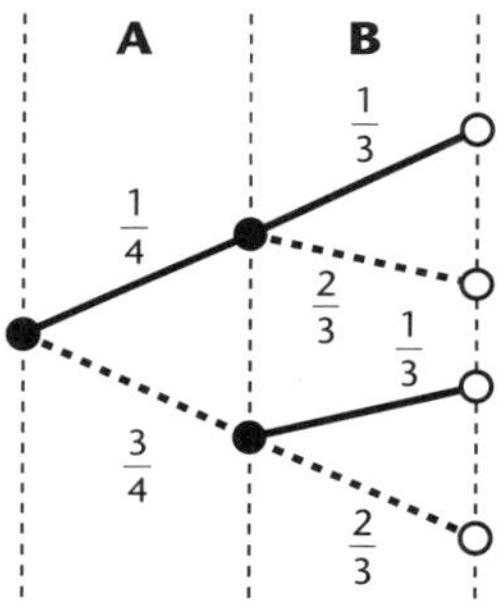

$P(\text{win A} + \text{win B}) = \frac{1}{4} \times \frac{1}{3} = \frac{1}{12}$

$P(\text{win A} + \text{lose B}) = \frac{1}{4} \times \frac{2}{3} = \frac{2}{12}$

$P(\text{lose A} + \text{win B}) = \frac{3}{4} \times \frac{1}{3} = \frac{3}{12}$

$P(\text{lose A} + \text{lose B}) = \frac{3}{4} \times \frac{2}{3} = \frac{6}{12}$

From the tree diagram (a) $\frac{1}{12}$ (b) $\frac{1}{2}$ (c) $\frac{2}{12} + \frac{3}{12} = \frac{5}{12}$

Exercise 67A

1 A machine part is tested twice for quality. The first test checks for size and there is a probability of $\frac{1}{3}$ of failing this test. The second test checks for strength and there is a probability of $\frac{2}{5}$ of failing this test.
(a) Draw a tree diagram to show the outcomes of the two tests.
(b) Use your tree diagram to find the probability of failure (i) on both tests (ii) on neither test (iii) on one test only.

2 A bag contains coloured discs, three red and seven blue. A disc is taken at random from the bag and *not* replaced. A second disc is taken at random from the bag.
(a) Draw a tree diagram to show the various outcomes.
(b) Use your tree diagram to find the probability of each of the following outcomes for the two discs.
(i) Both discs are red. (ii) Both discs are blue. (iii) There is one of each colour.

3 On the way to work I have to pass through two sets of traffic lights. The probability that the first light is red is 0.4. The probability that the second light is red is 0.3.
(a) Draw a tree diagram to show all the possible outcomes for the two lights.
(b) Use your tree diagram to find the probability of each of the following outcomes.
(i) Both lights are red. (ii) Both lights are green. (iii) Both lights are the same colour.
(iv) The lights are different colours.

4 A box contains 16 tickets. Three of these are winning tickets but the remainder are losers. Paul picks a ticket at random and does *not* replace it. Then Jaspal picks a ticket at random.
(a) State the probability of picking a winning ticket from the box.
(b) Draw a tree diagram to show the possible outcomes of Paul and Jaspal picking tickets and use this to find the probabilities of the following outcomes.
(i) Jaspal wins but Paul loses. (ii) Paul wins but Jaspal loses. (iii) Both win. (iv) Both lose.

5 The probability that Vijay oversleeps in the morning is 0.6. If he does oversleep, he has a probability of 0.75 of being late. If he does not oversleep, the probability that he is late is reduced to 0.2.
(a) Draw a tree diagram to show the possible outcomes of whether Vijay oversleeps or not and if he is late or not.
(b) Use your tree diagram to state the probability of each of the following outcomes.
(i) Vijay does not oversleep but is late.
(ii) Vijay oversleeps and is not late.
(iii) Vijay is late.
(iv) Vijay is not late.

6 Dave has two routes which he can use for getting to work. When he chooses the Ring Road, he has a probability of 0.7 of being held up in a traffic jam. When he chooses the route through the City Centre he has a probability of 0.5 of being held up in a traffic jam.
Dave chooses the Ring Road when it is sunny because the sun shining on the City Centre Road makes driving unpleasant. The probability that it is sunny is 0.25.
(a) Draw a tree diagram that shows whether Dave chooses the Ring Road or the City Centre route and whether he was held up in the traffic or not.
(b) Use your tree diagram to find the probability of the following outcomes.
(i) He chooses the Ring Road and is held up in traffic.
(ii) He chooses the City Centre and is not held up in traffic.
(iii) He is held up in traffic.
(iv) He is not held up in traffic.

7 A coin is tossed three times.
(a) Draw a tree diagram to show the possible outcomes for the three coins.
(b) Use your tree diagram to state the probability each of the following outcomes.
(i) 3 heads (ii) 3 tails (iii) 3 the same (iv) 2 heads or 2 tails

8 A game involves spinning the pointer in the diagram three times.

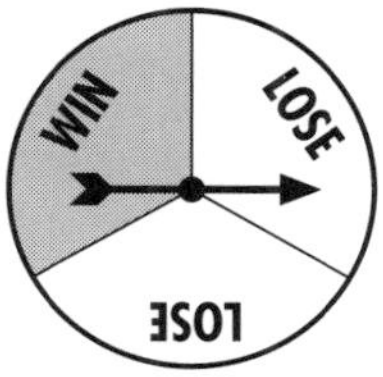

The prizes are as shown.

(a) Draw a tree diagram to show the possible outcomes of the three spins of the pointer.
(b) Use your tree diagram to find the probability of winning each of the prizes.
(c) What is the probability that a person will not win a prize?

9 The probability of a team winning is calculated to be $\frac{1}{2}$, for losing $\frac{3}{8}$ and for drawing $\frac{1}{8}$.
(a) Draw a tree diagram to show the possible outcomes of the next two games. You should assume that the probabilities do not change.
(b) Use your tree diagram to state the probability of each of the following for the next two games.
(i) Both are won. (ii) Both are drawn. (iii) Both are lost. (iv) Only one game is won.

10 A dart player is throwing at the 'treble 20'. She has a probability of 0.7 of hitting the' treble 20' with each dart. She throws three darts.
(a) Draw a tree diagram to show the possible outcomes of throwing the three darts.
(b) Use your tree diagram to state the probability that Sally hits the 'treble 20'
(i) with all three darts (ii) with none of the darts (iii) with two darts only (iv) with one dart only.

Exercise 67B

1 An athlete is to run two races. In the 100 metres race she thinks her probability of winning is $\frac{2}{3}$ and in the 200 metres race she thinks that her probability of winning is $\frac{3}{4}$.
(a) Draw a tree diagram to show the various outcomes.
(b) Use your tree diagram to find the probability of each of the following outcomes.
(i) She wins both. (ii) She does not win either race. (iii) She wins only one race.

2 Each player in a game of chance has two attempts at winning. The probability of winning on each attempt is only $\frac{1}{10}$.
(a) Draw a tree diagram to show the outcomes for two attempts.
(b) Use your tree diagram to find the probability that the player wins (i) twice (ii) once (iii) on neither attempt.

3 A bag contains coloured discs, four red and six blue. A disc is taken at random from the bag and *not* replaced. A second disc is taken at random from the bag.
(a) Draw a tree diagram to show the various outcomes.
(b) Use your tree diagram to find the probability of each of the following outcomes for the two discs.
(i) Both are red. (ii) Both are blue. (iii) There is one of each colour.

4 In order to pass an examination in science, Sally needs to pass in both Paper 1 and Paper 2. The probability of her passing Paper 1 is 0.8 and the probability of her passing Paper 2 is only 0.1.
(a) Draw a tree diagram to show the possible outcomes of Sally sitting Paper 1 and Paper 2.
(b) Use your tree diagram to state the probability of each of the following outcomes.
(i) Sally passes Paper 1 and fails Paper 2.
(ii) Sally passes both papers.
(iii) Sally fails both papers.
(iv) Sally fails one of the papers.

5 In a game two fair dice (A and B) are rolled. In order to win dice A needs to be odd and dice B needs to have a score that is greater than 4.
(a) State the probability that (i) dice A is odd (ii) dice B has a score greater than 4.
(b) Draw a tree diagram to show the possible outcomes of rolling the two dice.
(c) Use your tree diagram to find the probability of each of the following outcomes.
(i) A player wins.
(ii) Dice A is odd but dice B is not greater than 4.
(iii) Dice B is greater than 4 but dice A has even score.
(iv) Both dice are losers.

6 A bag contains coloured discs, two yellow and four green. A disc is taken at random from the bag and *not* replaced. A second disc is taken from the bag.
(a) Draw a tree diagram to show the various outcomes.
(b) Use your tree diagram to find the probability of each of the following outcomes for the two discs.
(i) Both are green. (ii) Both are yellow. (iii) There is one of each colour.

7 A coin is tossed three times.
(a) Draw a tree diagram to show the possible outcomes for the three coins.
(b) Use your tree diagram to state the probability of each of the following number of coins that come down heads.
(i) 3 (ii) 0 (iii) 2 (iv) 2 or more

8 The probability for each result of a game for a team are: win 0.3, draw 0.5 and lose 0.2.
(a) Draw a tree diagram to show the possible outcomes and their probabilities for the next two games.
(b) Use your tree diagram to state the probability of each of the following outcomes.
(i) Win both. (ii) Lose both. (iii) Draw both. (iv) Win one game.

9 (a) Jack has three 2p-coins and five 1p-coins in one pocket. If he takes one coin at random from his pocket, what is the probability that it is a 2p-coin?
(b) He has a 2p-coin and two 1p-coins in the other pocket. If he takes one coin at random from this pocket, what is the probability that it is a 2p-coin?
(c) He takes one coin at random from each pocket. Draw a tree diagram to show the probability of each of the possible outcomes.
(d) Use your tree diagram to find the probability of each of the following outcomes.
(i) Two 2p-coins (ii) Two 1p-coins (iii) 3p in total (iv) At least 3p

10 A card is picked at random from a pack of playing cards. It is *not* returned to the pack and another card is picked at random. Saul is seeing if each card is red or black.
(a) Draw a tree diagram to show the possible outcomes of whether each of the cards is red or black.
(b) Use your tree diagram to state the probability of each of the following number of red cards being picked.
(i) 2 (ii) 0 (iii) 1 (iv) at least 1

REVISION

Exercise H

1 Jason takes 20 coins at random from a large bag of change. He finds that he has £1.45. Estimate the value of the bag of change if it holds 800 coins.

2 Sarah Harris is one of two candidates in a local election. A survey of 100 voters taken at random gives her 28 votes more than the other candidate. Estimate how many votes more than the other candidate she will receive if 3200 people vote.

3 A bag contains coloured discs. Of these three are red, six are blue and eleven are green. One disc is removed from the bag.
State the probability that the disc is (a) red (b) red or blue (c) red or green (d) not red.

4 A card is taken from a standard pack of 52 playing cards. State the probability that the card is (a) the King of spades (b) a red 8 (c) a black 3 (d) an Ace.

5 Calculate the probability of getting a head as the result of spinning a coin and picking an Ace from a pack of playing cards.

6 If the probability of a sunny day is 0.9, what is the probability of a sunny day followed by another sunny day?

7 A bag contains coloured discs, thirteen red and seven blue. A disc is taken at random from the bag and then replaced. A second disc is taken from the bag.
(a) Draw a tree diagram to show the various outcomes.
(b) Use your tree diagram to find the probability of each of the following outcomes for the two discs.
(i) Both are red. (ii) Both are blue. (iii) There is one of each colour.

Exercise HH

1 The ages of the passengers on a trip to EuroDisney are noted and grouped to form the table.

Age group	Under 5	5–14	15–18	19–34	35 and over
Number of passengers	24	32	12	38	14

(a) What is the probability that a passenger taken at random is under 15 years old?
(b) If a passenger is over 18, what is the probability that the passenger is also 35 or over?
(c) What is the probability that a passenger taken at random is under 35 but over 14?
(d) Assuming that distribution of ages is the same, how many children's meals (under 15) will be required for 1200 people?

2 If a pentagonal spinner and a square spinner are spun, the probability for each total score on the two spinners is as follows.

Score	2	3	4	5	6	7	8	9
Probability	0.05	0.1	0.15	0.2	0.2	0.15	0.1	0.05

(a) State the probability that the score will be (i) 5 or 6 (ii) 6 or 7 (iii) less than 5 (iv) more than 6.
(b) State the probability of (i) an even score (ii) an odd score. Which is more likely?

3 A game involves spinning the pointer which has an equal probability of stopping in each of the four sections. The sections are marked WIN or LOSE as shown in the diagram. The game involves spinning the pointer twice.

Use the 'AND' rule to calculate the probability of each of the following.
(a) Both spins are WIN.
(b) Both spins are LOSE.
(c) The first spin is LOSE and the second is WIN.
(d) The first spin is WIN and the second is LOSE.

4 The probability for each result of a game for a team are: win 0.5, draw 0.35 and lose 0.15.
(a) Draw a tree diagram to show the possible outcomes and their probabilities for the next two games.
(b) Use your tree diagram to state the probability of each of the following outcomes.
(i) Win both. (ii) Lose both. (iii) Draw both. (iv) Win one game.